FrontPage® 98 Bible

FrontPage® 98 Bible

David Elderbrock with Paul Bodensiek

IDG Books Worldwide, Inc.
An International Data Group Company

Foster City, CA ✦ Chicago, IL ✦ Indianapolis, IN ✦ New York, NY

FrontPage® 98 Bible

Published by
IDG Books Worldwide, Inc.
An International Data Group Company
919 E. Hillsdale Blvd., Suite 400
Foster City, CA 94404
www.idgbooks.com (IDG Books Worldwide Web site)

Library of Congress Catalog Card No.: 97-071286

ISBN: 0-7645-3088-7

Printed in the United States of America

10 9 8 7 6 5 4 3 2 1

1E/RU/QV/ZY/FC

Distributed in the United States by IDG Books Worldwide, Inc.

Distributed by Macmillan Canada for Canada; by Transworld Publishers Limited in the United Kingdom; by IDG Norge Books for Norway; by IDG Sweden Books for Sweden; by Woodslane Pty. Ltd. for Australia; by Woodslane (NZ) Ltd. for New Zealand; by Addison Wesley Longman Singapore Pte Ltd. for Singapore, Malaysia, Thailand, Indonesia, and Korea; by Norma Comunicaciones S.A. for Colombia; by Intersoft for South Africa; by International Thomson Publishing for Germany, Austria, and Switzerland; by Toppan Company Ltd. for Japan; by Distribuidora Cuspide for Argentina; by Livraria Cultura for Brazil; by Ediciencia S.A. for Ecuador; by Ediciones ZETA S.C.R. Ltda. for Peru; by WS Computer Publishing Corporation, Inc., for the Philippines; by Unalis Corporation for Taiwan; by Contemporanea de Ediciones for Venezuela; by Computer Book & Magazine Store for Puerto Rico; by Express Computer Distributors for the Caribbean and West Indies. Authorized Sales Agent: Anthony Rudkin Associates for the Middle East and North Africa.

For general information on IDG Books Worldwide's books in the U.S., please call our Consumer Customer Service department at 800-762-2974. For reseller information, including discounts and premium sales, please call our Reseller Customer Service department at 800-434-3422.

For information on where to purchase IDG Books Worldwide's books outside the U.S., please contact our International Sales department at 650-655-3200 or fax 650-655-3297.

For information on foreign language translations, please contact our Foreign & Subsidiary Rights department at 650-655-3021 or fax 650-655-3281.

For sales inquiries and special prices for bulk quantities, please contact our Sales department at 650-655-3200 or write to the address above.

For information on using IDG Books Worldwide's books in the classroom or for ordering examination copies, please contact our Educational Sales department at 800-434-2086.

For press review copies, author interviews, or other publicity information, please contact our Public Relations department at 650-655-3000 or fax 650-655-3299.

For authorization to photocopy items for corporate, personal, or educational use, please contact Copyright Clearance Center, 222 Rosewood Drive, Danvers, MA 01923, or fax 978-750-4470.

is a trademark under exclusive license to IDG Books Worldwide, Inc., from International Data Group, Inc.

ABOUT IDG BOOKS WORLDWIDE

Welcome to the world of IDG Books Worldwide.

IDG Books Worldwide, Inc., is a subsidiary of International Data Group, the world's largest publisher of computer-related information and the leading global provider of information services on information technology. IDG was founded more than 25 years ago and now employs more than 8,500 people worldwide. IDG publishes more than 275 computer publications in over 75 countries (see listing below). More than 60 million people read one or more IDG publications each month.

Launched in 1990, IDG Books Worldwide is today the #1 publisher of best-selling computer books in the United States. We are proud to have received eight awards from the Computer Press Association in recognition of editorial excellence and three from *Computer Currents*' First Annual Readers' Choice Awards. Our best-selling *...For Dummies*® series has more than 30 million copies in print with translations in 30 languages. IDG Books Worldwide, through a joint venture with IDG's Hi-Tech Beijing, became the first U.S. publisher to publish a computer book in the People's Republic of China. In record time, IDG Books Worldwide has become the first choice for millions of readers around the world who want to learn how to better manage their businesses.

Our mission is simple: Every one of our books is designed to bring extra value and skill-building instructions to the reader. Our books are written by experts who understand and care about our readers. The knowledge base of our editorial staff comes from years of experience in publishing, education, and journalism — experience we use to produce books for the '90s. In short, we care about books, so we attract the best people. We devote special attention to details such as audience, interior design, use of icons, and illustrations. And because we use an efficient process of authoring, editing, and desktop publishing our books electronically, we can spend more time ensuring superior content and spend less time on the technicalities of making books.

You can count on our commitment to deliver high-quality books at competitive prices on topics you want to read about. At IDG Books Worldwide, we continue in the IDG tradition of delivering quality for more than 25 years. You'll find no better book on a subject than one from IDG Books Worldwide.

IDG BOOKS WORLDWIDE

John Kilcullen
CEO
IDG Books Worldwide, Inc.

Steven Berkowitz
President and Publisher
IDG Books Worldwide, Inc.

Eighth Annual Computer Press Awards ≥1992

WINNER
Ninth Annual Computer Press Awards ≥1993

WINNER
Tenth Annual Computer Press Awards ≥1994

WINNER
Eleventh Annual Computer Press Awards ≥1995

IDG Books Worldwide, Inc., is a subsidiary of International Data Group, the world's largest publisher of computer-related information and the leading global provider of information services on information technology. International Data Group publishes over 275 computer publications in over 75 countries. Sixty million people read one or more International Data Group publications each month. International Data Group's publications include: **ARGENTINA:** Buyer's Guide, Computerworld Argentina, PC World Argentina; **AUSTRALIA:** Australian Macworld, Australian PC World, Australian Reseller News, Computerworld, IT Casebook, Network World, Publish, Webmaster; **AUSTRIA:** Computerwelt Osterreich, Networks Austria, PC Tip Austria; **BANGLADESH:** PC World Bangladesh; **BELARUS:** PC World Belarus; **BELGIUM:** Data News; **BRAZIL:** Annuário de Informática, Computerworld, Connections, Macworld, PC Player, PC World, Publish, Reseller News, Supergamepower; **BULGARIA:** Computerworld Bulgaria, Network World Bulgaria, PC & MacWorld Bulgaria; **CANADA:** CIO Canada, Client/Server World, ComputerWorld Canada, InfoWorld Canada, NetworkWorld Canada, WebWorld; **CHILE:** Computerworld Chile, PC World Chile; **COLOMBIA:** Computerworld Colombia, PC World Colombia; **COSTA RICA:** PC World Centro America; **THE CZECH AND SLOVAK REPUBLICS:** Computerworld Czechoslovakia, Macworld Czech Republic, PC World Czechoslovakia; **DENMARK:** Communications World Danmark, Computerworld Danmark, Macworld Danmark, PC World Danmark, Techworld Denmark; **DOMINICAN REPUBLIC:** PC World Republica Dominicana; **ECUADOR:** PC World Ecuador; **EGYPT:** Computerworld Middle East, PC World Middle East; **EL SALVADOR:** PC World Centro America; **FINLAND:** MikroPC, Tietoverkko, Tietoviikko; **FRANCE:** Distributique, Hebdo, Info PC, Le Monde Informatique, Macworld, Reseaux & Telecoms, WebMaster France; **GERMANY:** Computer Partner, Computerwoche, Computerwoche Extra, Computerwoche FOCUS, Global Online, Macwelt, PC Welt; **GREECE:** Amiga Computing, GamePro Greece, Multimedia World; **GUATEMALA:** PC World Centro America; **HONDURAS:** PC World Centro America; **HONG KONG:** Computerworld Hong Kong, PC World Hong Kong, Publish in Asia; **HUNGARY:** ABCD CD-ROM, Computerworld Szamitastechnika, Internetto online Magazine, PC World Hungary, PC-X Magazin Hungary; **ICELAND:** Tolvuheimur PC World Island; **INDIA:** Information Communications World, Information Systems Computerworld, PC World India, Publish in Asia; **INDONESIA:** InfoKomputer PC World, Komputek Computerworld, Publish in Asia; **IRELAND:** ComputerScope, PC Live!; **ISRAEL:** Macworld Israel, People & Computers/Computerworld; **ITALY:** Computerworld Italia, Macworld Italia, Networking Italia, PC World Italia; **JAPAN:** DTP World, Macworld Japan, Nikkei Personal Computing, OS/2 World Japan, SunWorld Japan, Windows NT World, Windows World Japan; **KENYA:** PC World East African; **KOREA:** Hi-Tech Information, Macworld Korea, PC World Korea; **MACEDONIA:** PC World Macedonia; **MALAYSIA:** Computerworld Malaysia, PC World Malaysia, Publish in Asia; **MALTA:** PC World Malta; **MEXICO:** Computerworld Mexico, PC World Mexico; **MYANMAR:** PC World Myanmar; **NETHERLANDS:** Computer! Totaal, LAN Internetworking Magazine, LAN World Buyers Guide, Macworld Netherlands, Net, WebWereld; **NEW ZEALAND:** Absolute Beginners Guide and Plain & Simple Series, Computer Buyer, Computer Industry Directory, Computerworld New Zealand, MTB, Network World, PC World New Zealand; **NICARAGUA:** PC World Centro America; **NORWAY:** Computerworld Norge, CW Rapport, Datamagasinet, Financial Rapport, Kursguide Norge, Macworld Norge, Multimediaworld Norge, PC World Ekspress Norge, PC World Nettverk, PC World Norge, PC World ProduktGuide Norge; **PAKISTAN:** Computerworld Pakistan; **PANAMA:** PC World Panama; **PEOPLE'S REPUBLIC OF CHINA:** China Computer Users, China Computerworld, China InfoWorld, China Telecom World Weekly, Computer & Communication, Electronic Design China, Electronics Today, Electronics Weekly, Game Software, PC World China, Popular Computer Week, Software Weekly, Software World, Telecom World; **PERU:** Computerworld Peru, PC World Profesional Peru, PC World SoHo Peru; **PHILIPPINES:** Click!, Computerworld Philippines, PC World Philippines, Publish in Asia; **POLAND:** Computerworld Poland, Computerworld Special Report Poland, Cyber, Macworld Poland, Networld Poland, PC World Komputer; **PORTUGAL:** Cerebro/PC World, Computerworld/Correio Informático, Dealer World Portugal, Mac*In/PC*In Portugal, Multimedia World; **PUERTO RICO:** PC World Puerto Rico; **ROMANIA:** Computerworld Romania, PC World Romania, Telecom Romania; **RUSSIA:** Computerworld Russia, Mir PK, Publish, Seti; **SINGAPORE:** Computerworld Singapore, PC World Singapore, Publish in Asia; **SLOVENIA:** Monitor; **SOUTH AFRICA:** Computing SA, Network World SA, Software World SA; **SPAIN:** Communicaciones World España, Computerworld España, Dealer World España, Macworld España, PC World España; **SRI LANKA:** Infolink PC World; **SWEDEN:** CAP&Design, Computer Sweden, Corporate Computing Sweden, Internetworld Sweden, it.branschen, Macworld Sweden, MaxiData Sweden, MikroDatorn, Nätverk & Kommunikation, PC World Sweden, PCaktiv, Windows World Sweden; **SWITZERLAND:** Computerworld Schweiz, Macworld Schweiz, PCtip; **TAIWAN:** Computerworld Taiwan, Macworld Taiwan, NEW ViSiON/Publish, PC World Taiwan, Windows World Taiwan; **THAILAND:** Publish in Asia, Thai Computerworld; **TURKEY:** Computerworld Turkiye, Macworld Turkiye, Network World Turkiye, PC World Turkiye; **UKRAINE:** Computerworld Kiev, Multimedia World Ukraine, PC World Ukraine; **UNITED KINGDOM:** Acorn User UK, Amiga Action UK, Amiga Computing UK, Apple Talk UK, Computing, Macworld, Parents and Computers UK, PC Advisor, PC Home, PSX Pro, The WEB; **UNITED STATES:** Cable in the Classroom, CIO Magazine, Computerworld, DOS World, Federal Computer Week, GamePro Magazine, InfoWorld, I-Way, Macworld, Network World, PC Games, PC World, Publish, Video Event, THE WEB Magazine, and WebMaster; online webzines: JavaWorld, NetscapeWorld, and SunWorld Online; **URUGUAY:** InfoWorld Uruguay; **VENEZUELA:** Computerworld Venezuela, PC World Venezuela; and **VIETNAM:** PC World Vietnam. 3/24/97

Credits

Acquisitions Editor
Ellen Camm

Development Editors
Alex Miloradovich
Susannah Pfalzer

Technical Editor
Coletta Witherspoon

Copy Editors
Robert Campbell
Carolyn Welch

Project Coordinator
Tom Debolski

Book Designer
Murder By Design

**Graphics and
Production Specialists**
Jude Levinson
Linda Marousek
Hector Mendoza
Christopher Pimentel

Quality Control Specialists
Mick Arellano
Mark Schumann

Proofreader
Mary C. Barnack

Indexer
C² Editorial Services

About the Authors

David Elderbrock

David Elderbrock got his start as an Internet developer at the University of California at Berkeley, where he helped design an online reading and composition database for writing instructors while working on his Ph.D. in English. That was way back in the days when HTML was still an esoteric art practiced mainly in Switzerland. Mosaic was just an XWindows application written by some undergrads in the Midwest, and commerce on the Internet was still regarded as a big taboo.

Since then, David has worked as a commercial intranet and Internet consultant and Web application developer. He has helped design and develop over twenty Internet and intranet Web sites for Apple Computer, Pacific Bell, Citibank, Silicon Graphics, and Barclays Global Investors.

In addition to hammering out his share of Web pages, David has also done programming, mostly in Perl, JavaScript, and Java, and, more recently, a smattering of Visual Basic and C++. He has developed a number of online database applications, SQL and otherwise, on Macintosh, Windows, and UNIX platforms. He is the principal author of *Building Successful Internet Businesses* and a contributing author of *Producing Web Hits*, both IDG Books Worldwide publications.

Any day now, he swears, he is going to get around to designing his own Web site.

Paul Bodensiek

Paul Bodensiek is the owner of ParaGrafix, a Web publishing, graphics, technical writing, and engineering consulting company located just outside of Providence, Rhode Island. He honed all the skills required to make ParaGrafix a go during his 12-year tenure as the entire engineering, technical service, graphics, and training departments for a small manufacturing company. During his time with that company he also picked up five U.S. and over 25 foreign patents.

Paul has written, contributed to, or edited about 15 books on Web publishing, computer graphics, and computer gaming. He's also written over 100 user manuals for various hardware, software, and manufacturing companies. His most recent book is *Corel WebMaster Suite For Dummies*, published by IDG Books Worldwide.

To my wife, Tamar, for her constant support, and our sons, Eric and Evan, for their steadfast refusal to let a mere book have dibs on their dad. —*David Elderbrock*

To my wife, Mary, and daughter, Melissa, who have been fantastic throughout the writing of this and my other books. I'm grateful they have put up with my extended absences. —*Paul Bodensiek*

Preface

Just a few years ago, the Internet was a sleepy cow town on the virtual edge of reality. Then somebody built the information highway right down its main street, and behold, a new frontier was discovered. Go Web, young man! Today, the Web has transformed itself into a global metropolis, and many people and institutions have staked out their territory in this new world. That's where FrontPage 98 comes in — the most recent version of Microsoft's entry-level Web development and Web site management tool.

Why You Need This Book

On a basic level, FrontPage is easy to use, yet it can put a great deal of power in your hands — text searching, discussion forums, form submission, not to mention Java applets, ActiveX controls, and a host of other advanced, jargon-injected techniques. Suddenly, things aren't sounding so simple anymore. That's where this book comes in. Here's why:

+ **For new users:** *FrontPage 98 Bible* offers plenty of carefully explained, step-by-step examples. It's ideal for anyone who wants to create high-quality Web sites without focusing on the technical side.

+ **For the pros:** *FrontPage 98 Bible* pushes and prods FrontPage at every turn to take the application as far as *it* can go. It's for developers fluent in the ways of the Web, looking for the tools to become *more* productive and to expand their repertoire of technical expertise. It's for Web project teams, too, who need to coordinate the work of content editors, graphic designers, and programmers. This book offers sage advice on how to get the work done quickly, while ensuring a quality result.

+ **For all of us:** For the most part, the *FrontPage 98 Bible* is just good solid information presented in readable doses. It recognizes the serious nature of Web publishing yet, thankfully, retains the sense of fun — and occasional good-natured irreverence — that has characterized the Web from its inception.

How This Book Is Organized

Here's a brief description of what you'll find in the parts, chapters, and appendixes, and on the CD-ROM.

Part I: Building a Basic Web

The first chapter provides a quick-start tour of FrontPage by walking you through the steps to create a personal Web site. Only one chapter into the book, and already you have your own Web site! Chapters 2 and 3 examine the two main components of FrontPage in greater detail — the FrontPage Editor and Explorer. The fictional case studies that serve as the basis for most of the examples in the book are introduced here as well.

Part II: Enhancing the Look and Feel

Here we focus on ways to make your Web site more attractive and easy to navigate. Image Composer, the sprite-based image creation tool that Microsoft has packaged along with FrontPage 98, is covered. We show you how to use FrontPage to create image maps so fast it would make a Web old-timer cry. You'll also learn how to add life to the images on your Web site, convert PowerPoint animations, and use Microsoft's GIF Animator (included on the CD-ROM) in conjunction with Image Composer to generate sample animations.

Part III: HTML Layout and Design

In this part we turn to advanced page layout topics — formatting with tables and frames, HTML editing techniques, and using style sheets. Even simple things are covered in detail, and although these chapters speak, in part, to the HTML savvy, they also provide step-by-step examples using style sheets and frames that even the HTML-challenged can follow.

Part IV: Adding Interactivity

The Components have landed! FrontPage components (formerly referred to as WebBots) are the built-in, easy to install and customize Web programs that come with FrontPage 98. This part of the book puts these "Botsters" through their paces, demonstrating both how easy they are to set up and suggesting a number of ways to extend their usefulness. Topics such as creating and implementing forms, text searching, and discussion forums are addressed in the fullest.

Part V: Programming Elements

Part V looks at the variety of programming languages for which FrontPage provides at least a modicum of support — VBScript, JavaScript, ActiveX, and Java. Along the way, we sort through some of the issues relating to database connectivity. Special attention is given to the Script Wizard incorporated into FrontPage 98. We also look at some tools for bringing programming down to the level of the common user. Each chapter in this part of the book provides examples and references to additional resources.

Part VI: Administering and Maintaining Your Site

The last part of this book examines a number of issues relating to managing and publishing your Web project and administering your site. We discuss the ins and outs of adding the FrontPage server extensions to your Web server. We look at ways that FrontPage can be incorporated into team-based Web projects, including a discussion of linking FrontPage with Visual Source Safe, Microsoft's version control product. Finally, we review the major issues related to using FrontPage across a firewall or in conjunction with secure servers.

The appendixes

Appendix A provides easy-to-follow directions for those who would rather not plow through the official installation instructions. Appendix B covers upgrading from FrontPage 97. Appendix C deals with FrontPage server extensions, and Appendix D tells you all you need to know about using the CD-ROM attached to the back of this good book.

What's on the CD

The book includes a CD-ROM with all of the examples described in the book, as well as a number of other goodies (see Appendix D for details). There are content files that allow you to follow along with the examples and finished versions in case you are too impatient to do the examples yourself.

Conventions Used in This Book

All the components of the *FrontPage 98 Bible* are designed to work in concert. You can use the book (along with the wealth of examples and applications on the book's CD-ROM) as a cover-to-cover tutorial — beginning with the basics and proceeding to the advanced stages of FrontPage 98 and beyond. Or you can also use this book and the CD as a reference, dipping into it, topic-by-topic, as you deem necessary.

As an added feature for users who have upgraded to FrontPage 98 from FrontPage 97, look for icons like the one immediately to the left of this paragraph. The information found here clues you in to the new features, and occasional quirks, that are characteristic of the 98 version of FrontPage.

This is a note icon. It's a signpost to call your attention to especially insightful or just plain interesting factoids of various types. When you see the ⇨ symbol in this book (for example, select Edit ⇨ Current Color Fill) it's telling you in shorthand what path you need to follow to find a command under a menu. You'll find lots of notes like these in this book. They're sort of like asides in plays. Imagine the book is whispering them to you, so that those other people, over there, won't hear what it's saying.

The tip icon indicates a pearl of wisdom you could spend your life hunting for in vain. Tips are usually creative solutions to insoluble life problems, or at least thorny Web problems, if you'll pardon the mixed metaphor.

The caution icon alerts you to the presence of a don't-say-I-didn't-warn-you comment. Often cautions call your attention to an ever-so-slight shortcoming in FrontPage's ability to perform. Ignore these at your peril.

A few basic concepts

Sidebars, like this one, are a major feature of this book. They usually contain interesting technical asides and further information to support step-by-step processes. This sidebar informs you of the following important concepts:

✦ We assume you have a copy of FrontPage 98 and a Web server somewhere in the wings.

✦ In general you will glean the most from each chapter if you read it with FrontPage 98 up and running on your computer.

✦ Because FrontPage 98 ships with Microsoft's Personal Web Server, most of the book's examples focus on this combination.

✦ The operating system that receives the most attention in this book is Windows 95.

✦ UNIX Web servers and other Windows servers, such as O'Reilly's WebSite and Microsoft's own Windows NT-based Internet Information Server (IIS) are touched on in passing.

Taking the Next Step

At the end of each chapter, we pause to reflect on what we've learned and what adventures the next chapter holds. So here we are at the end of the preface. Now is the time to take the next step. If you haven't done so already, buy this book. Take it home or to the office. Better yet, take it to the beach or the woods, and then read it. (Personally, we never go out without our laptops, cell phones, portable faxes, and satellite dishes.) With FrontPage 98 and the information in this book (a good tan and some fresh mountain air), your Web site design and publishing experiences are bound to be good ones.

Acknowledgments

I would like to recognize and thank a number of dedicated and talented individuals who helped to bring this book into the world. Acquisitions editor Ellen Camm ensured the timely completion of the manuscript, supervising the writing schedule with unwavering kindness. My development editor, Alex Miloradovich, deserves two medals: one for helping maintain the structure and integrity of the book, and a second for his optimism and encouragement under all circumstances. I also want to thank Coletta Witherspoon, who helped to ensure the book's technical correctness, copyeditor Robert Campbell for repairing the damage I not infrequently wrought upon the English language, and Susannah Pfalzer, who helped put together the CD-ROM. I also owe a special thanks to my co-author, Paul Bodensiek, for his thorough and professionally written contributions.

Three other very special people—my wife, Tamar, and sons Eric and Evan—deserve credit and thanks for patiently supporting me through the long process of writing this book.

Contents at a Glance

Contents

· ·

Part II: Enhancing the Look and Feel   103

Part V: Programming Elements   349

Chapter 15: Scripting (VBScript and JavaScript) 351

Part VI: Administering and Maintaining Your Site   455

Chapter 18: Managing and Publishing Your Web Project 457

Building a Basic Web

Your First Web

This chapter is intended as a quick start for those who, like me, are impatient to dive right in to FrontPage. This chapter shows how easy it is to begin building your Web site with FrontPage even if you are not a veteran Web developer. Along the way, the chapter highlights some of the program's most prominent features, focusing on the tasks you would be likely to perform when designing a new Web site. By the end of the chapter you will have created your first Web—a simple, but serviceable, personal Web. If you prefer a more methodical approach, you may want to skip ahead to Chapter 2 and begin learning the FrontPage fundamentals. After you finish Part I, be sure to come back here and try your hand at building your first Web.

Introducing FrontPage

Microsoft FrontPage is a tool for creating, editing, publishing, and maintaining Web sites. It is designed for people who want to produce sophisticated Web sites quickly without necessarily becoming expert in all the technical details of Web development. Novices can use FrontPage to develop and maintain elegant, interactive Web sites. Professional developers can use FrontPage to increase their productivity, manage their projects more efficiently, and deliver cutting-edge, customized Web applications. You can use FrontPage to develop your own Internet-based business, a departmental Web as part of your company's intranet, or—as we illustrate in this chapter—your own personal Web site.

In the course of this book, we examine in detail each of FrontPage's many features. For those who are curious, here is a preview of some of FrontPage's capabilities:

✦ **Create new Webs and import existing Webs**—If you already have a Web, you can convert it to the FrontPage environment in a matter of minutes. If you don't yet have a Web, FrontPage provides wizards and templates to get you started quickly with a variety of different types of Webs.

✦ **Edit Web pages in a WYSIWYG environment**—"What you see is what you get" means that you can edit a Web page much as though it were a word processing document, without worrying about the technicalities of how it is created. Use the templates, themes, and wizards to develop professional-looking Webs quickly and painlessly.

✦ **Easily insert graphics, programming components, and other active elements** —Graphics can be added to a Web page as easily as importing a file or dragging an image onto the page. FrontPage components, such as text searching, discussion forums, and feedback forms, can also be added instantly.

✦ **Design Webs with such advanced layout features as tables and frames**—FrontPage 98 makes it easy to build even complicated table structures, and you can even build frames-based Web pages in WYSIWYG mode.

✦ **Designate shared borders for your Web pages and automatically generate a graphical navigation system**—Shared borders allow you to create consistent headers, footers, or side panels on all your pages. Edit a shared border once and see it reflected on all your Web pages.

✦ **Create cascading style sheets to maintain a consistent visual style across all your Web pages**—Create style sheets for your Web, ensuring a consistent look on all your pages.

✦ **Include cutting-edge technologies**—Even though FrontPage is easy to use, it offers room to expand. You can always add sophisticated applications coded in Visual Basic, JavaScript, ActiveX, Java, and a host of other Web programming languages. You can even use FrontPage to help you develop database applications. FrontPage 98 includes many new features that help you tap the power of Internet Explorer version 4.0.

✦ **Keep track of "to do" tasks**—FrontPage includes a Task List view that helps you be more productive. FrontPage can generate tasks automatically when they are needed; you can also add your own, mark them when completed, and keep a history of all the work you have done.

✦ **Publish and maintain your Web**—FrontPage includes tools for verifying hyperlinks as well as basic text maintenance tasks such as spell-checking. You can set up your Web with different levels of access or maintain multiple Webs with different access privileges. The FrontPage Publishing Wizard makes it easy to publish your Web to a remote Web server.

Learning the Key Concepts

I know you are eager to dive in (after all, that's what this chapter is about), but before you can get started building your first FrontPage Web, you need to understand a few key terms and concepts.

Defining a Web

A *Web,* in the FrontPage lexicon, is a set of Web pages and associated content contained in a single directory structure (that is, a top-level folder and all of its subfolders). The term "Web" can throw those of us who are used to referring to this same entity as a "Web site." So what's the difference between a FrontPage Web and the more common notion of a Web site? In most instances, the distinction is probably slight. Your FrontPage Web *is* your Web site. It is possible, however, to create multiple FrontPage Webs on the same Web site. You might want to think of a FrontPage "Web" as a "Web project"—a group of pages that are convenient to keep together because you are working on them as a unit. Over time, you might develop several different Web projects on your site. Or you might have different teams, each of which is responsible for maintaining one of the Webs on your site. To your visitors, the site appears to be a single entity. Only you know that it is in fact composed of multiple FrontPage Webs.

Defining a Web page

These days it is hard to find a person who has never seen a Web page. If you are mostly acquainted with Web pages from a user's perspective, however, you will find it helpful to review some of the characteristics of a Web page from a developer's standpoint. Even though FrontPage enables you to create Web pages without worrying about the technical details of their construction, you should have a basic familiarity with how a Web page is constituted so that you can better understand what you are doing. (If you *do* know a thing or two about Web page development, you will be happy to know that FrontPage gives you direct access to the Web page's HTML, so you can edit it manually if you prefer.)

Web pages under the hood

The Web page that you see in your Web browser is generated from an ordinary text file composed using a simple but powerful markup language called HTML (short for Hypertext Markup Language). HTML is called a markup language because it "marks up" the text to indicate how the page should be displayed. These markers are known as HTML "tags," and, in principle, they are much the same as the special formatting codes that word processors add to your text without showing you. Figure 1-1 shows an example of a simple Web page with a banner graphic and welcome text. Here is the same page as seen by a text editor with the HTML tags revealed:

```
<html>
<head>
<title>Welcome to this very simple Web page!</title>
</head>
<body bgcolor="#FFFFFF">
<p><img src="simple.gif" width="513" height="56"></p>
<p><font size="5"><strong>Welcome to this very simple Web
page!</strong></font></p>
</body>
</html>
```

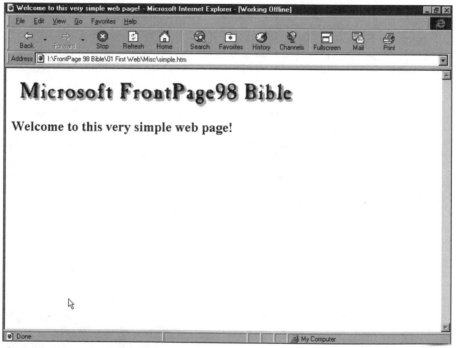

Figure 1-1: A very simple Web page as displayed by a Web browser

When you use FrontPage Editor, you will be constructing HTML pages without having to worry about how HTML tags work. You simply indicate that you want the text a certain size or placed in a certain way, and FrontPage will do the dirty work. What FrontPage produces, however, is the same HTML text file format that would be created if you did the work by hand. If you are curious, you can always check the HTML source—a great way to learn HTML painlessly!

The anatomy of an URL

A Web page creates links, known as *hyperlinks,* to other kinds of content, including graphics, video, and sound files as well as other Web pages. Hyperlinks are the Web's claim to fame, because they mean that any piece of content publicly accessible on the Web anywhere around the globe can be directly linked to any other piece of content. Now that's power! The only catch is that you have to know how to reference the page you want to link to. That's where Uniform Resource Locators (URLs) come in.

Every element on the World Wide Web has a unique identifier that amounts to its "address" on the Internet. That identifier is known as an URL (Uniform Resource Locator—pronounced "you-are-ell" by neophytes and "earl" by the cognoscenti). An URL works very much like a postal address. It is composed of several parts—analogous to the street number, street name, city, state, and postal code—organized hierarchically of the elements shown in Figure 1-2 (which you should come to know intimately).

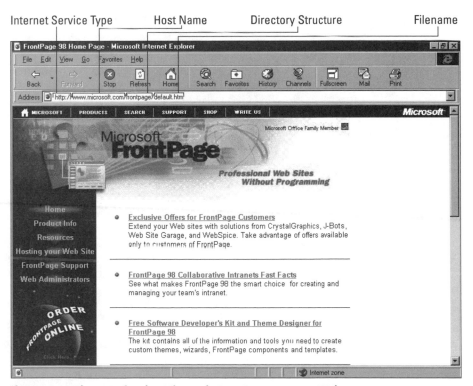

Figure 1-2: The URL for the Microsoft FrontPage support Web

✦ **Internet service type** (http://)—This first section of the URL identifies the type of Internet service being accessed. HTTP, short for Hypertext Transport Protocol, is the identifier for Web documents. Other commonly encountered service types include e-mail (mailto://), File Transfer Protocol (FTP, ftp://), and secure (encrypted) Web documents (https://).

✦ **Internet host name** (www.microsoft.com)—This identifier is the Internet name of the computer that hosts, or houses, this Web. The host name is itself composed of multiple parts, "www" being the individual host name, and "microsoft.com" naming a network or domain composed of many computers (presumably).

✦ **Computer port number** (default is :80)—After the host name, some URLs may include a port number. Each service on a host computer is assigned to a specific port, and every type of service has a default port number. In the case of Web servers, the default number is 80. If an URL does not include a port number, the default is assumed. If a Web server is running on some other port, you must include this number.

✦ **Directory structure** (/frontpage/)—Following the port number, or the domain name if no port is indicated, comes the directory path of the file we are referencing. In this case, the FrontPage Web page resides in a directory called (of all things!) "frontpage."

✦ **Filename** (default.htm)—The last element in the URL is the filename, which consists of the main part of the name and an extension (.htm or .html) that identifies the file type; in this case, it's an HTML file.

Enhanced Web page content

Now you may be wondering, how does an ordinary text file show up in my Web browser with graphics, animation, and even video? The answer is that the same URL addressing scheme that links one Web page to another also enables other kinds of content to be linked to your Web page. The only difference is that Web browsers know how to recognize certain kinds of nontext content and to embed that content directly into the page itself. In all cases, however, the additional content resides in a separate file that is referenced within the HTML of the Web page. (You may have noticed in your Web surfing that when a Web page is loaded, it loads each of the graphical and other content elements separately).

Note

Originally, graphics were the only type of embedded content. Now it seems the list of formats that browsers know how to display grows longer every day. For instance, a browser can easily be made to recognize additional content types by adding modules that help it deal with specialized content. In the Netscape world, these modules are known as "plug-ins"; in the Microsoft camp, they are called "controls." And although the two entities do not function in exactly the same way, they have basically the same goal—to make your browser smarter.

Distinguishing a Web page from a file

If you happen to be developing your Web on a local computer (as opposed to accessing your Web remotely over the Internet), you may find it hard to keep in mind the difference between your Web pages and the files in your file system (the files stored on your hard drive). Microsoft has to some extent encouraged this confusion by making FrontPage Explorer work very much like Windows Explorer (even giving them the same name). After all, you can see your Web files in Explorer just like any other files. What makes them any different?

The answer is that when you create Web pages or add other files as part of a FrontPage Web, FrontPage stores some special information about them. When you make changes to them, it stores information about the changes as well. In effect, FrontPage "registers" all of the files in your Web so that it can keep track of them. Now, if you make a change to a file outside FrontPage—say, for instance, you rename it using the Windows Explorer—FrontPage doesn't know about the change. Likewise, if you try to add files to your project directory, FrontPage doesn't know about them.

The moral of the story: You will avoid a lot of potential heartbreak (can you hear the voice of experience speaking here?) by remembering the distinction between your Web and your other files and by making sure to make all changes affecting the status of your Web via FrontPage.

From authoring to publishing

When you "author" a Web page, you create it and all of its links to other pages and content. You can create and view these Web pages using your own computer, even if you are not connected to the Internet. If you want the pages to be seen by the world at large, however, you need to "publish" them to a Web server that is connected to the Internet at all times.

What's in a Web server?

The notion of a Web server can be a somewhat slippery concept. Sometimes when people say "Web server," they mean the physical computer, or "host," that is connected to the Internet and that houses the Web files. More specifically, a Web server is a program that runs continually on the host computer and waits for requests for Web pages to come in.

The job of the Web server application is to interpret those requests and respond appropriately. When you "publish" your Web, you are making the Web pages and other files available to a Web server so that it can pass them on to all who request them, using their favorite Web browsers (sometimes called Web "clients").

Tip If the publishing concept is not crystal-clear to you yet, you will be happy to learn that FrontPage includes a Web Publishing Wizard that takes much of the pain out of publishing your Webs. This wizard is discussed in detail in Chapter 18.

Creating a Personal Web

Enough with preliminaries already. Let's create your first Web. The main goal in what follows is to introduce you to some of FrontPage's leading features as you do something practical. This chapter takes a step-by-step approach to the task at hand. It does not by any means cover all of FrontPage's features. For more thorough coverage, skip to the rest of the chapters in Part I. But come back here when you are done—this is the fun chapter!

Using the CD-ROM

The CD-ROM that accompanies this book includes all of the files used in the examples as well as several useful Web applications and utilities. The files from the book are located in two main folders: `Contents` contains the files necessary to reproduce all of the examples, if you like to learn by doing. If you would rather just view the finished results, these are contained in the `Examples` folder. Each of these directories is subdivided according to the chapters of the book.

You can use the example files in one of the following ways:

✦ Follow along using your Web browser. Open an HTML file directly from the CD-ROM using whatever method your browser supports for viewing local HTML files.

✦ Copy the files directly to your FrontPage Web directory.

✦ Import the files into your own FrontPage Web. (You learn how to do this in Chapter 2.)

Starting FrontPage

In this quick start chapter, I assume that you have installed FrontPage successfully and are ready to create your first Web. This Web is created and stored locally.

When you start FrontPage for the first time, you are prompted to wait while FrontPage determines the host name of your computer. This becomes the basis of the addressing scheme that FrontPage uses when you create a new Web.

Starting FrontPage Explorer

If you followed the default FrontPage installation, you can use the Windows 95 Start menu to access FrontPage by selecting Programs ➪ Microsoft FrontPage. This launches Microsoft FrontPage Explorer, where you create and maintain your Webs.

When you start the application, the FrontPage Explorer application opens. If this is the first time you have started the application, you may see a message alerting you that "FrontPage will now try to determine your host name."

Tip

The FrontPage list of recently accessed servers is stored in the `fpexplor.ini` file in the Windows directory. You can use a text editor to remove extraneous entries in this list.

Creating a new Web

After FrontPage has successfully completed its initial housekeeping, it presents you with the Getting Started dialog box as shown in Figure 1-3. Use this dialog box to open an existing Web or create a new one.

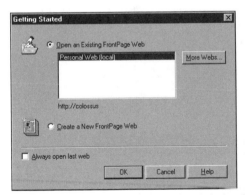

Figure 1-3: Use the Getting Started dialog box to create a new Web or load an existing one.

Tip

To prevent the Getting Started dialog box from appearing each time you start the application, select Options from the Explorer Tools menu and uncheck the Show Getting Started check box.

When it first installs itself, FrontPage creates a "root," or master, Web, identified as "<Root Web>" in the list of available Webs. If you plan to create only one Web on your Web site, you can use this. Figure 1-4 illustrates what the default root Web folder structure looks like in FrontPage Explorer. In this chapter, you create a new Web using the Personal Web template.

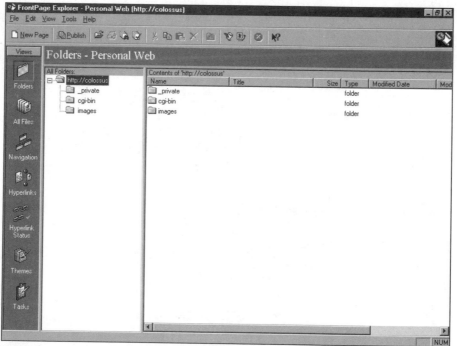

Figure 1-4: The root Web file structure as it appears in FrontPage 98

To start building your new Web, select the Create a New FrontPage Web option and click OK. This brings up the two-step New FrontPage Web dialog box (see Figure 1-5). In step 1, select the kind of Web you plan to develop. You have three basic options:

✦ **One Page Web**—This option creates a Web with a single, blank home page.

✦ **Import an Existing Web**—Use this option when you want to use FrontPage to maintain an existing Web site that was not built using FrontPage.

✦ **From Wizard or Template**—This option enables you to select one of FrontPage's numerous predefined Web structures.

Selecting the Personal Web option

To create your personal Web site, select From Wizard or Template from this dialog box, and then select the Personal Web option from the list of available templates and wizards.

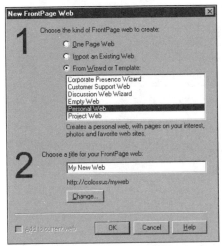

Figure 1-5: To create a new Web, select the kind of Web you want to create and give your new Web a title.

In part 2 of this dialog box, give your Web a title. Notice that as you type, FrontPage translates your Web title into the folder name that will contain your Web and displays this name just below the title input box. If you want to change the default folder name, select the Change button, and type the desired folder name in the Change Location dialog box.

FrontPage supports only Webs created one directory below the root directory. The application does not allow you to create a Web that is two directories deeper than the root Web.

Watching your Web as it builds

FrontPage now constructs the default pages for your personal Web. The view switches from Folders view to Navigation view, as shown in Figure 1-6, as the pages are loaded. You should see a box representing your home page at the top of the navigation map and three boxes linked below it. These boxes are labeled Interests, Photo Album, and Favorites. Below the diagram is the list of files and folders that form your new, personal Web.

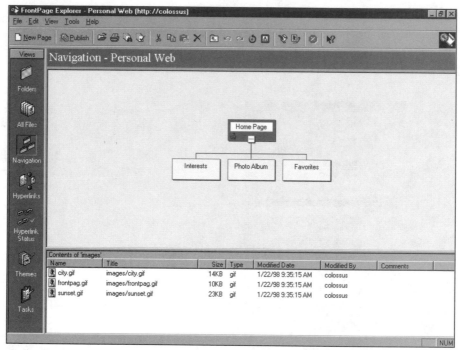

Figure 1-6: The first glimpse of your personal Web in FrontPage Navigation view

Introducing the Explorer workplace

At this point, you are looking at your new Web in FrontPage Explorer—the FrontPage component that takes care of organizing, managing, and publishing your Webs. Let's take a moment now to investigate the many ways Explorer lets you view your Web. Later in this chapter we examine some of Explorer's basic management and publishing capabilities. For detailed information on using Explorer, you can turn to the next chapter.

For some reason (lack of creativity?), Microsoft has apparently decided to give the name "Something-or-Other Explorer" to every third product it produces. For the sake of brevity, in this book, when I refer to "Explorer," I mean FrontPage Explorer. Any references to the other Explorers include their full name (for example, Internet Explorer or Windows 95 Explorer). Similarly, the other principle component of FrontPage, FrontPage Editor, is referred to as "Editor."

The Explorer workplace consists of the following three principle areas:

✦ **Menu and toolbar**—These provide quick access to the main functionality of the application. The icons on the main toolbar change when you change the view.

✦ **Views frame**—Arranged vertically down the left-hand column of the workplace, this set of seven icons provides access to the different ways you can view and interact with the content of your Web. To change the size of the icons in this frame, click anywhere inside it with the right mouse button and select the icon size, small or large, you prefer. The available views in Explorer include:

- **Folders**—As shown in Figure 1-7, Folders view looks very much like the Windows 95 Explorer. It shows a folder and file list of all of the items in your Web. Double-clicking a file icon launches it in Editor.

- **All Files**—The All Files view is similar to Folders view, except that it simply shows a flat list of all the files in the Web. Double-clicking a file icon launches it in Editor.

- **Navigation**—Navigation view is used to generate a customizable navigation bar for the site and organize your Web to see the relationships between your pages. This is a new feature in FrontPage 98. You can use Navigation view to launch pages in Editor.

- **Hyperlinks**—Hyperlinks view shows the links among the Web pages in a Web. It can be used to trace the interconnections among the various Web pages as well as to launch pages in Editor.

- **Hyperlink Status**—This shows a list of all hyperlinks and their validation status. It assists in the often burdensome task of link maintenance.

- **Themes**—Another new addition in FrontPage 98, *themes* are collections of styles and images that can be added to your Web automatically, ensuring a consistent look and feel.

- **Tasks**—A revised version of the To Do window in FrontPage 97, this facility aids in the management of larger Web projects, especially ones in whose development many people are involved.

✦ **The View window**—This main window, which is sometimes further subdivided, shows you the currently selected view of your Web. You can adjust the size of this window by clicking and dragging the frame borders of the window. In some views this window may itself be divided into multiple frames.

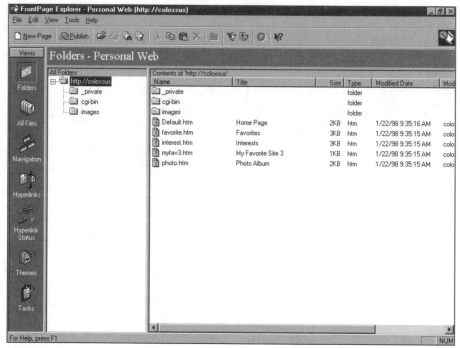

Figure 1-7: The Explorer workplace, showing the Folders view

In the next section, we take a quick spin through some of the more useful Web views. More thorough coverage of Explorer views is provided in Chapter 2.

Viewing your Web

By default, when you create your personal Web, it opens in Navigation view. Navigation view, as shown in Figure 1-6, consists of a diagrammatic flow chart of how to navigate your Web. Navigation view has two principle functions. The first is to create a map of your site, which you can manipulate and print. The second is to create a structure that FrontPage uses to automatically generate a navigation system for your pages.

Each box in the Navigation view represents one page in your Web. Lines connecting the boxes represent navigational hyperlinks from one page to the next. Each row represents a level of hierarchy in the Web. You can rearrange the structure of your Web's navigation by dragging a Web page box to another location in the diagram.

For example, click the Interests box and drag it until it is directly underneath the Photo Album box. Drag the Favorites box underneath the Interests box. The result is illustrated in Figure 1-8. Now the Favorites box is connected only to the Interests page, which is in turn connected only to the Photo Album page. Users would only traverse these pages in a linear sequence, which sort of defeats the purpose of hyperlinking. To restore navigation to its original status, you must drag each box back to its original position. Explorer does have an undo feature—but be careful, because it allows only one level of undoing (unlike the more generous Editor, which has 30 levels of undo!).

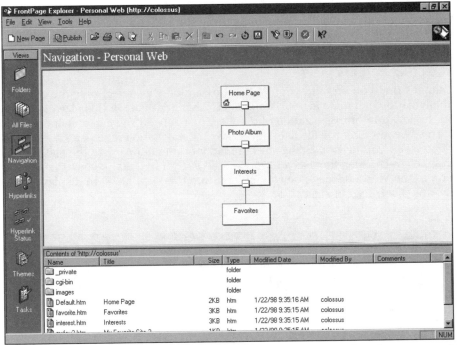

Figure 1-8: Fun with boxes—rearranging the navigational hierarchy of our personal Web

To reorient the flow chart, click anywhere in the View window with the right mouse button and select Rotate from the pop-up menu. Alternatively, use the Rotate icon on the toolbar to accomplish the same object. This pop-up menu also has options to Expand All levels of the diagram and to add a New Page. Click the minus (–) box on the Home Page icon to collapse the map and show only the top-level box. If your site is getting rather large but you still want to see the entire hierarchy, select View ⇨ Size to Fit—this makes the boxes smaller so that your entire Web appears in the View window.

You can also change the labels on each box. Click the Favorites box once to select it. Next click the text label to highlight it and enable it to be edited (if you click too quickly, FrontPage may interpret this action as a double-click and launch the page instead). Type in any new label you want, **Cool links**, for instance. In a few moments, you will see the results of this operation. Note that you can also right-click a filename and select Rename from the pop-up menu to avoid the double-click conundrum.

In my opinion, the Navigation view feature, added to FrontPage 98, alone is worth the price of the upgrade. Not only does it allow you to create a printable map of your site on the fly as you build it, it also automatically generates your navigation system for you.

We examine this view in more detail later in the chapter, after you learn how to edit your Web pages.

Selecting Folders view

Changes that you make to your Web in Navigation view affect only the construction of navigation elements in your Web pages. Changes made in this view have no effect on the location or organization of the files themselves. You can convince yourself of this by watching the file list pane below the navigation map pane in Navigation view. When you make a change to the map, nothing happens to the files. To make changes to the files themselves, you should switch to Folders view. Click the Folder icon in the Views frame or select Folders from the View menu to display the Folders view as illustrated in Figure 1-9.

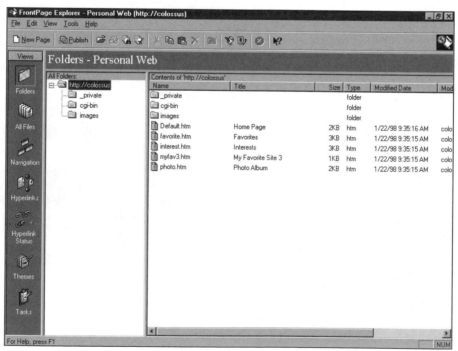

Figure 1-9: Folders view in Explorer

Folders view probably looks familiar to you—it mimics the interface used by Microsoft's Windows Explorer—although it displays only files and folders that have been either created by or imported into FrontPage. If you prefer to see a flat list of the files in your Web, select the All Files view instead.

Selecting Hyperlinks view

Now click the Hyperlinks View icon. In Hyperlinks view, the Explorer window is divided into two vertical frames. On the left side is a branching list of all of the Web pages and links in the Web. It is labeled "All Pages." The home page for your new Web is indicated with a House icon. Additional pages are indicated with document icons. Hyperlinks to other Web sites, of which there is one from your home page, are shown with a Globe icon. Graphics linked to the pages are also represented, as are links to other Web pages. Figure 1-10 shows the Personal Web list fully expanded.

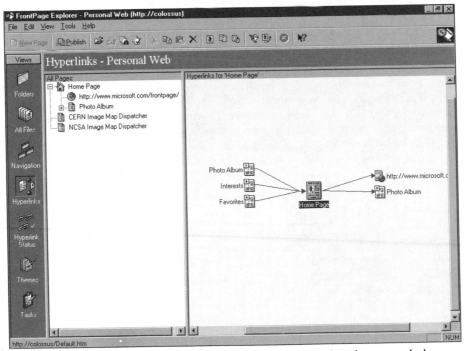

Figure 1-10: The personal Web from Hyperlinks view, showing the expanded branches of the hyperlinks

On the right side is a diagrammatic view that shows the currently selected Web page and all of its links. By default, the home page is the central page. It is identified with a Web page icon (showing an embedded image surrounded by text). All of the links contained on this page are shown as arrows pointing to smaller Web page icons with the Globe icon attached.

Click the minus sign next to the House icon in the All Pages frame. The branching tree collapses, showing only the Home Page icon with a plus sign next to it (the door of the House icon also turns red). Click the plus sign to expand the branch again.

Select a new item in the All Pages list. Move the mouse down the list of hyperlinks in your home page. Notice how each one is briefly underlined as you pass over it, indicating that the item is selected. When you select an item in the list, it becomes the central item in the diagrammatic view. Try clicking various pages. The diagram will look similar, except that the name of the hyperlinked document will change. Click the Home Page icon to return to the default view.

Locating your home page

Two of the views in Explorer, Navigation view and Hyperlinks view, call special attention to your Web's home page. For all practical purposes, you can think of the home page as the "top-level" page of your Web. It is also the default page for the Web, which means that anyone who points to your Web without requesting a particular page will get your home page. From a user's standpoint, a home page frequently serves to welcome visitors, introduce them to the contents of the Web, and provide links to all of the major sections of the site. In the next section we begin our editing of your Web with the home page.

Editing Web Pages

Viewing your Web from different perspectives is useful and informative, but at this point you are probably eager to get on with the task of building your Web pages. To this end, you must call on the services of the second half of the FrontPage dynamic duo—FrontPage Editor.

Editor is responsible for creating and editing individual Web pages. You can launch Editor in any of number of ways. You can open Editor from the Start menu (although by default FP98 only puts the Explorer application in the Start menu), or you can click the Editor icon in the Explorer toolbar. Both of these methods open Editor with a new, empty Web page.

More often than not, though, you want to call on Editor in order to edit a particular Web page. To do this, double-click an existing Web page from within Explorer from any of its views.

You were last in Hyperlinks view, so let's open your home page from there:

1. Switch to Hyperlinks view if you are not there already by clicking the Hyperlinks icon in the View window.

2. Select your Web's home page by clicking the House icon in the Web page list —the left-hand column of the View window. (Note that if you double-click this icon it will collapse or expand the branches underneath it.)

3. Select a page in this Hyperlinks list to move that page to the center of the Hyperlinks View window with a larger document icon and link arrows pointing into and out from this icon. Double-click this icon to launch Editor with this page. You should see a home page that resembles the one in Figure 1-11.

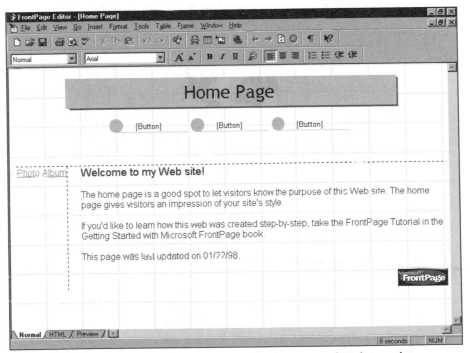

Figure 1-11: The default home page created by the personal Web template

You can use this same method of double-clicking the file icon to open Web pages from Navigation, Folders, or All Files view.

The Editor workplace

The Editor workplace consists of the following three main components:

✦ **Menu and toolbars**—In addition to its two default toolbars, the Standard toolbar and the Format toolbar, Editor has several specialized toolbars— Images, Forms, Advanced, and Tables. Each of these toolbars can be made visible or hidden. They can also be detached and made to float alongside the application.

✦ **The Document window**—This is the main area of Editor. It displays one of three representations of your Web page. The default, Normal view, shows a reasonable facsimile of what your page will look like from a Web browser. You use Normal view for most of your Web page authoring and editing.

✦ **View tabs**—In the bottom-left corner of the main Document window are three tabs that allow you to view your page from different perspectives. You can view your Web page in any of three ways by selecting one of these tabs:

• **Normal**—Normal view is where you do most of your editing. This view shows your page in WYSIWYG fashion. It also shows formatting marks and lines indicating the location of tables, frames, shared borders, forms, and such.

• **HTML**—Use this view to edit the HTML source of the Web page directly.

• **Preview**—This view shows the Web page more or less as it will appear online. This can be handy for making quick checks, but you should still preview your pages in at least one browser before publishing them, since not all elements can be displayed in Preview mode.

New in 98

The tab system in Editor is a new addition to FrontPage. The handy tabs make it easy to switch among WYSIWYG editing, direct HTML editing, and Preview modes.

The predefined elements of your home page

When you launch your Web page, you may be pleasantly surprised to discover that much of the design work for your home page has already been done for you. As you can see from Figure 1-11, your default home page has a background, a banner graphic, working navigational buttons, and text links. Open the other pages in the Web and notice that they have the same elements, all with the appropriate links. These elements are introduced here and discussed more fully later in the chapter.

Themes

FrontPage 98 comes with several sets of coordinated graphical elements and text styles: banners, buttons, bullets, and horizontal rules that together make up what FrontPage refers to as a *theme*. When you apply a theme to your Web, it automatically gives you the appropriately styled object whenever you insert that element into your page. By default your personal Web uses the "Global Marketing" theme.

New in 98

Themes are a new addition to the FrontPage repertoire. They are certainly fun and easy to use. It remains to be seen how many FrontPage users will actually use these themes in a production Web site.

Note

While the included themes are nice, it would be great to be able to design your own and gain the same functionality. Microsoft is a little sneaky—they've included a utility to do this but made no mention of it in any of their documentation. Luckily for you, you've purchased this book to find out tidbits like this. Chapter 4, "Graphics and Themes," includes instructions for installing and using this utility.

Changing the default theme

You can change or remove the theme either from your Web as a whole or from a given page. To change the default theme for your Web, you must first return to Explorer. You can switch between Explorer and Editor using their toolbar icons. Click the Explorer icon on the Editor toolbar to bring Explorer to the front.

In Explorer, select the Themes icon from the Views frame. The list of available themes with previews of their contents appears (see Figure 1-12). Select a theme name from the list to see its preview. In addition to changing the theme itself, you also have three other options:

- ✦ **Vivid Colors**—Add more colorful text to the theme styles.

- ✦ **Active Graphics**—Add animated "hover buttons" (that is, buttons that change their appearance when you pass the mouse cursor over them) to the theme.

- ✦ **Background Image**—Uncheck this option to include a solid-color background with the theme instead of a tiled background image.

To apply a new theme, first select it and then click Apply. The default theme for all of your pages is now changed. Use the Editor icon in the Explorer toolbar to return to your home page to see what a difference a style change can mean!

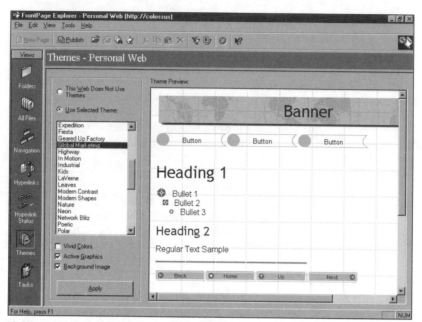

Figure 1-12: The Themes view from Explorer showing the Preview mode for the Global Marketing theme

Changing the theme on one page

You can also change the theme on a page-by-page basis. With your home page open in Editor, select Format ➪ Theme. Alternatively, click with the right mouse button anywhere on the page and select Themes from the pop-up menu. This action takes you to a dialog box version of the theme selection view (see Figure 1-13). The options are essentially the same as before, with the addition of the Use Selected Theme option. Select this to apply a separate theme to the current page. Click OK to accept the change and return to the page in Editor.

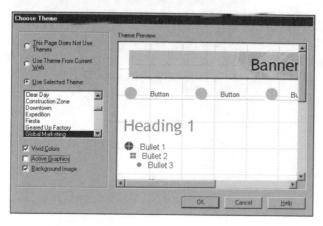

Figure 1-13: The Themes dialog box. Use this dialog box to attach a custom theme to a particular Web page in Editor.

Text styles

In addition to the shared graphical themes, your personal Web also comes with predefined text styles. A standard Web page uses a black Times Roman font for default text, blue highlighting for unvisited hyperlinks, and purple highlighting for hyperlinks that you have followed recently.

In contrast, your default home page uses a sans serif font with designer colors for the default text as well as the hyperlinked text. These styles are included with some of the themes. Be careful if you try to edit the text styles. You may find that you can override some of the style defaults. Others, however, may refuse to conform to your expectations.

Shared borders and navigation

Using a theme gives your Web a consistent look and feel throughout. When used in conjunction with *shared borders,* it ensures that the consistency extends to the function and location of the navigational elements as well.

Using shared borders, you can designate locations including any of the borders of your Web page—top, bottom, left, and right—where the content is to remain the same on every page. The beauty of this is that you can ensure that all pages are the same, and if you ever have reason to change a shared border area, you make one change and it updates every page!

Shared borders are a promising addition to FrontPage 98. My hunch is that the top and bottom shared borders are going to prove more popular than the left and right borders, simply because you cannot control the width of the vertical panels.

Selecting shared borders

Shared borders on your Web page are marked with dashed lines. You can set shared borders either for all pages in your Web or for individual pages. To adjust the shared borders for the Web as a whole, select Shared Borders from the Tools menu in Explorer. The Shared Borders dialog box appears, as shown in Figure 1-14. Select as many of the four border regions as you wish to use as shared borders. Similarly, to change the borders for a given page, open that page in Editor and select Shared Borders from the Editor Tools menu. A similar dialog box appears, allowing you to set the shared borders for this page.

Figure 1-14: The Shared Borders dialog box

Later in this chapter you learn how to edit the navigation bar and to control its appearance.

FrontPage components (a.k.a. WebBots)

Perhaps you have noticed a funny-looking robot icon as you passed your cursor over the navigation area of the Web page? This is the icon for the components formerly known as WebBots. A WebBot is (or was) a prebuilt programming component that added functionality to your FrontPage Web. Navigation bars are an example of a WebBot. In FrontPage 98 the official name for these entities has been changed to the more refined "FrontPage components." But the WebBot icon remains.

Speaking of FrontPage components, there is a small but useful one cleverly hidden on your home page. Can you find it? (Hint: Try using the cursor to hunt for WebBot icons.)

The component is found in the last paragraph of text on the home page. The date that your page was last modified is provided by the TimeStamp component. To add a timestamp to any page:

1. Open the page in Editor.

2. Place the cursor where you want the timestamp to appear.

3. Select Timestamp from the Insert menu.

The Timestamp Properties dialog box appears, as shown in Figure 1-15, enabling you to configure the appearance of the timestamp element.

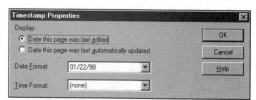

Figure 1-15: The Timestamp Properties dialog box is where you can select from a variety of time and date display formats.

To edit an existing timestamp element, like the one that comes predefined on your home page, simply double-click the component (that is, the text of the timestamp).

Basic editing techniques

As a WYSIWYG Web page editor, FrontPage behaves much like your favorite word processor application. This means that you probably already know how to use most of the basic text editing features in FrontPage. To take a simple example, use the mouse to select the " Welcome to my Web site!" heading at the top of your home page.

Note

If you are not familiar with selecting text in a word processor, you do this by clicking with the left mouse button at either end of the text string you wish to select and then dragging the mouse across the string to its other end. To select a single word, double-click it. To select an entire line of text, you can click once in the margin beside the line. To select an entire paragraph, hold down the Alt key and click the paragraph.

With the heading selected, type a new home page headline. The revised version replaces the old heading. Text editing in FrontPage is just that easy. And you didn't have to know an iota of HTML!

The following sections cover some of the basic editing techniques you can use in FrontPage.

Inserting text

First, let's add some real content to the home page. Locate the cursor at the beginning of the first paragraph of text on the page. Start typing. The text should appear in the same style as the existing text. Your writing wraps around to the next line when you reach the end of the page.

Hit enter to insert a paragraph return. Note that a paragraph return creates a double space between the two lines of text. To create a line break without space, hold down the Shift key and then hit Enter.

Tip

If you want to know where you have entered which kind of return, select Format Marks from the View menu to turn on paragraph marks (or click the Show/Hide button on the toolbar). A paragraph is marked with the paragraph symbol, a sort of backward *P*. Line breaks are marked with the return arrow symbol like the one on your keyboard's Enter key. To turn off Format Marks, select the menu item again.

Deleting text

Before you can begin to add serious text to your home page, you need to get rid of the placeholder text that is there by default. Place the cursor to the left of the beginning of the first paragraph and drag down and across to the end of the last paragraph. With the text selected, hit the Backspace key or the Delete key (or any key, for that matter). Bingo, text-be-gone.

Undoing things

This might be a good time to call attention to FrontPage Editor's Undo feature. According to the documentation, Editor has up to 30 levels of undo available — enough for even the most absent-minded developer. To undo the delete operation you just carried out, select Edit ➪ Undo or click the Undo icon (the curving backwards arrow) on the toolbar.

Cutting and pasting

Cutting and pasting refers to the process of moving a block of text into a temporary storage area known as the clipboard in order to put it back in a new location on the page.

To perform a cut-and-paste operation, select the block of text you wish to copy or move. Select Cut from the Edit menu to delete the text from its current position. Select Copy from the Edit menu if you wish to replicate the text block somewhere else. Move the cursor to the new location for the text block and click with the mouse button to position the cursor. Select Paste from the Edit menu. You can also use keyboard shortcuts for these operations. Use Ctrl+X to cut and Ctrl+C to copy. Ctrl+V pastes text in the new location. For even more options, you can use the Cut, Copy, and Paste buttons on the toolbar.

Dragging and dropping

Dragging and dropping is what I frequently find myself doing after a hard day's work, but it also refers to the act of selecting a block of text and dragging the selection with the mouse to a new location where you let go of the mouse button and "drop" the text. FrontPage 98 has full support for drag-and-drop operations, including all page elements, not just text. You can also drag and drop between applications, such as Microsoft Word and Windows Explorer, that support these operations.

Suppose you would like to move the Timestamp component from its current position at the end of the last sentence to a line by itself below the page headline. You can use cut and paste for this operation, but you can also use drag and drop. Select the Timestamp component by clicking it once. Now, click again and, holding the mouse down, move the mouse across the page. Notice how the mouse cursor has grown a little gray rectangular box at the end of its tail. This is the sign that your mouse is carrying a package. When you have arrived at the component's destination, release the mouse button. The timestamp jumps to its new location.

If you want to drag a copy of the selected item, hold down the Ctrl key before you release the mouse button. The gray box acquires a plus sign—your assurance that the element is being copied rather than moved.

Saving your creations

At this point you should finish editing the text of your home page. When you are satisfied, save your efforts. To save changes to the page, select Save from the File menu or click the Floppy Disk icon in the toolbar.

Moving around your Web pages

It is time to edit another page. There are several ways that you can get to another page in the current Web. The following sections cover the most commonly used.

Opening the file from within Editor

To open a file in Editor, select File⇨Open. The Open dialog box shown in Figure 1-16 appears. By default the dialog box shows you the pages in the current folder of your current Web. Select the page you wish to edit and click OK. The Open dialog box also has two additional ways of referencing files. If the file you want to open is not in the current Web, but it is on your local file directory, click the Folder icon in the lower-right corner of the dialog box. This button allows you to browse through all accessible file systems to locate the file you want.

You can also open a Web page directly via the Web. Click the Globe icon to start your Web browser. Locate the page you want to edit in the browser and then return to the Open dialog box. The URL of the desire Web page is entered in the URL input field. Click OK to load that file into your editor. (Of course the fact that you can open this file and change your local copy of it does not mean that you can change the file on a remote server—in case you were beginning to hatch some diabolical plans to that effect.)

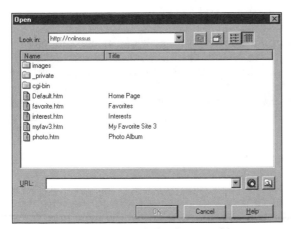

Figure 1-16: The Open dialog box enables you to open Web pages into Editor from a variety of sources, both local and remote.

Opening the file from Explorer

You already know how to open a file from Explorer. Simply switch back to Explorer and double-click the file icon of the file you wish to open.

Following a hyperlink

To follow a hyperlink is the most intuitive method. In fact, I predict, if you are at all accustomed to Web browsing, you will try to access a page by clicking its link before you remember that FrontPage is a Web *editor,* not a Web *browser.* Links do not automatically work in this environment. However, if you hold down the Ctrl key and click a link, it does operate just as it would if you were using a browser. The page you have linked opens in Editor, ready for action.

Moreover, once you have followed an initial hyperlink, you can use the back and forward buttons (the ones with the aqua-colored arrows) in the Editor toolbar to navigate among the pages you have already visited—much as you would in a real Web browser.

Using whichever method appeals to you most, try opening the Interests page of your personal Web. That is the page you work on in the next section.

Editing text formats

Being able to add, edit, and move around chunks of text is very useful, but I know what you really want to do is format that text—make it red, make it bigger, or (heaven forbid) make it blink. How to change the appearance of the text on the page is the subject of this section. Although these actions may also sound familiar if you have used word processors, you may want to keep in mind that you are now entering the territory where FrontPage is silently writing HTML code for you each time you add some formatting to your page. Be sure to take the time to express your appreciation.

Page properties

The page properties are those attributes of your Web page that apply to the whole page. If you have applied a theme to your Web, the page attributes you can control are actually somewhat limited. The most important one is the page title. The title consists of a short descriptive phrase that identifies the page. This title does not show up on the Web page itself. Typically it appears in the title bar of the browser window when the page is displayed. It is also the text that the browser uses when creating a bookmark for your page. For this reason it is very important not to forget about your page's title. (If you do forget, FrontPage assigns your page a default title, which it derives from the first line of text on the page.

There is a fine art to giving your page a title. It should be specific enough that a person who has bookmarked your page can look at the title and remember what it was. Consequently titles like "My little home in cyberspace" are probably not very useful. On the other hand, you need to be concise, since long titles are likely to get clipped.

You have several ways to edit the page properties. If you wait until you save your page, you are prompted to include the page title at that time. To access the full set of page properties, however, select Page Properties from the File menu or click with the right mouse button anywhere on the Web page and select Page Properties from the pop-up menu list that appears (on a page that contains shared borders, make sure you right-click in the main area of the page). Details on the Page Properties menu are provided in Chapter 2.

To practice, change the title of the Interests page, which by default is just "Interests." If you do not have the Interests page open in Editor, open it now using one of the methods just described. Select File ⇨ Page Properties and change the Title field on the General tab, as illustrated in Figure 1-17. Substitute whatever is an appropriate title for your page.

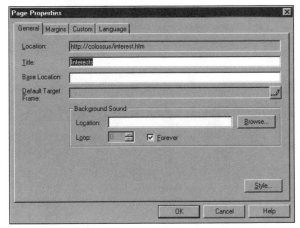

Figure 1-17: The Page Properties dialog box lets you control more than just a page's title.

Paragraph properties

The paragraph properties include the various heading levels styles as well as paragraph alignment properties. Heading levels are intended to be used in hierarchical fashion like the levels in an outline. A level-1 heading is the highest level; level 6 is the lowest. In practice a Web page rarely needs more than three or four heading levels. Many people use heading levels as shortcuts for other formatting styles, since the higher heading levels are usually displayed in large font sizes, and the lower levels, in smaller fonts. For example, it is fairly common to see people using a level-5 or -6 heading format for the small print at the bottom of their pages. How much of an HTML purist you want to be is your business. Keep in mind, however, that you are not guaranteed that a Web browser at the other end will display your text exactly as you formatted it. This is the beauty and frustration of publishing in the Web environment.

To apply a heading level style, locate the cursor anywhere in the paragraph you wish to format. Notice that you do *not* need to select the text—the style is applied to an entire line, because it is assumed to be a heading. Select the heading level you want from the Change Style pop-up menu at the far left side of the Format toolbar. If this toolbar is not visible, you can bring it back by selecting Format Toolbar from the View menu.

Alternatively, click with the right mouse button anywhere on the line of text and select Paragraph Properties from the pop-up menu. Select the heading level you want from the Paragraph Properties dialog box and click OK. You can also change the paragraph alignment using this dialog box. Alignment options are left, right, and center. These options can also be applied by clicking the alignment icons on the Format toolbar.

Let's change the first paragraph of text on the Interests page, the placeholder directions that begin "Here is a good place...." For some reason, this text is center-aligned by default—to ascertain that this is so, click the text and watch what happens to the alignment icons on the toolbar. The Centered Text button depresses.

For starters, remove the centered alignment by clicking the already depressed button. The text should jump to the left margin—the default alignment. Let's replace this text with a heading. Type in the text of your heading, and then with the cursor still on the line, select the heading level you want from the Change Styles pop-up menu. I personally prefer to start with heading 2, since heading 1 is usually displayed in an overly large font.

Making a list

The main content of the Interests page consists of a bulleted list using the custom bullets that accompany the theme you selected for your pages. To add an item to the existing list, place the cursor at the end of the previous bullet item and press the Enter key. A new bullet automatically appears.

To create a new list, first type the list items. Select the entire set of items. To create a simple list, click either the Bullet List icon or the Numbered List icon in the toolbar. To access the full range of list options in the Bullets and Numbering dialog box (see Figure 1-18), select Format ⇨ Bullets and Numbering. Once you have created a list, you can access the Bullets and Numbering dialog box via the right mouse button by clicking the list.

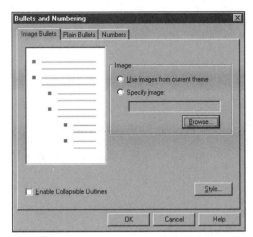

Figure 1-18: The Bullets and Numbering
dialog box

Font styles

FrontPage provides control over many aspects of fonts, including font style, size, and color. Most of the basic font and style properties are accessible from the Format toolbar. If the Format toolbar is not visible, you can show it by selecting View ➪ Format Toolbar. The toolbar has items for selecting the font; adding styles such as bold, italics, and underlining; altering the font size; and designating a text color. Alternatively, click with the right mouse button and select Font Properties in the pop-up menu to access the Font Properties dialog box. This dialog box is also accessible via the Format ➪ Font menu item.

The Font Properties dialog box also includes a Special Styles tab. Against my better judgment I will point out that among other things, this tab allows you to create blinking text. First select the text you want to blink. Access the Font Properties dialog box using one of the methods just described, and click the Special Styles tab. Use blinking text at your own discretion. Among the more useful items on this tab, by the way, are the superscript and subscript attributes.

New in 98

FrontPage 98 has added full support for cascading style sheets, a means of standardizing font styles over an entire Web. This is a much more efficient way to apply styles to your Web pages, but it also requires a bit more effort to learn. Details of this advanced topic are covered in Chapter 10.

Working with Hyperlinks

At the moment, the only hyperlinks in operation in your personal Web are the navigation buttons. To learn how to add and edit hyperlinks in FrontPage, open the Favorites page, the title of which you were invited to change to "Cool links" (or some label of your own devising) earlier in the chapter.

Note

By the way, if you *did* edit the label for this page, have you noticed how FrontPage has updated the text on the navigation buttons to reflect your change? When you open this page in Editor, you should notice that the banner title has also been updated.

Creating a new link

Let's start by adding a new link to the existing list of your favorite Web sites. Using what you learned about editing lists earlier in the chapter, create a new link item at the end of the predefined list. Type the text you want to link from, and then select the text. To add the hyperlink, click the Hyperlink icon in the toolbar (the globe with a chain link below it) or select the Insert ⇨ Hyperlink menu item. This brings up the Create Hyperlink dialog box shown in Figure 1-19.

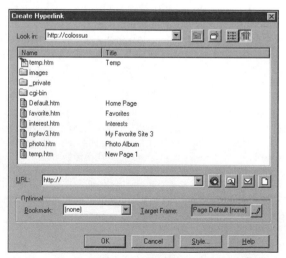

Figure 1-19: Creating a hyperlink in FrontPage is a snap, using the Create Hyperlink dialog box.

New in 98

The look and feel of the Create Hyperlink dialog box have changed in FrontPage 98. Gone are the tabs—they have been replaced by a set of buttons to access the various kinds of links you might want to generate.

You can use this dialog box to create one of several kinds of hyperlinks:

✦ **Link to a page currently open in Editor**—The currently open pages are listed at the top of the file list, marked with the Editor red quill pen icon. Select an open page and click OK to generate the hyperlink.

✦ **Link to another page in the current Web**—To do this, select the file to link to from the list of files shown. Click OK to create the link. Notice that if you have a file from the current Web open in Editor, it shows up twice in the dialog box. This is not harmful, just mildly disconcerting.

✦ **Link to another page on the Web**—If you know the URL of the page you want to link to, you can type it in. If not, click the Web icon to launch your Web browser, locate the Web page, and return to the dialog box. The page's URL is loaded in the input box. Click OK to accept this and create the hyperlink.

✦ **Link to a local file**—Click the File Folder icon and select the file from your directory structure to link to. Linking to a local file only works locally. You cannot link to a local file and then have others access that file via the Web.

✦ **Link to an e-mail address**—Click the Envelope icon to create a link to an e-mail address. When users click this link, it opens the e-mail sending portion of their Web browsers, enabling them to send e-mail to the designated recipient.

✦ **Link to a new page**—Click the New File icon to create a new Web page and automatically generate a link to it from the selected text. The available page templates for new pages are discussed in Chapter 3.

Editing existing links

Next let's edit the hyperlink from the "My Favorite Site" list item. Click anywhere on the text of this item and select Edit ➪ Hyperlink, click with the right mouse button and select Hyperlink Properties from the pop-up menu, or click the Create or Edit Hyperlink icon in the toolbar. The Edit Hyperlink dialog box opens with the current hyperlink displayed. Proceed as for adding a hyperlink as described earlier. Click OK to record your change.

New
in 98

One pleasant surprise in FrontPage 98 is the fact that you can now select a string of hyperlinked text, replace that text, and still have the hyperlink in place. In previous versions, editing the text of the hyperlink would result in the loss of the hyperlink, which could be mildly annoying to say the least.

Unlinking links

To remove a hyperlink from a string of text, select the linked text and select Edit ➪ Unlink from the menu bar. Of course, you can also open the Edit Hyperlink dialog box and clear the hyperlink.

Drag-and-drop linking

You can also use drag and drop to add or update a hyperlink. To do this, you need an application that supports dragging Web pages. Explorer supports this functionality, as does Netscape 4 and Internet Explorer 4. Internet Explorer 3 does not. For example, to drag and drop a hyperlink from Explorer to Editor, make sure that both applications are visible on your desktop. Select a page from your current Web in Explorer from All Files, Folders, or Hyperlinks view. Drag the file from Explorer and drop it on an existing hyperlink. Editor prompts you that you are about to replace the existing hyperlink with another link. If that is really what you want to do, click OK. The URL is updated. Similarly if you drag a Web page icon onto a blank space of the page, it will create a new hyperlink using the Web page title as the default link text.

Enhancing Web Page Design

Navigation buttons are only one of FrontPage's nifty add-ons that you can use to make your site easier to navigate and more interesting. In this section, we briefly look at how to change the appearance of your navigation bars, as well as how to add two of the most popular active elements: hover buttons and marquees.

Configuring navigation buttons

Return to the home page for a moment. Perhaps you noticed earlier that the graphical buttons on this page have generic (button) titles rather than the actual page names. Similarly on the remaining pages, although the buttons are correctly labeled, the text navigation buttons in the left border have generic titles. Fixing this requires editing the properties of the navigation bar element.

As you saw earlier in the chapter, FrontPage generates the navigation for your Web automatically, using the information you provide in the Navigation view of Explorer. On each of the pages in your personal Web, there are two instances of the navigation bar component—one at the top of the page and another on the left. Select the top buttons on the home page first, since they are the ones whose labels need fixing. To edit the navigation bar, double-click the FrontPage component that controls it. This brings up the Navigation Bar Properties dialog box shown in Figure 1-20.

This dialog box enables you to configure three aspects of the navigation bars. The most important of these is to designate which hyperlinks to include. By default the home page buttons are set to the Same Level. Since this is the home page, however, there are no other pages at the same level, which is why the buttons have no label. Select Child Level to have the buttons correspond to the remaining pages in the

Web. In addition to controlling the hyperlinks for the buttons, this dialog box also allows you to select either text or graphical navigation elements and a horizontal or vertical orientation. Because these navigation buttons are located in the shared border area of the page, changing them on one page automatically changes them for all the other pages in your Web. (By the way, when your pages are viewed in a browser, buttons that don't have a label are not displayed.)

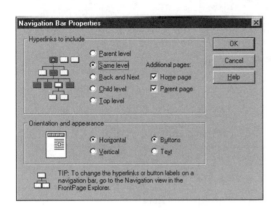

Figure 1-20: The Navigation Bar Properties dialog box allows you to configure the buttons automatically added to your personal Web pages.

Chapter 8 contains more complete instructions for creating and using navigation buttons, including using them without shared borders.

Active elements

We have covered a great deal already, but this chapter would not be complete if it didn't call your attention to some of FrontPage's coolest Web page features. These are elements whose primary purpose is to call attention to themselves. Most of these are collected under the Active Elements menu items on the Insert menu in Editor. This chapter does not have time to introduce all of these elements — jump ahead to Chapter 6 if you can't wait — but we will briefly introduce two of these elements — just to whet your appetite.

Adding hover buttons

In FrontPage lingo, a *hover button* is a button that changes when you pass the mouse cursor over it. You can create hover buttons as part of your theme by selecting the Active Graphics option. In addition, you can add your own customized buttons.

To add a hover button, place the cursor where you want the button to appear, and select Insert ➪ Active Elements ➪ Hover button. This opens the Hover Button dialog box (see Figure 1-21), which has extensive customization options, as follows:

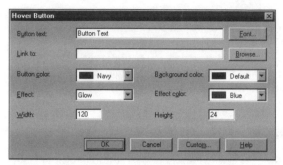

Figure 1-21: Use the Hover Button dialog box to create a custom animated button that changes when you pass the mouse cursor over it.

✦ **Button Text**—This is the text that appears on the button.

✦ **Font**—You can set the exact font to be displayed in the button.

✦ **Link To**—This is the URL of the page that the button is linked to.

✦ **Button Color**—This is the color of the button itself.

✦ **Background Color**—This is the color of the background behind the button.

✦ **Effect**—Available effects include color fill, color average, glow, reverse glow, light glow, bevel out, bevel in.

✦ **Effect Color**—This choice customizes the effect.

✦ **Width and Height**—These options designate the dimensions of the button.

If these options are not enough, you can also select the Custom button to add sounds to the two states of the button and optionally to use custom-designed graphics as the basis of the button states.

Just for fun, let's replace that garish blue "Site created with Microsoft FrontPage" logo on your home page with a more appealing hover button. (Of course, you will want to replace the official logo before you publish your site!) Return to the home page, if you are not there. Select the logo button by clicking it once. Then press Backspace or Delete to eliminate the button. Poof. (Don't worry, the file is still there on your hard drive!)

Open the Hover Button properties dialog box. Type **Site created with Microsoft FrontPage** and adjust the font size to a reasonably small one, so that the text will actually fit. Select some eye-pleasing colors for button, background, and effect. Select the glow effect—this works best with two complementary colors. That's it. Select OK to create the button. Notice that FrontPage Editor is not capable of displaying the hover button effect. To view your handiwork, you need to preview your Web page as described at the end of the chapter.

Note

The hover buttons are actually Java applets, which means that they work equally well in Netscape or Microsoft browsers.

Inserting a marquee

While we are on an interactive roll, how about adding a scrolling marquee to your home page? It's not exactly an essential component, but the process illustrates how easy it can be to add special effects to dazzle your friends and amaze your coworkers.

Caution

The marquee element is a Microsoft-specific feature. Viewers of your Web page who use another browser, such as Netscape Navigator, see the marquee text as regular text.

A *marquee* is a text string that scrolls across your Web page. It can scroll once or loop continuously. To add a marquee to your home page, first open your home page in FrontPage Editor. Add an extra space after the heading at the top of the page and place the cursor in this open area. Select Insert ➪ Active Elements ➪ Marquee. The Marquee Properties dialog box opens, as shown in Figure 1-22.

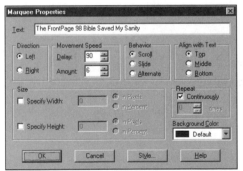

Figure 1-22: The Marquee Properties dialog box

Type the text you want in your marquee message into the text input box. Change the background color from its default to white. You can leave the rest of the options as they are or experiment with them if you wish. Click OK, and the marquee element appears on the page with its borders highlighted. If you change your mind about the text, double-click the marquee to reopen its property dialog box and edit the text.

That's all there is to it, unless you want to reposition the marquee. By default the marquee window covers the entire width of the page. To resize the marquee, click it to select it. This will activate its selection handles—small black rectangles around the perimeter of the marquee. Drag the black rectangle on the right side toward the middle, shrinking the width of the window, and then click the Align Center icon in the toolbar to center the marquee element on the page.

Chapter 6 includes a complete discussion of all the marquee options available.

Viewing Your Handiwork

After all this work, you are probably eager to view the fruit of your labor as the rest of the world will see it. The following sections cover the two methods for doing this.

Using the Preview tab in Editor

To switch to Preview mode, click the Preview tab in the lower-left corner of the Editor window. Preview mode is a good, quick way to check your work. However, it is not a substitute for a real browser. For example, if you view your home page—although your marquee runs correctly, the hover button you added may not display correctly because of Preview's limited capabilities. To see your page more accurately, preview it in a Web browser as outlined next.

Using the Preview in Browser option

To preview your work in any available Web browser, first make sure that you have saved all of the files in your Web by selecting File ⇨ Save All. Make your home page the current window in FrontPage Editor and select File ⇨ Preview in Browser to see a dialog box that lists the available Web browsers on your computer. You can add new Web browsers to the selection list. Select the browser of your choice and click OK. The browser opens to your home page. If you have selected Microsoft Internet Explorer as your browser, you should see the text of your marquee scrolling across the center of the page. Pass your cursor over the hover button to watch it change states. Pretty amazing what you have accomplished in only one chapter! Try your navigation links and the hyperlinks you added to the Favorites page to see if they work as expected, and then sit back and bask in the glow of a job well done. But don't forget to keep reading—there's still more fun and Web excitement ahead!

Taking the Next Step

This chapter has taken you on a whirlwind tour of some of FrontPage's leading features. You have seen how easy FrontPage is to use. In the following chapters, we will explore in more detail the two main components of FrontPage, Explorer and Editor.

✦   ✦   ✦

Working with FrontPage Editor

This chapter focuses on using the FrontPage Editor application to create and edit Web pages. It begins with an introduction to the Editor environment and its principle toolbars. In the course of the chapter, you will learn to identify Editor's text editing and formatting features as well to explore its ability to add and edit hyperlinks.

Introducing FrontPage Editor

The easiest way to open Editor is to open Explorer from the Start menu as described in Chapter 1: Start Explorer, open the Web you want to work with (if it didn't automatically open), and then double-click the page you want to edit. Editor now starts and displays the page you selected.

Note

You may wonder why you need to go through Explorer to get to Editor. The answer is that you don't. If you open Editor directly, however, you have to designate a Web in which to save your work the first time you try to save a new Web page. Opening a Web in Explorer first saves that later step. Of course Microsoft, in its wisdom, no longer puts Editor on the Start menu automatically. If you want to add Editor, use the Start Menu Programs tab of the Taskbar Properties dialog box.

Before diving into the many features that Editor offers you as a Web page designer, I would like to take a moment to identify the main components of the application itself.

The environment

Editor, like Explorer, has a menu bar, toolbars, a main window, and a status line. The window is a single frame that resembles Microsoft Word a good deal. That is good news to anyone who is familiar with the way Word functions. One of the slick features of the Editor environment is that you can drop content on it from somewhere else, such as Windows Explorer or Internet Explorer. One shortcut for importing a file is to drag its icon from Windows Explorer to the Editor. Images can be imported in this fashion as well. Even hyperlinks can be dragged and dropped onto a page in Editor.

The toolbars

The most prominent set of features, however, is the Editor's collection of toolbars. In this chapter we focus on the Standard and Format toolbars—the two that are present by default (see Figure 2-1). In later chapters, we return to these toolbars and discuss the Images, Forms, Advanced, and Tables toolbars, which are described in brief as follows:

✦ **Images toolbar**—This contains a set of functions for working with images (covered in Chapters 4 and 5).

✦ **Forms toolbar**—This contains tools for building forms.

✦ **Advanced toolbar**—This contains items for inserting custom programming modules such as Java applets and ActiveX controls into FrontPage.

✦ **Tables toolbar**—This contains items for inserting and editing tables.

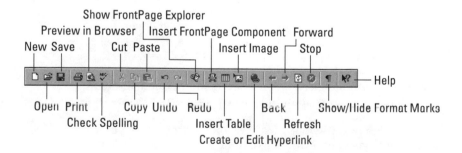

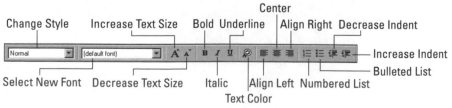

Figure 2-1: The Editor's Standard toolbar (top) and Format toolbar (bottom)

How it works

Most of the page commands used by FrontPage Editor are eminently familiar to anyone who uses a word processor such as Microsoft Word. Because we are dealing with Web pages that may reside locally or remotely on a Web server, however, these familiar commands have a few new wrinkles.

Working with the File Menu

The following sections describe the File menu commands that FrontPage may treat a bit differently than you're used to.

Creating new files or pages

To create a new page, select File ➪ New and choose one from among the available page templates and wizards. By default, FrontPage comes with a long list of page templates of varying degrees of usefulness. To begin with a relatively clean slate, select the Normal Page template. Clicking the New File icon in the toolbar creates a normal page as well. (For more information on templates, see Chapter 10.)

Opening existing files or pages

To open an existing file or Web page, select File ➪ Open or click the Open File icon on the toolbar to access the Open dialog box, as shown in Figure 2-2.

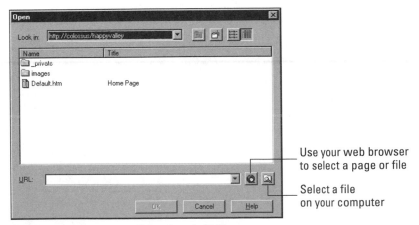

Figure 2-2: The Open dialog box in Editor

You have three basic options when opening a file:

✦ To open a file from the current Web, select a file from the directory listing, and click OK.

✦ To open a file from another location, press the Select a File on Your Computer button to open the Select File dialog box. Use this dialog box as you would any Open dialog box for a word processing program. You can open files in a variety of formats, including text (.txt) various hypertext formats (.htm, .html), word processor formats (Word, WordPerfect, WordStar, Works), and Excel worksheets. Click OK. All formats are automatically converted to HTML when they are opened.

✦ The final option is to open a file from a remote Web server. Press the Use Your Web Browser button to select a page or file button to open your Web browser, and then browse to the page you want to open in Editor. Close your browser or switch back to Editor—the page's URL is now listed in the URL text box. Press the OK button to open the page in Editor. Note that the page is not saved on your hard drive—if you want to save the page locally, do so normally as outlined in the next section, "The Save and Save As options."

The Save and Save As options

If the open page in Editor is a Web page from an existing FrontPage Web or a local file, select File⇨Save or click the Save icon to save the file to its existing location. Select File⇨Save All to perform a save operation on all open files. To save a copy of the file or to change its format, select File⇨Save As. The dialog box shown in Figure 2-3 appears.

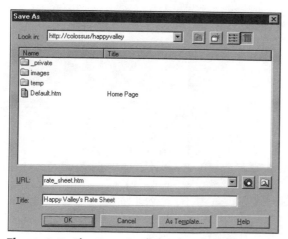

Figure 2-3: The Save As dialog box in Editor

Also, if you attempt to save a file that you opened from a non-FrontPage Web server or a file converted from another format, the Save As dialog box appears. This dialog box provides the following options:

✦ **Save in the Current Web**—This is the default. Give the page a title if it does not already have one. (The title of a Web page typically appears in the title bar of the browser window.) Editor automatically gives the page a filename based on the page's title (this may not be the page's original filename), though you can enter any filename you'd like. Use the standard Save options to navigate your Web to locate the folder you want to save the page in and press the OK button.

✦ **Save as a File**—Click the Select a File on Your Computer button to open the Save As File dialog box, shown in Figure 2-4. Select a folder name and a filename for the file. Select a type from among the three options: Hypertext (.htm), Preprocessed HTML (.htx, .asp), or Hypertext Template (.htt). Click OK.

Figure 2-4: The Save As File dialog box

✦ **Save as Template**—This option allows you to save the current file as a template like those in the New File dialog box. Click As Template. Give the template a title and a description—its name appears in the Template list. Select the Browse button to see a list of currently available templates.

Tip There is no way to delete a template file from within FrontPage; however, you can delete them from outside FrontPage using Windows Explorer. This is a good idea if you don't plan to use all of the canned templates Microsoft supplies. Templates are stored in *.tem directories in the Pages subdirectory of the FrontPage application directory (by default, this is C:\Program Files\Microsoft FrontPage). You can move the folders to another location to remove them from the list without deleting them.

Print and Print Preview

These functions work the same way they do in any Windows application. Select
File⇨Print to open the Windows Print dialog box. Or bypass the dialog box by
clicking the Print icon in the toolbar. Select File⇨Print Preview to view the current
page as it should look printed. In the Print Preview window, you can zoom in on
the page by clicking with the mouse (note the magnifying glass cursor). FrontPage
supports three zoom levels. Click twice to zoom to the greatest possible
magnification. Click again to return the page to its smallest size.

Page Setup

This command offers a modicum of control over how the page is printed. Select
File⇨Page Setup to access the dialog box shown in Figure 2-5.

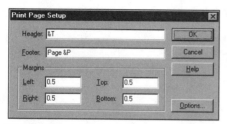

Figure 2-5: The Print Page Setup dialog box

By default, Page Setup places the file title (&T) in the header and the page number
(Page &P) in the footer. Use this dialog box to alter the header and footer and
adjust the print margins. Page Setup stays in effect for all pages printed in
FrontPage Editor, not just the current page.

Creating and Editing Text

You can create and edit text in FrontPage Editor very much as you would in a
standard word processor. You do not need any knowledge of HTML to use
FrontPage effectively. As with anything else, of course, the more you understand
about the technologies you are using, the more you are able to tap their power. In
this section, however, we confine ourselves to the basics. If you are eager to know
how FrontPage works with HTML, check out Chapter 9.

Adding and selecting text

You add text to a Web page by typing at the insertion point (that is, at the location of the vertical, blinking cursor). Word wrap applies in this context just as it would in a typical word processor. You can select a range of text by dragging the I-beam cursor from the beginning of the range to the end. To select a single word, double-click the word. To select a line of text, move the cursor to the left margin—the cursor changes to an arrow—and click the line to select it, or double-click to select the entire paragraph. You can select the entire page by selecting Edit ⇨ Select All or by using the key command shortcut, Ctrl+A. Once text has been selected, you can edit it using any standard text editing and formatting techniques.

Cutting, copying, clearing, and pasting

These text editing functions also work as they do in most word processors. To cut or copy text, first select the text using one of the methods described in the previous section. To cut the selected text from its current location and store it in the clipboard, select Edit ⇨ Cut, click the Cut icon, or use the key command shortcut Ctrl+X. To copy the currently selected text to the clipboard, select Edit ⇨ Copy, click the Copy icon, or use the key command shortcut Ctrl+C. To permanently delete the selected text, select Edit ⇨ Clear or use the Delete or Backspace keys.

To paste a cut or copied selection to a new location, move the cursor to the beginning of the text's new location by clicking with the mouse button's I-beam cursor. Select Edit ⇨ Paste, click the Paste icon, or use the key command shortcut Ctrl+V to place the text.

Dragging and dropping

You can also use the drag-and-drop method of cutting and pasting text. To cut and paste text using this method, hold the mouse button down over the selected text and drag the mouse pointer to the new location. The mouse arrow cursor includes a gray box at its tail, indicating that it is carrying the selected text with it. A gray, vertical cursor identifies the insertion point. Drag the cursor until the gray insertion point is located at the new spot for the text, and release the mouse button. To copy and paste text, use the same method, holding down the Ctrl key as you drag the selected text. The mouse cursor now displays a plus sign, indicating that you are copying rather than moving the selection.

Any of these methods can be used to edit text between two documents as well as between two points within the same document, even if the documents are open in different applications (as long as they support editing operations). When text is cut and pasted in this fashion, it loses any formatting styles associated with it and acquires the style of its new location. This method can also be used to cut and paste other items, including hypertext links and images.

Finding and replacing

Select Edit ➪ Find or use the shortcut, Ctrl+F, to open the Find dialog box (see Figure 2-6). All text in the current page is searched. To find a text string, type it into the Find What field and click the Find Next button. You can search for text either forward (down) or backward (up) from the current cursor location. By default, searching is done on any matching string of text. To limit matches to complete words, check the Match Whole Word Only box—a complete word has a space before it and a space or punctuation mark after it. To specify the exact capitalization of letters, check the Match Case box.

Figure 2-6: The Find dialog box

The replace text function, as shown in Figure 2-7, works similarly, with the difference that you can substitute one string of text for another. Notice that the Replace command does not offer search direction options. To open the Replace dialog box, select Edit ➪ Replace, or use the shortcut Ctrl+H.

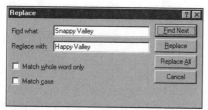

Figure 2-7: The Replace dialog box

Searching is always in a forward direction. Type the string to find in the Find What field. Type the replacement string in the Replace With field. To replace the next instance of the string, click the Replace button. Click Replace All to automatically replace all instances of the string. Specify whole word and case matching as previously described for the Find command. To perform an interactive find and replace, click Find Next, examine the selected match in the page, and then use the Replace button if desired. Click Find Next to continue examining matches.

Undoing and redoing

FrontPage Editor allows up to 30 actions to be undone. Select Edit ⇨ Undo, click the Undo icon, or use the shortcut, Ctrl+Z, to undo an action. To redo an action that has been undone, select Edit ⇨ Redo, click the Redo icon, or use the shortcut, Ctrl+Y.

Setting Page Preferences

You can access the Page Properties dialog box (see Figure 2-8) by selecting File ⇨ Page Properties or by right-clicking the page itself and selecting Page Properties from the pop-up menu. It contains five tabs, each of which controls some element or set of elements, as follows:

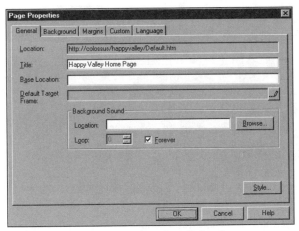

Figure 2-8: The Page Properties dialog box

✦ **General**—This tab includes the capabilities to edit the page's title and to indicate a base location (for instance, the top of your company's Web page hierarchy). It also enables you to designate a sound to play on the page.

✦ **Background**—This very useful section allows you to designate background and text colors or to define a custom background image. Background images tile, so a good one takes up very little file space. This tab does not appear if your page incorporates a theme.

✦ **Margins**—Margins can be designated as horizontal and vertical pixel counts. The Top Margin setting also sets the bottom margin, and the Left Margin setting also sets the right margin. This seems like a fairly primitive mechanism to anyone who has used a recent word processor.

✦ **Custom**—The Custom tab allows users to enter custom meta-tags and add them to their Web page.

✦ **Language**—This tab contains controls for setting the encoding for special characters, such as accented letters, used in foreign languages. Typically you will want to leave these settings alone.

Using Formatting Techniques

So far, most of Editor's operations resemble the basic operations of a standard word processor (at least a standard Microsoft word processor) fairly closely. In the following sections, we begin to look at the Editor functions that enable the user to create a sophisticated HTML Web page without worrying about the underlying technical language.

Some disconcerting aspects

The ability to create HTML as if you were creating a printed document is quite powerful. However, you may find the following aspects of text formatting in this environment somewhat disconcerting:

✦ HTML is more limited as a page description language than are most word processing languages. If you have spent any time doing even simple desktop publishing with a word processor, you immediately realize that FrontPage's capabilities are very limited in comparison with these types of applications. The reason for this has mainly to do with the limitations of HTML, which is not primarily a page description language, although it is being pushed increasingly in that direction by current demands for more finely controlled document layout and formatting.

✦ FrontPage has a mixture of standard HTML formatting and word processor–like formatting, resulting in some redundancy of function. Even though FrontPage may seem to be limited in its functionality, at times you will find several ways to accomplish the same formatting task. This, too, is the product of the evolution of HTML. For example, select a string of text and apply the Heading 1 style to it. Then select a second text string, click Increase Font Size three times, and then click the Bold icon. The second string of text looks very much like the first, although they were created with two entirely different mechanisms, using very different HTML.

✦ White space is largely ignored in this environment. If you are accustomed to fudging the formatting of your word processing documents by using extra spaces and tabs, you may be alarmed to learn that HTML ignores all such characters, providing only for single spaces between characters. If you don't believe me, try typing some text and then inserting a tab or two (or twenty) into the middle of it. Nothing happens. Don't worry; you'll get used to it.

Paragraph styles

Paragraph styles pertain by default to an entire paragraph. In other words, you do not need to select any text to operate this command. Simply place the cursor somewhere in the string of text, click the right mouse button, and select Paragraph Properties from the pop-up menu. This menu provides direct access to both paragraph styles and alignments. The paragraph style options are also accessible from the Change Style drop-down selection list on the far-left side of the Format toolbar. The alignment options (left, center, and right) are also accessible from icon buttons on the Format toolbar.

Paragraph styles define a particular kind of text without identifying how that text should look. Different browsers avail themselves of different methods of displaying these styles, although there are common conventions for each. You may be dismayed by the fact that you have little or no control over how each of these elements is displayed. For example, compare the two screen shots from Microsoft Internet Explorer and Netscape Navigator as shown in Figure 2-9.

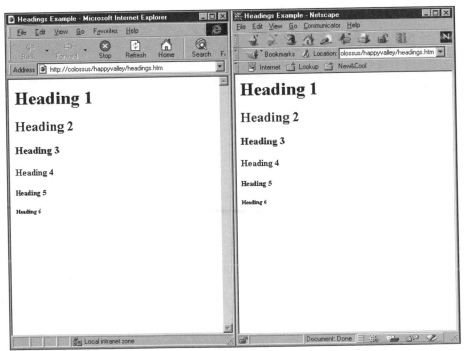

Figure 2-9: Note the difference in distance between heading levels in Netscape Navigator and Microsoft Internet Explorer.

Note

Be very sparing when using formats from the Change Style drop-down selection list. Each browser displays the styles slightly differently, so you can never be exactly sure how your page will look. If you are creating a "quick and dirty" page and don't really care about the aesthetics, go ahead and use them—if you want better control over your page's appearance, use the other formatting options for font, character style, and so forth that are outlined later in this chapter.

Available styles from the Change Style drop-down selection list on the Format toolbar include:

✦ **Address**—This is a paragraph style intended for formatting an address such as might be found at the bottom of corporate Web page. It is displayed in a normal italicized font.

✦ **Bulleted List**—This is a nonnumbered list. The appearance of the bullet (circle, square, open, or filled) depends on the browser used to view your page. A method for changing the bullet type is described later in this chapter in the section "Bulleted and numbered lists," although the exact bullet displayed still depends on the browser. In any case, each bulleted item is displayed indented with a line break following it.

✦ **Definition List, Defined Term, Definition**—A *definition list* consists of a list of words or short phrases, each accompanied by a longer description, a summary paragraph, or an explanation. Properly constructed, a definition list should consist of a series of words with indented definitions. For example:

  • **Fish**—A water-dwelling animal with fins and gills

  • **Fowl**—A land-dwelling animal with feathers and a beak

  • **Fern**—A green, shade-loving plant with frilly leaves

✦ **Formatted**—This one may throw some people. At least it did me. I mean, isn't every text style formatted? Actually, the proper HTML name for the style referred to here is "preformatted." Originally, text marked in this fashion was meant to be displayed just as it appeared. The idea was to use this as a way of retaining simple text formatting, such as the tabbed indents used in programming code. Remember, we are talking about preformatted plain text, not fancy word processed text. This is why the default font for this style is usually Courier. Before tables appeared in the HTML code, this was also one way to display text in columns. This style is essentially outmoded and should be used sparingly, but in a pinch, it is one of the only ways to make tabs and extra spaces show up.

✦ **Heading 1–6**—The six heading levels were intended to allow information in documents to be structured in a hierarchical manner (that is, outline-style). Ideally, each heading level should appear as a subheading of the level above it. For this reason, the headings are typically displayed in decreasing font sizes. In reality, few documents contain more than one or two levels of subheadings. Still, people use the heading styles for other purposes. For instance, it is not uncommon to see a Heading 6 style applied to text that the Web developer wants to appear smaller than normal.

✦ **Menu List**—This is another, relatively obscure, list format. It is ostensibly intended for unordered lists of short items, but browsers mostly ignore it. As a result, most menu lists end up looking exactly like standard unordered bullet lists.

✦ **Normal**—This text is unformatted, in the sense that it is not marked up with any HTML encoding. It is displayed in the Web browser's default font size and style.

✦ **Numbered List**—Otherwise known as an ordered list, this list has formatting similar to a bulleted list except that each item is numbered. Default numbers are 1, 2, 3, and so on.

Paragraph margins

HTML control over margins and indents is primitive at best. FrontPage has chosen to hide this deficiency by creating two indent options on the Format toolbar that mimic the options available in Microsoft Word. It is also possible to adjust the page margins, using the Paragraph Properties dialog box described in a later section.

✦ **Increase Indent**—Use this button on the Format toolbar to cause a currently selected paragraph to be indented as a block. Click multiple times to increase the quantity of indentation.

✦ **Decrease Indent**—This essentially strips an indented text block of its indentations. Click multiple times to remove multiple indentations.

Caution

These functions use the HTML `<BLOCKQUOTE>` tag, which, as the name implies, was designed only as a way of indenting large, block quotes. It was not really envisioned as a general-purpose method of indenting text, so you have no precise control over how much your text is indented—I would recommend using it only for the purposes for which it was intended. Typically block quotes are also displayed with an automatic paragraph break.

Paragraph alignment

Paragraph alignment in the Web page environment is also relatively limited. By default, all text is left justified. Options are: left-justified text (that is, text that lines up flush with the left margin), centered text, or right-justified text (that is, text that lines up flush with the right margin). There is no mechanism here for creating fully justified text (that is, text that is both left and right justified). To align a paragraph of text:

1. Place the cursor somewhere in the paragraph.

2. Click the Align Left, Center, or Align Right icon on the toolbar or press Ctrl+L, Ctrl+E, or Ctrl+R respectively. (The alignment options are also accessible through the Paragraph Properties dialog box discussed in the next section.)

The Paragraph Properties dialog box

The Paragraph Properties dialog box (see Figure 2-10) is available either by right-clicking the paragraph you want to format and selecting Paragraph Properties or by selecting Format ⇨ Paragraph. This dialog box repeats a subset of the styles available for paragraphs in the Change Style drop-down selection list discussed earlier.

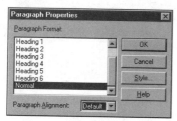

Figure 2-10: The Paragraph Properties dialog box

In addition to these standard options, the Paragraph Properties dialog box in FrontPage 98 now also provides access to advanced formatting options for cascading style sheets. To view and use these options, press the Style button to open the Style dialog box. Note that cascading style sheets are not supported by older browsers. Cascading style sheets and the use of the Style dialog box are discussed at length in Chapter 10.

Font styles

In the beginning, HTML was blissfully unaware of the existence of fonts. What fonts were displayed depended entirely on the settings made in the browser. As sophistication of page display has become an increasing concern, the need for HTML to recognize and display specific fonts has become apparent. At the moment, most browsers are capable of recognizing font information, but the ability to designate a font size is still relatively crude. That is why Editor has two Format toolbar font icons—to increase font size and decrease font size—rather than the standard method of selecting a font size by point size. There are a total of seven font sizes available in FrontPage.

✦ **Increase font size**—To increase the font size, select the text whose size you want to increase and click the Increase Text Size icon on the Format toolbar. If you begin with default-sized text, you can click this icon four times in succession and increase the font size each time.

✦ **Decrease font size**—To decrease the font size, select the text whose size you want to decrease and click the Decrease Text Size icon on the Format toolbar. If you begin with default-sized text, you can click this icon twice in succession and decrease the font size each time.

✦ **Select a new font**—FrontPage allows you to adjust the font face of your Web page to any font resident on your computer. Think twice before peppering your Web pages with stylish fonts. Remember, for your visitors to see the page as you intend, they have to have identical fonts resident on their computers. (This is likely to change in the near future, as methods of downloading and rendering fonts on the fly are perfected.)

✦ **Text color**—To change the color of text, select the text to change and click the Text Color icon on the Format toolbar. Select a basic color from the available options or use the color wheel to define a custom color.

✦ **Additional font styles**—The standard styles (bold, italic, and underline) can also be applied to fonts.

These formatting options are also available in the Font dialog box described in the next section.

Tip

Different users have different fonts installed on their computers, and different types of computers (PCs, Macs, and so on) have different variations of the same fonts. If you want to have more control over the exact fonts used in your Web pages, consider using Microsoft's Web Fonts. You can find these fonts at `www.microsoft.com/truetype/fontpack`—simply download and install the desired fonts on your computer. Note, however, that for your site's visitors to see these fonts, they'll also have to download and install the fonts, so you'll want to include a link to this page in your site.

The Font dialog box

For more detailed control over fonts, you can use the Font dialog box. Select Format ⇨ Font, or select the text to change, click with the right mouse button anywhere on the page, and select Font Properties. The Font dialog box is shown in Figure 2-11.

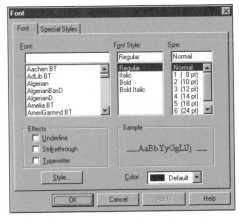

Figure 2-11: The Font dialog box

The Font dialog box has two tabs. The Font tab provides control over all the basic font attributes: Font (also called the typeface), Font Style, Size, Effects, and Color. The second tab is Special Styles. Each of these represents an HTML tag that could not be subsumed into a familiar interface—as with the paragraph formats, these special styles give control of the exact appearance of your text to the browser and should be used only when you don't specifically care how the page looks. The list of special styles includes:

✦ **Citation**—This style formats text appropriately for a title or bibliographic citation, typically rendered in italics.

✦ **Sample**—This formats text as it literally appears, usually rendered in Courier (typewriter font).

✦ **Definition**—This indicates a definition, typically in italics.

✦ **Blink**—This causes selected text to blink in some browsers.

✦ **Code**—This renders text literally in Courier (typewriter font).

✦ **Variable**—This formats text as a variable name, typically in italics.

✦ **Bold**—This formats text in standard bold formatting.

✦ **Italic**—This formats text in standard italics.

✦ **Keyboard**—This indicates keyboard entry, usually rendered in typewriter font.

In addition, the Style button provides access to controls for using cascading style sheets. See Chapter 10 for complete information about using style sheets in FrontPage.

Bulleted and numbered lists

FrontPage provides support for the two principle types of HTML lists: bulleted (unordered) lists and numbered (ordered) lists.

Creating a list

You have two basic methods for creating lists in FrontPage:

✦ Create the items that compose the list, select all the items, and apply the desired list style.

✦ Create the first item in the list, apply the desired list style, press Enter to prepare for the next list item, and type the item. Press Enter twice in succession to end the list.

Applying list styles

There are several ways to apply a list style. For each, begin by placing the cursor somewhere on the line of text to which you want to apply the style. To apply the style, do one of the following:

✦ Select the desired style from the Change Style drop-down list on the toolbar.

✦ Click either the Numbered List icon or the Bulleted List icon on the toolbar.

✦ Select Format ➪ Bullets and Numbering to display the dialog box shown in Figure 2-12.

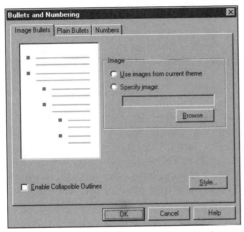

Figure 2-12: The Bullets and Numbering dialog box

Note

The Bullets and Numbering dialog box provides more detailed control over lists than that offered by the Format toolbar. The Bullets and Numbering dialog box includes a sample of four different styles for bulleted lists and six options for numbered lists. Also, a box allows users to set the starting number for a numbered list. The upcoming section, "Using image bullets," details the use of pictures in place of dots in a bulleted list. If you select text that is already in a list and open the Bullets and Numbering dialog box, an additional tab, Other, is available that lets you specify the list as a Definition, a Directory, or a Menu—these three types of list are out of date and rarely used. The Bullets and Numbering dialog box is also accessible by selecting Font ➪ Bullets and Numbering.

Using image bullets

As noted earlier in this chapter (the section entitled "Paragraph styles"), you have essentially no control over the appearance of standard bullets in your page—the specific type of bullet used is entirely up to the browser. To regain control over your bullets' appearance, select the Image Bullets tab in the List Properties dialog box, check the Specify Image radio button, and enter the name and path of the bullet image you want to use in the text box directly under that button or click the Browse button and select the image file using the Select Image dialog box.

Note that if your list is multileveled (as detailed in the next section, "Adding list levels"), then you need to add the image (or a different image) to each level of the list individually.

Adding list levels

Often a list will have more than one level of hierarchy—an item may have several items underneath it in indented bullets. To add additional hierarchical levels to your list, select the item(s) you want set in a level and then press the Increase Indent button on the toolbar and press the Numbered List or Bulleted List button (as appropriate). The item(s) now appear indented under the item above.

Creating collapsible lists

New
in 98

Collapsible lists are a new feature, both of FrontPage and the Web. A *collapsible list* lets your site's visitors collapse a hierarchical list (as detailed in "Adding list levels") so that they see only higher-level information. Both bulleted and numbered lists can be made collapsible. To make a list collapsible, open the List Properties dialog box and check the Enable Collapsible Outlines check box in the appropriate tab.

As of this writing, only Internet Explorer 4 supports collapsible lists—Netscape Navigator does not. A visitor who views your page in a browser other than Internet Explorer 4 sees the list normally, the only difference being that the list will not collapse.

The Refresh command

This command, the icon for which looks more like the poster for a recycling center, *refreshes* the page. Typically, to refresh a page means to update it, but here Refresh is really more like a revert function. Click the Refresh icon on the Standard toolbar or select View ⇨ Refresh. A dialog box appears, asking whether or not you wish to save changes to the page. Click the Yes button, and the current page is saved in its current incarnation. Click the No button, and the page reverts to its state the last time it was saved. Click the Cancel button to forget the whole thing.

Showing format marks

This handy command, located on the right end of the Standard toolbar, acts as a toggle to show and hide various formatting symbols—blue dotted lines under text indicate a bookmark, a return arrow indicates a line break, paragraph marks indicate paragraph ends, and long dashed lines mark the boundaries of a form element. Alternatively, you can access this function by selecting View➪Format Marks.

Removing formatting

The Remove Formatting command is not found on the toolbar. It is accessed by selecting Format➪Remove Formatting from the menus. Use this command to return text you have selected to the default text style. Note that this does not remove paragraph formatting, only text formatting, such as font, bold, or italic.

Inserting line breaks

Here is another case where standard word processing practice differs from FrontPage practice. FrontPage records a paragraph break (essentially a double line break) when the Enter key is pressed. In order to insert a single line break, it is necessary to select Insert➪Line Break. There are four options, indicated in Figure 2-13.

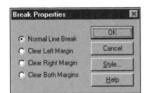

Figure 2-13: The Break Properties dialog box

The Normal Line Break causes a simple line break (<BR>) to be placed at the cursor location—you can quickly add a normal line break without using the dialog box by pressing Shift+Enter instead of Enter at the end of a line. The clear margin options are used when text has been aligned to wrap around images. For more information on aligning text around images, see Chapter 4. If you have selected the Format Marks option, you see a right-angle-arrow pointer appear to designate the presence of the line break. To turn Format Marks on, select View➪Format Marks or click the Show/Hide ¶ icon.

Inserting horizontal lines

Everyone has seen the horizontal ruled lines that appear on many Web pages. They may look like images, but in fact they are inserted using HTML, making them a low-bandwidth method of dressing up a page. To insert a horizontal line, select Insert ⇨ Horizontal Line. To adjust the look of the line, select it and open the Horizontal Line Properties dialog box, either by selecting Edit ⇨ Horizontal Line Properties or by clicking the line with the right mouse button and selecting Horizontal Line Properties from the pop-up menu.

Inserting symbols

Select Insert ⇨ Symbol from the menu bar to access a list of available symbols you can add to your Web page. These are primarily accented text characters and a few common symbols, such as the copyright symbol, trademark, and paragraph sign. Be advised, however, that FrontPage simply inserts the symbol character, not the HTML version of the symbol. As a result, symbols inserted in this way may not appear correctly on all computers.

Inserting comments

FrontPage uses a component (WebBot) to provide special handling for comments. Comments appear in FrontPage as highlighted text in the color of visited hyperlinks (by default this is purple). Comments do not appear when a Web browser displays the Web page. To insert a comment, select Insert ⇨ FrontPage Component and then highlight Comment from the list and press OK. Type your comment into the dialog box. Click OK to return to Editor.

Inserting text files

You can insert a file directly into your Web page. This file may be an HTML file or any of the other text formats that FrontPage supports. Editor converts the file to HTML when it inserts it. To insert a file, select Insert ⇨ File, select the appropriate format, locate the file to add, and click OK.

Creating Hyperlinks and Bookmarks

Hyperlinks are the glue that ties your Web pages together and to other resources on the World Wide Web. A hyperlink is just an embedded pointer to another Web page's URL. A *bookmark* is a named label placed at a given location on a page that allows a hyperlink to jump precisely to that point. In a Web page URL, a bookmark appears preceded by a hash mark (#) at the end of the URL. For example, http://www.myserver.com/webpage.html#coolbookmark.

Editor makes it quite easy to add and edit hyperlinks and bookmarks without worrying about the HTML code necessary to make the links work correctly. Even better, you never have to remember the name of the URL you want to link to, a real plus for those like me who may be prone to writing URLs on scraps of paper that always manage to disappear right before you want them.

Inserting a hyperlink

To create a hyperlink:

1. Type and select the text to be linked.
2. Click the Hyperlink icon on the Standard toolbar, select Insert ➯ Hyperlink, or press Ctrl+K.
3. Indicate the URL of the Web page or bookmark to link to, using the Create Hyperlink dialog box, shown in Figure 2-14.
4. Press OK to close the dialog box and return to Editor.

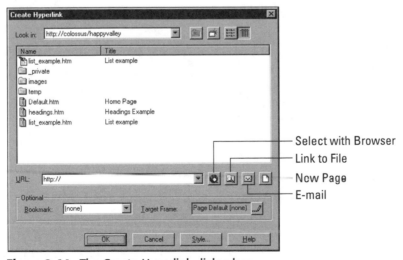

Figure 2-14: The Create Hyperlink dialog box

A number of types of hyperlinks can be inserted into your page using the Create Hyperlink dialog box. The main list box in the dialog box displays your Web, with all of its files—all currently open pages look like documents with quill pens on them, while pages that aren't open don't have the pens. You can navigate through your Web as you would using any standard Open dialog box.

In addition, the four buttons next to the URL text box provide even more options:

✦ To use your browser to select a file from the Web, click the Select with Browser button and then navigate to the page you want to link to, switch back to Editor, and press OK.

✦ To link to a file on your computer other than a Web page, press the Link to File button, select the file using the Select File dialog box, and press OK in both dialog boxes to return to Editor.

✦ To add an e-mail link, press the E-Mail button, and then enter the e-mail address you'd like mail sent to and press OK in both dialog boxes to return to Editor.

✦ To link to a new page, press the New Page button. The New dialog box opens, and you set up a new page just as you would normally (as described at the beginning of this chapter in "Creating new files or pages").

Editing hyperlinks

Edit hyperlinks via the Edit Hyperlink dialog box (also accessible as the Hyperlink Properties dialog box). Editing a hyperlink is very similar to adding one. To edit a hyperlink:

1. Click anywhere within the hyperlinked text (no need to select the text).

2. Click the Hyperlink icon on the Standard toolbar; select Edit ⇨ Hyperlink, Edit ⇨ Hyperlink Properties, or Insert ⇨ Hyperlink; click with the right mouse button and select Hyperlink Properties; or (in case that's not enough possibilities) use either of the two shortcuts, Ctrl+K or Alt+Enter.

3. In the Edit Hyperlinks dialog box, revise the link pointer, as previously described in the section "Inserting a hyperlink."

Following hyperlinks

Once you have created a hyperlink in Editor, the text changes to look like it *may* look in any Web browser. As you may have guessed, this is one instance when what you see is not exactly what you get. If you try to click a hyperlink in Editor, nothing happens. (You can see the URL of the hyperlink in the status bar at the bottom of the window. To toggle the status bar on or off, select View ⇨ Status Bar.)

It is possible to simulate the experience of following hyperlinks in Editor. To do this, click the hyperlinked text with the right mouse button. The pop-up menu that appears has two items of interest: Hyperlink Properties and Follow Hyperlink. Select Hyperlink Properties to edit the hyperlink. If you select Follow Hyperlink, the linked page is opened in the Editor window, whether it is a page in the current Web or a page on a remote Web server (assuming that you have an active Internet connection).

Once you have followed a hyperlink, the Back and Forward icons in the Standard toolbar become activated. Click the Back icon, or select Go ⇨ Back to return to the page containing the hyperlink. After you have gone back, you can use the Forward icon or select Go ⇨ Forward to repeat the initial Follow Hyperlink action. You can follow multiple links in this manner, just as you would in a standard Web browser.

Adding and editing a bookmark

Adding a bookmark to a page enables you to link to that exact location from a hyperlink somewhere else on the same page, from another page in the same Web, or from another Web altogether. To someone visiting your page, the bookmark looks no different than any other piece of text. To create a bookmark:

1. Select the text with which you wish to associate the bookmark. If you do not want the bookmark associated with any text, place the cursor at the spot where you want the bookmark to be located.

2. Select Edit ⇨ Bookmark.

3. In the Bookmark dialog box provide a name for the bookmark.

4. By default, Editor displays the selected text as the bookmark name. Editor also displays the names of any other bookmarks currently on the page. A bookmark must be unique for that page, and Editor prompts you with an error message if you attempt to create two identical bookmarks.

   Never create a bookmark name with spaces. Most browsers ignore any characters after the first space, causing any links to your bookmark to fail. Internet Explorer is an exception to this, so if you were to preview your Web with it, you would not realize the potential problem.

5. Click OK. Your bookmark is denoted by a dotted blue line underneath the bookmark text. If you added a bookmark without any text, it is only visible when you turn Format Marks on, in which case it appears as a small flag. (To toggle Format Marks on or off, select View ⇨ Format Marks or click the Format Marks icon on the Standard toolbar.)

To edit an existing bookmark, place the cursor within the bookmarked text and select Edit ⇨ Bookmark, select Edit ⇨ Bookmark Properties, click the right mouse button and select Bookmark Properties, or use the shortcut for the active property, Alt+Enter. Proceed in the manner previously described.

Linking to a bookmark

Create a link to a bookmark using the same procedure as for creating any hyperlink. This process is easiest if you have opened the page containing the bookmark to which you want to link, but this is not required:

1. Select the text for the hyperlink.

2. Open the Create Hyperlink dialog box using one of the methods described earlier under "Inserting a hyperlink."

3. Select the page and the bookmark.

4. If the page containing the bookmark is open, highlight it and then select the bookmark name from the Bookmark list.

5. If the page containing the bookmark is not currently open, highlight it in the file list. Type the bookmark you wish to link to in the Bookmark field. Click OK.

6. If you want to link to the bookmark on a page located in another Web or on the World Wide Web, press the Select with Browser button, browse to the page and the appropriate bookmark, and then switch back to Editor and press OK.

Working with FrontPage Tables

Tables are an increasingly important part of Web page design. Begun as a simple way of presenting tabular information, tables are now used as integral parts of pages for aligning text and graphics. Chances are, if a page has columns or looks particularly intricate, it was designed using tables.

FrontPage provides excellent table support, from the most basic to the most advanced options. To create a simple table, place the insertion point where you want the table to go, press the Insert Table button in the toolbar, and then highlight the number of rows and columns you want the table to have in the drop-down list. The table now appears on your page, pretty much how you want it to.

New in 98

To create more advanced tables and use all of Editor's table editing capabilities, you need to view the Table toolbar. To view this toolbar, select View ➪ Table Toolbar. With the Table toolbar, draw new cells by pressing the Draw Table button on the toolbar (the cursor changes to a Pencil icon) and clicking and dragging the size of the cell you want. You can split cells by drawing a vertical or horizontal line in an existing cell. When you are done with the Draw Table tool, press its toolbar button again, and the cursor returns to the standard word processing cursor.

To edit an existing table or cell, place the cursor within the cell or table and select Table ➪ Cell Properties or Table Properties as appropriate. Chapter 7 provides complete details on all facets of table formatting.

Viewing Pages

While editing pages in Editor, you will notice many underlines, dashed lines, and highlights that don't appear when the pages are viewed in a browser (see Figure 2-15). While these help greatly during your editing, you will often want to be able to see a "browser's-eye view" of your page, or you may need to delve deep into your page's underlying HTML codes to give it that extra tweak. To actually view your page in your computer's default browser, press the Preview in Browser button on the toolbar.

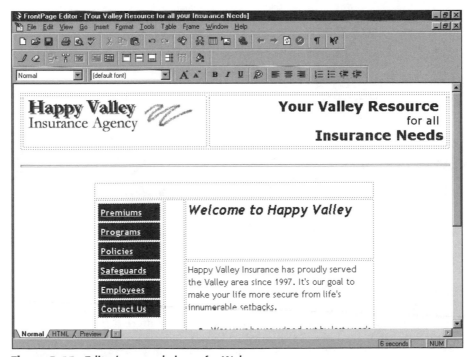

Figure 2-15: Editor's normal view of a Web page

To view your page approximately as it will appear in Microsoft Internet Explorer 4, click the Preview tab at the bottom of the Editor screen (see Figure 2-16). Note that some advanced page elements, such as components, do not preview correctly in Editor.

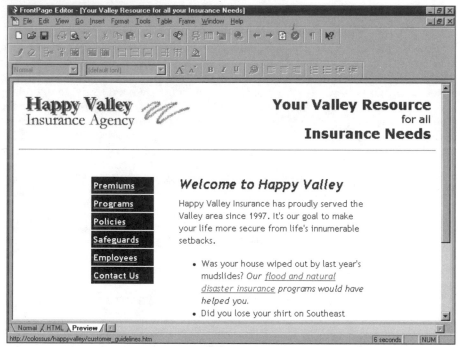

Figure 2-16: The Preview view of the same Web page shown in Figure 2-15

To view (and edit, if you desire) a Web page's HTML code, press the HTML tab at the bottom of the Editor screen. Chapter 9, "HTML Editing Techniques," provides an introduction to HTML code and how to edit it in FrontPage.

Tip

Throughout this chapter, and most of the others in this book, notice is given when a command or format looks different depending on the browser used. It's an excellent idea to preview your Webs in a number of different browsers (or different versions of the same browser) to ensure that they look as you want, or expect, them to look. At the very least, all Webs should be previewed in Microsoft Internet Explorer and Netscape Navigator.

Working with Frames

New in 98

Frames provide a way of displaying multiple Web pages in one browser. Using frames can make your Web easier to navigate, as well as more visually interesting. FrontPage 98 adds complete frame editing capabilities that reduce this once difficult option to mere child's play (comparatively). The following sections provide a brief introduction to FrontPage's frames options—for a complete description, see Chapter 8, "Working with Frames."

Creating a frame page

Creating a frame page is nearly identical to creating a nonframed ("standard")
Web page.

To create a new frame page:

1. Select File ⇨ New to open the New dialog box, and press the Frames tab.

2. Choose one from among the available frame page templates (descriptions of
   the various templates are provided in the Description box at the right side of
   the dialog box).

3. Press the OK button to close the dialog box. The new frame set is displayed
   (see Figure 2-17).

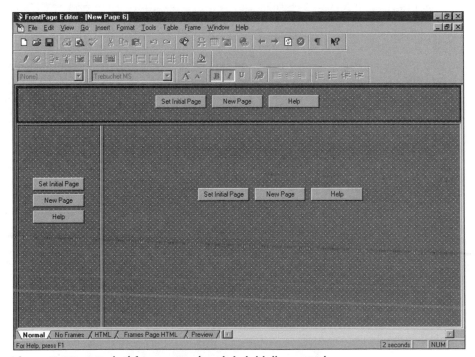

Figure 2-17: A typical frame set when it is initially created

4. Each frame in the frame set contains a different page. To specify the page
   that will be displayed in each frame, press either the Set Initial Page button
   or the New Page button in each frame.

   • **Set Initial Page**—Press this button when you want to have an existing
     page open in the frame. Although the Create Hyperlink dialog box opens
     when you press this button, the page, rather than a hyperlink to it, is
     actually loaded into the frame.

• **New Page**—Press this button to create a new page for the frame. The new page is a standard blank Web page.

5. Save your page normally.

Using the frames view options

When a frame set is open in Editor, two new view tabs appear at the bottom of the page: No Frames and Frames Page HTML.

The No Frames tab shows the page that is displayed when this page is visited by a browser that can't display frames. By default, the message "This page uses frames, but your browser doesn't support them" is displayed in this area. You can remove this message and create a new page if you want to give your "browser impaired" visitors a more satisfying message. The No Frames page can incorporate any standard Web features (tables, horizontal lines, fonts, ActiveX controls, and so on), but you should bear in mind that if the browser doesn't support frames, it is unlikely to support other advanced features.

The Frames Page HTML tab allows you to view and edit the code that creates the frame set (the HTML code for the No Frames page is contained within this code). The standard HTML tab now displays the code for the currently selected page within the frame set—the currently selected page is displayed with a dark outline around it.

Taking the Next Step

You've learned how to edit your Web pages, format them, add tables and frames, and create hypertext links and bookmarks. The next step is keeping your files organized and up to date. Chapter 3 tells you how to manage the files within your Web using Explorer.

✦   ✦   ✦

Using FrontPage Explorer

This chapter introduces Explorer, FrontPage's Web creation and site management application. After a brief overview of the Explorer environment, the chapter demonstrates how to create a new Web by importing existing Web content or by using one of Explorer's many Web templates and wizards. The chapter demonstrates the uses of the many "views" that Explorer provides for navigating around your Web. It shows how Explorer can help you give your Web a consistent design and navigational structure and how you can use Explorer's Task view to manage Web tasks, such as verifying links and checking spelling.

Note

This chapter also introduces the first of the two hypothetical companies that the book uses to illustrate FrontPage in action. These fictional "case studies" dramatize how companies of different sizes, with varying resources and ambitions, might use FrontPage to help them develop their Web presence. The case studies are intended to be both instructional and entertaining, but they are entirely fictional. Any resemblance to real enterprises or individuals anywhere is utterly coincidental.

Introducing FrontPage Explorer

FrontPage Explorer is the starting point and center of activity in FrontPage. When you start FrontPage, it is Explorer that launches, enabling you to create a new Web or to work with an existing one. All other FrontPage components, including Editor and Image Composer, can be accessed from within Explorer. Any activity that involves your Web as a whole, you conduct in Explorer. Once you have developed an initial Web, you are likely to use FrontPage Editor more often than Explorer, since most of your time is spent on specific Web pages, but you will continually come back to Explorer to perform basic Web management tasks — opening Web pages, deleting pages, reorganizing pages, checking the Web for problems, and publishing and updating the production version of your Web. This chapter focuses on using Explorer to create, view, and manage Webs. Chapter 2 describes the use of FrontPage Editor to develop individual Web pages.

FrontPage Explorer has a new look and many new features in the 98 version, all of which make it a more productive site management tool. Featured in this chapter are discussions of using the Navigation view to create shared navigation systems, creating graphic themes, and using the improved Web Publishing Wizard.

Creating an empty Web

Let's begin by creating a blank FrontPage Web — not very exciting perhaps, but it gives us a chance to survey the Explorer environment. After a basic overview, we create more interesting Webs using the Import Wizard and the Corporate Presence Wizard:

1. Start FrontPage. If you have followed the standard installation process, you can start FrontPage by clicking the Windows Start button and selecting Programs ➪ Microsoft FrontPage. (For more information on installing FrontPage, see Appendixes A and B.)

2. By default, unless you have disabled it, the Getting Started dialog box appears. (If you wish to prevent FrontPage from displaying this dialog box in the future, select Tools ➪ Options from the Explorer menu bar, click the General tab if it is not already on top, and click the Show Getting Started dialog box to uncheck this option.) This dialog box, shown in Figure 3-1, enables you to create a new Web or resume work on an existing one. Select the Create a New FrontPage Web option and click OK.

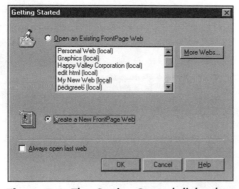

Figure 3-1: The Getting Started dialog box displays a list of existing Webs for easy access and an option to create a new Web.

3. If the Getting Started dialog box does not appear, you can create a new Web by selecting File ➪ New ➪ FrontPage Web. This brings up the New FrontPage Web dialog box (Figure 3-2).

4. Select the type of Web you want to create. Select the From Wizard or Template option and then select Empty Web from the list of templates and wizards.

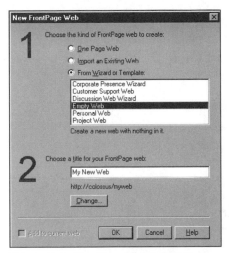

Figure 3-2: The New FrontPage Web combines the two steps of creating a new Web — selecting the kind of Web and giving it a title.

Note

Keep in mind that an "empty" FrontPage is not really empty — it just doesn't have any Web pages yet. Selecting the Empty Page option instructs FrontPage to build the directory structure for a new Web, including all the support files that are generated automatically.

5. Give your new Web a title. This can be somewhat confusing, because you are really doing two things at once. The *title* you designate becomes the descriptive title for the Web. You can put spaces in it, capitalize words, and make it really long if you like. At the same time, FrontPage uses the title to create the *name* for this Web's top-level folder — but it omits all the spaces and capitals and stops after fourteen characters.

Tip

You can change the value of either the Web title or the directory name at any time from within Explorer by selecting Tools ➪ Web Settings from the menu bar and choosing the Configuration tab. The Web Title input field updates the descriptive title; the Web Name updates the directory name.

6. By default, FrontPage assumes you want to create this Web on the last accessed Web server (the name of the current Web location is indicated under the title input field). To change this location and save this Web somewhere else, select the Change button. This brings up the Change Location dialog box, illustrated in Figure 3-3. Use this dialog box to select from the known hosts or type a new name into the input field. If you are running a Web server on your computer, you can select that, or if you are connected to the Internet, you can select a remote server to which you have access. Alternatively, you can select a local file directory for use without a Web server (although not all FrontPage functionality is available in this circumstance). Click OK to accept your changes.

7. When you have correctly identified the new Web, click OK to create it.

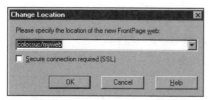

Figure 3-3: To designate an alternate location for your new Web, select an existing location or type the name of a new one into the Change Location dialog box.

The environment

What you see now should resemble Figure 3-4 — a brand new Web, not very awe-inspiring to look at, perhaps, but just think of the endless possibilities it presents! You can reflect on this while we get acquainted with Explorer's principal features.

The windows

The main elements of the Explorer window (refer to Figure 3-4) are:

✦ A menu bar consisting of File, Edit, View, Tools, and Help menu items

✦ A toolbar (described in detail in the following section)

✦ A Views icon palette that runs vertically down the left side of the Explorer window

✦ A main window that displays the contents of the current Web according to the selected view

✦ A status bar, the thin gray band at the bottom of the window, which displays helpful messages such as "For Help, press F1."

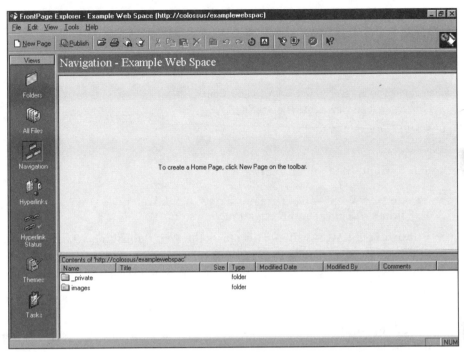

Figure 3-4: A view of an empty Web in Explorer — a vast, uncharted frontier

Note

In the upper-right corner of the application is also an enlarged Explorer icon (in previous versions of FrontPage this looked more like a fireworks display). This icon functions like similar icons in Web browsers. When Explorer is accessing a Web, this icon animates to reassure you that something is happening. When it stops, it signals that a transfer has ended.

The toolbar

The main Explorer toolbar consists of fourteen main items, which are identified and briefly described here. To familiarize yourself with their locations, refer to Figure 3-5. Note that at times some of the icons may be "grayed out" and inaccessible. Also, the exact composition of the toolbar changes when you switch to another view in Explorer. The icons that appear in particular views are described following the main toolbar description.

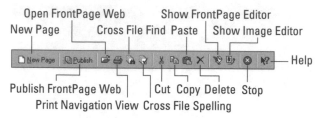

Figure 3-5: The Explorer toolbar

From left to right, the toolbar items are:

✦ **Create New Page** — This creates a new, blank Web page (this button is active in Folders, All Files, and Navigation views only).

✦ **Publish FrontPage Web** — This starts the Web Publishing Wizard to help you copy your Web contents to another server or other remote location.

✦ **Open FrontPage Web** — This opens the Open FrontPage Web dialog box.

✦ **Print Navigation View** — Only enabled when the Navigation view is active, this enables you to print the Navigation view schematic.

✦ **Cross File Find** — This performs a find across all or selected pages in the current Web.

✦ **Cross File Spelling** — This performs a spelling check in all or selected pages in the open Web.

✦ **Cut** — This removes the selected item and copies it to the clipboard for pasting.

✦ **Copy** — This copies the selected item to the clipboard for pasting.

✦ **Paste** — This inserts the contents of the clipboard at the selected location.

✦ **Delete** — This deletes the selected item.

✦ **Show FrontPage Editor** — This launches the Editor application or brings it to the foreground.

✦ **Show Image Editor** — This launches the designated image editor (by default, Image Composer) or brings it to the foreground.

✦ **Stop** — This halts the loading of a Web in progress.

✦ **Help** — This is the interactive help function.

Tip   To get context-sensitive help, click the Help button and then click an item you would like to learn about. The help file launches and opens to the section describing the feature you designate.

View specific toolbar items

When you switch to a new view by clicking one of the view icons, the toolbar may change to provide access to views of specific functions. The following list, arranged by view, identifies these icons and briefly describes their functions (see Figures 3-6 through 3-9). Except where noted, these buttons appear between the Cut and Paste buttons and the Show Editor/Image Editor buttons.

Navigation view

✦ **Up One Level** — When enabled, this moves the current view up one level in the folder structure.

✦ **Undo** — This enables you to undo the most recent action performed on the navigation schematic.

✦ **Redo** — This undoes the most recent undo action.

✦ **Rotate** — This toggles the schematic view from top-down to left-to-right orientation.

✦ **Size To Fit** — This resizes the schematic to fit in the current window (handy for large sites).

Figure 3-6: Additional toolbar icons in Navigation view

Hyperlinks view

✦ **Hyperlinks to Images** — This displays links to images as well as Web pages.

✦ **Repeated Hyperlinks** — This shows the actual number of links to a particular page (when this isn't selected, only one link to each page is shown regardless of how many links are actually located in the currently selected page).

✦ **Hyperlinks Inside Page** — This shows hyperlinks within a page — that is, links that incorporate bookmarks.

Figure 3-7: Additional toolbar icons in Hyperlinks view

Hyperlink Status view

✦ **Verify Hyperlinks** — This starts the process of checking that all selected hyperlinks go where they are supposed to.

Figure 3-8: The Verify Hyperlinks button on the Hyperlink Status toolbar

Tasks view

✦ **Create New Task** — This icon, which replaces the Create New Page icon in Tasks view, enables you to add a task to the current list.

Figure 3-9: The Create New Task button on the Task View toolbar

Before we embark on a tour of the Explorer views, it would be helpful to have some content. It is time to add some to our hitherto empty Web. In the sections that follow, we first import an existing Web page into our empty Web and then show how to import a Web when you first create it. After that we introduce the FrontPage Web templates and wizards and use the Corporate Presence Wizard to create a full-blown Web almost instantly!

Planning a new Web project

FrontPage makes the process of creating a Web site so easy, it is tempting just to start right in without worrying too much about a plan for the project. Because this book focuses on using the application, it may foster the sense that you should dive right in and start building your Web. So, for the record, this is not the process this author advocates.

If you have little or no Web experience and are just learning FrontPage, your best bet is probably to start by experimenting with FrontPage and the various templates that it includes. This helps to give you a sense of what is possible. At the same time, start paying attention to how other people have organized their Web sites and what kinds of information they have included. You might even create some trial Webs, just to start to get a feel for the medium.

At the same time, give some serious thought to these basic questions:

✦ *What existing content do you have that would be appropriate for Web use?* There are two sides to this question. On the one hand, nothing slows down a Web development project more than the need to invent new content. Any existing suitable content you have gets you up and running faster. On the other hand, Web pages that have been created simply by converting a print document to Web format are often exceedingly clunky and annoying.

✦ *What is your reason for wanting a Web site?* Some typical reasons include impressing and/or attracting potential customers, providing a convenient source for your product or support information, increasing sales, providing services for existing clients, or expanding your business into a new arena. Whatever your reasons, continually ask yourself how each element you are placing on the Web site speaks to your purpose.

✦ *Who is likely to use your Web site? If you build it, will they come?* This question is an important reality check. Is your target audience using the Web at all? When they want information, are they more likely to pick up a phone, write a letter, or dial up the Internet? Don't assume just because the whole world appears to have gone gonzo over the Web (or is that only in California?) that your target audience will too.

Finally, before getting down to serious Web page development, diagram your vision of how the site should be organized and how the various sections will be linked. You can use an existing diagramming tool like Visio to do this, or use the built-in capability of FrontPage's Navigation view, which has the advantage of actually building your Web as you design it!

Importing a Web

There are two ways to import content into a FrontPage Web. The first is to add them to an existing Web, and the second is to add them using the Import Wizard when you create your Web. In this section we describe the process of importing files into an existing Web.

Note

If you wish to duplicate the actions suggested in the following sections, look on the CD-ROM that accompanies this book. There you will find the files needed for the exercises in this chapter and throughout the remainder of this book. For information on installing and using the CD-ROM, see Appendix D.

Importing pages into an existing Web

To illustrate the process of importing a Web page into an existing Web, we use an early draft of the Happy Valley Insurance Company home page, designed before they had discovered the virtues of FrontPage.

Creating a list of import files

You can import files from any of the four main Web views: Folders, All Files, Navigation, and Hyperlinks. For now, let's use Folders view. Switch to Folders view by clicking the Folders icon in the View palette. Make sure that you are currently at the top of your empty Web. By default, FrontPage imports all files into the current directory. Select File ⇨ Import to open the Import File to FrontPage Web dialog box. This dialog box invites you to build a list of files to import.

To use the files on the CD-ROM that accompany this book, locate the `Contents/ ch03` folder on the CD-ROM. For additional information on using the CD-ROM, consult Appendix D.

You can select files individually, a folder at a time, or from the Web. If you select the Add File button, the Add File to Import List dialog box opens, enabling you to select one or more files. Selecting Add Folder opens the Browse for Folder dialog box. Select a folder, and all of its contents are added to the import list. If you select the From Web button, the Import Web Wizard (discussed later) appears to walk you through the steps of accessing a remote Web site to download files.

New in 98

In FrontPage 97, only files could be added to the import list. The ability to add entire folders and to download files from a remote server has made the import process much more flexible. Note that if you import a folder containing a complete FrontPage Web, you will be informed that the configuration folders contained in the Web will not be imported — press the OK button to acknowledge this and carry on.

Even though we are only importing one Web page, we select the Add Folder button. Why? Because the Web page we want, like most Web pages, is actually composed of its HTML file and several associated graphics files. Currently, if you import an HTML file, FrontPage does not prompt you to add any associated pages.

Click the Add Folder button and locate the folder that contains the Happy Valley Web page associated with this chapter (see Appendix D for information on locating these files on the CD-ROM that accompanies this book). Select the folder and click OK. The files appear listed in the Import File dialog box.

Editing the import list

At this point you could selectively add more files to the list using the same methods or remove files from the list by selecting the files and clicking Remove.

One complication results from our having added an entire folder to the list of files to import. By default, FrontPage recreates that folder with all of the files in it. In many cases, this is exactly the behavior you would like. In this case, however, it is not. We want these files in the main directory of our Web. To accomplish this, we need to edit the target URL for each page.

Select the home page, default.htm in the list of files, and click the Edit URL button. Remove any folder names associated with the file, so that the URL is simply "default.htm." Click OK to save your changes. Repeat this procedure for each of the files in the list, and then click OK to import the files into your Web.

Note

Actually, it would be nice at this point to be able to move the images into the images folder that FrontPage so conveniently made for us when we created our empty Web. If we do this, however, the HTML will no longer be able to find its graphics. Once the files are all imported, we can move the files and FrontPage will manage any associations that need to be updated. But it does not know how to do this when you are importing.

Checking the import results

FrontPage loads the file into Explorer, showing it in the current view. If you have been following along, you should see the five files listed in Folders view just as they appear in Figure 3-10. Of course, seeing the files' names in a list is really not that satisfying. What you really want to see is the Web page itself. To check the Web page and to ensure that all of its associated files have been imported correctly, double-click the HTML file in Folders, All Files, Navigation, or Hyperlinks view. The page should open in FrontPage Editor, as shown in Figure 3-11.

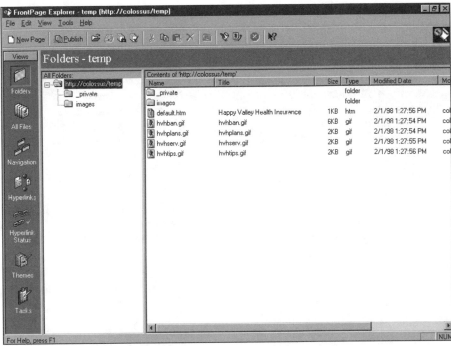

Figure 3-10: The Happy Valley home page listed in Folders view

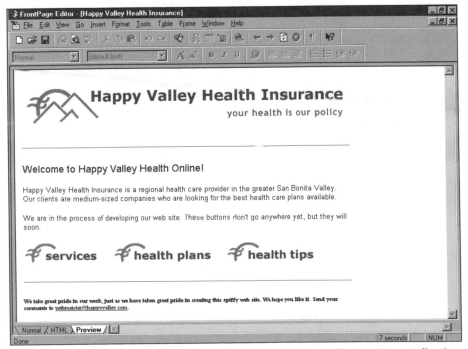

Figure 3-11: The imported Happy Valley home page as seen in FrontPage Editor's Preview mode

Welcome to Happy Valley

As we build our Web sites throughout this book, one of the fictional companies you'll be seeing is Happy Valley Insurance. Happy Valley is a prosperous insurance company whose headquarters is located somewhere in the sun belt. They provide insurance benefits to other institutions. Although not yet a major player in the insurance arena, they are a rapidly growing company, looking to ride the wave of cybermania into the twenty-first century. Currently they have over 60 employees, the majority of whom work at a single main office. The rest are divided among three branch offices. There is also a small but growing telecommuting sales force.

Happy Valley has already created a simple Web site to promote its services. Designed by the CEO in her spare time, it is pretty basic. But at least it's a start. This year, the company has provided an actual budget to enhance and maintain the Web site. They've hired a Web site project coordinator, whose task is to identify the various departments of the company who might contribute content to the Web site and then to make the whole thing happen.

Happy Valley is looking to FrontPage as a way to distribute the development responsibilities to the various contributing departments and also to help coordinate their efforts. The administrative staff has the job of updating content, so FrontPage is an excellent choice. Although the administrators are not trained as Web developers, they are already using other Microsoft Office products.

Importing formatted content files

You can also use the import feature to copy files of any type into your Web. Be aware, however, that the import function does not make any conversions. It assumes that you want to copy the content directly in its existing format. So for example, if you have a set of document files in Microsoft Word format, you cannot import them into your Web converted to HTML files (wouldn't it be pretty to think so, though?). You need to use Editor to perform this task, one file at a time. We illustrate the process in Chapter 2.

Importing a Web with the Import Wizard

Having successfully added a Web page and its associated graphics to our Web, we now illustrate an alternative. You can also import an entire existing Web into a new FrontPage Web at the time you create it.

To do this, save and close any currently open Web — FrontPage can only handle one open Web at a time. Select File ➪ New ➪ FrontPage Web. In the New FrontPage Web dialog box, select the Import an Existing Web option, and give the new Web a title as described earlier in the chapter. Click OK to continue.

The Import Web Wizard appears as shown in Figure 3-12. You can elect to import files from your local computer or from a computer to which you are connected via a local area network (LAN). Alternatively, you can import files from a remote Web server. To select files from a local system, select the From a Source Directory of Files option and click the Browse button to locate the folder containing the files you wish to import.

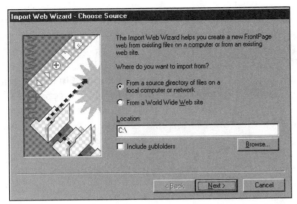

Figure 3-12: Select where you want to import your Web from using the first screen of the Import Web Wizard.

To use the files on the CD-ROM that accompanies this book, locate the `Contents/ ch03` folder on the CD-ROM. For additional information on using the CD-ROM, consult Appendix D.

When you have selected the appropriate folder in the Browse for Folder dialog box, click OK to return to the wizard. If the Web you want to import has subfolders, you will need to check the Include Subfolders check box. Click the Next button to continue.

The wizard shows you a list of the files in the folder you have selected, much like the list we saw earlier. You can remove one or more files from this list by selecting the offending files and clicking the Exclude button. Click Next when you are happy with the list. In the final wizard screen, click Finish to import the files into your Web. The selected files are imported into Explorer. Check the results as described in the previous section on importing files.

Importing a Web from the Web

As noted earlier, you can also use the Import Wizard to import a Web from the World Wide Web. Follow the same procedure initially that you did to import files using the wizard. In the first wizard screen, select the From a World Wide Web Site option and type the name of the Web server in the input field provided. (Note that if the Web you want to import is contained in a directory on the server, you need to enter the folder name as well, and depending upon your Internet account setup, you may have to begin your Internet connection before beginning this procedure.) Click Next to continue.

If you do not give it an exact filename, the Import Wizard looks for a `default.htm` file on the designated Web server. If it finds instead an `index.html` file, it grabs this instead and converts it to `default.htm` at the other end.

The next wizard screen, as you can see from Figure 3-13, enables you to limit the type and number of files that the wizard tries to retrieve. You can limit how deep into a Web site's directory structure the Import Wizard probes. To do this, check the Limit to This Page Plus box and select a number from the Levels Below list. You can limit the quantity of files that the wizard imports by checking the Limit To option and indicating a maximum file size. Finally, you can limit the types of files downloaded to text and graphics, thereby avoiding the long download times required for, say, twenty-megabyte digitized video presentations. When you've finished your selections, click Next to proceed to the final screen. Click Finish when you are ready to start importing. The selected files import into Explorer. Check the results as described in the earlier section on importing files.

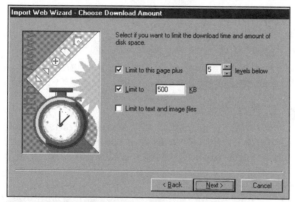

Figure 3-13: Specify how many pages and files you want to import.

The Import Web Wizard is useful but not particularly discriminating when it downloads files from a World Wide Web server. By default it grabs all the files it can find. It would be nice to be able to add and exclude files in the manner of the other Import Wizard. Also note that you will probably run into some problems when trying to import a Web that incorporates frames — either you get only the no-frames pages or you get the frame set with no content pages.

Using Web Templates and Wizards

FrontPage's Web templates and wizards make short work of creating new Webs out of thin air. The results are pretty generic, however, so you will still need to use Editor to update and "personalize" the pages in your new Web.

To create a new Web using a template or wizard, select File⇨New⇨FrontPage Web in Explorer to open the New FrontPage Web dialog box shown in Figure 3-14. Make your choice of which wizard or template to use, enter a title for your new Web, and press the OK button. The following two sections, "The FrontPage templates" and "The smarter Web wizards," describe the types of Webs available.

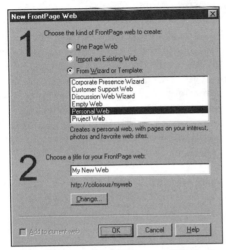

Figure 3-14: Select the type of Web you want to create in the New FrontPage Web dialog box.

The FrontPage templates

In FrontPage terminology, a *Web template* is a generic set of predesigned Web pages collected into a single Web. If you followed along in Chapter 1, where we created a personal Web, you have already seen a good example of a simple FrontPage template in action. The Personal Web template is a single Web page with placeholder content and prompts for content appropriate to a page of personal information. In addition to the Personal Web template, the other templates that come with FrontPage 97 include:

✦ **Empty Web** — This template generates a new Web without any pages in it yet.

✦ **One Page Web** — This template, created if you select the One Page Web radio button, generates a Web with a single, blank home page. (This is also the Web that is created if you choose to create a new, blank FrontPage Web from the Getting Started dialog box.)

✦ **Customer Support** — This more elaborate template includes a home page and links to several additional pages: a welcome page, What's New, a FAQ, and a page for downloading customer information. In addition, it has prebuilt forms for collecting bug report information and customer suggestions. There is also a customer support discussion section and a search function.

✦ **Project Web** — This Web consists of a welcome page, a page listing project team members, a schedule page, an index of status report pages, and an archive page that links to individual project pages. This Web also includes a search function and a discussion section. It is intended to serve as a point of communication for the members of a project team.

Templates can help you get started quickly, but to be brutally honest, the templates provided with FrontPage are of marginal value at best. To use one, you first create the Web using the template and then edit the generic contents, replacing them with your own information. One useful feature of the templates is their prebuilt functionality, including search engines and discussions. Once you have learned to add these elements yourself, even this value diminishes. Overall, the templates that come with FrontPage are probably most valuable as learning tools. (Speaking of learning tools, FrontPage comes with a tutorial. To follow the tutorial, open the Learning FrontPage template.)

Tip

Once you have built a few practice Webs, you will find it just as easy to start with a blank Web and fill it with content of your own devising. Templates become a powerful feature when you begin to create your own, a process described in Chapter 18.

The smarter Web wizards

A wizard is similar to a template, only smarter. Rather than create a Web with all generic content, the FrontPage wizards first ask you to answer some probing questions, such as "What is your name?" The wizard then places your answer in the appropriate spot in the template. When you first open a wizard-generated Web, it is already filled with customized content based on your answers. This feature can save you some real time, although again you are likely to want to customize the pages to your liking. Here too, the most useful wizards are the ones you build yourself, a topic covered in Chapter 18.

The wizards included with FrontPage are:

✦ **Corporate Presence Wizard** — This wizard creates a basic site for communicating information about a company. This is the most elaborate wizard included with FrontPage. We walk through the steps of creating a corporate Web toward the end of this chapter.

✦ **Discussion Web Wizard** — This wizard generates a fully threaded, searchable discussion group. We return to this wizard in Chapter 14. (Jargon alert: When we speak of an online discussion, a thread refers to a message in the discussion and any replies to that message.)

Getting Around in Explorer

Now that we have imported some content into our Web, it is time to explore Explorer (I just had to say that). In this section we examine some of Explorer's general-purpose functions — these are basic actions that can be performed from most or all of the Explorer views. Following that, we look at the specific capabilities of each of the seven Explorer views. Later in the chapter, we examine the particulars of using Explorer to update and maintain your Webs.

General Web functions

Explorer gives you the ability to perform two kinds of Web management functions. The first are operations performed on the Web as a whole. The second are operations performed on individual elements, typically files, that make up your Web. Most of the file-related functions in Explorer involve "housekeeping" tasks. The actual work of editing files is done by other applications, including FrontPage Editor, introduced in Chapter 2, and Image Composer, discussed in Chapter 5.

Customizing your workspace

There is not much you can do to alter the Explorer workspace, but there are a few noteworthy ways to customize your workspace:

✦ **Adjusting the size of the Views icons** — Right-click anywhere in the Views bar and select small or large icons.

✦ **Resizing window panes or columns** — Click and drag any of the vertical or horizontal window panes to resize the corresponding windows. Use the same procedure to resize individual columns in those views that include file lists.

✦ **Sorting file lists** — In those views that include a list of files, you can sort the files by any column by clicking the name of the column at the top of the list. Clicking a second time on the same column sorts it in opposite order.

Configuring workspace options

The Options dialog box (select Tools ⇨ Options) contains a number of settings that you can use to customize the Explorer environment. The Options dialog box consists of three tabs.

General

The General tab consists of a number of check box options, including the capability to hide or show the initial Getting Started dialog box, to show or hide the toolbar or status bar, and to enable or disable a variety of warning messages. Refer to Figure 3-15.

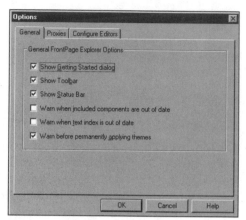

Figure 3-15: The Explorer Options dialog box, showing the General tab

Proxies

A *proxy server* is a gateway server that enables you to access Internet services on the opposite side of a firewall, the security system that restricts access to a given Internet domain or host. Typically, you will need to configure FrontPage to use a proxy server if you are working on a network that has a firewall and you need to access a Web server that is external to that firewall, or conversely, if you are working remotely and need to access a server that is inside the firewall.

To configure FrontPage to use a proxy server, select the Proxies tab and enter the URL of the proxy host in the designated input field. By default, FrontPage always attempts to use any proxy host you list here. If you also access servers that are not on the opposite side of a firewall, you can identify them in the List of Hosts without Proxies input area. If you are working on a network that has a firewall, you can turn off proxy access to all internal servers by checking the Do Not Use Proxy Server for Local (Intranet) Addresses option. The proxy settings are usually available from your network administrator.

Configure Editors

This Options tab enables you to tell Explorer what application to launch when you double-click a particular file format. By default, this option associates all HTML and HTML-related files with FrontPage Editor, graphics with Image Composer, and general-purpose text files (including cascading style sheets and channel definition files — discussed in later chapters) with Notepad.

You can add, modify, or remove items in this list. For example, to change the association for cascading style sheet files to your favorite text editor, select this item and click the Modify button, bringing up the dialog box shown in Figure 3-16. You can change the descriptive name of the associated application and identify its location. Use the Browse button to find the application if need be. Click OK to accept the changes and return to the Options tab. Click OK again to apply the changes and return to Explorer.

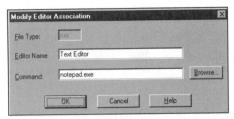

Figure 3-16: The Modify Editor Association dialog box lets you specify the program used to edit particular types of files.

By default, Explorer associates files either with programs included with FrontPage (for example, Editor) or with Notepad. The types of files initially associated include:

- ✦ **HTM** and **HTML** — Standard Web pages
- ✦ **SHTM** and **SHTML** — Web pages that incorporate server-side includes
- ✦ **HTX** — Preprocessed HTML files
- ✦ **ASP** — Microsoft's active server page files
- ✦ **CSS** — Cascading style sheets
- ✦ **IDC** — Database connection files
- ✦ **CDF** — Channel definition files
- ✦ **GIF** and **JPG** — The two standard World Wide Web image files
- ✦ **.** — Files without any extension

Opening and deleting FrontPage Webs

Earlier in the chapter, we described the process for creating new Webs. You can open an existing Web at any time from within Explorer by selecting File ⇨ Open FrontPage Web. Note that you can open only one Web at a time.

You can also delete an entire Web from within Explorer. To do this, simply select File ⇨ Delete FrontPage Web. Be certain that you know what you are doing, since you cannot undo this action.

Caution

Speaking from personal experience, I would like to point out that it is very easy, if you are not paying close attention, to confuse the operation of deleting a *Web* with the operation of deleting a Web *page*. Think twice before clicking the OK button on the confirmation prompt as deleting a Web cannot be undone!

Web settings

The Web Settings menu item enables you to configure a variety of parameters related to the currently open Web (see Figure 3-17). Select Tools ➪ Web Settings to open the dialog box. Alternatively, you can click with the right mouse button in the open space of any view's main window (with the exception of the Themes view) and select Web Settings from the pop-up menu. Many of these settings affect functions that are described elsewhere in the book. Most of the time, you use this item to modify the title of your Web.

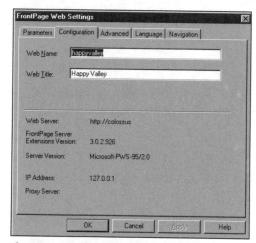

Figure 3-17: The Web Settings dialog box, showing the Configuration tab, with options to modify the name and title of the current Web

✦ **Parameters** — Use this tab to define variables for the Substitution component. The Substitution component is discussed in Chapter 12, "FrontPage Components."

✦ **Configuration** — This tab allows you to change the name and title of the current Web. Recall that the Web title is its descriptive name — you may have noticed that this title appears in the title bar of the main Explorer window. The name is the actual name of the folder that houses this Web on the server. This tab also presents some information that cannot be changed, such as the IP address of the host computer, the Web server address, and the server extension version, if appropriate. If you have set up your server to use Microsoft's Visual Source Safe, you see an additional option here that allows you to set up a Source Safe project for the current Web.

✦ **Advanced** — This tab contains settings for advanced FrontPage options. These include: image map styles (covered in Chapter 5), validation script options (Chapter 15), an option to display files in hidden directories (that is, directories whose names begin with an underscore), and settings to indicate when included pages or a text-search engine should be recalculated.

✦ **Language** — This tab enables users to customize the FrontPage environment with multiple-language support.

✦ **Navigation** — If you are using the FrontPage navigation bar capability, this tab enables you to define the labels that appear on some of the general-purpose buttons. You learn more about this in the section "Navigation view" later in this chapter.

Working with Explorer's Web Views

One of Explorer's primary functions is to show you your Web from various angles. That is the purpose of its seven "views" — each offers a slightly different perspective on your Web and gives you the ability to modify your Web accordingly. The first four views in the Explorer Views bar — Folders, All Files, Navigation, and Hyperlinks — are views of your Web and its contents. The last three items — Hyperlink Status, Themes, and Tasks — provide views of different operations that you can perform in the course of managing your Web. In this section we discuss the four main Web views. The others are detailed in Chapter 18, "Managing and Publishing Your Web Project."

If you have already imported the Happy Valley Web page as described earlier in the chapter, open that page now to follow along in the next section. If you have not imported this Web, you can find a copy of it in the Contents/ch03 folder of the CD-ROM that accompanies this book. For additional directions on using the CD-ROM, consult Appendix D.

New in 98

The concept of "views" in FrontPage is greatly expanded in FrontPage 98. Previously, Explorer consisted of two views, Folders and Hyperlinks, along with a variety of miscellaneous functions, such as means of calculating links and creating "to do" tasks. Now these are all consolidated into the Views bar, and the All Files, Navigation, and Themes views have been added.

Folders view

To switch to Folders view, click the Folders view icon in the Views bar or select View ⇨ Folders View in the menu bar. Figure 3-18 illustrates what you should see.

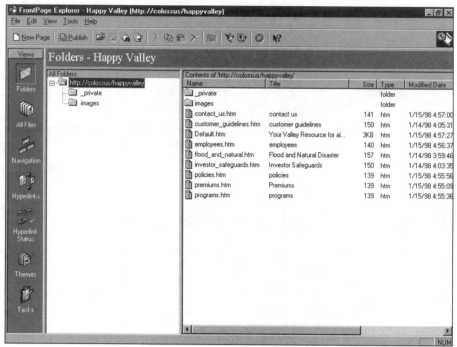

Figure 3-18: Folders view provides a Windows Explorer–esque depiction of a Web.

Folders view resembles a standard directory listing in Windows Explorer. In the left pane, labeled "All Folders," is a hierarchical listing of the folders contained in the Web. On the right, in a pane labeled "Contents of" and the name of the current folder, are the files and folders contained in the folder currently selected in the left column. The top-level folder in the hierarchy is the root Web. It is designated with its absolute URL.

Getting around

Navigating around Folders view should be very familiar to you if you have used Windows 95. Click the plus sign (+) next to a folder in the All Folders pane to expand the branch of the folder. Click the minus sign (–) to collapse an expanded branch. Click the folder icon once in the All Folders pane to display its contents in the Contents pane. Double-clicking a folder in the Contents pane performs the same function. The current folder is indicated with an open folder icon in the All Folders pane.

Use the Up One Level button in the toolbar to move to the parent folder of the current folder. If this icon is grayed out, you are currently at the highest-level folder of the Web.

Opening files

Generally, you open a file by double-clicking it in the Contents pane. Alternatively, select the page in the Contents pane and select Edit ➪ Open. How the file is launched depends on (1) what type of file it is and (2) what application it is associated with in Explorer. By default Web pages (ending in .html or .htm) open in FrontPage Editor. Graphics (ending in .gif or .jpg) open in Image Composer. Standard text files open in Notepad. If you attempt to launch a file with an unrecognized file ending, FrontPage complains and asks if you would like to save the file to a different filename before continuing.

To change the application associated with a particular file type, use the Configure Editors tab of the Options dialog box, described earlier in the chapter in the section entitled "Configure Editors." To access this menu item, select Tools ➪ Options.

If you want to open a file in an alternate application or open an unrecognized file type, highlight the file and select Edit ➪ Open With or right-click the file and select Open With from the pop-up menu. Unfortunately, there is no way to pick an editor that is not listed in the Options dialog box.

One way around the limitation in Explorer's Open With function is to add all of your favorite editing applications and associate them with alternate or even bogus file endings. So for example, you might add Adobe Photoshop to the list and associate it with its native file type, .psd. If you want to edit a GIF image in Photoshop, simply select Open With and select Photoshop from the list of available editors.

Adding files and folders

To add a new page in Folders view, select the folder to which you want to add the file and click the New Page icon in the toolbar. Alternatively, select File ➪ New ➪ Page. Better still, click with the right mouse button in the Contents pane and select New Page from the pop-up menu. A blank HTML file is added to the folder, with its default name highlighted, ready for renaming.

To add a new folder, select File ➪ New ➪ Folder, right-click in the Contents pane, and select New Folder from the pop-up menu. Again, the name is highlighted, waiting for you to fill in a new name.

Moving and copying files

You move and copy files in Explorer just as you do in Windows Explorer. To move a file to a new folder, select it in the Contents pane, drag it until it is over the folder where you want it to go, and drop the file. To copy a file, use the same procedure, holding down the Ctrl key as you drag. You should see a plus (+) sign next to the file, denoting the fact that you are copying rather than moving the file. If you copy a file within the same folder, the new file has "copy" tagged onto the end of its name.

You can also use the Cut, Copy, and Paste commands to move and copy files in Folders view. Select the files you want and click the Cut icon in the toolbar to move or the Copy icon to copy. Alternatively, select these items from the Edit menu. Note that if you use Cut, the file icon grays out to indicate that it is about to move somewhere else. Select the new location for the files and click the Paste button.

All of these file-related actions — Open, Open With, Cut, Copy, Rename, and Delete — can be accessed by clicking the file icon with the right mouse button.

You can copy or move multiple files in one of two ways. Use the Shift key if you want to select a range of files that are all together. Select the first file, hold the Shift key down, and select the last file to select it and all of the intervening files. Use the Ctrl key to select a series of files. Hold the Ctrl key and select the desired files one at a time. In either case, once you have selected the files you wish to move or copy, drag one of the files (the rest follow along) as described previously.

The good news is that when you move files, FrontPage automatically updates any pointers to these files in your HTML pages, so that moving files never causes links to break. To demonstrate this, open the top level of Happy Valley Web, select the four image files (ending in .gif), and move them into the images folder. Then check on the status of the HTML page by double-clicking it. It opens in Editor — and the images are still intact!

Renaming files

To rename a file, select the file and then click it a second time to highlight the text of the name for editing. Type the new name for the file. Press the Enter key or click anywhere in the window to accept this new name.

There is a fine art to clicking at just the right tempo to highlight the filename without launching the file. If you would rather avoid the challenge, use the F2 button on the keyboard as a shortcut. This automatically highlights the filename for editing. If all else fails, select Edit ➪ Rename to produce the same effect.

If the file whose name you have changed is linked to other files, FrontPage alerts you to the number of instances where the file is referenced on your Web. Select Yes to allow FrontPage to update your links. Select No to rename the file without updating the links (for example if you want to save an older draft of the file). Select Cancel to bail out of the whole thing and return the file to its initial name.

Deleting files

Deleting files is so simple, you could do it in your sleep — but watch out that you don't, since the delete action cannot be undone. Fortunately, FrontPage does prompt you before letting you delete files.

To delete one or more files, select all of the files and click the Delete icon on the toolbar, press the Delete key, or select Edit ➪ Delete. Click Yes, or Yes to All if you have selected a large number of files to delete and are feeling lucky (or impatient), or No if you get cold feet.

Accessing folder and file properties

Another task that you can perform in Folders view is to set access privileges to specific folders in your Web. To do this, select the folder in either pane and select Edit ➪ Properties or click the folder with the right mouse button and select Properties from the pop-up menu. The Folder Properties dialog box, shown in Figure 3-19, appears. This dialog box displays general information about the folder: its name, type, location, and contents. It also provides a means of designating what kind of access to this file is allowed. Options are:

✦ Allow Scripts or Programs to Be Run

✦ Allow Files to Be Browsed

Check the first option only for those folders where you plan to store scripts or programs that need to be called from a Web page. General HTML directories should have this option unchecked as a general security measure. Uncheck both options to create a file that is inaccessible to Web browsers.

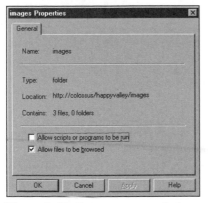

Figure 3-19: Set access permission using the Folder Properties dialog box.

Tip

If you want, you can hide the folder as well. Simply rename it with an underscore character at the beginning of the name (for example, "_bigsecrets"). Of course this only hides the file from FrontPage — which means that you may only be hiding it from yourself! By the way, you can show hidden files (is this an oxymoron?) by checking the Show Documents in Hidden Directories check box option on the Advanced tab of the Web Settings dialog box.

All Files view

All Files view is similar to Folders view in that it lists all of the files in your Web. It differs in that it pulls all of the files out of their directory structure and places them all into a single, flattened directory. Although at first this might seem like a rather pointless exercise, there are some reasons you might plausibly want to use All Files view:

✦ If you want to locate all of the files on your Web of a certain type or modification date, say audio clips created after the last blue moon, you can do so (assuming you know the date of the last blue moon).

✦ One column in the All Files display indicates whether files are "orphans" or not. In Web lingo, an orphan is a Web page that is not referenced from any other pages in the Web. It is, metaphorically speaking, parentless. These files are often suitable candidates for removal, since they are not directly reachable from within the Web site. (Of course there are plenty of legitimate reasons for having orphan pages in your Web, so don't just blithely delete an orphan any time you encounter one.)

✦ All Files view has the virtue of displaying files even in the "invisible" folders that FrontPage creates. These folders are indicated with an initial underscore character, as in "_private." You can use this view to access files that are otherwise sometimes inaccessible

New
in 98

The All Files view is All New. Help Microsoft think of a reason for having invented it.

Navigation view

Navigation view is a new addition to FrontPage 98. It serves three primary purposes: (1) to help organize your Web, (2) to create a printable schematic of your Web's structure, and (3) to create shared borders with an automatically configured navigation system, either text-based or graphical. Each of these functions is introduced later. Shared borders are described in detail in Chapter 8, "Working with Frames."

Getting around in Navigation view

To see Navigation view in action, open the Happy Valley Web page as described earlier in the chapter, and click the Navigation button in the Views bar. The Navigation window consists of two panes. The upper pane shows a schematic representation of your Web. Web pages are represented as rectangular boxes, and connecting lines represent links between pages. The bottom pane lists the files and folders in the current folder — the equivalent of the folder Contents pane in Folders view (see Figure 3-20).

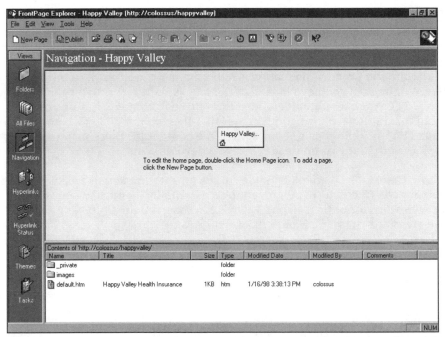

Figure 3-20: Navigation view, showing the default view of the Happy Valley Web page

The Contents pane works much as it does in Folders view, the biggest difference being that you must use the Up One Level icon (or its right mouse button equivalent) in order to navigate up through the folder hierarchy. The purpose of this pane is not so much to replicate the Folders view, however, as to provide a convenient way of adding files to the Navigation view window.

Customizing Navigation view

In addition to being able to resize the Navigation window panes, you can also customize the look of the map pane. Options include:

✦ **Rotate the map** — Click the Rotate button on the toolbar, select View ➪ Rotate, or click using the right mouse button and select Rotate to toggle between horizontal and vertical orientations of your schematic.

✦ **Expand/collapse levels** — Each page rectangle that is connected to a lower level contains an expand/collapse button. Click the plus (+) sign to expand the level. Click the minus (–) sign to collapse an expanded level.

✦ **Size to fit** — Use this command if you have a large Web that scrolls off the screen or if you have a small Web and have enlarged the bottom pane to the point that it covers the Web. Select the Size to Fit icon on the toolbar, select View ➪ Size to Fit, or right-click in the Map window and select Size to Fit from the pop-up menu. The contents of the window resize to the available screen size.

Mapping your Web

If you are creating a new Web, you can use the Navigation view to generate a working schematic of your site even as you create placeholders for the Web pages.

To illustrate the process of creating a Web schematic, we return to our Happy Valley Web page. If you have looked at the page in Editor (or if you glanced at Figure 3-11), you undoubtedly noticed that the page contains buttons ostensibly leading to additional information, except that they do not go anywhere yet. That is because Happy Valley has not yet written the content for these pages — it is always the content that holds up your Web development!

For now, then, let's create placeholder pages for the three areas we know Happy Valley intends to create. (The procedure is essentially identical when working with your own Web rather than Happy Valley's.) In case you aren't looking at the page, those areas are: Services, Health Plans, and Health Tips.

To create a new page and add it to the map:

1. Open the Happy Valley Web (see the discussion earlier in the chapter if you need help here).

2. Make sure the top level of the Web is current and switch to Navigation view by clicking the Navigation icon in the Views bar.

3. Create an empty file:

   • Click anywhere in the Contents pane in Navigation view and select File ⇨ New ⇨ Page or click the New Page icon on the toolbar. This adds a new file to the file list, just as it does in Folders view. It does not add it to the map.

   • Rename the new page **services.htm**.

   • Drag the page onto the map pane. As you drag, notice that when the mouse cursor gets near the home page currently in the pane, an outline of the new file appears with a connection attaching it to the Home Page. Since that is what you want to have happen, when that outline appears, drop the file.

4. The first time you add a file to the schematic, Explorer prompts if you want to use shared borders or not. If you say Yes, the shared borders are automatically added to both pages using the default settings. If you say No, FrontPage ceases to hound you, and you can add pages to the map to your heart's content. For now, just say No to shared borders. The upcoming section, "Introducing shared borders," details adding and formatting shared borders.

5. You may be somewhat surprised to note that when you drop the new services.htm file onto the map, it shows up as "New page 1" (assuming this is the first new page you have created in this Web). The reason for this is that the two panes — map and folder contents — operate semi-independently. You can add files to the folder list without having them appear in the map.

Adding files to the Navigation pane automatically creates the files in the file list.

6. Just to prove this last point, select the Happy Valley home page icon in the map view (it turns a pretty shade of blue, except for the label). Use any of the methods described earlier to create two more new pages. Because you selected the home page in the map, these pages show up linked to that page parallel with the first page. The result of these actions should look like Figure 3-21. If you do not immediately see the two new pages in the file menu, select View ⇨ Refresh from the menu bar to update the file list pane.

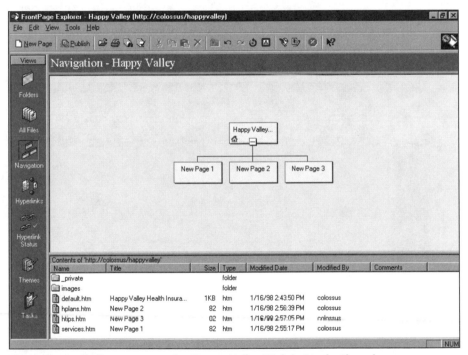

Figure 3-21: Adding pages to the Happy Valley Web in Navigation view

7. Next you need to update the filenames and the map labels. The first file is already named `services.htm`, so label it **Services**. Name the second file **hplans.htm** and label it **Health Plans**. Call the third file **htips.htm** and label it **Health Tips**. Just for fun, click the Rotate button.

8. As a final step, let's add some real content pages to create a third level in the hierarchy. As it turns out, Happy Valley does have some health tips content more or less ready to add to the Web. It's not much to look at yet, but it's a start. You can find these pages in `Contents/ch03/import2` on the CD-ROM. If you need additional help locating these files, consult Appendix D.

9. To import these tips, first create a new folder in your Web, named **tips**. You can switch to Folders view to do this if you like, or stay in Navigation view — if you use Navigation view, make sure the lower folder Contents pane is selected. When the map is the active pane, the New ⇨ Folder menu item is grayed out.

10. Make `tips` the current folder by double-clicking it from Navigation view or clicking it in Folders view. Select File ⇨ Import and add the `import2` folder to the list of files to import, following the directions given earlier in the chapter.

11. Use the Edit URL option to remove the extra folder name, and then click OK. The five new files — `accident.htm`, `dieting.htm`, `doctors.htm`, `exercise.htm`, and `vacation.htm` — are now in the `tips` folder.

12. Select all of these files (you can use the keyboard shortcut, Ctrl+A) and drag them onto the Health Tips box. The results are shown in Figure 3-22.

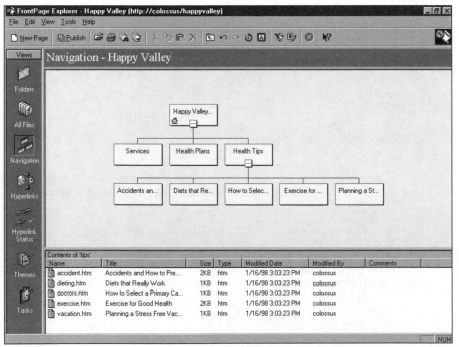

Figure 3-22: The expanding Happy Valley Web, showing five new tips pages added to the Navigation view

Note   A Web's map is not imported with it — if you import a Web, you will have to incorporate it into your existing Web's map using the preceding instructions.

Printing your map

To print your schematic map, select the Print icon on the toolbar or select File➪ Print Navigation View. Use Print Preview to see what the printout will look like before you commit. In Print Preview, you can zoom in on the page to check it for details or zoom out to see how it fits on the page. If your Web map occupies multiple pages, you can page through them in Preview mode. Use Page Setup to alter general print options, particularly if you want to reorient the map in landscape mode (that is, to print the long way on the paper).

Printing is available only in Navigation view even though the icon remains on the toolbar at all times (unlike the other view-specific icons, which appear only when their view becomes active).

To test the Navigation view's printing capabilities, try printing the Happy Valley Web map we created in the previous section.

Introducing shared borders

A *shared border* in FrontPage refers to a section of each Web page that is repeated on every page. Most pages have an area that repeats on every page, and shared borders can make it easy to create and maintain that area. When you want to update the shared section, you only need to change it once, and the change is immediately reflected on every page.

This is a nice feature, although earlier versions already had an Include component that could be used to accomplish a similar effect. The real power of shared borders, however, emerges when it is combined with the new Navigation Bar component. As it turns out, some areas of your Web page, most notably borders and navigation buttons, are very similar from page to page but not exactly the same. The shared borders used with the Navigation Bar component are designed to make it easy to create these elements.

Shared borders and the navigation bar are discussed in detail in Part IV of this book. For now we can only demonstrate how to designate default shared borders for your entire Web from within Explorer.

Adding shared borders

To add a default shared border to all Web pages, you use the shared border command in Explorer. To add a shared border only to a subset of your pages, use Editor's shared borders command for that purpose.

To add a shared border to the Happy Valley Web we created in the previous section, first open the Web in Navigation view and select Tools➪ Shared Borders. The Shared Borders dialog box, Figure 3-23, appears. Designate the areas you wish to use for shared borders. Different regions contain different default elements:

✦ **Top** — This is a banner and navigational bar with links to other pages at the same level.

✦ **Left** — This is a vertically oriented navigation bar with links to pages at the next lower level.

✦ **Right** — This is a blank space for inserting content of your choosing.

✦ **Bottom** — This is a blank space for inserting content of your choosing.

Figure 3-23: Use this dialog box to add shared borders.

Click OK to accept your changes, and you are done. See Figure 3-24 for a peek at one of the Happy Valley tips pages with all four shared borders. All new pages that you create in this Web now inherit the shared borders you designated. If you want to change the shared borders at any time, these changes are reflected in all pages.

Note that if you want to import a Web that incorporates shared borders, you need to change your existing Web's settings to show documents in hidden directories before you import the new Web. This also means that you need to create a new blank Web before you can import an existing one that incorporates shared borders rather than doing the creation and importing in one step as outlined earlier in this chapter in "Importing a Web with the Import Wizard." To make this setting: select Tools ⇨ Web Settings, click the Advanced tab, and check the Show Documents in Hidden Directories check box.

Hyperlinks view

By default, new Webs are first displayed in Hyperlinks view. Hyperlinks view is a two-pane display with a hierarchical list of Web pages and their links in the left-hand pane and a schematic view of the selected Web page (represented with a page icon) and its links in the right-hand pane. The hierarchical branches in Hyperlinks view can be expanded and collapsed — when there are branches available.

Hyperlinks view can be used to see how a Web's pages are linked together as well as what other kinds of content, such as graphics, are linked to them.

Figure 3-24: Shared borders allow you to quickly incorporate repeating content in some or all of your pages.

Taking the Next Step

This chapter introduced the basics of using FrontPage Explorer to create a new Web, view a Web, import pages and complete Webs, and map a Web. When you add what you learned in Chapter 2, "Working with FrontPage Editor," you now have the basic knowledge to create a Web. The next step is to incorporate other types of content, such as graphics and multimedia files. Part II of this book shows you how to do this. Laying out your pages using tables, frames, and style sheets is covered in Part III. When your Web meets your exacting standards, it's time to publish it on the World Wide Web. Chapter 18 shows you how to do this.

✦   ✦   ✦

Enhancing the Look and Feel

Graphics and Themes

So far we have covered FrontPage features that probably have you convinced that it is just a glorified word processor. Sure, it can format text, add styles, change the font, or even make bulleted lists. Big deal. Well, things are about to heat up. Beginning with this chapter, we start exploring aspects of FrontPage that really show off its abilities as a Web development tool. Here is where you also learn some Web development skills that allow you to make really compelling Web pages instead of just rehashing your Word documents.

Understanding Web Graphics Formats

This chapter is about using FrontPage to add graphics to your Web pages. The adding part is easy, but it is also fairly useless unless you know a little bit about the graphics themselves. Between the concepts introduced in this chapter and Chapter 5, "Creating and Editing Images," you may not turn into a digital artist, but you can come to understand a little about what goes into the graphics you add to your Web pages—*and* how to judge goods images from bad ones. Throughout, we emphasize two basic principles of Web graphic design:

✦ Images on a Web page make for a visually attractive, highly compelling Web experience.

✦ Images on a Web page make for a slow, highly tedious Web experience.

It is the ability to reconcile these two principles that makes for the best Web pages.

Getting in line

When most people think of Web graphics, they think of inline images, that is, graphics that appear as part of a Web page. This may seem like a mundane concept these days, but, after the capability to hyperlink, it was this capability that initially made the Web such a revolutionary medium.

Graphics are not physically embedded in a Web page, except when they are displayed. All graphics on a page are stored externally as separate files and linked to a particular location in the page. When a browser requests a Web page that contains one or more graphics, it requests all of the linked files as well. These are downloaded to you one at a time; the browser then assembles them for you according to the instructions embedded in the Web page.

A format primer

Graphics can be created in a variety of formats, each one having a slightly different method of storing the information necessary for a computer to render a bunch of 0s and 1s as a full-color image on your monitor. At the moment, almost all Web graphics are stored either as GIFs (GIF is variously pronounced "jiff," as in "I'll be there in a jiff," or "giff," as in "Giff 'em an inch and they'll take a mile") or as JPEGs (JPEG is always pronounced "jay-peg"). These two formats are very different, and each has its virtues in certain circumstances, but they share three characteristics that make them both well-suited to the Web:

✦ They are not proprietary formats.

✦ They are not specific to any computer platform.

✦ They use compression to create reasonably small file sizes (although sometimes you wonder).

GIF images

GIF (short for Graphic Interchange Format) was a cross-platform graphics format invented by CompuServe to enable people to transfer graphic files easily over dial-up connections. This was the first graphics format used on the Web, and it continues to be the most prevalent—even though all of the more recent Web browsers now support both GIF and JPEG formats. Because of its compression techniques, the GIF format is particularly well-suited to graphics that have horizontal bands of color or large areas of similar colors. Thus, it works well for most banners, buttons, and basic illustrations.

GIF images also have two interesting characteristics:

✦ Any single color in a GIF image may be "transparent," allowing the background of your Web page to show through—these images are called *transparent GIFs*.

✦ A single GIF image can actually be composed of a number of individual pictures that are shown in sequence, giving the appearance of motion—these images are called *animated GIFs*.

Unfortunately, because of GIF's limit of 256 individual colors (called the *palette,* which is discussed in Chapter 5) and because of its compression technique, GIF images are not particularly well-suited to photographic images, which is where JPEGs come in.

JPEG images

JPEG stands for Joint Photographic Experts Group, the name of the organization that created the format. The JPEG standard was devised as a method of compressing digitized photographs. Like the GIF format, it is a cross-platform standard. Although it is used less frequently than GIFs on the Web, you will see it used for complex images and for larger background images. One interesting aspect of JPEG images is that they can be created with varying amounts of compression, whereas a GIF is just a GIF. This is because JPEGs are compressed basically by throwing out some of the information in the image — in theory enough to make the file smaller but not enough that anyone would notice without a magnifying glass. The more information you throw out, the smaller the file is and the more degradation to the image quality results. For the technical-minded, this is called "lossy" compression (not to be confused with "lousy" compression).

Armed with this basic understanding, you are now ready to turn to the task of adding graphics to your Web pages. In the following section, we cover the basics of adding graphics without worrying about such details as where the graphics might come from. That comes later.

Importing Images

When you add a graphic (or any other content for that matter) to your Web pages, FrontPage stores that element as part of the current Web. This means that the process of adding a graphic always involves two steps:

> ✦ Importing the graphic into the current Web
>
> ✦ Adding it to a Web page

The order in which you perform these steps is entirely up to you. We illustrate both, starting with a methodology that has you import your graphics first and add them second.

The import/add method

Importing images into a FrontPage Web is simply a fancy way of saying that you are copying them into the folders where your Web content is stored. You can do this from Explorer by selecting File ➪ Import and then adding any images you want to import to the dialog box shown in Figure 4-1. In this manner, you can add individual files or whole folders. So, for example, you might create a folder of images and then import them all at once when you are ready to begin adding them to your pages. (Chapter 3, "Using FrontPage Explorer," includes a more in-depth discussion of importing files into your Web.)

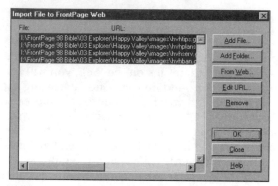

Figure 4-1: Use the Import File to FrontPage Web dialog box to copy images into your Web.

There is nothing magical about the FrontPage import function, and you can accomplish the same task simply by copying the image files or folders into the folder for the current Web using the Windows Explorer or any similar file-management application, if you find that easier.

Tip

You may have noticed when you created your Web that FrontPage created an empty folder called images. This is a convenient place to store your images if you have a relatively small Web. With a larger Web, you may want to divide your graphics up further in order to make it easier to locate them later.

Adding graphics to pages

Once you have imported all the graphics you plan to use for now, you can begin to add them to your Web page. Adding a graphic is a simple process. Open the Web page in Editor. Place the cursor at the spot where you would like the graphic to appear and select Insert ⇨ Image. Select the Current FrontPage Web tab and select the image to add. Click OK, and the image is added to the page at the cursor location.

Cutting and pasting

In situations where you have a graphic already loaded into another application, you can use the standard cut-and-paste procedure to insert an image into your Web page. With the graphic open in the other application, select Edit ⇨ Copy. Switch to Editor, place the cursor where you want the image to appear, and select Edit ⇨ Paste. When you next save the Web page, you are prompted to save the image as part of your Web.

Using drag and drop

You can also drag and drop your image into the Web page from Explorer. If you are in Folders view, simply select the image file you wish to add and drag it to the location on the Web page opened in Editor. You can also drag and drop images from Hyperlinks view. First make sure that images are displayed in Explorer. If they are not, select View ➪ Hyperlinks to Images or click the Hyperlinks to Images button on the toolbar. This displays all graphics linked to Web pages in the left-hand column of the display. Drag a graphic from the left-hand column onto the Web page.

The drag-and-drop method works from other applications as well, including Windows Explorer, Internet Explorer, and Image Composer (discussed in detail later in this chapter).

The add/save method

The second method for incorporating graphics into your Web reverses the order of the process. First, add a graphic that is stored outside your Web. To do this, open the Web page in Editor and select Insert ➪ Image. The image is added in exactly the same manner. The only difference is that, at the moment, the file still lives elsewhere. When you select File ➪ Save to save the Web page, FrontPage asks you if you would like to save the image to the current Web. In most cases, you want to say yes.

Perhaps you are wondering what happens if you say no? FrontPage saves the Web page with the reference to the image altered as if you had copied the image to the current Web anyway. It just doesn't copy the image. When you attempt to close the file, it asks you if you want to save changes, which might confuse you if you haven't made any changes since you last saved. What it wants to do is copy the image before quitting. If you still say no, the next time you open the Web page, you get a missing image icon. Why does FrontPage bother to give you a choice of saving or not saving if it is basically going to force you to save it anyway? Welcome to the Microsoft way.

Working with Image Objects

Once you have inserted an image into your Web page, it exists as a separate object on the page, allowing you to alter it in a number of different ways, which are detailed in the following sections.

Resizing images

Select the image by clicking it. Notice how little black rectangles appear around it. These are its handles. You can resize the graphic any way you like by dragging these handles. If you drag from one of the corners, you can resize the graphic in two directions at once. Figure 4-2 shows a resized copy of an image next to its original.

Figure 4-2: The top image was resized only in the vertical direction.

Caution

Think twice before resizing graphics in this manner. You are likely to distort the image by doing this. It is usually better to resize the graphic using an image processing application that maintains its aspect ratio (that is, its proportions) and then insert it into FrontPage.

Positioning images

If you have any experience with inserting graphics into documents, you may be disappointed to learn that you have only limited ability to move a graphic once you have inserted it into your Web page. You can move it as you would a selection of text, from one location to another within a section of text. You can also move it vertically, but you cannot position the image arbitrarily on the Web page, as you might in a Microsoft Word document. This is a constraint imposed in part by the limits of HTML. An upcoming section, "Alignment options," details the ways that you can position an image in relation to text and other images in your Web pages.

Converting image formats

FrontPage automatically converts graphics from several common formats for you when you save them to your Web. Supported formats include BMP, TIF, TGA, RAS, EPS, PCX, and WMF. If you have images in some other format, you will need to use an image conversion utility such as HiJaak Pro or an image editing program to save the image in one of these formats (or, better yet, directly in GIF or JPEG format).

An Image resizing tip

You can also resize an image using the Appearance tab of the Image Properties dialog box — open this dialog box by highlighting the image and then selecting Edit⇨Image Properties. This allows you to enter an exact size (either in pixels or as a percent of the browser screen size).

The big tip, however, is to check the Specify Size check box but leave the default values in the Width and Height text boxes (the original size of the image). This tells your visitor's browsers the size of the image before it's downloaded so that your page doesn't redraw to accommodate the image's actual size each time an image is downloaded — this isn't a big thing, but it can make your pages easier to view.

Working with Image Properties

Once you have inserted an image in your Web page, you can modify it using the Image Properties dialog box, shown in Figure 4-3. To access the image properties, click the image once to select it (double-clicking the image opens it in the assigned image editor, by default, Image Composer). Select Edit ⇨ Image Properties, click the selected image with the right mouse button, and select Image Properties from the pop-up menu, or highlight the image and press Alt+Enter.

The Image Properties dialog box gives you direct access to all of the image properties in HTML. The dialog box is divided into three tabs: General, Video, and Appearance. The Video tab, which contains properties specific to video images, is discussed in the next chapter. Let's look in detail at the options on the other two tabs.

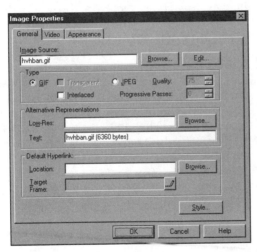

Figure 4-3: The Image Properties dialog box in Editor

General properties

The General tab of the Image Properties dialog box allows you to edit some basic characteristics of the image, including the name of the image file, its format type, alternative representations that can be presented to users, and any hyperlink associated with the image.

The image source

The Image Source field displays the filename of the currently selected image. You can use this field to replace the current image with another. Click Browse, locate a new image file, and click OK. When you close the Image Properties dialog box, the new image appears in place of the former one. You can also load the image into an editing application from this field. Click Edit, and the image file is opened in the designated image editor, by default Image Composer. (You can also open Image Composer with the graphic loaded by double-clicking the image.)

The image type

The Type option indicates the image format of the selected image. Click either GIF or JPEG to change the image format. If the image is GIF format, two additional attributes of the image are indicated:

✦ **Transparent**—This enables you to designate one color in the graphic, typically the background color, that can be rendered transparent, allowing any background on the Web page to show through. We show how to control transparency on a GIF image in the next chapter. You cannot edit this property from the Image Properties dialog box. If the image contains a transparent color, the Transparent check box is checked. Otherwise, it is grayed out.

✦ **Interlaced**—This refers to an alternative way of storing the information about a GIF image. Some browsers are capable of displaying interlaced GIFs differently from noninterlaced images. By default, most Web browsers display images as they are downloaded. If the images are small, they appear to pop into the page. If they are larger, they draw in from top to bottom, which can be somewhat irksome if you happen to be the impatient type. Interlaced images can be displayed so that the entire image appears as the image is still downloading. The image at first appears blurry and becomes increasingly focused as more of its information is downloaded. The effect is of an image materializing out of a haze of color. Interlacing was first introduced as a way of displaying the entirety of an image map quickly, so that the user could click some dimly recognized area in the image map without having to wait for the entire image to load. It is up to you to decide whether this is really a useful feature. In practice, interlacing produces a pleasing effect for certain kinds of images, including photographs and illustrations. It can also be annoying, so use your judgment.

If the image type is JPEG, then two text boxes open up allowing you to specify more information:

✦ **Quality**—Adjust the quality of the image as a percentage from 0 to 100. The higher the number, the higher the quality of the image and the larger the file size. See the earlier discussion of the JPEG format for more information on how JPEGs work.

✦ **Progressive Passes**—This is essentially the same as "interlace" for GIF images. You do, however have one advantage—you can specify the number of steps it takes to go from the extremely fuzzy version of your image to full version. The number of steps can vary from 0 to 100.

Alternative representations

There are several reasons why HTML includes provision for designating alternative representations of images. One is that not all Web browsers are actually capable of displaying inline images (the most prominent example of a nongraphic Web browser is the popular UNIX Lynx browser). In addition, all Web browsers include an option to turn off the automatic display of images. This feature enables users with slower Internet connections, or users who might (heaven forbid!) find the images distracting rather than useful, to browse the Web without waiting for images to download. FrontPage provides the following ways to address the needs of those for whom large graphics are either burdensome or just inaccessible:

✦ **Inclusion of substitute text**—The first method enables you to include text that serves as a substitute for those browsers that either cannot display images or have images turned off. This alternative is quite useful, and you should get in the habit of including text for all of your image files. To do this, simply type the alternative text into the Text field of the Alternative Representations section.

This text is beginning to be used in other ways by browsers that are quite capable of displaying images. Some display the text as a temporary substitute for images as they are downloading. Some display this text any time you place the cursor over an image. Selecting appropriate text is something of an art form.

✦ **Inclusion of low-resolution version**—The second alternative is less widely supported but can be used to interesting effect. It enables you to designate a temporary, lower-resolution version of an image that is displayed first while the real image is still downloading. When the real image has completely downloaded, it replaces the temporary image. To make use of this feature, simply designate the image file to be used as the Low-Res version. Click the Browse button next to the Low-Res field in the Alternative Representations section to select an image for this purpose. (The Low-Res image and the main image must have the same dimensions.)

This feature can be used to create interesting effects—the equivalent of a two-frame animation. One popular technique is to use a black-and-white version of an image as the low-resolution version. When the color version appears, it looks as if it is painting color into the image.

The default hyperlink

You can associate an image with a hyperlink in the same way that you associate a string of text with a hyperlink. For details on creating hyperlinks, refer to Chapter 2. When users click the image, they jump to the hyperlinked location. This is the standard method of creating graphical "buttons" on your Web page (unlike conventional computer interface buttons, though, these simple buttons do not change when you click them).

If you have associated your image with a hyperlink, that information appears in the Image Properties dialog box as well. Alternatively, you can use the Image Properties dialog box to create and/or edit an image's hyperlink. To add a hyperlink to an image, click the Browse button next to the Location field in the Default Hyperlink section. Locate the file and click OK.

Appearance issues

The Appearance tab contains image properties that directly affect the way the selected image is displayed. The Layout section of the Appearance tab contains the following options:

Alignment options

The alignment options affect how an image is aligned in relation to the text around it. Generally speaking, images are positioned on a page as if they were part of the line of text. Text before and after the image is aligned according to the alignment type (top, bottom, middle, and so on), but a new line of text begins beneath the image (see Figure 4-4). The two exceptions to this are left and right alignment, which allow text to wrap around an image.

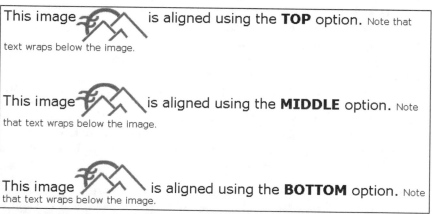

Figure 4-4: Some options for aligning an image with HTML text

When you use left or right alignment to wrap text, you can use special versions of a line break to discontinue wrapping text. Select Insert ➪ Break. Select Clear Left Margin to discontinue wrapping text around an image aligned left. Select Clear Right Margin to discontinue wrapping text around an image aligned right. Choose Clear Both Margins to discontinue any wrapping of text.

Horizontal and vertical spacing

Use the Vertical Spacing and Horizontal Spacing options to affect how much white space appears between an image and the surrounding text. These options are particularly useful when used in conjunction with the left- and right-alignment options to control how text wraps around an image.

Border thickness

If you associate an image with a hyperlink, then by default it displays with a thin border the color of the other hyperlinks on the page around it. You can use the Border option to hide this border or control its width. In addition, you can use the Border option to add a border to nonhyperlinked images. To add a border to an image, simply designate its thickness as measured in screen pixels. The border displays in the color of the default text on the Web page.

Size options

The Size section of the Appearance tab indicates the width and height of the current image, designated in screen pixels. By default, these values are grayed out. You can alter them directly by first checking the Specify Size check box. This is the equivalent of resizing the image. Values for the size property can be given either in pixels or in percentages. If you select percentages, the size of an image changes in relation to the size of the Web browser window (see Figure 4-5).

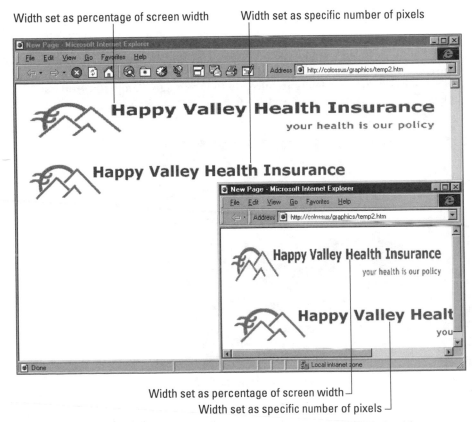

Figure 4-5: The effects of resizing browser windows with graphics sized by percentage and by pixel

Finding Existing Images

You know how to work with an image once it is in FrontPage, but perhaps you are wondering how you are going to fill your Web pages with beautiful artwork and interface elements like the ones you see on all the best professional Web sites? In the next chapter, we introduce Image Composer, the Microsoft image creation application that comes with FrontPage 98. Image Composer makes it easy to create your own professional-looking graphical compositions. But, let's say for the sake of argument that you don't have time to take up graphic design yourself and your budget does not include provision for professional art production. What do you do?

Fortunately, there are many resources at your fingertips for locating images—from art that is free to take and use, to professional stock houses that provide images at prices that vary sharply but that are generally well below the price of custom-designed graphics. This section briefly outlines some of the places you can look for images.

FrontPage sample art

FrontPage comes with its own library of clip art, which it installs in the FrontPage Clip Art folder. Editor's Image dialog box has a special Clip Gallery that allows you to preview thumbnails of the images (see Figure 4-6). To access the Clip Gallery, select Insert ➪ Clip Art. If you are already in the Image dialog box, you can also click the Clip Art button to access the Clip Gallery as well.

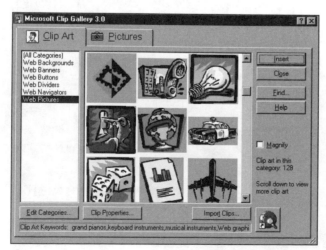

Figure 4-6: You can access clip art in FrontPage.

To add your own images to the clip art list, open the Clip Gallery, and then press the Import Clips button. Now locate the image you want to include in the gallery and press Open. A dialog box now opens asking which category or categories you want the image included in and a list of keywords that you can use to search for the image later. Press OK and the image now appears in the Clip Gallery—note that the image is still in its original location, not in the clip art folder.

In addition, FrontPage 98 with Bonus Pack comes with more images on the CD-ROM. Located in the `ImgComp` folder is a subfolder called `MMFiles`. In this folder are many media files in the default Composer format (`.mic`). These can be opened in Composer and added to your Web.

Tip

If you happen to be the owner of Office 97, it too ships with a huge array of clip art, including links to the Web sites of the media companies who have provided royalty-free clips. One good way to browse the collection is by running a PowerPoint presentation called `Overview.pps`. You can find this presentation in the `Valupack` subfolder on the Office 97 CD.

Online resources

In addition to the clip art included with FrontPage, Microsoft also maintains online resources that include sample media files and pointers to additional media resources. Two locations to check out are:

✦ **FrontPage Resources**—`http://www.microsoft.com/frontpage/documents/resources.htm`

✦ **Sitebuilder Gallery**—`http://www.microsoft.com/gallery/default.asp`

Of course, you need not rely on Microsoft for everything. The Web has a store of freely available art that is expanding all the time. To get a sense of the possibilities, check out Yahoo's listing of sites offering graphics. Point your browser to:

`http://www.yahoo.com/Computers_and_Internet/Internet/World_Wide
_Web/Page_Design_and_Layout/Graphics/`

Another site that deserves special mention for its thoroughness as well as for the quality of its links is Gina Schmitz's Cool Graphics on the Web, located at `http://www.geocities.com/SiliconValley/Heights/1272/index.html`.

Saving images from the Web

Some people think it is one of the Web's greatest virtues, others think it is downright criminal, but the fact remains that it is astoundingly easy to copy images from Web sites. (In fact, merely in the process of requesting a Web page, your Web browser automatically copies the images to a temporary location on your computer). If you have ever saved images from your Web browser, though, you know that you can only save one image at a time. What if you want to save all of the images from a page? FrontPage makes this easy.

You already know this, but I have to say it anyway: Under no circumstances should you make use of images that you find on the Web for your own profit, either directly or indirectly, unless those images come with explicit permission to do so. Doing so is illegal, and it threatens to undermine the whole spirit of the Internet.

To save images from a Web page:

1. Select File ⇨ Open from the Editor menu.

2. In the Open File dialog box, choose the Other Location tab and check the From Location radio button.

3. Type the URL of the Web page you want to open into the From Location field. Note that this can be any publicly accessible URL.

4. Click OK. The Web page opens in Editor (don't worry, you can't make changes to the original).

5. Select File ⇨ Save. FrontPage prompts you to save the page to the current Web, including the HTML file and any inline graphics.

If you want images that are displayed on many pages of the same Web, you can import some, or all, of the Web site using the technique detailed in Chapter 3.

Stock houses

You may notice that free images on the Web are of varying quality. In general, you can find lots of nice background textures (and some garish ones), and trinket art, such as ruled lines and bullets. You are harder pressed to find decent illustrative art. Even nice buttons and icons are a rare commodity. If you have some money to spare and want to add professional-quality illustrations to your Web pages, you might want to investigate some of the many stock photography and digital art companies. Here are two large, representative examples of stock houses:

✦ **PhotoDisc** — http://www.photodisc.com/index.asp — This service specializes in photographic images and lots of them. These images are royalty free, meaning that you pay for them once and then use them for their designated purpose as long as you like.

✦ **ImageClub** — http://www.imageclub.com — Affiliated with Adobe Corporation, this is a source for your clip art needs. They have line art, icons, and fonts, as well as photography.

Working with Themes

Themes are an easy way to ensure that all of your pages have a similar "look and feel." Every page that incorporates the same theme automatically uses the same font, font size, text color, background, and even bullet images so that you don't have to go through all the trouble of adding them yourself. The downside to themes is that they are static—FrontPage comes with 54 premade themes in a variety of styles.

In an undocumented piece of charity, Microsoft has included Theme Designer on the FrontPage 98 CD-ROM—Theme Designer lets you create your own themes quickly and easily. For an introduction to Theme Designer, see "Creating new themes" later in this chapter.

For quick-and-dirty pages that are still impressive looking, though, themes are an excellent resource.

Cascading style sheets, explained in Chapter 10, provide much of the ease of use of themes with the added benefit of your having complete control over every aspect of your pages' design. Web templates also provide an easy way to make consistent-looking pages, except that pages don't automatically update to the new styles if you change the layout of the original template. Saving a page as a template is explained in Chapter 2.

Adding a theme to an entire Web

In general, you'll want to have an entire Web use the same theme. This way every page will incorporate all of the same graphic elements and type styles.

To add a theme to an existing Web or change a Web's theme:

1. Open the Web in FrontPage Explorer.
2. Select Themes view.
3. Check the Use Selected Theme radio button.
4. Select the theme you want to use from the menu list. The various elements in the theme are shown in the preview window (see Figure 4-7).

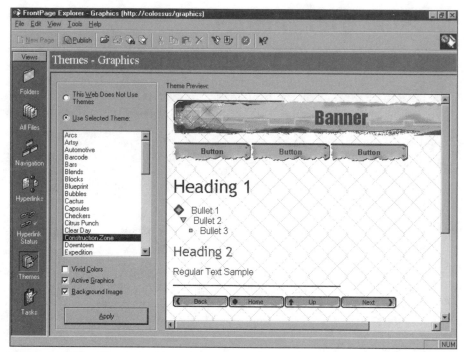

Figure 4-7: The Theme Preview shows examples of all the elements of a particular style.

5. Select the elements you want included in your pages:

- **Vivid Colors** uses brighter colors for the graphics and text.
- **Active Graphics** incorporates animated images for banners and buttons.
- **Background Image** adds an image "behind" your pages' text.

6. Press the Apply button. After a few moments, all of the pages of your Web are updated to include the new elements.

To remove a theme from a Web, check the This Web Does Not Use Themes radio button in Themes view.

Note

If you added a theme to a Web that did not incorporate one before, you'll notice that your pages do not incorporate the banners or navigation buttons that are shown in the Theme Preview. These are elements used by shared borders. To learn more about shared borders, see Chapter 8. There is also a brief introduction to shared borders in the section "Navigation view" in Chapter 3 that can quickly get you up and running using them.

Adding or changing a page's theme

There is no law that says every page in your Web must use the same theme. Depending on the type of Web you're putting together, it may be more advantageous for you to incorporate a couple of different themes that highlight different pages' content.

Adding or changing a page's theme is very similar to the steps taken for an entire Web:

1. Open the page in Editor.

2. Select Format ⇨ Theme to open the Choose Theme dialog box.

3. Select the theme you want to use with the page:

    - **This Page Does Not Use Themes**—Checking this radio button removes the theme from the current page.

    - **Use Theme From Current Web**—Checking this radio button incorporates the default theme for the Web (the one specified in the previous section).

    - **Use Selected Theme**—Checking this radio button incorporates the theme that is highlighted in the selection list.

4. Select the elements you want included in your pages: Vivid Colors, Active Graphics, and/or Background Image.

5. Press the OK button. The dialog box closes, and the page is updated to reflect the choices made.

Again, incorporating banners and navigation buttons into your page requires shared borders. See Chapters 3 and 8 for more information on shared borders.

Creating new themes

As noted earlier, you can create your own themes using Theme Designer. This is an amazingly easy-to-use way to create brand-new themes. For some reason, Microsoft decided not to mention Theme Designer in their documentation, but because you bought this book, we're letting you in on the secret.

To install Theme Designer, insert the FrontPage 98 CD in your drive. When the FrontPage 98 screen opens, click the Exit button. Now open the Start menu and select Run. Enter *D*:**\SDK\Themes\Designer\tdsetup.exe** (where *D*: is your CD-ROM drive) and click OK. When asked if you want to install Theme Designer, click OK, and the program will be installed in your FrontPage folder.

To start Theme Designer, start Explorer and select Tools ⇨ Show Theme Designer. With Theme Designer, you can create a new theme, update an existing theme, or update the theme of the Web currently loaded in Explorer.

✦ To create a new theme, select File ➪ New Theme. A representation of all of the objects available for customizing appears — this window looks very similar to Explorer's Theme Preview.

✦ To update an existing theme, select File ➪ Open Theme and select a theme from the list.

✦ To update the theme of the current Web, select File ➪ Open Web Themes.

You now have complete control over all of the theme properties. To change any of the displayed object properties, double-click an item and update its properties in the Properties dialog box that opens. When you click OK to close the dialog box, your changes are shown in the preview. (To change the background options, double-click anywhere in the open white space.) You can also select an item to be changed from the Properties menu.

To save your theme, select File ➪ Save Theme, or File ➪ Save Theme As if you want to change its filename. When your theme meets your requirements and you want to include it in the list of available themes in Explorer and Editor, select File ➪ Package for Download.

Taking the Next Step

After completing this chapter, you should begin to feel like a Web developer and less like a glorified word processor on the Web. You have learned how to insert images and incorporate themes in your pages. In Chapter 5, we really get down to some serious graphic creation. You may be surprised to learn, though, how easy it is to make your own Web page images — just like the pros! (Depending on your drawing ability, of course.)

✦   ✦   ✦

Creating and Editing Images

CHAPTER

✦ ✦ ✦ ✦

In This Chapter

Introducing Web graphics

Learning Image Composer basics

Making an image from scratch

Building image maps

Creating backgrounds

✦ ✦ ✦ ✦

You can easily create nice-looking Web pages using preexisting images, but sooner or later you may feel the urge to create your own graphics. The following sections help you get started. They introduce some of the important characteristics of Web graphics and then dive into a brief explanation of using Image Composer, the new Microsoft image creation and editing application that accompanies FrontPage 98 with Bonus Pack.

You can also create Web graphics in any graphics application, such as Adobe Photoshop and Corel PhotoPaint, which are both professional commercial tools. You can also use Paint Shop Pro, a shareware application that includes many of the same features as the more expensive products.

I have elected to focus on using Microsoft Image Composer in this book for the following reasons:

+ It comes with FrontPage, so I know you have it.

+ It is a new application and may be unfamiliar even to those who have used other tools.

+ FrontPage comes with no documentation on how to use it (at least not in the release I have).

+ As graphics applications go, it is different from either standard paint programs (like Photoshop) or drawing programs (like CorelDRAW!).

Introducing Web Graphics

Besides understanding Web graphics formats (a topic we covered in the last chapter), you need to know a little bit about how images are stored if you want to create successful Web graphics. Designing Web graphics has two principle challenges:

✦ Given the number of bandwidth-constrained users, the smaller and simpler the graphics, the happier the viewer. Unfortunately, it is much easier to create stunning big graphics with lots of subtle color variations than stunning little graphics with a limited number of colors, unless you know how to get more for less with your graphics.

✦ Because the Web is a cross-platform, multibrowser world, graphics that look gorgeous on one monitor can look dreadful on another, unless you know how to minimize differences.

The following is an overview of some of the key concepts involved in creating great graphics for the Web.

File size

In general, the larger the dimensions of an image, the larger the file size of the image. One way to decrease the file size of an image, then, is to decrease its physical dimensions. A good rule of thumb is to create your images so that they look good when displayed *in a Web page* on a 640 × 480 pixel screen. Remember that most new computers come with their resolution set to 640 × 480 (even though many can display in excess of 1280 × 1024 pixels) and many people new to surfing the Web don't know how to change this setting. Don't forget, though, that even a 640 × 480 pixel image can take a *long* time to download, so you generally won't want to fill the entire page.

Note that changing the dimensions of images within FrontPage does not affect the file size. That is because FrontPage resizes the image only after reading it into memory. It then takes the information it has and stretches it or squeezes it, but file size is unaffected.

Color depth

The color depth of an image refers to the number of colors available in the graphic. GIF images have a limit of 256 colors, which corresponds to an eight-bit color depth (basically because it takes eight bits of data to define a color that is one of 256 possible colors). Not all graphics use 256 colors, but if the image is saved as an eight-bit GIF, it is still the same file size as an image that did use all 256 colors. In such circumstances, you may reduce the bit depth of an image to the actual number of colors used (conversely, one way to design smaller graphic files is to limit yourself to a smaller range of colors). JPEGs are typically saved with more than 256 colors, since they are often photographic images. You may be able to reduce the number of colors in your JPEGs without adversely affecting their appearance. Trial and error is a good method.

A few words on palette problems

What if the computer can display only 256 colors? Well, if it only has to display one image at a time, it can disguise the fact that it only knows how to display 256 colors by switching its own palette between the first image and the second. This little trick is what sometimes causes your monitor to flash as it tries to change palettes without your realizing it.

However, if it has to display both images at once, your computer resorts to another trick, called dithering. *Dithering* is the art of substituting colors that are close to the actual colors but within the range of colors that the computer has to work with. You know you are looking at a dithered image when you see little dots of color sprinkled around a graphic. This is the attempt to put several colors close to one another in order to fool your eye into seeing a different color. Sometimes dithered images are OK, other times they are awful, but the main problem is that the designer is going to have limited control over how his or her images are dithered on any given computer.

There are additional reasons why Web graphics need to pay attention to palettes, but this is enough to demonstrate the general problem. How to solve it? One way is to limit your Web graphics to a "safe palette," a designated set of 216 colors that any browser can show on any monitor capable of displaying 256 colors without dithering.

In case you are wondering why 216 and not 256, it is because the other slots are reserved for Windows system colors—the colors that are used in your desktop graphical elements. Leaving some slots in the palette empty ensures that the computer has room for these colors as well.

In just a moment, we demonstrate how to ensure that your graphics use this safe palette. Of course, using these colors may be too constraining at times, and that is fine, but if you want the best assurance that your graphics look the same for everyone, the safe palette is the best approach.

Palettes

An image's *palette* is the index of colors that it uses or has available for its use. A 256-color image has 256 colors in its palette. This does not mean, however, that one 256-color image has the same 256 colors as the next. If two images on a Web page do not have the same 256 colors, however, you begin to run into trouble when the images are displayed, because now the computer displaying these images has to be able to display up to 512 colors in order to render both images correctly.

Learning Image Composer Basics

This brief section does not pretend to cover all of Image Composer's features. Its main intention is to demonstrate how to make simple images and insert them into your Web pages. Along the way, you learn enough about Image Composer to be dangerous, or at least to whet your appetite for more. Should you want more information, your best bet is to check the Microsoft Web site at http://www.microsoft.com/imagecomposer/. This site has links to other resources.

In this chapter, you use Image Composer to create three images—a logo, a background, and an image map. In the next chapter, we use Image Composer in conjunction with Microsoft's GIF Animator utility to create a simple animated graphic.

Image Composer is an image creation and editing application that creates graphical compositions designed primarily for the Web. In Image Composer, the basic graphical unit is the sprite. A *sprite* is a self-contained graphical object that has its own properties and can be manipulated separately as long as the image is stored in the Image Composer format (.mic). Put one or more sprites together, and you have a composition that can be converted to a GIF or JPEG and transferred to your Web page.

The Image Composer workspace is shown in Figure 5-1 with a composition in process. It has two important elements in addition to the standard menus and toolbar. To the left is a vertical strip of icon buttons called the *toolbox*. The toolbox contains the principal tools for image manipulation, which are named in the figure.

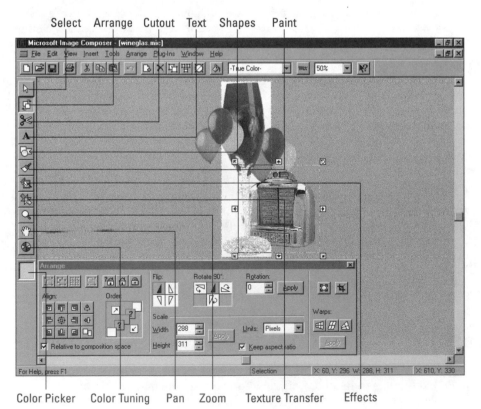

Figure 5-1: Would you like an olive with your champagne? (Oooh, this is some party!)

Most tools in the toolbox have dialog boxes with multiple options (the dialog box for the Arrange tool is shown in the figure.) In addition, many of the principle tool features are accessible from the menus and/or toolbar. In the main workspace is a white area referred to as the Composition Guide. This is the area that is retained if the image is converted to another format, such as a GIF image, or if it is printed. The composition includes the Composition Guide as well as the rest of the workspace. For example, in Figure 5-1, you see that there are balloons floating outside the white area of the Composition Guide. These balloons remain part of the composition saved in Image Composer format. However, if this composition is saved as a GIF or JPEG, it saves only the sprites inside the white area, as illustrated by the image imported into Editor in Figure 5-2.

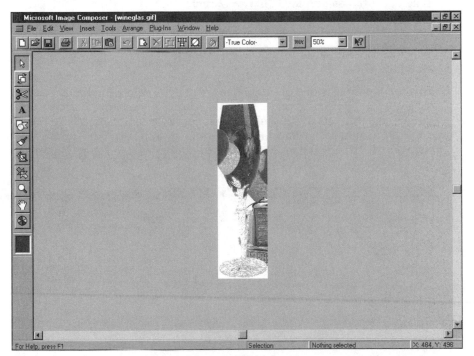

Figure 5-2: The Composition Guide as a GIF image

Making your first image

In this section, you create a simple banner with a logo for the Happy Valley Health Web to illustrate some basic Image Composer techniques. This graphic consists of a banner with some illustrative art, a logo, and the Happy Valley name. To create a simple logo banner for Happy Valley Health:

1. Open Image Composer.

2. Select the Shapes tool from the toolbox to display the Shapes dialog box. In the Shapes dialog box, click the Rectangle button and drag a long, thin rectangle in the workspace. When you release the mouse, a shape sprite is created. To fill the shape with the default color, click the Create button in the Shapes dialog box.

3. Check to make sure the color format is set to Web (Dithered). To do this, select Web (Dithered) from the Color Format drop-down menu, located on the right side of the toolbar.

4. Change the fill color. First, click the default color swatch below the toolbox and select the Custom Palette tab. In the color table, select a color by clicking one of the squares. Alternatively you can designate a color by switching to the True Color tab and typing RGB (Red-Green-Blue) values in the Red, Green, and Blue input fields. If you are color challenged, try R: 204 G: 204 B: 255. Click OK to close the dialog box and change the default color swatch.

5. Select Edit ➪ Current Color Fill. The rectangle is now filled with the color you selected.

6. To alter the dimensions of the banner rectangle, select the banner sprite and drag one of the handles on its bounding box. For exact pixel control, select the Arrange tool, uncheck the Keep Aspect Ratio option, and type the exact dimensions you desire into the width and height boxes. You can try Width: 560 Height: 120 if you like. The results should resemble Figure 5-3.

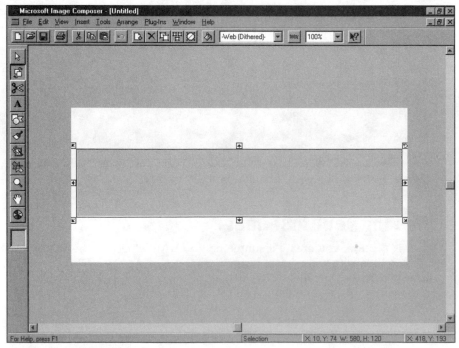

Figure 5-3: A fairly plain lavender banner

7. To liven up the banner, add some preexisting art from the FrontPage CD-ROM. Select Insert ⇨ from File and locate the folder of plant images on the CD-ROM (its directory path is illustrated in Figure 5-4). Select the sunflower image, `sunflwr1.mic`. Click OK to add this image as a new sprite to your composition.

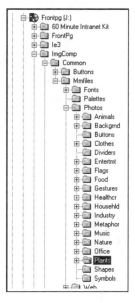

Figure 5-4: The menu path of the Plants folder on the Insert from File dialog box

8. Notice that the image is a wee bit too large for our purposes. We can resize it using the Arrange tool. This time make sure Keep Aspect Ratio is checked and change the height of the sprite to 190. This makes it large enough to extend over the edges of the lavender banner.

9. Finally, to give everything a professional edge, we add a drop shadow. Select the sunflower sprite, and click the Effects button in the toolbar. Select Outlines from the Category list, and Shadow from the thumbnail list. Click the Details tab, set the distance to 3, and click Apply. Voila! A shadow. Repeat the process for the banner itself if you like. The result should resemble Figure 5-5.

Figure 5-5: A healthy-looking banner

Next we are going to create a simple logo for the left side of the banner. This logo is just a background with some letters. Stay tuned—in the next chapter, we animate this logo. Woo, hoo!

1. Create the letters by selecting the text tool, clicking the crosshair cursor near the left edge of the box, and typing **H** in the small box that appears. We are creating each letter as a separate sprite, so that in the next chapter we can animate this logo.

2. Select a font from the Font list in the Text dialog box. Our example shows Britannic Bold—blocky but with a little style.

3. Set the size to 72.

4. To select a color for the text, click the Color rectangle in the lower-right corner of the dialog box. In the Color Picker dialog box, select the Custom Palette tab. Select a soothing, healthy color by clicking a square in the color table (or switch to the True Color tab and insert R: 153, G: 0, B: 51. This makes a deep red, cranberry color). Click OK to accept the color.

5. Click the Select Tool to create the letter sprite in the currently selected font and color. Do not close the Text dialog box yet.

6. To create the next letter, select the H and pick Duplicate from the Edit menu. A copy of the H now appears below and to the right of the original.

7. Click the text tool and click the new H. The text box opens again—remove the H and replace it with a V.

8. To create the second H, just duplicate the first letter. Select the H and select Edit⇨Duplicate, or use the key command shortcut, Ctrl+D.

9. To create the background, create a square for the logo using the same procedure we used earlier for the banner. Make the square slightly smaller than the height of the purple banner background. H: 106 works nicely.

10. Since we want the color to complement the sunflower, find a matching color with the Color Picker dropper tool, located on the Color Picker dialog box. Click the color swatch and click the Eyedropper button. Move the cursor over the sunflower, watching the changes to the Color Picker–selected color. Select an appropriate complementary color for this logo square. Fill the square with the color (select Edit⇨Current Color Fill).

11. Now let's add a texture to this square. Select the Effects tool. Choose Surface from the Category list and Rough Texture from the thumbnail list. Click Apply. Give this texturized square a drop shadow and add it to the banner, as shown in Figure 5-6.

Figure 5-6: The banner with a texturized square with a drop shadow too

12. Add the HVH letters to the square (you can use Figure 5-7 as a guide or be creative).

Tip

Remember that each of the pieces of your composition is a sprite. Each sprite lives in a separate layer on the composition workspace. If you move one sprite on top of another and it seems to disappear, that is because the sprite you want to be on top is currently in a lower layer than the sprite you want to be beneath it. To correct this problem, select the sprite you want to put on the top and then select Arrange⇨Bring to Front.

13. To add some text to our banner, select the text tool in the toolbox and click the crosshair cursor on the image. Select a font (we selected Arial because it was easy to read) and set the size to 12. Type **Happy Valley** into the Text box and select the Pick tool. Repeat this step and type **Health Insurance** as the second text block (press Enter before typing "Insurance").

14. Before copying the logo banner into the Happy Valley Web, you need to save a copy of the Image Composer version of the graphic, in case we want to do additional editing later. Select File⇨Save. Make sure the Microsoft Image Composer (.mic) format is selected and give the composition a name. Click OK to save your work. You can compare your results with Figure 5-7.

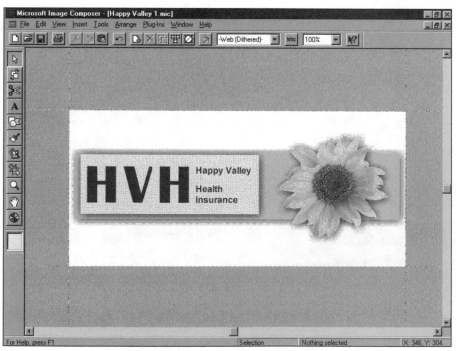

Figure 5-7: The completed banner

Transferring images to pages

You have are two methods for copying an image from Image Composer to your Web page. One is easy; the other, cumbersome. I present both methods for consistency, but also because the hard method should not be as hard as it is. To copy and paste an image to the Web page, first open the designated Web page in Editor. Select all sprites in the logo. You can click each sprite while holding down the mouse key, select Edit ⇨ Select All, click the Select All button from the toolbar, or press Ctrl+A. Copy the selection to the clipboard by selecting Edit ⇨ Copy, clicking the Copy button in the toolbar, or pressing Crtl+C. Switch to FrontPage, place the cursor at the point where you want to insert the image, and select Edit ⇨ Paste. This image needs to be saved when you next save the Web page.

Saving your compositions as GIFs

You can also save your Image Composer compositions as GIF files and insert them into your Web page. This turns out to be a somewhat cumbersome method if you are working with a graphic created in Image Composer, due to the fact that Image Composer saves your sprites as well as the entire Composition Guide, which is clearly not the desired effect. Here is a workaround:

1. Select the image to be saved using one of the methods previously described.

2. Group the selected images. Select Arrange ⇨ Group from the menu or click the Arrange toolbox icon and click the Group button.

3. Select Edit ⇨ Properties or click the selection with the right mouse button and select Properties from the pop-up menu.

4. Note the height (H) and width (W) of the selection, and click OK or Cancel to close the Properties window.

5. With the image still selected, select Arrange ⇨ Return to Home Position, or click the Arrange tool button in the toolbar and click the house icon. This places the selected image in the upper-left corner of the composition guide.

6. Select File ⇨ Composition Setup or click with the right mouse button anywhere on the white Composition Guide. Change the height and width parameters to equal the previously selected image. Click OK to change the size of the Composition Guide to equal the size of the image. This effectively eliminates the white background when you save the image as a GIF.

7. Select File ⇨ Save As so that you do not accidentally overwrite your .mic version of the file.

8. In the Save as Type box, select CompuServe GIF. For Color Format, select Web (Dithered). You can also designate a transparent color in this dialog box.

9. Click Save. You can then import the GIF into your Web page using the standard Insert ⇨ Image method.

Tip

In general, you will want to create images with a specific size (say a 30 × 30 pixel button, or a 500 × 120 pixel banner). By setting the appropriate size in the Composition Setup dialog box before you begin creating your image, not only can you avoid some of these steps, but the Composition Guide also helps you gauge how your image will look when you're done.

Making transparent images

At the moment, the Happy Valley logo banner integrates nicely into the Web page. That is because the background of the image is white and so is the background of the Web page. What if the background of the Web page was changed to, say, lime green? (Not that we are recommending this, by the way). Suddenly we have a problem, as illustrated in Figure 5-8. Now the white background of the image shows up all too plainly.

Figure 5-8: The Happy Valley banner, showing its white background

The solution to this problem is to make the background transparent. You can do this using Image Composer, but it is actually easier to use FrontPage. If you have not done so already, create a new Web page in Editor and insert the GIF version of the Happy Valley banner. Select the image by clicking it once. The image handles become visible, and the Image toolbar appears. We return to this image toolbar in a moment to discuss its image mapping features, but for now, we are interested in only one icon on the toolbar. It looks sort of like an eraser being poked into a sideways *V*, but trust me, it is the transparency tool. Select this tool, and your cursor turns into an eraser with a thin arrow sticking out. With this arrow, click any white spot on the graphic. The white disappears, and the background color shows through (see Figure 5-9). Your image now works equally well on any color background.

Figure 5-9: The Happy Valley banner with a transparent background

Note

After making the banner transparent, you may notice some artifacts of white that look like little solar flares erupting from the sunflower image. These are the result of some drop-shadow pixels not conforming exactly to the background color. They can be eliminated with a little elbow grease and know-how, but the lazy man's solution is to keep the background white.

Making an Image from Scratch

Image Composer, as its name implies, is really more of a tool for composing Web graphics using existing images. While it's all well and good to be able to slap a couple of pieces of clip art together, add some text, and say you've got an image, you also want to be able to create custom artwork for your pages. Make no mistake, if you want true professional-quality images for your pages, you'll have to use a professional-quality editor such as Photoshop, but for quick buttons and banners, Image Composer can do the job nicely.

Painting on sprites

If you're familiar with paint programs (even Windows Paint, which comes with Windows 95), you're used to being able to select the paint tool and begin drawing as soon as the program starts. This is not the way that Image Composer works. Instead, you can only paint on existing sprites.

While having to paint on sprites may seem like a totally bad thing, it is more of a mixed blessing—if you have a complicated image, the ability to work on a single sprite means that you don't have to worry about ruining sprites that you want to leave alone.

To paint on a sprite, select the sprite you want to use and open the Paint palette by clicking the Paint Palette button in the toolbar. Select a paintbrush and begin painting on your sprite. If the tools in the Paint palette (see Figure 5-10) are gray, then you have not selected a sprite, or you have selected a group of sprites. The next section, "Combining sprites," tells you how to group, ungroup, and flatten (combine) sprites to make working with them easier.

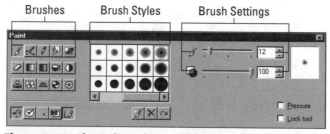

Figure 5-10: The Paint palette provides control over how you paint on a sprite.

Select the brush that you want to paint with from the left-hand table of brushes. The middle, brush styles, list contains a number of preset sizes for the brushes—the fuzzy brushes in the top two rows indicate that these brushes paint with soft, more natural edges. The brush settings section contains a number of ways to customize each brush—these settings change depending on which brush you select.

The color shown in the Color Picker box at the bottom of the toolbar is the color that you'll be painting with. If you want to change the paint color, click the Color Picker and select the new color from the dialog box that opens.

As shown in Figure 5-10, the Paint palette contains 15 different standard brushes. Unlike most other paint programs, Image Composer includes a number of special effects brushes in addition to the standard brush, spray gun, and pencil.

All brushes can be used at various sizes set using the Brush Size slider in the brush settings section of the palette. This lets you set brush sizes from 1 to 100 pixels in diameter.

Most brushes include the Opacity slider. This slider ranges from 0 to 100—a setting of 0 means that the paint or effect being applied is nearly invisible, whereas 100 means that the effect obscures what's being painted over.

Here is a list of the brushes and a short description of the capabilities of each one:

✦ **Paintbrush**—This is the typical paintbrush. Selecting this brush lets you paint with solid colors.

✦ **Air brush**—This tool paints like an artist's air brush. The faster you move this tool, the lighter the paint is.

✦ **Pencil**—As the name implies, this tool makes a hard, solid line when used.

✦ **Smear**—This tool doesn't actually paint anything but rather smears the paint already on the sprite.

✦ **Impression**—This tool adds an impressionistic "spottiness" when applied.

✦ **Erase**—Unlike the erase tool in most paint programs, this eraser actually removes portions of the sprite. You can't paint on any area that's been erased. Be very careful when using this tool.

✦ **Tint**—This tool tints the opaque areas of a sprite with the current color.

✦ **Color fill**—Similar to tint, this tool applies the current color without affecting the brightness of the underlying paint.

✦ **Dodge/burn**—This tool darkens (dodges) or lightens (burns) the colors in the sprite. Use the Burn ... Dodge slider to set the amount of darkening/lightening. If the slider is left in its default position, the tool has no affect.

✦ **Step contrast**—This tool changes the contrast of the painted area (the difference between the darkest and lightest areas). Low settings on the Low ... High slider bring the darkness levels closer together, while higher settings increase the contrast between dark and light.

✦ **Rubber stamp**—Use this tool to duplicate small areas. Click the area to be duplicated once and then click again in another area to "drop" a copy of it.

✦ **Pick source**—This is similar to the rubber stamp brush except that the source for the "paint" is another sprite. Select the sprite you want to paint on and then select the pick source brush. Now click the sprite whose paint you want to copy and click the original sprite where you want the copy placed.

✦ **Mesa**—This tool distorts the area that it is used on by either pulling in or pushing out the center area. Set the amount of distortion in the Radius Factor % text box and the direction (in or out) in the Warp Direction area.

✦ **Vortex**—This tool distorts the area that it is used on by swirling the colors to resemble a whirlpool. Set the "speed" of the whirlpool in the Angle text box.

✦ **Spoke inversion**—This tool distorts the area it's used on by pinching it toward the center. Set the amount of "pinching" in the Value text box.

Combining sprites

Sprites are the basic objects used in Image Composer. A sprite can be anything from a string of text that you've inserted to a picture that you've imported from a clip art CD or the World Wide Web. Individually, sprites are very powerful tools, but you also have a number of ways to use them together.

✦ **Grouping**—Grouping sprites makes them easy to move around or resize in your composition while maintaining the relative positions and sizes. Grouped sprites retain their own identities so that you can ungroup them later.

To group a number of sprites, select them using the standard Windows Shift+Click combination, drag a marquee box around them, or, to select all of the sprites in a composition, press Ctrl+A and then press Ctrl+G (or select Arrange ⇨ Group). To ungroup a collection of sprites, select the group and press Ctrl+U (or select Arrange ⇨ Ungroup). Note that you can't paint on a group of sprites.

You can even group groups of sprites. To do this, select the groups as though they were individual sprites and press Ctrl+G. When you ungroup a group of sprites, the original groups are still intact. To return a group of groups to its individual sprites all at once, press Ctrl+E or select Arrange ⇨ Explode Group.

✦ **Flattening**—Flattening, as opposed to grouping, a selection of sprites combines the individual sprites into one single sprite. (Users of vector graphics programs such as CorelDRAW! know "flattening" as "combining.") This can be advantageous if you want to create an intricately shaped sprite or need to paint all of the sprites at once. One downside to flattening sprites is that you cannot unflatten them to get back the original sprites.

To flatten a number of sprites, select them as just outlined and Press Ctrl+F or select Arrange ⇨ Flatten Selection.

The cutout tool

The cutout tool makes it easy to cut and paste only certain areas of a sprite. There are four main cutout tools: the rectangle, oval, curve, and polygon tools. The rectangle and oval tools allow you to copy simple geometric shapes, whereas the curve and polygon tools let you copy more intricate shapes. In addition, you can select areas to copy based on their colors using the Select Color Region tab of the Cutout palette.

To select an area to copy using the rectangle or oval tool:

1. Select the sprite you want to copy an area from.
2. Click the Cutout icon in the toolbar to open the Cutout palette.

3. Select either the Rectangle or Oval icon at the left-hand side of the Cutout Tools tab.

4. Click and drag the cursor over the sprite to define the area you want to copy. You can constrain the shape to a square (or circle) by pressing either the Shift or Ctrl key while dragging. Release the mouse button when your shape is defined.

To select an area using the curve or polygon tool:

1. Select the sprite you want to copy an area from.

2. Click the Cutout icon in the toolbar to open the Cutout palette.

3. Select either the Curve or Polygon icon at the left-hand side of the Cutout Tools tab.

4. Click points on the sprite to define the outline of the shape you want to copy.

5. To edit the shape that you have defined, click one of the three icons in the Edit curve or polygon area of the palette. The icon with a plus sign in it adds points to your curve wherever you click it. To remove points from your curve (or vertices from a polygon), click the icon with a minus sign, and then click a point (the points are highlighted with small boxes when you move the cursor near them). To move a point or vertex, click the blank icon and then click the point and drag it to its new location.

To select an area by its color:

1. Select the sprite you want to copy an area from.

2. Click the Cutout icon in the toolbar to open the Cutout palette.

3. Click the Select Color Region tab.

   • Set the "sharpness" of the selection's edge using the Hard ... Soft slider. The further to the right this slider is, the more "fuzzy" the edge of the selection will be.

   • Set the tolerance (or closeness of color) for your selection using the Hue, Whiteness, and Blackness sliders — the smaller these settings, the smaller the difference in colors that will be selected.

   • To select all matching colors within the sprite, check the Global radio button. To pick only those matching colors that are in direct contact with the point where you click, check the Local radio button.

4. Click the Magic Wand icon on the left-hand side of the palette and click the area of the sprite you want to copy.

5. Add areas to your selection by checking the Add radio button and clicking another area within the sprite. Remove areas from your selection by checking the Delete radio button, tightening the Hue, Whiteness, and Blackness settings (making them closer to zero) and clicking the area you want to remove.

To make the selection into a new sprite, press the Cut Out button (this button is on both the Cutout Tolls tab and the Select Color Region tab). The area you selected now appears as a new sprite and is already selected. You can paint, copy, distort, or otherwise treat this new sprite just like any other.

To cut the selection from the sprite, press the Erase button. The sprite now has a hole the shape of the selected area.

Building Image Maps

An *image map* is a graphical image in which one or more areas within the image are designated as hotspots—areas that, if clicked, send the user to a designated hyperlinked page. To create an image map requires three basic steps:

✦ Create the image.

✦ Identify the hotspots on the image.

✦ Link each hotspot to its target location.

In the old days, before applications like FrontPage, creating an image map took some time and headaches. Using the Image Mapping toolbar makes life much easier. In this example, we are creating a simple Pill Pop Quiz (not to be confused with a Pill Popping Quiz). The goal is to identify each of the pills on the image. For now we are not worried about the quiz part. We simply link each pill to a page of information describing it. To follow along, use these steps:

1. Start Image Composer and create a new file.

2. Create the pill image. Open the `pillmap.mic` file located on the CD-ROM that accompanies this book. This file is located in the `Contents/ch05` folder on the CD-ROM. (Note: `pillmap.mic` is derived from `pills.mic` included on the FrontPage CD-ROM.)

3. Each pill in `pillmap.mic` is a separate sprite. If you like, you can rearrange them (see Figure 5-11). If you move the pills, don't forget to save your changes.

4. Once you have the pills arranged to your liking on the Composition Guide, select all of the pills. A nice shortcut for selecting a number of items is to drag a rectangle that encompasses all of the images. When you release the mouse button, all of the images are selected.

5. Select Edit ➪ Copy. Then open a new Web page in Editor and select Edit ➪ Paste. The results are shown in Figure 5-12.

Figure 5-11: The Pill Quiz cast of characters

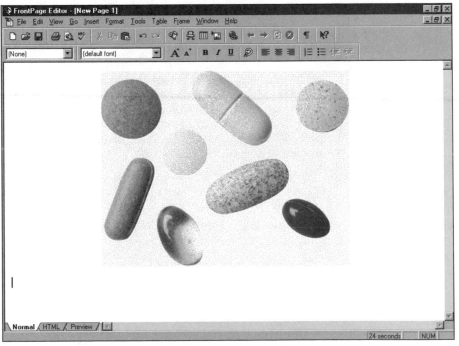

Figure 5-12: The Pill Quiz image map graphic in Editor

Image map varieties

There are two principal kinds of image maps: client-side image maps, in which the map information is contained in the HTML page itself and sent along to be interpreted by the browser, and server-side image maps, in which the map information is stored on the server and processed there.

The first image maps were all server-side image maps. Because all processing is done by the server, this form of image mapping is browser-independent. It is also slow. Client-side image maps are more efficient and easier to develop (especially with FrontPage!). At this point, most browsers support client-side image mapping, which is a part of the latest HTML standard.

By default, FrontPage creates client-side image maps. If you need to generate an image map file for server-side image mapping, you can do this too. In Explorer, select Tools⇨Web Settings. Click the Advanced tab. By default, FrontPage creates image maps in FrontPage style (that is, by using a component), and it generates only client-side image maps. To change the style of image maps to server-side, select the server-side style appropriate for your Web server (typically either NCSA or CERN). In the Prefix field, indicate the path to the server-side program that handles image maps. If you want both client-side and server-side image maps, check the Generate Client-Side Image Maps box. Otherwise uncheck this box. If you use both kinds of image maps, client-side is the default. If the user's browser does not recognize the client-side information, then the server-side image map is used.

Note

Once we have our image, we need to create the hotspots and indicate what they link to. This is the purpose of the other Image toolbar. The three main tools on the toolbar are the Rectangle, the Circle, and the Polygon. With these we mark the hotspots on the image. If we were feeling lazy, we could use the rectangle to create hotspots around the pills, even though they are not rectangular. But we want to be exact, so we use the circle tool for the round pills and the polygon tool for the elliptical pills. The polygonal hotspot tool works similarly, with one distinction. When you create a polygonal hotspot, it can have any number of edges. Each time you click the mouse button and release, it creates another edge of the polygon. To complete the process, you must connect the polygon back to the initial starting point.

6. To make a circular image map hotspot, select the circle tool on the Image toolbar. Position the pencil cursor at the center of the first round pill and drag with the mouse to the edge to create a circular hotspot.

7. When you release the mouse button, the hotspot is created and the Create Hyperlink dialog box appears. Link the hotspot to pill1.htm, included in the

Examples/ch05 folder on the CD-ROM. Or leave the hyperlink blank for now. If you want to revise the hotlink later, double-click the hotspot; the Edit Hyperlink dialog box appears. Click OK to close the Create Hyperlink dialog box.

8. Don't worry if you missed the pill with the hotspot. To move or resize the hotspot, simply select it with the selection tool (the arrow button) and you can move or resize it to your heart's content. You can also delete it while it is selected by clicking the Delete or Backspace key.

9. Link each pill to its respective page: pill2.htm through pill8.htm, left to right and top to bottom. The result should resemble Figure 5-13.

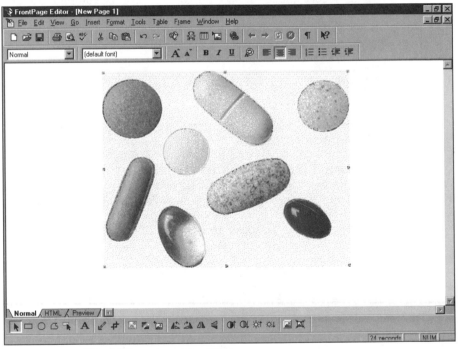

Figure 5-13: Pills with hot spots identified

Note

If you want to define a default hotspot, one that is in effect if the user clicks anywhere outside of the hotspots, select Image Properties and type the hotlink into the Default Hyperlink option or select it using the Browse button.

Creating Backgrounds

A Web page background works much like the wallpaper tiles on a Windows computer. A small image is repeated, horizontally and vertically, to fill the space defined by the window. We have already discussed how to insert a background into a Web page using the Page Properties dialog box. If you missed it, review Chapter 2. In this section, we use Image Composer to create three common variations on the background concept.

Tip

Used judiciously, a background can add a great deal to the look and feel of a page without adding a lot of overhead. Used rampantly, however, backgrounds, like blinking text, access counters, and looping animations, can be more of a distraction than an enhancement to your Web page. Backgrounds and textures are things that you can find plenty of on the Web. Check out one of the references provided earlier in the chapter.

Basic textures

The most common type of background is the simple tile, usually composed of a repeatable texture or pattern. You can use Image Composer to create a variety of textured backgrounds.

Tip

The power users in the crowd may be interested to know that Image Composer, just like Photoshop, is capable of working with third-party plug-ins such as Kai's Power Tools. Image Composer comes with an Impressionist filter installed.

The easiest backgrounds to make are ones that do not need to repeat. Here is one suggested method. You can find many more:

1. Make a square approximately 80 × 80 pixels.

2. Fill it with a color (for example, R: 102 G: 153 B: 102).

3. Select the effects tool in the toolbox. In the Effects palette, select Photographic in the Category drop-down menu and pick Film Grain from the list of effects. With the square selected, click Apply. The result is a grassy looking texture, as shown in Figure 5-14.

4. Save the image. Saved as a GIF, this background is 3K. As a JPEG saved with quality of 50 percent, it's 1K (see Figure 5-15).

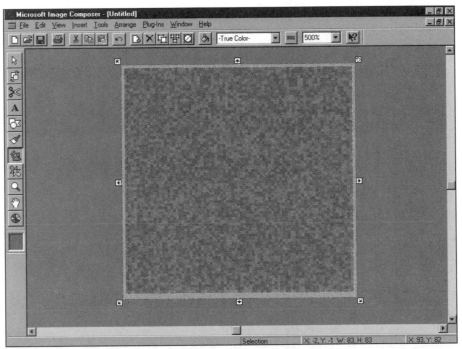

Figure 5-14: Creating a simple texture

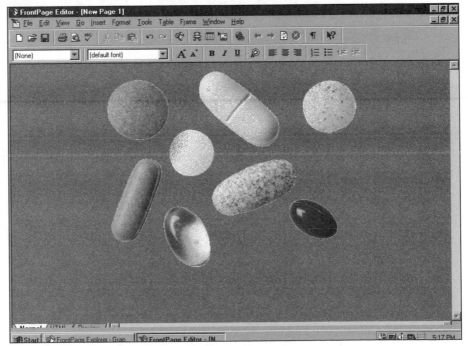

Figure 5-15: The Pills Quiz with a new background

Background stripes

This section and the next cover techniques that are variations on the standard background format. At this point, you should be able to create the backgrounds without detailed directions, so they are presented with a brief overview and an example. We leave the execution up to you.

You have seen Web pages that have a narrow band of color along either the left- or right-hand column, usually for the purpose of the main navigation or table of contents. The main section of the page is a contrasting color. This effect can be achieved in one of two ways. The first is through use of frames, a technique we cover in Chapter 8. The second method is to use a striped background in conjunction with a table-based layout to produce a frame-like effect without the complexity of a frames-based site.

Striped backgrounds exploit the tiling effect of background images by creating a very long, thin, solid-colored background image that is repeated down the page. As a variation on this theme, we have created a horizontally banded background image. Figure 5-16 shows a portion of the background image loaded as an inline image. Figure 5-17 shows the background in action.

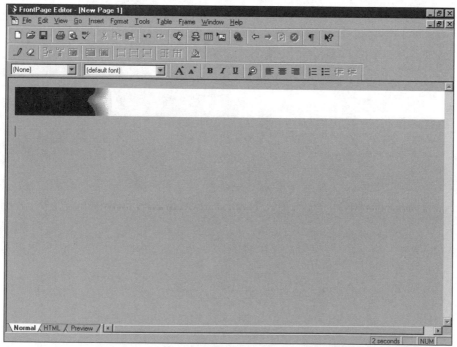

Figure 5-16: This thin background tiles horizontally to create a banded effect.

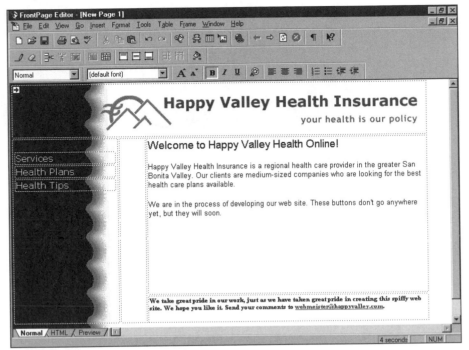

Figure 5-17: The background in action

Tip

In theory, this background image need be only one pixel wide. It turns out that working with one-pixel sprites in Image Composer is rather unwieldy and produces unreliable results when copied over to a Web page. I recommend using a standard paint program for any such backgrounds you might be contemplating.

Large images as backgrounds

A final background technique is to place a large, centrally located image into a background tile. The goal of this image is to defeat the tiling effect that is built into the background feature. There is currently no way to indicate whether a background image should be tiled or just centered on the page. The only way around this, given that it is impossible to predict monitor size and page length, is to create an image with enough white space around it to keep it from tiling (see Figure 5-18). You can keep the background image from scrolling, however, by checking the Watermark check box in the Background tab of the Page Properties dialog box.

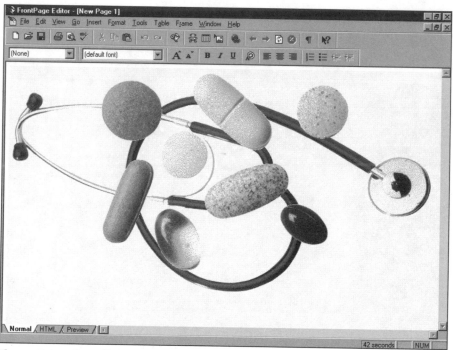

Figure 5-18: The Pill Recognition Test with a single image background

Taking the Next Step

Although you may not feel like the next digital Degas when you've finished reading this chapter, you have, at least, been introduced to the main aspects of Image Composer and can begin to create your own Web pictures. You can also make image maps that let your visitors quickly and easily navigate your Web. You now have all the basic skills necessary to begin learning how to add multimedia content such as animation and sound to your Web. Multimedia is introduced in the next chapter.

✦   ✦   ✦

Adding Multimedia Elements

This chapter looks at some of the ways FrontPage supports the inclusion of multimedia content. We are also going to look briefly at some of the main kinds of multimedia content currently available. It is not possible in an introductory chapter to provide information on how to create all the different kinds of content described here. This chapter does not turn you into an overnight multimedia developer, but It can help you recognize the important types of multimedia currently available on the Web and understand what is involved in producing and delivering them.

Working with GIF Animations

A GIF animation is a sequence of GIF images that have been collected together into a single GIF file. As we mentioned in Chapter 5, the GIF image format was initially developed by CompuServe as a convenient cross-platform format for transferring graphics over dial-up phone lines. In its most recent version, GIF89a, the GIF format also contains a provision for embedding multiple images in a single file. The main reason for doing this is compressibility. If you have five images that repeat much of the same graphical information, it is more convenient to put all five images in a single file where you only have to store the common information once. The GIF format was not initially intended for animations, but it did not take long for some smart folks to realize that if the format was convenient for storing the information, it could also be read out and the images played like a sequence of movie frames. Thus, more or less, was born the concept of GIF animation.

Simple animations have become ubiquitous on the Web, thanks largely to the spread of advertising banners among commercial sites. Animations are a relatively simple, low-bandwidth way to add life to your Web pages and to draw a reader's attention to particular elements on the Web page.

Inserting an existing GIF animation

Adding a GIF animation to a Web page is no different than adding a GIF image, a topic we discussed in detail in Chapter 5. Let's take a simple example. Open a page from the personal Web you created in Chapter 1—for example the page of hotlinks, favorite.htm. Place the cursor at the beginning of the first paragraph of text. We are going to insert a simple GIF animation to jazz up the top of the page. Open the Web page in Editor, and select Insert ➪ Image. Click the Select a File on Your Computer button and navigate to the folder shown in Figure 6-1. Select the image new.gif and press OK.

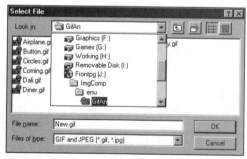

Figure 6-1: Inserting a GIF animation is as easy as inserting a standard image file.

The image is now displayed on your page (see Figure 6-2). Save your work, and click OK when FrontPage prompts you to save the GIF animation file as part of the Web. You may be interested to discover that this animation file takes up a whopping 17K.

Inserting multiple copies of the same graphic in a Web page or even on the same Web is a good way to conserve bandwidth. A given image is only downloaded once from the Web server. Any subsequent copy of the image is taken from your browser's local cache, resulting in negligible download times under reasonable circumstances.

You may notice that nothing animated happens when you insert this image. FrontPage merely displays the first frame of the graphic. This, by the way, is what most browsers that are not capable of showing GIF animation files do with this image, as well. This means that you do not have to do anything different for those folks, a nice side benefit of the GIF animation format. To see your page in motion, simply select the Preview tab.

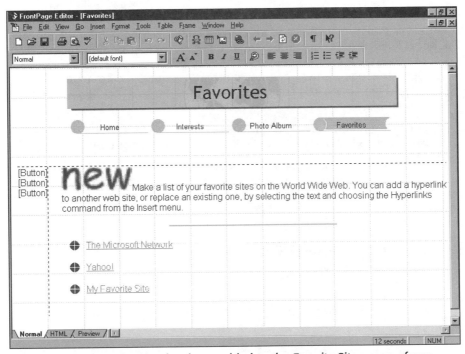

Figure 6-2: A GIF animation has been added to the Favorite Sites page of our personal Web.

Image Composer and Gif Animator

There are plenty of nifty GIF animations available for adding in your Web pages, but sooner or later you are going to want to create some of your own. The good news is that creating your own GIF animation is fairly easy. If you can imagine an animation, you can build it. The other good news is that you already have all the tools you need to make GIF animations: Image Composer and Gif Animator (catchy name!). Image Composer is detailed in Chapter 5.

Animating the Happy Valley logo

In Chapter 5 we used Image Composer to create a simple banner and logo for the Happy Valley Health Insurance Company. At the time, we insisted on saving the graphic in Composer's native .mic format, retaining each of the sprites. This enables us to manipulate the logo and create an animated version from the original.

Our plan is to create a sequence of spinning letters, first the H, then the V, then the H—not the most compelling animation, perhaps, but it serves to demonstrate the technique. Each spin takes four frames, with a 90-degree turn in each frame. Add in the initial start frame, and that makes a total of 13 frames. Here's how:

All example files used in this chapter can be found on the CD-ROM that accompanies the book. Files for this chapter are located in the Contents/ch06 folder.

1. Open the logo file hvh_logo.mic in Image Composer. To open an image, select File⇨Open and select the file using standard techniques for the Open dialog box.

2. Start Gif Animator from within Image Composer by selecting Tools⇨ Microsoft Gif Animator. Its default interface is illustrated in Figure 6-3.

To aid in your editing, check the Main Dialog Window Always on Top check box in the Options tab. This makes it easier to drag and drop animation frames from Image Composer to Gif Animator. At this point only the Options tab is visible, but as you add frames to your animation, other tabs appear.

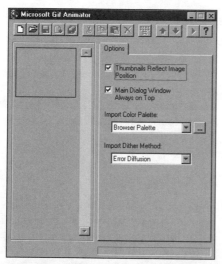

Figure 6-3: The Microsoft Gif Animator interface (unanimated)

3. We already have the first frame of our animation, so let's go ahead and add it to the Gif Animator. Select all of the logo sprites—the easiest way to do this is to click the Select All button on the toolbar.

4. Then drag the logo into the empty rectangular box in the upper-left corner of Gif Animator. A thumbnail version of the image appears in the box, labeled Frame #1, and a new empty rectangle appears beneath it as shown in Figure 6-4.

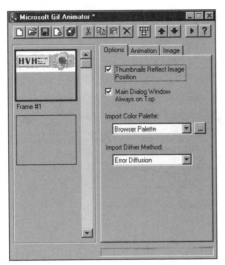

Figure 6-4: The first frame of the logo animation

5. Select the first letter H in Image Composer.

6. Open the Arrange dialog box by clicking the Arrange tool button on the left side.

7. Click the Rotate Right 90 degrees button in the Rotate square. Then repeat the steps to drag this version into the second frame box in Gif Animator. Repeat this step until you have all 13 frames of the animation, rotating the V and the other H completely around, in turn.

8. Save the animation file by clicking the Save icon (note that there are no menu items in this utility).

Note

You may notice that the H, by virtue of the fact that it is a block letter, really only has two different states. If you are lazy, you can simply copy the first frame into the third and fifth frames and the second into the fourth. Then do the same for the four frames of the last H. To copy a frame in Gif Animator, select the frame and drag the image while holding down the Ctrl key.

Previewing your creation

Once you have all of the frames collected, it is time to preview the animation. Select the Preview icon, on the far right of the toolbar. It looks like the play button of a VCR. This opens the Preview window (see Figure 6-5) that allows you to play your animation, step through it one frame at a time, rewind it, or fast-forward it.

Figure 6-5: The animation Preview window

Controlling animation speed

One thing you may notice is that the animation plays very fast. Let's slow it down a little. To control the speed, use the Duration field on the Image tab. Choose the Image tab to bring it to the front. Then select all frames by clicking the Select All button. You should see the dark blue selection highlight around each frame. Then change the duration to $^{25}\!/_{100}$ of a second. Run Preview again, and this time the letters should spin more slowly. Finally, click the Animation tab and check the Looping check box and the Repeat Forever check box. This should drive people sufficiently crazy.

Adding it to your Web

To add the new, animated version of the Happy Valley logo to their Web, open the HVH Web in Explorer and open the default page. Replace the static version of the logo with this one. To preview the results, select the Preview tab. Be sure to save the animation to the Web when FrontPage prompts you to do so.

Animating with horizontal movement

Our second GIF animation example demonstrates one way to create horizontal movement across your Web page. For this example, we are going to work with the Pedigree Pets Web. Open the Armadillo page, `Examples/ch06/Adillo1.htm`, located on the CD-ROM that accompanies this book. This page features purebred Texas armadillos. Our plan is to add an animated armadillo to the page pictured in Figure 6-6. To do so, follow these steps:

1. Open the Armadillo GIF in a new Composer window.

2. Mask the armadillo so that he can run on the background. To do this, select the Cutout tool from the Image Composer toolbox or select Tools ⇨ Cutout from the menu bar.

3. Select the armadillo sprite. Using the magic wand tool (located on the Select Color Region tab), click in the white area around the armadillo. This fills the white with the current foreground color.

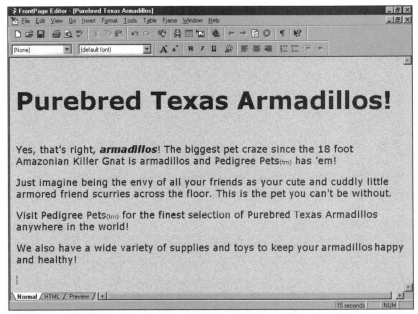

Figure 6-6: The Armadillo product page, before animation

4. Click the Erase button and this color is erased from the sprite, leaving the armadillo on a transparent background.

5. Next we create the background for the armadillo to run on. Using the shapes tool again, click the Rectangle button and drag a long, thin rectangle, approximately 500 pixels wide by 80 pixels high (high enough for the armadillo to fit).

6. We want to fill this rectangle with the same background pattern used on the page. This background file is `Contents/ch06/brntxtr1.gif`. Fill the rectangle with the color Red: 102, Green: 153, Blue: 102 (instructions on how to do this are in Chapter 5).

7. Now texturize the rectangle by selecting the grain effect in the Photographic category of the effects tool. The result is shown in Figure 6-7.

Figure 6-7: Mr. Armadillo, ready to race

8. With the armadillo and the background, we can create the animation by duplicating the sprite combination and moving the armadillo ahead in each frame before copying both the armadillo and background into Gif Animator. The procedure is:

   • Select both armadillo sprite and background.

   • Drag the two sprites into the next Gif Animator frame box.

   • Deselect the background.

   • Reposition the armadillo sprite.

   • Repeat the previous four operations to create as many frames as necessary.

9. Select all frames in Gif Animator, set the duration to $^{15}/_{100}$ sec to slow down the speeding armadillo, and set the looping to Repeat Forever (guaranteed to drive anyone who uses the page to distraction, which is probably the only circumstance under which one might purchase an armadillo).

10. Finally, save the images as a GIF file and insert them into the Armadillo page.

In Figure 6-8, the resulting GIF animation is shown in Editor's preview mode with the frisky armadillo caught midway across the page.

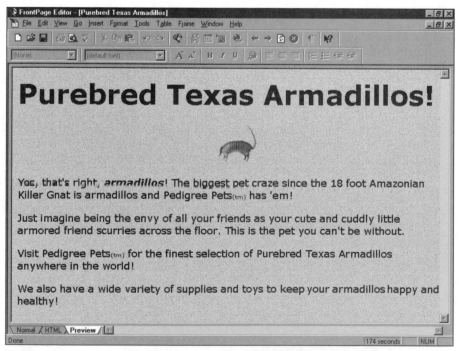

Figure 6-8: Mr. Armadillo, well on his way to a Web page near you

All example files used in this chapter can be found on the CD-ROM that accompanies the book. Content files for this chapter are located in the `Contents/ch06` folder. The completed version of the armadillo animation, `pro2anim.htm`, can be found in `Examples/ch06`.

Additional GIF animation tools

Microsoft's Gif Animator is convenient because it works so nicely in conjunction with Image Composer. It also comes free with FrontPage, which is always an attraction. It is not the only GIF animation tool in town, however. We close this section with a reference to three other tools, all of which are shareware products that are far more robust than Gif Animator. They are also easy to use, but, like any feature-rich products, they take a little more time to learn.

✦ **VideoCraft GIF Animator:** This product from Andover Advanced Technologies includes a vast array of animation effects, including morphing of images. Curious folk may want to experiment with Andover's online banner maker, at `http://www.mediabuilder.com/abm.html. http://www.andatech.com/vidcraft/banners.html`. This Web-based form allows users to create a simple GIF animation banner using their own text and one of a long list of effects. Although it is essentially a promotion for their GIF animation product, you may find the banner maker useful in its own right.

✦ **Ulead GIF Animator:** This is one of several shareware Web utilities offered by Ulead, a maker of graphics applications. Their application, also called GIF Animator, contains many custom effects. It also has very good optimization capabilities—leaving you with smaller animation files, always a good thing. Check out their product line at `http://www.ulead.com`.

✦ **GIF Construction Set:** Besides the obvious virtue of having an original name, GIF Construction Set, from Alchemy Mindworks, is also a highly respected animation program that has been in use longer than the two previously mentioned products. You can find out more about GIF Construction Set from the Alchemy Mindworks Web site, `http://www.mindworkshop.com/alchemy/alchemy.html`.

Creating PowerPoint Animations

In the last year, Microsoft has made impressive efforts to convert all of their business applications into Web tools. The Office 97 suite is the first realization of this. With Office 97 you can edit and view Web pages directly in Word, create tables in Excel, and convert PowerPoint presentations to HTML. In the context of multimedia, one of the niftiest new features is the ability to create and play PowerPoint animations in your Web page. In this section we briefly illustrate the ability to display standard PowerPoint slide shows in a Web browser, and then we turn to PowerPoint animations.

Installing the PowerPoint Animation Player

In order to view the PowerPoint application, you need to install the current version of the PowerPoint Animation Player plug-in (`axplayer.exe`), available from the Microsoft Web site at `http://www.microsoft.com/powerpoint/`.

To install the plug-in:

1. Download the player installation file, `axplayer.exe`.
2. Start the installation, either by double-clicking it in Explorer or by selecting Run from the Start menu, locating the installation application, and running it.
3. The installation program installs the ActiveX version of the player in Internet Explorer and/or the plug-in version in Netscape.

Using the AutoContent Wizard

PowerPoint 97's AutoContent Wizard is a quick way to create a presentation. If you were really creating a presentation, you would probably want to customize the presentation that the wizard generates, put in new graphics, perhaps add a few custom pages, and so on. For our purposes, however, the generic version does suffice.

Tip

If you do not have the current version of PowerPoint, you can create a slide show in an earlier version. In fact, the current plug-in only supports the prior version of PowerPoint anyway.

To create an instant presentation using the AutoContent Wizard in PowerPoint 97:

1. Launch PowerPoint and the AutoContent Wizard.
2. Select a presentation type. We are going to create a product overview for Pedigree Pets. Click the Presentation Type button, and then select Product/Services Overview (see Figure 6-9).

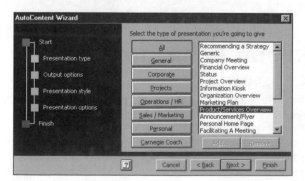

Figure 6-9: Selecting a template type in the PowerPoint AutoContent Wizard

3. Press the Output Options button and select Internet/Kiosk. Notice that the current version of PowerPoint is designed to save PowerPoint presentations optimized for the bandwidth of the Internet.

4. Press the Presentation Options button and add custom copyright information and an e-mail address, and you are finished with the template.

This creates the template for a seven-slide presentation, the opening screen of which is shown in Figure 6-10. You can edit the content as much as you like. When you are finished, it is time to transfer the presentation to the Pedigree Web.

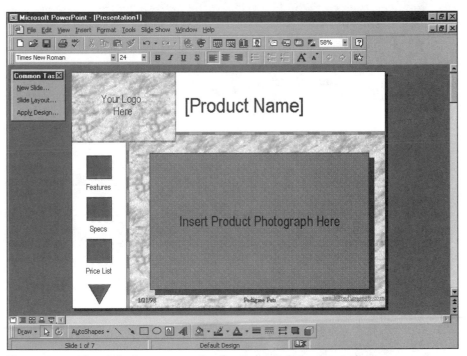

Figure 6-10: The default start page for the PowerPoint presentation

Inserting a PowerPoint presentation

Inserting your PowerPoint presentation is a slightly more complicated procedure than you might imagine. If you use the following steps, however, your Web page may make its point more powerfully.

1. Save your PowerPoint presentation.

Note

Before you insert the slide show, you need to decide in what version of PowerPoint to save your slide show. If you have PowerPoint 97, part of the Office 97 distribution, the slide show saves by default as PP97 format. However, the current version of the PowerPoint plug-in only supports the previous version of PowerPoint. Saving in the current format may limit your audience (or require that they download an updated version before they can view your presentation). If you prefer to save in PowerPoint 95 format, select that option from the Save menu in PowerPoint.

2. Open the Web page in Editor that includes the slide show. Before you begin, you need to decide whether to insert the ActiveX control version of the presentation or the plug-in. Some considerations:

   • FrontPage makes it very easy to insert ActiveX components. It even lists all of the currently installed ActiveX controls on your system.

   • ActiveX controls, however, currently only work in Internet Explorer. Both Internet Explorer and Netscape Navigator support the plug-in version.

3. To insert the animation as a plug-in, select Insert ➪ Advanced ➪ Plug-In. To insert the animation as an ActiveX control, select Insert ➪ Advanced ➪ ActiveX Control.

4. If you choose to insert the animation as a plug-in, you will see the Plug-In Properties dialog box shown in Figure 6-11.

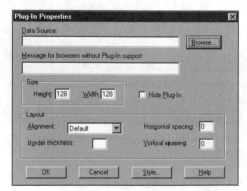

Figure 6-11: Tough decisions at the front lines of the browser war

Tip

If you do use the ActiveX version, be sure to include some text in the Alternative Representation field in the ActiveX Properties dialog box (see Figure 6-12). This text, which can be any valid HTML, appears if the user's browser is incapable of displaying the ActiveX control.

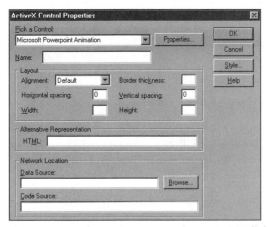

Figure 6-12: The ActiveX Control Properties dialog box

5. Set the parameters for the animation.

- For the plug-in version, enter the name and path of the animation in the Data Source text box (or find it using Browse) and press OK. The presentation now appears as a representation of a plug (funny how that works). Note that you can also set other properties such as the animation's size and alignment, and you can even add a message that is displayed for people who don't have the plug-in.

- For the ActiveX version, select Microsoft Powerpoint Animation in the Pick a Control list box and enter the name and path of the animation in the Data Source text box (or find it using Browse) and press OK. The presentation now appears as a spiffy *X* logo on your page. Note that you can also set other properties such as the animation's size and alignment, and you can even add a message that is displayed for people whose browsers don't support ActiveX.

6. Save the file and preview. The result is a completely functional presentation available on the Web (see Figure 6-13).

Figure 6-13: The Pedigree Pets presentation ready for content

Creating a PowerPoint animation

In addition to serving up full-blown presentations, PowerPoint can be used to create simple animations, much like the GIF animations we practiced earlier. The difference is that PowerPoint has some built-in animation features that make creating more sophisticated animation effects quite easy.

To create the animation:

1. Select File ⇨ New in PowerPoint and select a blank presentation.

2. Select File ⇨ Page Setup and reduce the page dimensions from full screen to banner width (1 inch × 8 inches).

3. Select Insert ⇨ Picture ⇨ From File and insert the armadillo image.

4. Select Insert ⇨ Text Box and type in a message.

5. Select Slide Show ⇨ Custom Animation to access PowerPoint's animation tools (see Figure 6-14).

6. Select the text object in the list and check the Animate radio button. Repeat for the picture object. They now appear in the Animation order list with the picture first.

7. Select the text object and choose an animation effect, for example, Fly from Right, from the Effects tab.

8. Switch to the Timing tab and click the Automatically radio button. By default, the animation occurs on a mouse click, which is not what we want for this animation.

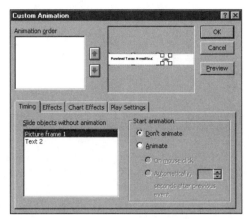

Figure 6-14: The Custom Animation dialog box in PowerPoint

9. Select the picture object and repeat the process, selecting an effect (Crawl from Right works well) and setting the timing to run automatically.

10. Save the animation as before. Remember to save it as a Windows 95 presentation rather than the default, PowerPoint 97 version, which the Animation Player does not currently support.

11. Return to FrontPage and insert the PowerPoint animation as previously detailed, with one difference. By default, PowerPoint inserts plug-ins at 128 × 128. You need to change the dimensions of the plug-in space in the Plug-In Properties window (W: 590 H: 74 works nicely for the banner size).

12. Preview your work in a browser. Compare this to the static version in Figure 6-15.

The Animation Player does not always do a flawless job of translating animation objects. For example, note the black line artifacts introduced around the armadillo in Figure 6-15. They are not present in the PowerPoint version. Attempting to use the transparent version of the armadillo image produces even worse results. Moral: Let the animator beware.

Purebred Texas Armadillos!

Figure 6-15: Static armadillos aren't nearly as nifty as animated pets

Using Macromedia Shockwave

One additional animation plug-in that deserves mention in this context is Macromedia's Shockwave. Shockwave began as a simple plug-in for Macromedia Director applications. It has evolved into a family of plug-ins, supporting many of the Macromedia multimedia products, including Authorware and FreeHand.

The latest addition to the Shockwave family is Flash, a vector-based animation application that creates animations that download quickly and run smoothly. The Shockwave ActiveX control and plug-in are free for downloading. The Flash development application, of course, is a commercial product. However, you can download a trial version of the latest release, 2.0 as of this writing, from Macromedia's Web site, http://www.macromedia.com.

Adding Background Audio

As Web pages continue to evolve in the direction of multimedia titles and interactive television programming, the ability to add background audio has become an increasingly prevalent element of multimedia Web pages. FrontPage includes support for a Microsoft-specific HTML extension that enables developers to embed an audio file in a Web page. When the page is requested, this audio file loads and plays automatically.

Note

This feature is easy to implement, although it does not offer much in the way of user control. Remember, it is also Microsoft-specific, and it is not supported by all browsers. (Most notably, it is not currently supported by Netscape's browsers.)

A primer on digital audio formats

The background audio feature supports several digital audio formats. Without attempting to go into detail, here are the formats:

✦ *Wave Sound (WAV):* This is the Windows standard audio format.

✦ *AIFF Sound (AIF, AIFC, AIFF):* This is the Macintosh equivalent of WAV files.

✦ *AU Sound (AU, SND):* This is a Sun audio format that is widely used on the Web and has gained limited cross-platform acceptance.

✦ *MIDI:* This stands for Musical Instrument Digital Interface. It is the format generated by synthesizers.

The first three formats are sampled audio, also known as waveform audio. Waveform audio formats record, or "sample," sounds much as a tape recorder does. MIDI, unlike sampled sound format, records a set of instructions about how to recreate, or "synthesize," a particular sound. As a result, MIDI has a more limited repertoire than waveform audio, which can copy any sound you feed into a microphone. MIDI is, however, far more economical in the size of its files than is waveform audio. Most musical compositions are created in MIDI format.

Getting audio files

In order to add background audio, we need an audio file. Fortunately, Microsoft has made available a number of audio samples on its Web site, at http://www. microsoft.com/gallery/files/sounds/default.htm. Let's select a nice little number from the Musical section called Caribbean, shown in Figure 6-16—just say no to door slams, cat screeches, and other audio samples commonly known as noise. Follow the directions on the Caribbean page to download and save this MIDI file (only 27K).

Turn down your stereo speaker before you check out the sound samples page listed here. It provides a good example of why unannounced sounds on Web pages is a bad idea. I jump out of my skin every time I go there.

Figure 6-16: The Caribbean at your fingertips courtesy of the Microsoft Sound Sample site

Inserting audio files in your Web pages

Once you have copied the file to your local drive, it is time to add it to your Web page. Let's add this to the Pedigree Armadillo page, since it provides a complementary backdrop to our scuttling armadillo animation. To insert a background audio into a Web page:

1. Open the Web page in Editor.

2. Select File ➪ Page Properties The dialog box shown in Figure 6-17 appears.

3. Press the Browse button and select the file, either from the current Web or from another location.

4. Click OK.

5. Save the Web page. You are prompted to add the sound file to your Web if it is not already there.

6. Preview the sound in your Web browser and dance along with the armadillo.

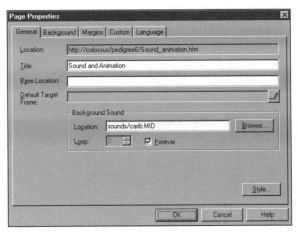

Figure 6-17: Inserting a background sound into your
Web page using Page Properties

Setting audio properties

Once you have created a background sound, there are a couple of properties you
can control. For instance, as with GIF animations, you can set the sound file to loop
a designated number of times. To do this, select File⇨Page Properties, and in the
General tab, indicate the number of times to loop the sound file. You can also use
the Page Properties dialog box to change the name of the background sound.

Additional sound ways and means

If you are looking for sound bytes to add to your Web, or if you would like to learn more
about sound formats, there are several Web resources you may want to investigate:

✦ *WWW Virtual Library:* The WWW Virtual Library maintains lists of Internet resources
   on a variety of topics. Each topic is maintained by a volunteer. The library's list of
   audio resources is located at `http://www.comlab.ox.ac.uk/archive
   /audio.html`. It contains links to sound archives, software, newsgroups, and
   online radio.

✦ *Harmony Central:* This is an excellent site for MIDI resources and information,
   including everything from MIDI forums to software and links to MIDI archives:
   `http://www.harmony-central.com/MIDI/`.

✦ *The MIDI Farm:* This is another full-service MIDI site with a well-organized potpourri
   of MIDI related content: `http://www.midifarm.com/`.

(continued)

(continued)

✦ *Geek-Girl's Site with Audio Clips:* Including links to sounds, music, and voice, this site is somewhat dated, but it still has one of the best indexes for sounds on the Net: `http://snhungar.kings.edu/Sndroom.html`.

✦ *Whoopie!:* This is a searchable archive of links to vast quantities of general multimedia on the Web, including music and audio. Entries are rated from 1–5 exclamation points: Whoopie! `http://www.whoopie.com`.

✦ *IUMA (Internet Underground Music Archive):* If you are looking for music on the Web, this should be your first stop. Lots of audio, and a way-cool, award-winning interface: `http://www.iuma.com`.

If you are serious about audio, you may want to investigate some of the other technologies for adding audio to your Web. Here are some of the leading contenders:

✦ *Netscape LiveAudio:* Netscape Navigator ships with an audio plug-in called LiveAudio. It is capable of playing audio in a variety of formats, including AIFF, MIDI, WAV, and AU. The LiveAudio plug-in can be controlled via JavaScript. Information on Netscape Navigator is available at `http://www.netscape.com`.

✦ *QuickTime Audio:* Apple Computer's video format can also be used to prepare audio only. QuickTime files can be saved for fast-start, allowing the QuickTime to begin playing as it downloads. For more information, see the QuickTime Webmaster's Page, `http://www.quicktime.com/dev/devweb.html`.

✦ *RealAudio:* This is the original streaming audio format, and still the most popular. Unlike the standard audio formats, which require users to download an entire file and then listen to it, streaming audio plays as it downloads. It can even be used to broadcast audio in real time. RealAudio has its own player application, available in free and Plus versions: `http://www.realaudio.com`.

✦ *Crescendo:* Crescendo is a MIDI plug-in from LiveUpdate available in Netscape and Microsoft versions. It is available in a free version and as a Plus version, which can provide streaming of MIDI files: `http://www.liveupdate.com`.

✦ *Liquid MusicPlayer from Liquid Audio:* This is another plug-in format, designed to allow users to download and play CD-quality audio, as well as to view art, lyrics, and credits: `http://www.liquidaudio.com`.

Adding Inline Video Clips

In addition to providing basic support for background sounds, FrontPage supports the ability to add video clips to your Web pages. This feature is simple to implement but limited in its flexibility. FrontPage supports inline video in AVI format, the standard Windows video format. Although there are players for AVI video format on all major computer platforms, AVI is not considered a cross-platform standard. Nor does it have the best compression methods available. Even relatively short video clips are likely to be 300K and larger—more than the average user is going to want to confront unannounced on a Web page.

Inserting video clips into your Web pages

Select Insert ➪ Active Elements ➪ Video, locate the AVI file you want to include, and click OK. A preview of the video appears in the Web page, showing the initial frame of the video clip (see Figure 6-18).

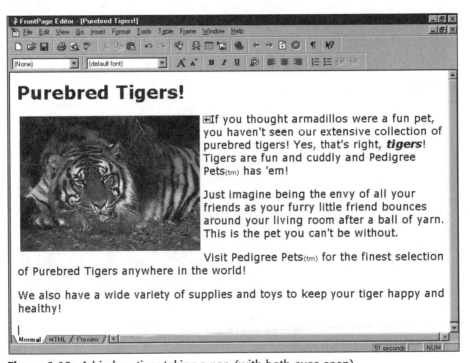

Figure 6-18: A big lazy tiger taking a nap (with both eyes open)

You now have video in your Web page. When you save the page, you are prompted to save the video in the current Web (if that wasn't its original location). To preview, select the Editor's Preview tab.

Setting video properties

The properties for video clips are located on a tab in the Image Properties dialog box. Select the video preview and select Edit ➪ Image Properties, or click the image with the right mouse button and select Image Properties from the pop-up menu. The Video tab of the Image Properties dialog box is shown in Figure 6-19. You can control how the video is displayed with these items:

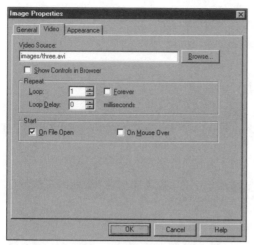

Figure 6-19: The video clip properties you can control

✦ **Video Source**—As with other inserted objects, you can alter the source name, effectively substituting another video for the current one.

✦ **Show Controls in Browser**—This check box item enables you to insert simple playback controls into the Web page. Another way to see the controls is to insert the animation as a plug-in using the same procedure as outlined earlier in the chapter for the PowerPoint presentation—an animation inserted as a plug-in automatically has the controls. See Figure 6-20.

Caution

For some reason, when you elect to include the controls, FrontPage does not adjust the size of the space reserved for the video to compensate. If you do not enlarge the dimensions of the video, it is scrunched (that's a technical term) by the controls.

✦ **Repeat**—Just as with animation and sound, you can elect to loop the video clip as many times as you want to subject the poor user to the sequence.

✦ **Start**—By default, the video begins to play when the file loads. Alternatively, you can have it begin when the user passes the mouse over the video. If you use this option, you might want to prompt the users as to what to do. Unless you just want them to guess for themselves.

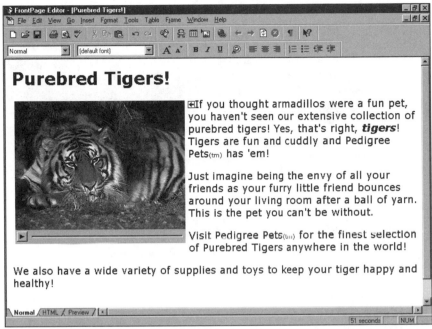

Figure 6-20: Inserting the playback controls enables users to step through the video clip.

Video viewing alternatives

If you have a mind to post your home movies for the world to enjoy or to broadcast your full-length documentary film, a variety of technologies can help you do it. Internet video technologies have made great strides in the past few years, which means that the video they generate is almost watchable, even if you don't happen to have a T3 line or a cable modem.

Several of the technologies described earlier in the sidebar titled "Additional sound ways and means" can be used to create and/or deliver video content. These include Netscape's MediaPlayer plug-in, RealAudio, which now includes streaming video, and Apple's QuickTime. In addition, a number of other technologies merit investigating. These include:

✦ *Microsoft NetShow:* NetShow is Microsoft's entry in the streaming multimedia category. (For a definition of streaming audio, see the discussion of RealAudio in the "Additional sound ways and means" sidebar). NetShow content is created in ActiveX Streaming Format (ASF) or broadcast in real time from an audio/video source. NetShow can be used in conjunction with Internet Information Server (IIS), which is the Microsoft Windows NT Web server. For more information on NetShow or to download the free NetShow Player go to http://www.microsoft .com/netshow.

(continued)

(continued)

✦ *VDOLive:* VDOLive is a streaming video technology from VDONet. It uses a separate VDOLive On-Demand server to deliver quality real-time video, even at dial-up connection speeds. For more information or to download the VDOLive plug-in for either Netscape or Microsoft, visit `http://www.vdo.net`.

✦ *VivoActive:* VivoActive is a serverless streaming video technology from Vivo Software, Inc. Use the VivoActive Producer to convert your video to VivoActive format, and then use a standard Web server to deliver the content. The VivoActive Player is free for downloading from the VivoActive Web site, `http://www.vivo.com`.

Adding Active Elements

Active elements, even more than their name implies, add activity *and* interactivity to your pages. From light-up buttons to text search features to animated text, active elements provide an easy way to make your pages seem more exciting. The following sections detail all of the active elements—except video, which was outlined in the last section.

Hover buttons

"Hover button" sounds like something you press on a helicopter, but in fact it's a way to make relatively boring text buttons more interesting. When visitors to your page pass the cursor over a hover button, one of several effects (from a glowing look to a changing color) alerts them that the button is available. You can even specify images and sounds to use for the button to provide a more interactive look and feel to your pages. It's a little thing, but it can make a page seem more snazzy.

To add a hover button, select Insert ⇨ Active Elements ⇨ Hover Button. The Hover Button dialog box (shown in Figure 6-21) opens to let you specify the button's properties.

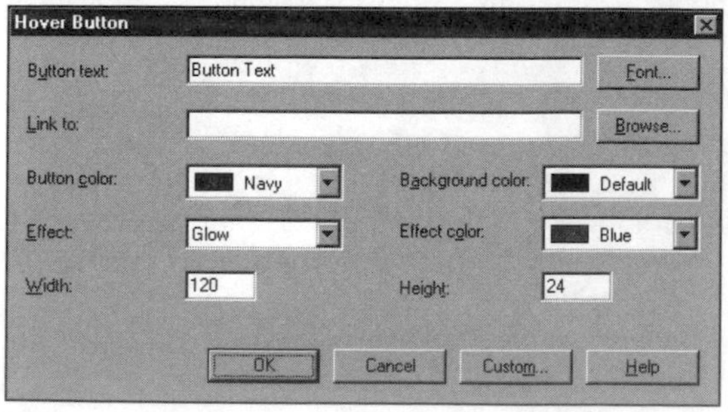

Figure 6-21: The Hover Button dialog box

You have the following selections:

✦ **Button text**—This is the text that's displayed on the button's face. You can change the font, color, style, and size by pressing the Font button. This text is visible even if you use a graphic image in your button.

✦ **Link To**—This is the page or file that is opened when the button is clicked. Enter the URL directly in the text box, or click the Browse button to select the page as you normally would.

✦ **Width**—This is the button's width, in pixels. Note that this does not automatically change if you have a long string of text or large image—you have to update it manually to compensate.

✦ **Height**—This is the button's height, in pixels. Note that this does not automatically change if you have selected a large font size or large image—you have to update it manually to compensate.

✦ **Button Color**—This is the button's "static" color when you don't use an image, that is, the color when the cursor is not over it.

✦ **Background Color**—This is the color for the button's background. Unfortunately, this color shows through even if you use a transparent GIF as a button image.

✦ **Effect Color**—This is the button's "hover" color when you don't use an image, that is, the color when the cursor passes over it. How the color shows up depends on what effect is selected.

✦ **Effect**—The following are the effects available:

   • **Color Fill**—The entire button changes to the effect color.

   • **Color Average**—The entire button changes to a color halfway between the button color and the effect color.

   • **Glow**—The center of the button changes to the effect color, with the color fading toward the edges.

   • **Reverse Glow**—The center of the button remains the button color, but it fades to the effect color at the outside edges.

   • **Light Glow**—This is a muted version of Glow.

   • **Bevel Out**—The button takes on a 3-D appearance as if it's sticking out of the page. Note that this effect works best with relatively light button colors.

   • **Bevel In**—The same as Bevel Out, except that the button looks indented into the screen.

To add graphic or sound elements to the button, click the Custom button and either enter the name and path of the element you want to include or press the appropriate browse button and select it normally.

Banner ads

Banner ads—those wide, short graphics that change periodically to keep your attention—are familiar to just about everyone who surfs the Web. You could make GIF animations to deal with incorporating a banner ad on your page, but just think about how big the file would be! An easier way to do this is to use the Banner Ad Manager. In addition to keeping your image size much smaller, the Banner Ad Manager also allows you to incorporate transition effects (such as fades) between images without having to try to create them in, say, Image Composer.

Unfortunately, there is one small drawback to the banner ad element—each image links to the same URL. This means that each image should, preferably, be advertising the same thing.

To add a banner ad, select Insert ➪ Active Elements ➪ Banner Ad Manager. To add images to your banner, press the Add button and search normally. The image name appears in the Images to Display list. When visitors view your page, the images appear in the order shown in this list. To move an image up or down in the order, highlight it and press the Move Up or Move Down button, as appropriate. Note that the height and width settings do not automatically update to reflect the size of the image(s) you're using, so you'll have to make these settings manually.

Marquees

A *marquee* is a block of text that scrolls across your page like the big Times Square news sign in New York City. Adding a marquee is fairly straightforward: select Insert ➪ Active Elements ➪ Marquee to open the Marquee Properties dialog box, type the text you want displayed in the (appropriately named) Text text box, and press OK to accept the default options.

To customize the size or action of your marquee, double-click an existing marquee in Editor, or make the settings when you add it. The available settings are:

- ✦ **Direction**—This is the direction that the text moves. You can choose Left or Right.

- ✦ **Movement Speed**—As the name implies, this controls how fast the text moves. Play with the two settings, Delay and Amount, to create the speed you want.

- ✦ **Delay** is the length of time that the text appears at a certain spot (in thousandths of a second).

- ✦ **Amount** is the distance the text moves between each delay.

- ✦ **Behavior**—This controls the way that the text in the marquee moves.

✦ **Scroll**—The text starts at the right (unless you have Right set in Direction) and moves to the left until all of the text has gone off the screen; it then repeats.

✦ **Slide**—This is similar to Scroll, except that when the first letter hits the left edge of the marquee, the text disappears and starts again from the right.

✦ **Alternate**—This makes the text bounce back and forth between the left and right edges of the marquee.

✦ **Align with Text**—This controls how the marquee aligns with other (nonmarquee) text on the same line. These options behave the same way as those for graphics.

✦ **Size**—The Specify Height and Specify Width settings control the size of the marquee. Both can be specified either in pixels or as a percentage of the screen size.

✦ **Repeat**—This controls how many times the text scrolls across the screen. The default is continuously, but if you uncheck this check box, you can specify a specific number.

✦ **Background Color**—By default, this is the background color of your page (or clear, if you use a background image). You can pick any other color, or create a custom color, using the color list. Note that if you change the background color, your text might not show up well—you can change the text color to compensate by highlighting the marquee and setting the text color normally. You can also set the marquee text style as you would any other text.

Search forms

Search forms make it possible for visitors to search your Web for a particular word, or words, and then go directly to the page that contains it. Unlike with a standard form (as detailed in Chapter 11), you don't have to set up any custom CGI (Common Gateway Interface) scripting to make this element work—just insert it, make whatever settings you want, and you're done.

To add a search form, select Insert ➪ Active Elements ➪ Search Form and either change the default settings or just press the OK button. Figure 6-22 shows the results of a search using the default settings.

The options available for the Search Form element are limited, but that doesn't detract from the power and ease of use of the finished product. By default, only the names of the matching pages are listed after a search is completed. You can also add columns telling your visitor how close the matching pages are to what was searched for, when the page was created, and even the size of the page. To add these options to the output, click the Search Results tab and check the appropriate check box.

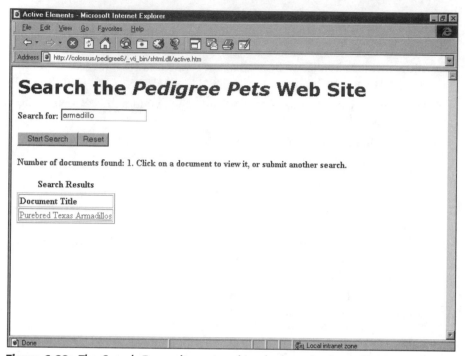

Figure 6-22: The Search Form element makes short work of creating a search engine for your Web.

In addition, you can limit the scope of the search. By default your entire Web is searched, but if you have a discussion group in your Web, you can limit the search to the discussion group listings, by entering the name of the discussion group folder in the Word List to Search text box. Chapter 14 includes complete instructions for adding a discussion group as well as other types of custom forms.

Hit counters

Hit counters help you keep track of your Web's traffic by listing the number of times a page is visited. To add a hit counter, select Insert ⇨ Active Elements ⇨ Hit Counter, pick the style counter numbers you want to use, and press the OK button.

You can also use a custom set of numbers by selecting the Custom Image radio button and entering the name of a GIF image. Note that the GIF image must be a GIF image, 10 times wider than it is tall, with each digit evenly spaced (zero through nine) in sequence.

By default, the counter uses only as many digits as are required to count the number of hits received. You can also have the counter look like a car odometer by specifying the exact number of digits used—if a page has received 32 hits and if the number of digits is fixed at 5, its counter would read "00032."

To set the counter to a specific number, check the Reset Counter To radio button and enter the number you want in the text box next to it. (Not that I advocate lying, but you can make a page look far more popular than it is by setting the initial number to some large amount.)

Taking the Next Step

In this chapter we have taken a whirlwind tour of the various ways that FrontPage simplifies the task of adding sound, action, and interactivity to your Web. We have focused on using additional Microsoft products to create animation and have called attention to other resources and methods you can use to make yourself look like a multimedia guru (at least after you've had a chance to practice with them). In the next chapter, we return to page layout issues. We discuss in detail an advanced HTML element for making pages bend to your will: tables. We discover that FrontPage makes these a snap to implement.

✦   ✦   ✦

HTML Layout and Design

Formatting with Tables

By now, you are able to use FrontPage to create and edit your Web pages and to enhance them with oodles of exciting multimedia content—from simple images to animations, with audio and video. This chapter looks at some slightly more advanced ways of controlling the layout of information on your Web pages. HTML tables can be used to format tabular data or to control the layout of information on the page.

Creating a Table

If you are at all familiar with spreadsheet applications such as Microsoft Excel, you should have no trouble understanding the basic principles behind the construction of tables in HTML. Tables were added to HTML in order to display structured information, that is to say, data that you want to line up in nice neat rows and columns. At present, because HTML offers limited control over the placement of elements on the Web page, tables also provide one of the best available means of specifying the location of objects on the page. In this chapter we explore both kinds of table functions.

You have three ways to create a table in FrontPage. The first two, inserting and drawing, are detailed in the next two sections. The third, using the Table icon in the toolbar, is explained afterward in a tip.

Another intuitive inroad

Recently, schemes for instituting more precise control over the layout of objects on the page have begun to spring up. Why, you may ask, did this not happen sooner? Mainly because HTML was not born as a page description language, such as PostScript, for example.

HTML is officially a *structural* markup language. It defines structural elements on a page, such as lists or header levels, but it does not dictate what those elements should look like or where they should be when they are displayed. HTML purists are fighting a losing battle.

Inserting a table

Inserting a table using the Insert Table dialog box (shown in Figure 7-1) provides excellent control over the initial appearance of your table. While not every table option is available in this dialog box, enough options are there to make setting up your table easier. These options, as well as others, are explained in detail later in this chapter in the section entitled "Setting overall table properties."

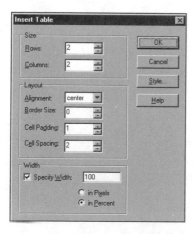

Figure 7-1: Use the Insert Table dialog box to make short work of creating a table.

The main options of initial concern are located in the size and width sections of the dialog box. These options let you specify how many rows and columns your table has and its overall width.

To insert a table:

1. Select Table ⇨ Insert Table to open the Insert Table dialog box.
2. Set the size, layout, and width options.

3. Press OK to insert the table.

Once the table has been inserted, it can be manipulated in any of the ways detailed in the rest of this chapter.

Drawing a table

With tables' increasing use as a page layout tool, Microsoft has vastly upgraded the tools for creating and editing tables in FrontPage 98. The Tables toolbar (shown in Figure 7-2) provides quick access to many of the most frequently used table formatting tools. The function of each of these tools is explained later in this chapter (all are detailed in the section "Adjusting Table Structure," except the background color tool, which is explained in "Editing Table Properties").

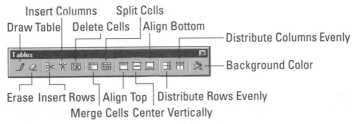

Figure 7-2: The new Tables toolbar

For now, the important tool is the draw table tool. Appropriately named, this tool lets you create a table by simply drawing its structure in your page. To create a table using the draw table tool:

1. Select the draw table tool from the Tables toolbar, or if the toolbar isn't visible, select Table ⇨ Draw Table. The cursor changes to a pencil, and the Tables toolbar is open.

2. Click and drag the cursor to define the overall rectangular shape of the table you want to create. When the table is the size you want, release the mouse button.

3. Add rows and columns to your table by simply drawing them in (see Figure 7-3).

4. When you are done creating your table, click the draw table tool in the toolbar again to deselect it. The cursor returns to normal.

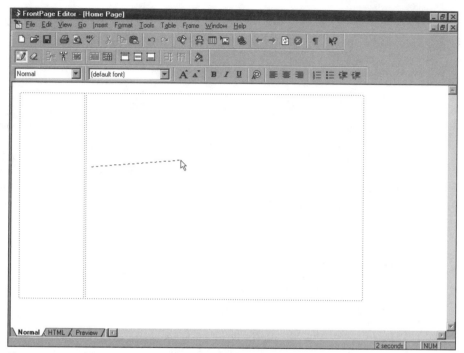

Figure 7-3: Adding cells using the draw table tool

A quick table tip

If you are not fussy about the table properties, or if you are willing to edit them later, you can create a table more quickly via the Table icon on the toolbar. Click this button and a grid palette pops down beneath it (as shown here).

Select the cells in the grid that correspond to the number of rows and columns you want in your table. If you want a table that is larger than the 4 × 5 grid that appears by default, just keep dragging the mouse down and over. The table grid grows as you do so. This table is created with the properties that were last in effect.

Placing content in a table

Adding content (text, graphics, form fields, what have you) is exactly the same as adding it anywhere else on a page: Place the cursor where you want to add the content and type or insert it. Voilà.

Importing a spreadsheet table

Suppose you already have a carefully formatted spreadsheet full of data that you'd like to include in a Web page. Wouldn't it be nice if you could just copy and paste the table into FrontPage and have it automatically convert to HTML? Well, sometimes wishes do come true. Figure 7-4 shows a spreadsheet created in Microsoft Excel.

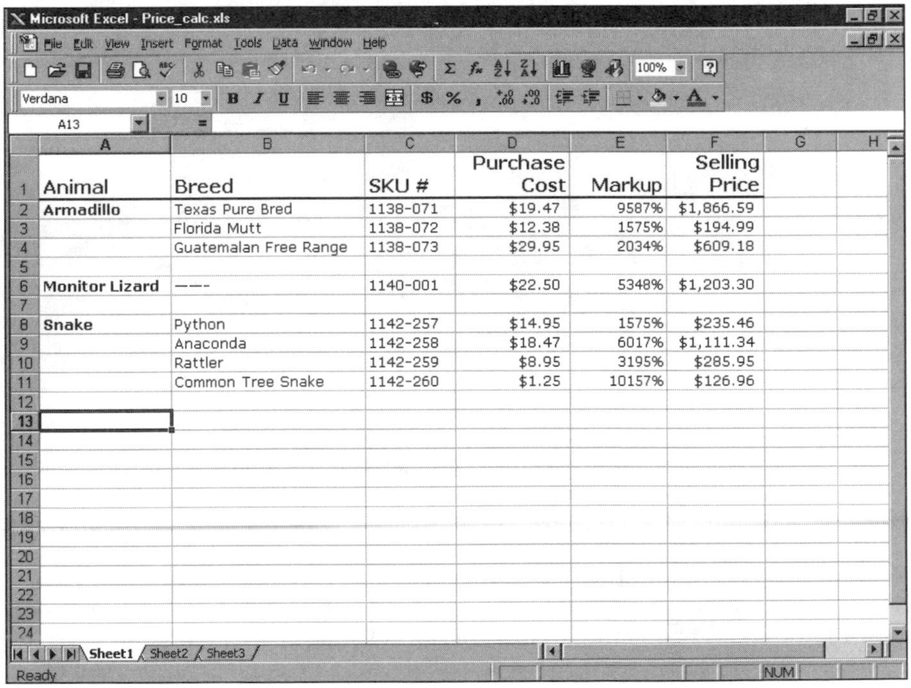

Figure 7-4: A carefully formatted table in Excel. If only it were in HTML.

To create the FrontPage version:

1. Start Excel and load a spreadsheet. The spreadsheet shown in this example is available on the CD that came with this book. You can find the file, `Price_ calc.xls`, in the `Contents/ch07` subdirectory of the CD.

2. Highlight the cells you want to include in your page and copy the selection by selecting Edit ⇨ Copy or using the Ctrl-key shortcut, Ctrl+C.

3. Place the cursor where you want the table to be placed and select Edit ⇨ Paste or use the Ctrl-key shortcut, Ctrl+V, to paste the table into FrontPage. The untouched results are shown in Figure 7-5.

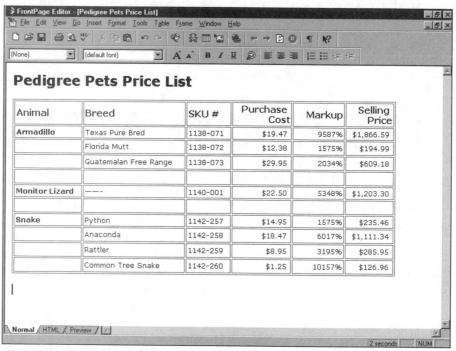

Figure 7-5: Your spreadsheet transformed into HTML!

Not bad for instant HTML! Granted this is a relatively simple table. For more complex tables, count on some manual labor to clean it up. Even this table could use some cleaning up—note that all of the cells between the first and last are copied, even if you only selected some of them to be copied. In the example spreadsheet, it's unlikely that Pedigree Pets would want to advertise their purchase price and markup, so these columns would have to be removed as outlined later in this chapter, under "Adjusting Table Structure."

This example also demonstrates another interesting aspect of tables: If some cells are empty and the table has a border (which an imported table does automatically), then there is no border around those cells. Figure 7-6 demonstrates this. Note that this doesn't happen when you create a table from scratch—FrontPage inserts a special HTML code (called a nonbreaking space) to effectively fill the space until you decide to add text or a graphic of your own.

Tip When you copy a spreadsheet that includes calculation cells, Excel replaces the calculation with its value before completing the copy. If you need to retain the calculation, you need to rewrite the calculation using one of the client-side scripting languages discussed in Chapter 15.

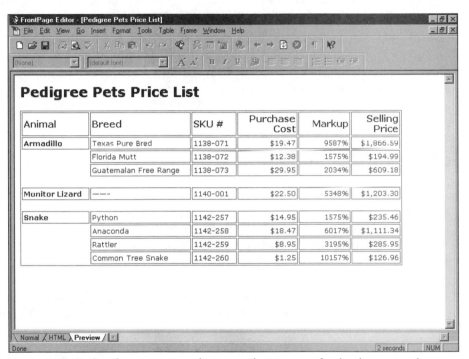

Figure 7-6: Notice the open space between the groups of animals as seen in Preview mode.

Table captions

A *caption* is a short phrase that is associated with a table. When you select the Insert Caption option, Editor automatically places it above the table. If you would prefer that the caption be under the table, select the table caption and select Table ▷ Caption Properties to display the dialog box. This dialog box allows you to designate the location for the caption, either at the top or the bottom of the table.

Although you can format caption text normally, exactly how it displays (how far away from the table it is, how it's aligned to the table, and so on) is up to the browser. For this reason I suggest that you ignore captions.

Editing Table Properties

As shown in the previous section, tables can have borders around the cells, or not. This is only the most basic of the formatting options available. You have (almost) complete control over how text aligns within cells, what color the cells are, and how much space there is between the cells. The next two sections, "Setting overall table properties" and "Setting Individual Cell Properties," detail these options and many others.

Many of the options detailed in the upcoming sections can be performed on individual cells, columns or rows of cells, or the entire table (the exception being overall table properties, which only apply to the table as a whole). To make selecting the cells you want to work with easier, use the options in the Table menu: Select Cell, Select Row, Select Column, and Select Table.

Setting overall table properties

The Table Properties dialog box, shown in Figure 7-7, provides quick access to all of the formatting options available for the table as a whole. To open this dialog box, place the cursor within the table and then select Table ⇨ Table Properties or right-click within the table and select Table Properties from the pop-up menu. The following sections detail each portion of this dialog box.

Layout

This section of the Table Properties dialog box provides settings governing how other text interacts with the table and how individual cells are spaced within the table. The options in this area are:

✦ **Alignment**—This setting determines where the table is located. Left places the table against the left margin, Right places it against the right margin, and Center aligns the table between the left and right margins. The default option typically places the table against the left margin, but this placement is determined by the browser.

✦ **Float**—This option lets you wrap text next to the table, just as you can wrap it next to an image.

✦ **Border Size**—This setting specifies the width of the outline placed around the table. A setting of 0 means that no border is displayed in a browser, though you can still see the dashed border when editing the page. Note that the thickness only applies to the outside border—when the border is active, only a thin line is placed between cells.

✦ **Cell Padding**—This option specifies the space, in pixels, between the contents of a cell and the border around it. This option may be set whether or not the border is visible (whether its size is greater than 0 or not—see Figure 7-8).

✦ **Cell Spacing**—This setting determines the spacing between individual cells.

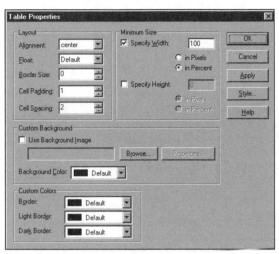

Figure 7-7: The Table Properties dialog box

Cell padding
Cell spacing

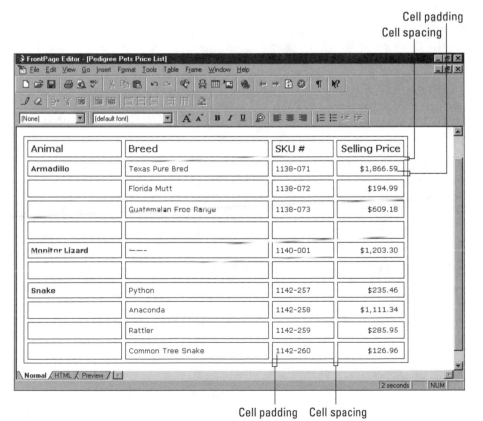

Cell padding   Cell spacing

Figure 7-8: Cell spacing and padding specify how cells and their contents interact.

Minimum size

This area allows you to specify the overall height and width of a table. The height and width can be set either in pixels or as a percentage of the screen width. If the width check box is not checked, then the table will typically be 100 percent of the browser window width. If the height check box is not checked, then the table will be whatever minimum height is required to display everything in your cells.

There is a very important word to notice in the name of this area: "minimum." If you set a table to be 50 percent of the height of the browser window, but the window is resized so that 50 percent of the height would not allow all of the contents to be displayed, the table will be larger than this setting.

Custom background

This area gives you the option of adding a background color or image to your entire table, much as you can add a background to an entire page. By default, the table is transparent, so that whatever background you have on your page shows through. Background images tile the same way that they do for entire pages.

Custom colors

In addition to setting the color of the table as a whole, you can also set the color for the table's border. There are three settings: Border, Light Border, and Dark Border. The Border setting lets you set a single color for the entire border.

The Light Border and Dark Border settings allow you to specify colors for the top-and-left and bottom-and-right edges of the border respectively. This can help you give your table a 3-D look. Setting either of these overrides the Border setting for that area.

If you set Light Border to a dark color and Dark Border to a light color, your table will look as though it's indented into your page rather than sticking out from it.

Note that if you leave all of these settings on Default, most browsers will display your table as though Light Border is set to silver and Dark Border is set to gray.

Setting individual cell properties

The Cell Properties dialog box, shown in Figure 7-9, provides quick access to all of the formatting options available for individual cells within the table. To open this dialog box, place the cursor within the cell you want to edit and then select Table ⇨ Cell Properties or right-click within the cell and select Cell Properties from the pop-up menu. The following sections detail each portion of this dialog box.

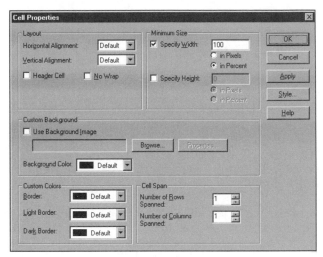

Figure 7-9: The Cell Properties dialog box

Tip   If you want to format all of the cells within the table, do not use the Table⇨Select Table command as this causes the Cell Properties option to become inactive.

Layout

This section determines how text and graphics are placed within the cell. The four settings in this area are:

✦ **Horizontal Alignment**—This determines where the text or graphic is placed horizontally within the cell. The options are Default, Left, Right, and Center. Typically browsers display the default setting as left. You can also perform this alignment using the Align Left, Center, and Align Right icons on the toolbar.

✦ **Vertical Alignment**—This determines where the text or graphic is placed vertically within the cell. The options are Default, Top, Middle, Baseline, and Bottom. Baseline makes the bottoms of all letters in the row line up, no matter what the size. In general, most browsers display the default setting as Middle. You can also perform these alignments (with the exception of Default) using the Align Top, Center Vertically, and Align Bottom icons on the Table toolbar.

✦ **Header Cell**—This typically makes the text within the cell bold, though how it is actually displayed depends on the browser being used. I recommend that you don't bother using this setting.

✦ **No Wrap**—This forces text to remain on one line. Note that this setting overrides the minimum size settings for other columns. Minimum size is discussed in the next section.

Minimum Size

As with the overall table size, this area sets the *minimum* width and height for the cell. Note that the width setting applies to all cells in a particular column, and the height applies to all cells in a row.

Some browsers cannot display tables if the height and width settings do not make mathematical sense. For instance, if the overall width of the table is 500 pixels and the width of the individual columns (*plus* the cell padding and cell spacing for each column) is 510, then the browser may display the table erratically or even crash. A good rule of thumb is: If you specify your table width or height in pixels, set the columns and rows in pixels as well. Another rule of thumb: Be very careful when setting the heights and widths in tables.

To quickly make a number of columns the same width, highlight cells in two or more columns and select Table⇨Distribute Columns Evenly or click the Distribute Columns Evenly icon in the Table toolbar. To quickly make a number of rows the same height, highlight two or more rows and select Table⇨Distribute Rows Evenly or click the Distribute Rows Evenly icon in the Table toolbar.

Custom background

As with the table and page, individual cells can have background images or colors. If you select more than one cell and apply a tiling background image, the image will tile seamlessly between the cells.

Custom colors

The three options in this section allow you to set the colors for the border of an individual cell, rather than the table as a whole. Note that Light Border refers to the bottom and right edges of the cell and Dark Border refers to the top and left edges of the cell—this is the opposite of their positions for the table's outline. If the table border is set to 0 width, then these settings have no effect.

Cell span

Spanning cells are ones that take the space of two or more cells. As shown in Figure 7-10, a spanning cell can make a table more visually interesting and easier to read.

The tools in FrontPage 98's new Table toolbar make using the Cell Properties dialog box to deal with cell and row spanning a thing of the past. I would suggest that you ignore these settings and use the techniques outlined in the next section, "Adjusting Table Structure."

Spanning cells   Spanning cells

Figure 7-10: Spanning cells help add style to a table.

Adjusting Table Structure

With the inclusion of the Table toolbar in FrontPage 98, working with tables is almost a snap. While the toolbar doesn't provide the complete control afforded by using the menu options, it does make handling tables faster and more intuitive. This can greatly increase your productivity and creativity—especially when you use your tables for page layout as explained in the next section.

Inserting rows, columns, and cells

To insert a row using the toolbar, highlight the row *below* where you'd like to add the new row and click the Insert Rows icon. A new row appears. Each cell of the new row has settings identical to the one below it (the one you highlighted).

To insert a column using the toolbar, highlight the column to the *right* of where you'd like to add the new column and click the Insert Column icon. A new column appears. Each cell of the new column has settings identical to the one to its right.

To insert a row or column using the menu options, select Table⇨Insert Rows or Columns. The Insert Rows or Columns dialog box opens, as shown in Figure 7-11, which allows you to add additional rows and/or columns to the table. New rows or columns can be inserted above or below the selected row, and left or right of a selected column. You can insert one or many rows or columns at one time.

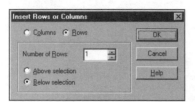

Figure 7-11: The Insert Rows or Columns dialog box

If the row or column you selected includes spanning cells, the structure of your table can get messed up, as shown in Figure 7-12. In this figure, a row was inserted above the Florida Mutt. Notice in the figure that the three cells for Guatemalan Free Range Armadillo now start all the way to the left and that a blank area has appeared at the right side of the row. To fix this problem, select the spanning cell (Armadillo), then select Table⇨Cell Properties, and increase the row spanning option to 4.

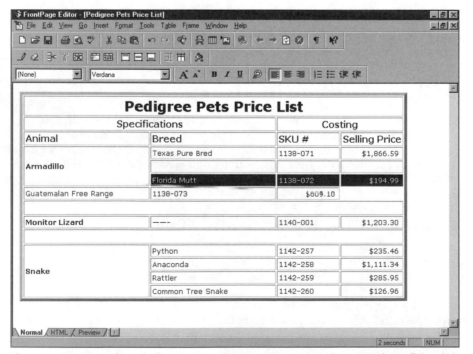

Figure 7-12: Even though the Guatemalan Free Range row is messed up, fixing it is easy.

To insert a cell, highlight the cell to the right of where you'd like the new cell and select Table⇨Insert Cell. A new cell with the original cell's properties appears.

An alternative way to create new cells is to split a single cell in two. To split a cell, simply place the cursor inside the cell (or highlight a number of cells) and select Table⇨Split Cells or click the Split Cells icon on the Table toolbar. This opens the Split Cells dialog box, shown in Figure 7-13. Select the options you want from this dialog box and press OK to split all of the highlighted cells.

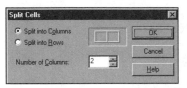

Figure 7-13: Splitting cells is better than splitting hairs.

As shown earlier in this chapter, you can also split cells using the draw table tool available on the Table toolbar. Simply select the tool and draw a vertical or horizontal line in the cell, or cells, you want to split.

Removing cells, rows, and columns

Actually, this section should be called "Reducing the number of cells, rows, and columns" since many of the options presented remove the table's cells but not the text or graphics inside of them. That title doesn't flow very well, however, so this one was used instead.

That said, the first thing to be discussed is how to delete a row or a column. To do this, select the row or column to be deleted and select Table⇨Delete Cells. All of the highlighted cells are removed.

Merging cells is a nondestructive alternative to deleting cells. When this option is used, all of the text or graphics from the merged cells is placed within the new cell. To merge cells, highlight the cells you want merged and then select Table⇨Merge Cells or click the Merge Cells icon on the Table toolbar.

Using Tables for Page Layout

In addition to organizing tabular information, tables can be used to provide more layout control over the HTML page. These days almost every major Web page is designed using tables. Creating columns, aligning text and graphics, and creating an almost magazine-like appearance are all possible with tables.

Look at Figures 7-14 and 7-15 and notice how Microsoft's designers were able to create a very intricate-looking page using fairly simple table techniques. One of the nice things about this Web is that it was produced using FrontPage 98 — if they can make a great-looking site, so can you. You're only limited by your imagination.

Notice that the top navigation bar and the link buttons on the left do not appear in Figure 7-14, because only this individual page was downloaded, not the entire FrontPage site, which includes the appropriate shared border definitions and component art.

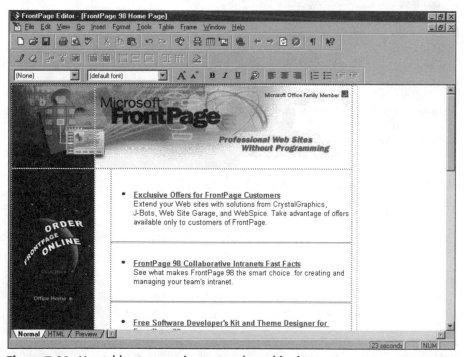

Figure 7-14: Use tables to organize text and graphics in a page.

Taking the Next Step

Tables provide excellent control for almost any aspect of page layout and design — you can use tables to create intricate columns and borders and even to line up tabular data, if you're so inclined. With the completion of this chapter, you have learned all of the basic tools for creating Web pages. Starting in Chapter 8, "Working with Frames," you begin to learn more advanced techniques for laying out your Web and organizing your pages.

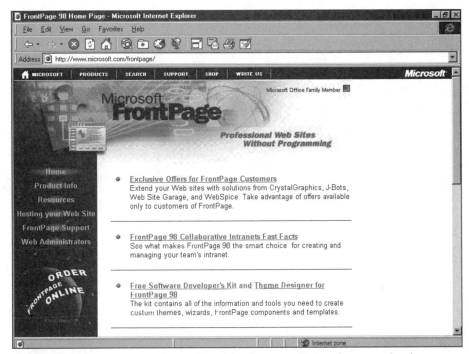

Figure 7-15: In Internet Explorer, the table elements fit together seamlessly.

✦   ✦   ✦

Working with Frames

An HTML frame set is an HTML entity that enables multiple subwindows to coexist within the space of a single browser window. In effect what happens is that multiple HTML pages are displayed simultaneously, each in a fixed portion of the main window. In practice, frames are used primarily as a way to present immovable interface elements. Using frames, one can select additional information from the Web site without losing the navigation mechanism. Without frames, all HTML elements, including graphics, hyperlink lists, and other such elements, scroll with the page.

FrontPage 98 now includes full frame editing capabilities. Gone are the bad old days of the Frames Wizard and editing individual pages and having to preview a frame set in your browser to see if it looks even remotely like what you intended. Now you can create and edit frame sets as easily as you work with "normal" pages.

Creating a Frame Set

A frames environment consists of two or more HTML pages displayed in separate subwindows (that is, frames) within a single window of a Web browser. The set of Web pages displayed in this fashion is called a *frame set.* In Chapter 9, "HTML Editing Techniques," we look at ways to customize your frames if you are willing to roll up your sleeves and do some simple HTML editing.

Those infuriating frames!

For some reason, some people find frames infuriating. There are entire Web sites devoted to spleen venting on the topic of how frames suck. Frankly, this seems like an overreaction. Granted, there are better and worse ways to implement frames, and frames can be annoying if they are overused or forced on people without a choice, but these problems are avoidable.

Still it is worth knowing that a few people seem to have a very strong emotional response to frames. Be forewarned and see the additional sidebar on this subject toward the end of the chapter.

Creating a new frame set

If you're familiar with FrontPage 97, you'll really like this new approach to creating frame sets. Now all you need to do to create a frame set is:

1. Start Editor.

2. Select File ⇨ New or press Ctrl+N. The New dialog box opens. (Do not press the New button in the toolbar, as this automatically creates a new blank page, not a frame set).

3. Click the Frames tab to display the available predesigned frame sets (see Figure 8-1). Note that these are just a starting point; you can make changes to any of the frame sets once you have created the new page.

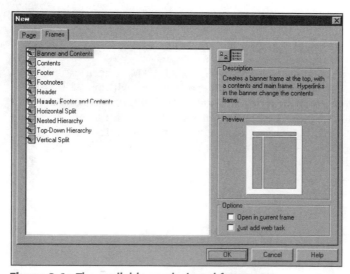

Figure 8-1: The available predesigned frame sets

4. Select one of the frame sets from the list at the left, noting the layout as shown in the right-hand Preview window. For help in making your decision, read the description of the frame set in the Description area. The default way that links work within the frame set is noted in this description—if you are unfamiliar with the way links work in a frame set, see the section "Creating Hyperlinks in Frame Sets" later in this chapter.

5. If you are already editing a page in a frame set, you can check the Open in Current Frame check box to have the new frame set loaded as a page, replacing the currently selected page.

6. Press OK to close the dialog box and open your new frame set. A typical frame set is shown in Figure 8-2. Notice the two new tabs at the bottom of the page, No Frames and Frames Page HTML—these tabs allow you to view attributes only available in frames pages. These tabs are explained in the "Editing Frame Set Properties" section later in this chapter.

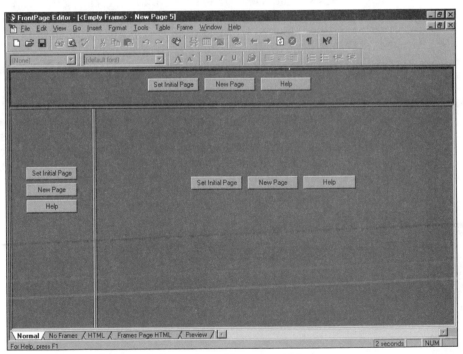

Figure 8-2: A typical new frame set awaiting your design prowess

The new frame set looks a little empty, doesn't it? Well, not for long. The next section, "Adding pages to a new frame set," shows you how to build or include pages in your set.

Adding pages to a new frame set

As you can see in Figure 8-2, each frame area in a new frame set contains three buttons: Set Initial Page, New Page, and Help. You will use these buttons to include an existing page or create a new page in the current frame (or get help about either option).

The current frame is the one indicated by the dark blue border running around it. You can change the current frame by clicking in another frame to select it.

✦ To create a new page to be displayed in a frame, click the New Page button. A clean, blank page appears. If you'd rather include a frame set in a frame (called a nested frame), select the frame and then repeat the steps involved in the last section, "Creating a new frame set," making sure to check the Open in Current Frame check box mentioned in step 5.

Tip

Note that FrontPage does not accurately display nested frames in Editor but instead shows a new View Frames Page button. Pressing this button changes Editor's view to display the frame set that's in the current frame. If you are editing a nested frame set, change the size of the Editor window to more accurately reflect the size of the frame in which the set is displayed in the main frame set. This will help you picture how the frames will look in a browser. Also, Preview mode does display nested frames properly.

✦ To include an existing page in a frame, press the Set Initial Page button. Use the Create Hyperlink dialog box (shown in Figure 8-3) to pick the page that will be displayed in this frame. You can use any of the standard methods used for opening a page described in Chapter 2, "Working with FrontPage Editor." Don't worry that this dialog box is called "Create Hyperlink," you did press the correct button and when you've made your selection, the page is displayed in the frame.

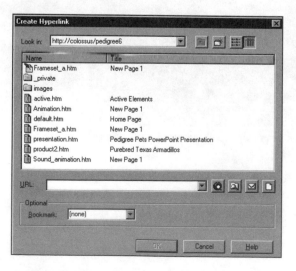

Figure 8-3: Use the oddly named Create Hyperlink dialog box to pick a page to be displayed in the current frame.

Once you have created or added pages to your frame set, you can edit them as you would any normal page. Notice that when you select a different frame to edit, the dark blue border shifts to that frame and its filename appears in the FrontPage title bar.

Changing frame contents

The pages that you initially insert in your frame set are only the first pages to be displayed. The links in each frame can modify the contents of the frame, or any other frame. To learn more about the way that links operate in a frame set, see the section "Creating Hyperlinks in Frame Sets" later in this chapter.

To change the page that is initially displayed in a frame, select Frame ➪ Edit Initial Page. The (still oddly named) Edit Hyperlink dialog box opens. Select the page you want to display in the current frame and press OK.

Editing Frame Set Properties

Chances are, the frame set that you create using the New dialog box won't exactly fit your needs. Either the frames won't be exactly the right size, or the space around the frame documents won't be quite right, or you will want to get rid of those pesky borders between each frame. All of these attributes, and more, are available for you to edit.

Removing frame borders

The borders between frames are not required. You can turn them off by selecting Frame ➪ Frames Page Properties. The Page Properties dialog box opens and displays the Frame tab. This tab has only two options: the Frame Spacing text box and the Show Borders check box. To turn off the borders, uncheck the Show Borders check box.

Notice that the Frame Spacing value drops to 0 when you uncheck this box. The Frame Spacing value determines the width of the frame borders. If you give this property a value (other than 0) with borders turned off, then blank space is displayed between the frames of the frame set. Typically you will want to leave Frame Spacing as 0 when borders are turned off and 2 when they are turned on.

Adjusting individual frame properties

You can also change the size of frames numerically using the Frame Properties dialog box shown in Figure 8-4. This dialog box (accessed by selecting Frame ➪ Frame Properties or right-clicking within the frame and selecting Frame Properties from the pop-up menu) also contains other options relating to the frame.

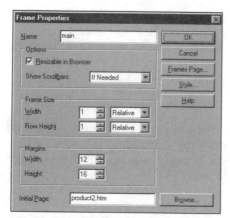

Figure 8-4: Control many frame properties in this dialog box.

The following options are available:

✦ **Name**—This is the name given to the frame. The name is important because it is used to indicate the "target" for any hyperlink that may be intended for this frame.

✦ **Resizable in Browser**—This is used to allow users to resize the frame windows by dragging the divider bars. By default all frames are resizable.

✦ **Show Scrollbars**—Choices are Always, which forces a scroll bar to be always present; Never, which forces no scrolling bar; and If Needed, which includes a scroll bar if necessary but does not show one if it is not. If Needed is the default option.

✦ **Frame Size Width and Row Height**—These two options determine the size of the frame. As with tables (discussed in Chapter 7) changing the width or height of a frame will affect other frames in the same row or column. Select units from the right-hand list box and set the size in the left-hand text box. The units available for frame sizing are:

  • **Percent**—This sets the frame's size as a percentage of the browser screen height or width.

  • **Pixels**—This sets the frame's size as a specific number of pixels.

  • **Relative**—This option sets the frame's size relative to the setting for other frames in the row or column, as long as they are using one of the other options. When using this option, set the amount in the left-hand text box to 1. By default, the leftmost frame in a row and the topmost frame in a column are set in pixels, whereas the other frames are set to relative.

You can also change the frame size "manually". Place the cursor over the frame border (or, on the area where the frame border would be if you have turned them off). When the cursor changes to a two-headed arrow, drag the cursor to the new size.

✦ **Margin Width**—This adjusts the marginal space between vertical frame dividers and any content in the frame.

✦ **Margin Height**—This adjusts the marginal space between horizontal frame dividers and any content in the frame.

✦ **Initial Page**—This is the filename of the frame. Changing this changes the file that is initially loaded into the frame set. You can also change the initial page by selecting Frame ⇨ Set Initial Page and picking the page from the Edit Hyperlink dialog box.

Adding and deleting frames

If you need to add an additional frame to a frame set, you will "split" an existing frame into two new frames. One of these two frames will contain the contents of the original frame, while the other will display the Set Initial Page, New Page, and Help buttons shown when the frame set was originally created. There are two ways to split a frame:

✦ Select the frame you want to split and select Frame ⇨ Split Frame to open the Split Frame dialog box. Select either the Split into Columns or Split into Rows radio button and press the OK button.

✦ Select the frame you want to split and place the cursor over any border (including the four borders around the Editor window) so that the cursor changes to a two-headed arrow and control-drag to create the new frame.

If you want to create a new frame the full height or width of the browser window, but you don't have an existing frame to split in this way, you can still do it if you follow this procedure. Split any existing frame using the Frame ⇨ Split Frame command, and then immediately select Edit ⇨ Undo. The dark blue border denoting which frame is selected now goes around the entire frame set. Now split the entire frame set using one of the two methods just described. (Generally, though, using the menu command is easier although you are limited to placing the new frame on the right or bottom of the page.)

The two extra view tabs

Earlier in this chapter I mentioned that there are two additional view tabs at the bottom of the Editor screen. These new tabs, No Frames and Frames Page HTML, provide additional control over your frame set.

The No Frames tab displays the contents of the page shown on browsers that do not support frames. By default, this page contains only the not-so-helpful message "This page uses frames, but your browser doesn't support them" as shown in Figure 8-5.

You will rarely leave this message as is, but rather you will use this page as the beginning of a no-frames version of the same information displayed in the frame set pages. The no-frames page can be edited exactly like any other page—it is a good idea to keep in mind, though, that browsers that are unable to display frames generally can't handle other "high-tech" Web items such as tables, Java scripts, shared borders, and ActiveX controls, so you will want to avoid or limit their use. An easy way to fill the no-frames page is to copy the contents of your main frame and paste it into the no-frames page.

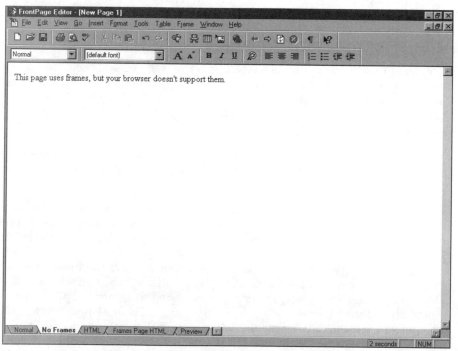

Figure 8-5: The no-frames page is displayed on browsers that don't understand frames.

The Frames Page HTML tab displays the HTML codes that define your frame set (see Figure 8-6). Notice that the no-frames page codes are also contained here, between the tags `<noframes>` and `</noframes>`—in this case, the no-frames page only has the default message.

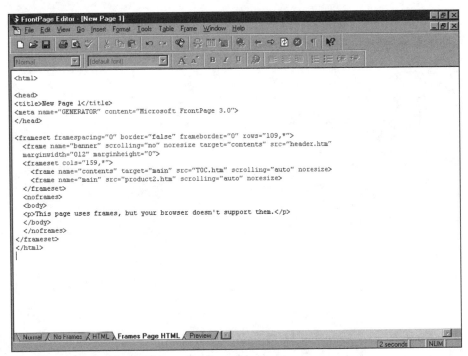

Figure 8-6: The typical HTML codes for a frame set

Creating Hyperlinks in Frame Sets

Creating hyperlinks within a frame set poses some new challenges. You need to be able to indicate not only what page to link to but what frame the page should appear in.

How it works

By default, each FrontPage sets up each link in a frame to automatically open a new page in a different frame. For example, in the frame set banner and contents (see Figure 8-7), clicking a link in the banner frame changes the page displayed in the contents frame, while clicking a link in the contents frame changes the page shown in the main frame. Clicking a link in the main frame, however, only changes the contents of the main frame.

Banner frame

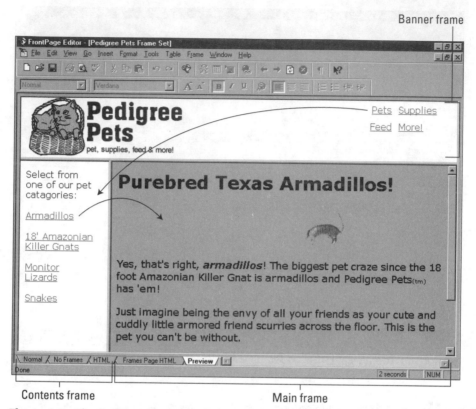

Contents frame

Main frame

Figure 8-7: The link/frame relationship in a typical frame set

Note

This behavior calls attention to the fact that you do not need to create a frame set for every Web page. In fact, that is the whole idea behind frames. You create the frame set once, and then you only change the content frame as needed.

Hitting the target

How does the frame set know to behave this way? An HTML code located in the frames page sets the default way for links to work. Looking back to Figure 8-6, notice that the tags defining the banner and contents frames (`<frame name="banner"` ... and `<frame name="contents"` ... respectively) each contain the code `target="..."`. The name inside the quotation marks indicates the frame that should be opened when you click a link. The target information is also placed in each page's HTML code—click the HTML tab and notice the tag that reads `<base target="...">` near the top of the banner and contents frames.

FrontPage automatically adds the base target tag to your pages, whether you created them from scratch when you made the frame set or you set them as the initial pages later on.

Changing the default target

Changing the default target for a particular frame is a two-step procedure. You must change the default target for both the page itself *and* the frame.

To change the default target for a page:

1. Open the frame set in Editor.
2. Select any link in the frame whose default target you want to change.
3. Select Insert ⇨ Hyperlink or click the Create or Edit Hyperlink button on the toolbar to open the Edit Hyperlink dialog box.
4. Click the Change Target Frame icon (the small pencil icon next to the Target Frame text box) to open the Target Frame dialog box shown in Figure 8-8.

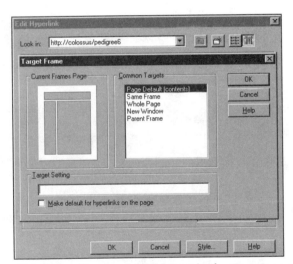

Figure 8-8: Set the default target in the Target Frame dialog box.

5. Select the new target frame either by clicking one of the frames in the left-hand Current Frames Page area or by selecting one of the options in the Common Targets list. The common targets are described in the later section called, appropriately enough, "Common targets."
6. Check the Make Default for Hyperlinks on the Page check box.
7. Click OK in both the Target Frame and Edit Hyperlink dialog boxes to return to Editor.
8. Select the Frames Page HTML tab.

9. Highlight and delete the text that reads `target="..."` in the frame you are working with (the text between the quotation marks should be the old default target frame's name).

10. Save your frame set. You will notice that some extra time is taken to save—this is FrontPage automatically changing the HTML code in the frames page.

11. Switch to another view and then switch back to the Frames Page HTML view. Notice that `target="..."` has been inserted back in the code, only now the target's name matches the name you selected in step 5.

Caution

If you change the default target for a frame, make sure you really want to do it. FrontPage does not automatically update all of the pages that are opened in a particular frame, so you must do this manually on a page-by-page basis. For a large site, this can be quite time consuming.

Avoiding frames hate mail

As we mentioned earlier, not everyone appreciates the virtues of frames. People can become annoyed if they are not capable of viewing frames, if the frames are not implemented properly, or if the use of frames makes navigating your Web more difficult than it would have been without the frames. Even if you create a perfect implementation of frames, however, a few people may gripe, just because they don't like frames. Here are some of the ways you can reduce complaints from the non–frames enthusiasts among us:

✦ Always have a no-frames alternative built into each page. Having a no-frames option deals with those people whose browsers simply do not handle frames.

✦ Some people have frames-capable browsers, but they would rather not use frames. Consider giving users the option—at least from the home page and potentially from other appropriate locations as well—to choose between a frames version and a no-frames version.

✦ Do not overdo the number of frames. The more you break up the main window into little frames, the more cluttered your interface becomes. Reserve as much space as possible for the main content window of your frame set.

✦ Be sure you have a better reason for using frames than the desire to show you know how. You should be able to explain why you have chosen to use frames rather than a simpler approach. If nothing else, it helps you write snappy answers to your hate mail.

✦ Avoid multiple frame sets in a single Web. The whole point of using a frame set is to create a consistent interface. If you are using multiple frame sets, you are defeating the purpose.

✦ Be sure that all hyperlinks target the correct frame windows. Avoid any circumstances that might result in a frame set document being opened in a frame window.

Specifying the target for individual links

You can also override the frame's default target for individual links. This is useful if you are making a link to an external page.

To specify the target frame for a single link:

1. Open the frame set in Editor.

2. Select the link whose target you want to change.

3. Select Insert ⇨ Hyperlink or click the Create or Edit Hyperlink button on the toolbar to open the Edit Hyperlink dialog box.

4. Click the Change Target Frame icon to open the Target Frame dialog box.

5. Select the new target frame either by clicking one of the frames in the left-hand Current Frames Page area or by selecting one of the options in the Common Targets list.

6. Click OK in both the Target Frame and Edit Hyperlink dialog boxes to return to Editor.

Common targets

In addition to the frames within the current frame set, five common targets also provide added flexibility:

✦ **Page Default**—This makes the linked page open in the default frame for the page.

✦ **Same Frame**—This automatically opens the linked page in the same frame as the link.

✦ **Whole Page**—This clears the current frame set from the browser and opens the linked page in the full browser window. This is the best option to use when you are linking to an external page.

✦ **New Window**—This option starts another instance of your visitor's browser and opens the linked page in it.

✦ **Parent Frame**—If the link is within a nested frame, then this option opens the linked page in the frame containing the subframe set. If the link is not in a nested frame, then this link will behave just like the Whole Page option.

Working with Shared Borders

Chapter 3 introduced shared borders and indicated that they were, for the most part, a way to quickly add a couple of navigation features to your Web. They are far more than that—in a way, shared borders can be thought of as a proprietary Microsoft style of frames. Although the default shared borders contain only navigation bars (see Figure 8-9), you have as much control over the contents of the shared borders as you do of any other Web page. This section provides complete details on adding, and updating, shared borders in your Web.

Shared border

Shared border

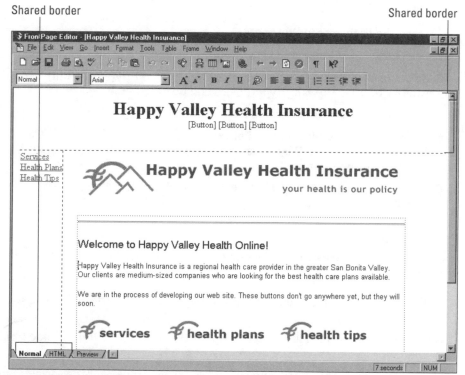

Figure 8-9: These shared borders provide navigation bars and a basic banner.

Note

Unfortunately, you can only have one design of shared borders per Web. Because of this limitation, frequently frames are a better alternative than shared borders. If you want to use the navigation bars without shared borders, see the section "Navigation bars" later in this chapter.

Adding shared borders

As you saw in Chapter 3, adding shared borders can be a two-step process: Organize your Web using Navigation view in Explorer and then add shared borders. Strictly speaking, organizing your Web is only necessary if you are going to be using the automatic navigation bars. To recap the method for adding shared borders to your Web:

1. Open your Web (or create a new one) in Explorer.

2. Switch to Navigation view and organize your site (see Figure 8-10). This procedure is discussed in detail in Chapter 3.

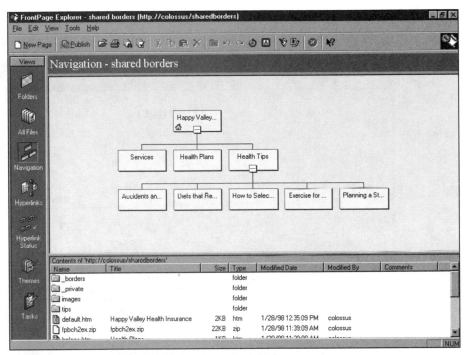

Figure 8-10: The Navigation view of a typical Web

3. Select Tools ➪ Shared Borders to open the Shared Borders dialog box shown in Figure 8-11.

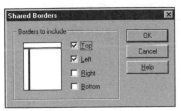

Figure 8-11: The Shared Borders dialog box

4. Select which borders you want included in your Web. Note that the Top and Left borders automatically include navigation bars, whereas the Right and Bottom borders are empty.

5. Click OK to close the dialog box. In Explorer, your Web looks no different, but when you open a page, the new shared borders are now displayed. Figure 8-12 shows a blank page with all four shared borders active.

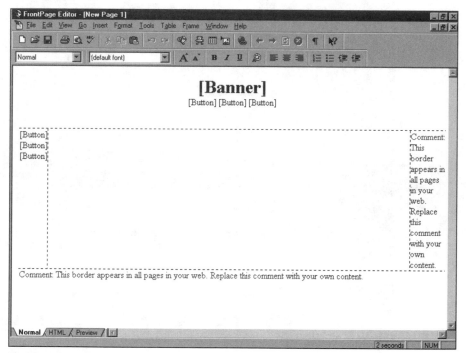

Figure 8-12: The four default shared borders

Changing the shared borders' content

As you can see in Figure 8-12, the right and bottom shared borders contain comments that you are urged to replace with text (or a graphic) of your own choosing. There are a couple of ways to do this.

Edit the shared borders in place

Open a page incorporating shared borders in Editor and edit the shared border portion(s) as you normally would. When you save the page, you are prompted to save the changes made to the shared borders.

This is an excellent option if you don't plan on doing very much editing to the borders. By editing in place, you can see exactly how the borders will appear. Unfortunately, you have no control over the HTML code that makes up the shared borders, so it makes them difficult to fully "tweak."

Edit the shared borders individually

You can also open the pages that make up the shared borders in Editor and edit them as you would any other page. Before you can edit these pages, however, you have to give Editor access to them (the border pages are located in a hidden folder in your Web).

To allow direct access to your shared border pages:

1. Open your Web in Explorer.

2. Select Tools ➪ Web Settings to open the FrontPage Web Settings dialog box.

3. Select the Advanced tab and check the Show Documents in Hidden Directories check box.

4. Click OK to close the dialog box. A new dialog box opens asking if you want to refresh the view of your Web. Click Yes, and you'll notice that a new folder, _borders, appears. The shared border pages are included in this folder. Each file is named for the border it represents.

You can now open and edit these pages in Editor. One downside to editing shared border pages in Editor, however, is that unlike with frames you have no direct control over the size of your borders, so it is difficult to gauge whether your edits will look good in your Web's pages.

Shared borders and individual pages

You have two alternatives if you want to incorporate shared borders in only some of your Web's pages: either have shared borders for all of your pages and turn them off for specific pages, or only turn on shared borders for specific pages.

To turn shared borders on or off in an individual page:

1. Open the page in Editor.

2. Select Tools ➪ Shared Borders to open the Page Borders dialog box. This is essentially the same as the Shared Borders dialog box, except for the addition of the Use Web Default and Set for This Page Only radio buttons.

3. Check the Set for This Page Only radio button. The four shared border check boxes cease to be grayed and become active.

4. Turn on or off specific borders for this page by checking or unchecking the appropriate check box.

5. Click OK to close the dialog box and apply your changes.

Navigation bars

Navigation bars provide a quick method for creating links within your Web, provided that you have organized the Web using Navigation view. Navigation bars are not restricted to use within shared borders; you can add them anyplace within a page.

To add a navigation bar:

1. In Editor, open the page in which you want to add navigation bars.

2. Select Insert ➪ Navigation bar. The Navigation Bar Properties dialog box opens (see Figure 8-13).

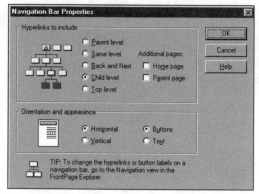

Figure 8-13: Add a navigation bar or edit its properties in this dialog box.

3. Set the options for the navigation bar and click OK. The options are detailed next.

You have a number of options available when creating a navigation bar.

In the Hyperlinks to Include section, choose from:

✦ **Parent Level**—This provides links to all pages in the level above the current page.

✦ **Same Level**—This provides links to all pages in the same level as the current page.

✦ **Back and Next**—This creates links to the pages in the current level on either side of the current page.

✦ **Child Level**—This option adds links to all pages in the level below the current page.

✦ **Top Level**—This provides links to all pages at the top level of the Web. Typically this is the home page, though there may be other pages at this level as well.

✦ **Home Page**—This check box adds an additional button for the Web's home page.

✦ **Parent Page**—This check box adds an additional button for the page in the level above that links to the current page.

In the Orientation and Appearance section, you can choose from:

✦ **Horizontal** or **Vertical**—These options produce a row or column of buttons, respectively.

✦ **Buttons** or **Text**—If your page incorporates a theme, checking the Buttons radio button uses the theme's button image. If your page doesn't incorporate a theme, the Buttons option displays a standard text link. The Text option displays standard text links whether or not your page incorporates a theme.

Tip

If you want to include navigation bars within a frame set, organize all of the pages you want displayed in the target in the level below your contents frame page (using Navigation view in Explorer). Then add a navigation bar with the Child Level option set.

Taking the Next Step

This chapter detailed the construction and use of frame sets within a FrontPage Web. If you were familiar with FrontPage 97, you noticed how much easier and powerful these tasks are in FrontPage 98. In addition, the use of shared borders and navigation bars was covered. With the conclusion of this chapter, you can create Webs that are extremely easy to navigate and maintain. Using these techniques, you can make large-scale changes to your Web's structure without having to duplicate a lot of effort to link your pages together. The next chapter, "HTML Editing Techniques," examines the ways FrontPage enables you to edit and extend HTML directly. It also looks at some relatively simple enhancements to frames and to page layout that necessitate making changes to the HTML of your Web pages.

✦   ✦   ✦

HTML Editing Techniques

As we have seen in the first eight chapters, FrontPage makes it possible to create professional-looking Webs without having to learn or worry about HTML. However, some effects can only be achieved by directly editing the HTML code. This chapter examines the ways FrontPage enables you to edit and extend HTML directly. For those who are already familiar with HTML and would like to be able to use FrontPage in conjunction with other HTML editing tools, this chapter provides the basic information on how FrontPage deals with HTML. We also look at some relatively simple enhancements to frames and to page layout that necessitate making changes to the HTML of your Web pages.

Dealing with HTML

This chapter looks at how FrontPage deals with, and in some cases does not deal with, HTML code. If you bought FrontPage precisely because you didn't want to have to know anything about technical stuff, you may happily skip this chapter. Sooner or later, though, the time will come when you want to produce an effect on your Web page that you have seen on other Web sites but FrontPage doesn't provide a way to do. That's when you'll come back to this chapter.

This chapter is directed primarily at those who either are familiar with HTML or would like to be. This chapter does not pretend to instruct you in the use of HTML. If you would like to learn more about HTML, there are several good books on this topic, for a wide range of audiences. If you are looking for an introductory-level book, one excellent choice is *Creating Cool HTML 4 Web Pages* by Dave Taylor (published by IDG Books Worldwide).

The main questions we address in this chapter are:

✦ Can I coordinate FrontPage with the other development applications I already use?

✦ Can I edit HTML directly in order to take advantage of HTML elements not directly supported in FrontPage?

✦ Can I use FrontPage to do <name your favorite state-of-the-art HTML technique>?

✦ Can FrontPage help with compatibility and validation of HTML?

Caution   If your Web will be posted to a UNIX-based server, you have to make absolutely certain that any HTML code you add involving filenames or URLs is properly capitalized. To a UNIX computer, "`filename.htm`," "`Filename.HTM`," and "`FILENAME.HTM`" are three totally different files.

Viewing FrontPage HTML

Unlike some of its competitors, FrontPage does allow users to access and edit HTML directly. FrontPage has a fairly usable, if somewhat bare-bones, text editor built into the main Editor application.

To access the HTML for the current Web page, click the HTML tab at the bottom of the Editor screen (or the Frames Page HTML tab if you want to edit the HTML codes for a frame set). HTML is displayed with color coding to tag the various elements, attribute names, and values (see Figure 9-1).

This view in Editor performs basic text editing functions. It makes available simple cutting and pasting actions, including control-key actions such as Ctrl+A to select all, Ctrl+X to cut, Ctrl+C to copy, and Ctrl+V to paste, as well as drag and drop both internally and across windows.

In addition, the Find and Replace features are active in HTML view to help you quickly find or replace HTML code in your pages. These features work just as they do in Normal view (or your favorite word processor):

✦ To use the Find dialog box, select Edit⇨Find or press Ctrl+F, and then enter the text you're looking for in the Find What text box and press the Find Next button. The text (if it exists on your page) is now highlighted.

✦ To use the Replace dialog box, select Edit⇨Replace or press Ctrl+H, and then enter the text you want to replace in the Find What text box and the text you want to replace it with in the Replace With text box. To review each change before it's made, click the Find Next button to highlight the text you're looking for; if it should be changed, click the Replace button—Replace changes the text and then highlights the next instance of the text. To replace all instances of the text at once, click the Replace All button.

✦ Both Find and Replace support matching whole words and case via the Match Whole Word Only and Match Case check boxes, respectively.

✦ If you enter **alt** and check Match Whole Word Only, then "alternative" will not be found. Note that the whole word does not include punctuation or functions such as the equals sign—in other words, entering **Bob** will return instances of "Bob's," and entering **alt** will return instances of "alt=." This is both a blessing and a curse; it makes it important that you be very careful using Replace All.

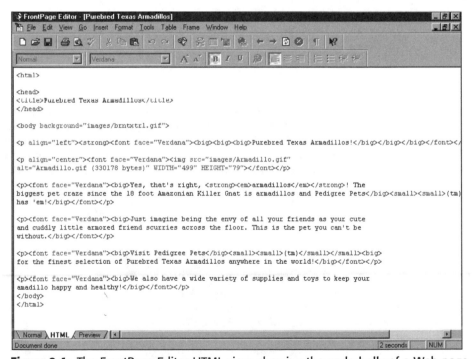

Figure 9-1: The FrontPage Editor HTML view, showing the underbelly of a Web page

In HTML view, you can enter any HTML you like, valid or otherwise. FrontPage is somewhat persnickety about some aspects of HTML, though, and may alter your code to its liking or remove it altogether (see the later section, "Dealing with FrontPage's HTML Oddities"). Occasionally it silently corrects errors. More often than not it refuses to permit perfectly valid HTML.

Using the HTML Markup Component

In addition to using the built-in HTML editor, another way to enter HTML directly into your Web page in Editor is via the HTML Markup dialog box. Select Insert ⇨ FrontPage Component, then select Insert HTML, and click OK (or click the Insert HTML button on the Advanced toolbar) to open the HTML Markup dialog box, shown in Figure 9-2.

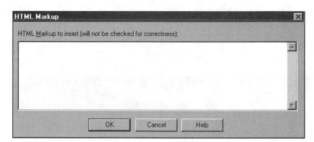

Figure 9-2: The HTML Markup component allows you to enter custom HTML.

You can type any HTML you like, valid or otherwise, into this dialog box. This feature is controlled by a FrontPage component (components—previously known as WebBots—are covered in detail in Chapter 12). Unfortunately, this markup is not parsed by Editor. Even if it is valid, it will show up with the HTML markup icon, a yellow highlighted exclamation point inside tag brackets—and then only when you view format marks. Valid HTML entered in this fashion will display correctly in the Preview tab or a standard Web browser, but if you want to add valid HTML, you are probably better off adding it via the HTML editor directly.

A couple of useful HTML tips

When you view a page using the HTML tab, all the HTML markup in a page can make it difficult to find the exact location where you want to insert a code. An easy way to insert HTML code at exactly the right location is to use the Insert HTML dialog box in Normal view, then switch to HTML view, and (using the handy Find feature, which still works in HTML mode) find bot="HTMLMarkup". Now delete the two Component commands before and after your new code. The command before your code includes the statement startspan, and the command after it includes endspan. Once these two Component commands are gone, your new code will function normally in Editor (assuming that it's a code that Editor recognizes and can display).

One useful function for the HTML Markup component is to insert comments into your HTML text. To insert a standard HTML comment tag, begin the comment with <!--, then type the comment, and end the tag with -->. A comment formulated in this manner will be less obtrusive in Editor than if you use the FrontPage Comment component. On the other hand, you will have to click the Markup component symbol to read your comment. If you import an HTML page that contains standard HTML comments, FrontPage will convert it to the HTML Markup component.

Working with Meta-Tags

Whenever you add or edit a Web page in FrontPage, you are working primarily with the body section of the page. Web pages also contain a head section, which stores information about the page that typically does not display. (One exception is the Web page title. This tag appears in the head element and is displayed in the window title bar of the current Web page.)

Meta-tags are one of the kinds of HTML tags located in the nondisplaying, head portion of an HTML Web page. Meta-tags contain useful information about the HTML page, its creation date, the application that created it, the author, and such. This information is contained in the file but invisible to anyone who views the page in his or her browser.

By default, FrontPage adds the following meta-tags to the header of every HTML document:

```
<meta name="GENERATOR" content="Microsoft FrontPage 3.0">
```

In FrontPage 97, if you attempted to remove this information, FrontPage put it right back. FrontPage 98, however, allows you to remove this tag without any consequences. There's no real reason to delete this, however, unless you are attempting to make an amazingly lean and clean page where every byte counts.

You can also add your own meta-tag information in the Custom tab of the Page Properties dialog box. One common use of the meta-tag is to create a list of keywords that text engines can use to index your Web pages. You can also include a short description of your site, which some search engines will display with your URL when a search query matches your Web site.

To add keywords and descriptions to the meta-tags on a page, select File ⇨ Page Properties. Click the Custom tab in the Page Properties dialog box. You should see options to add, modify, or remove two kinds of meta-tags: *system variables,* which are standardized variables parsed by the Web server, and *user variables,* which are user defined. We will add the keyword and description meta-tags to the System Variables section.

To add a meta-tag, click the Add button next to the System Variables window. In the dialog box that appears, type **KEYWORDS** as the Name and a comma-separated list of keywords or phrases as the Value. Use Figure 9-3 for comparison. Click OK to add the keywords attribute. Repeat the process, using **DESCRIPTION** and a short paragraph that describes your site. Click OK in the Page Properties dialog box to accept your changes. Save the page.

To check the results, select the HTML tab. You should see the new meta-tags added to the header of the HTML file, as shown in Figure 9-4.

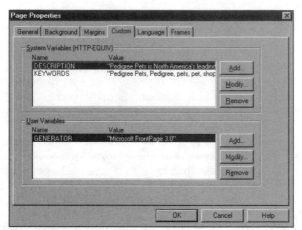

Figure 9-3: Add meta-tags in the Custom tab of the Page Properties dialog box.

New meta tags

```
<html>

<head>
<meta http-equiv="DESCRIPTION"
content="Pedigree Pets is North America's leading supplier of weird and wonderful pets. If you're looking for it,
<meta http-equiv="KEYWORDS"
content="Pedigree Pets, Pedigree, pets, pet, shop, fee, accessories, profit, armadillo, snake, python, rattler,
<meta name="GENERATOR" content="Microsoft FrontPage 3.0">
<title>Pedigree Pets Frame Set</title>
</head>

<frameset framespacing="0" border="false" rows="109,*" frameborder="0">
  <frame name="banner" scrolling="no" noresize target="contents" src="header.htm"
  marginwidth="012" marginheight="0">
  <frameset cols="159,*">
    <frame name="contents" src="TOC.htm" scrolling="auto" target="banner">
    <frame name="main" src="product2.htm" scrolling="auto">
  </frameset>
  <noframes>
  <body>
  <p>This page uses frames, but your browser doesn't support them.</p>
  </body>
  </noframes>
</frameset>
</html>
```

Figure 9-4: Your HTML page with custom meta-tags

If you want to add meta-tags to a frame set page, select Frame➪Frame Page Properties and then the Custom tab.

Opening a Web page in a different editor

If you are accustomed to using a particular text editor to edit HTML, it would be nice if you could substitute this application for the simple text editor built into FrontPage. Unfortunately, there is no direct way to do this. You could, of course, cut and paste HTML back and forth between your application and the FrontPage editor, but this is an unwieldy alternative.

One option is to use the Open With... facility in Explorer to open Web pages into your editor. In either Hyperlink or Folder view, you can select a file and select Edit ⇨ Open With... or click with the right mouse button and select Open With... from the pop-up menu to access a list of editors that FrontPage recognizes.

The trick is to get FrontPage to add your editor to this list. To do this, select Tools ⇨ Options from Explorer. Click the Configure Editors tab. Here you see the list of editors that FrontPage recognizes, each one associated with a particular file type. You might think that you would substitute your editor in place of FrontPage Editor for files of type htm/html, but this would effectively disable your ability to open pages in Editor.

In fact, it does not matter what extension you associate with your editor, since all you want to do is get it added to the list of options that FrontPage displays. One way to do this would be to make up an extension (xyz, for instance) and associate your editor with that. Alternatively, substitute your editor for Windows Notepad (unless of course your favorite editor *is* Notepad), which by default is associated with extension type (.), that is, no extension, and also with style sheets. Now when you use the Open With... function, your editor will be one of the options, and you can open the file directly.

Dealing with FrontPage's HTML Oddities

If you are accustomed to writing HTML using a text editor, you probably have a set of conventions you use to make your HTML more readable. Perhaps you use capital letters for all tags and attributes to distinguish them from the content. You probably divide the lines of HTML and perhaps indent them in order to make them easy to read. You may add comments internally to help you identify major sections of more complex pages. All of these are standard HTML developer practices, but when you use FrontPage, you will find that it has its own ideas about some of these things. This section highlights some of the idiosyncrasies of the application.

Formatting

In general FrontPage does a fair if not stellar job of formatting HTML. It does typically isolate a single tag on a line (notable exceptions include image tags and hyperlink references). However, it does insist on rendering HTML tags in lowercase and placing dividing lines where it wants to. If you attempt to change either of these formats by hand, FrontPage will silently but definitively change them back.

On the other hand, FrontPage does a very nice job of color-coding HTML for easy recognition. The following colors are used by FrontPage:

✦ **Black** indicates text that is displayed on your page.

✦ **Green** indicates comments.

✦ **Purple** indicates an HTML tag (command).

✦ **Red** indicates an HTML attribute and modifies a tag.

✦ **Blue** indicates the value for an HTML attribute.

List item tags

Items in a bulleted or numbered list are indicated with a list item tag (<li>). FrontPage also ends each list item with an end list tag (</li>), which is unconventional, since it is not necessary to determine where one item in the list ends and the next begins. This is another format that FrontPage insists on. It will add the end list tag to any lists you import, and it will reinstate any end list tags you delete. This behavior, though peculiar, is harmless.

Nonbreaking spaces

It is possible to indicate a nonbreaking space character in HTML using the entity reference . This character can be inserted to force browsers to display space characters where they would normally ignore them. Not all browsers recognize this entity reference, however, so it is not always advisable to use it. FrontPage uses it in a variety of circumstances.

FrontPage writes this symbol into blank paragraphs if, for example, you create two paragraph breaks in a row. It also often inserts it into blank table cells. The only cure for this is to avoid such constructions in FrontPage or to delete the references by hand. Note that FrontPage doesn't always allow you to delete these references and may replace them when your back is turned.

Symbol entity references

HTML entity references are used to insert nonstandard ASCII characters into an HTML page. FrontPage correctly translates most typed characters, such as greater-than and less-than signs, or quotation marks, into their proper entity references. However, it does not translate any of the characters that it inserts as symbols. This includes all of the accented characters used in romance languages as well as symbols such as the copyright and trademark signs. Instead it simply inserts the PC ASCII symbol character. In practice, this means that browsers on Windows platforms may see the character you intended, but results are unpredictable on other platforms. Even worse, if you manually insert any of these characters into the HTML as entity references, FrontPage will translate them back into Windows symbols.

Enhancing Frames

In Chapter 8, you learned how to use FrontPage to create frame sets visually without having to write or understand the intricacies of HTML. The current version of the Frames Wizard cannot handle a few specialized features of frame sets, however, such as customizing frame borders beyond FrontPage's "Internet Explorer–centrism."

Directions for performing these operations are given here. However, providing complete information on creating frame sets in HTML is beyond the scope of this section.

The frame and frame set attributes that control color are relatively new innovations. You should always test them in several browsers to ensure that they produce the effect you want.

The frame and frame set HTML tags have several attributes that you can set to customize how the frame borders appear. These attributes can be added either to the `<frameset>` tag or to individual `<frame>` tags. Adding border attributes to the frame set is generally easier, since it avoids "border conflicts" if, for example, you designate the border color of one frame to be purple and the color of an adjacent frame to be green. Here are the attributes you can use:

- ✦ `BORDERCOLOR=#rrggbb` — This attribute was introduced by Netscape in version 3.0 of their browser and then inexplicably dropped in version 4. Just to keep things interesting, however, it is now supported in Microsoft Internet Explorer 4.0, though users of earlier versions will not see this color. You can designate a color either using the standard hexadecimal RGB value, or, for more standard colors, you can use an English equivalent (for instance, "purple," "blue," "pink").

- ✦ `FRAMEBORDER="yes|no"` *or* `"0|1"` — This attribute is used in conjunction with one or the other of the next two attributes to designate the presence or absence of a frame border. This attribute is supported by both Netscape and Microsoft as of version 3 of their respective browsers.

- ✦ `FRAMESPACING=number` — This is currently the preferred method for designating the thickness of frame borders. It is equivalent to the `CELLSPACING` property of tables. It designates the distance between frames in pixels, effectively the thickness of the border. Note that any change in the border spacing will produce a flat border line in older browsers, not the 3-D beveled version that is the default.

- ✦ `BORDER=number` — This attribute is used by Netscape 3.x and greater browsers to indicate border thickness. Internet Explorer simply ignores this attribute and uses the `FRAMESPACING` attribute instead. To create frames that look the same in both browsers, you will need to use both attributes.

Caution   Entering the BORDER=*number* attribute in Editor's HTML view does a very interesting thing: It sets the FRAMEBORDER attribute to "0," effectively eliminating your border. This means that if you want a frame to have a border with a thickness different than the default, you need to enter the HTML code in an alternative editor, such as Notepad. This is a major annoyance and makes it extremely unwieldy to deal with border widths. On the other hand, I can't really think of a reason to use different width borders.

Making Graphical Form Buttons

You may have noticed that some forms on the World Wide Web don't use the usual faintly 3-D buttons but instead have spiffy graphics for you to click. Although FrontPage gives you a fair amount of control over the appearance of a form button, you aren't able to directly use a graphic for it. To make a standard form button into a graphical button:

1. Insert the button in your form as you normally would (this procedure is detailed in Chapter 11).

2. Highlight the button and switch to HTML view. The HTML code that creates the button should be highlighted. This code will look something like the following definition for a submit button:

   `<input type="submit" value="Submit" name="B1"`

3. Change type to "image" and value to the filename of the image you want to appear as the button.

4. Add a new attribute called src and set its value to the filename *and* path of the image. For example: `src="images/image.gif"`.

5. Save your changes and view the page in Normal or Preview mode to see your new graphic.

Note   Note that you cannot make either button in a Search Form component graphical, since they are not specified the same way.

Linking to or embedding a style sheet

Style sheets (covered in detail in the next chapter) provide an extremely powerful and easy way to add a consistent look to all of your Web pages, while reducing the amount of time you need to spend formatting (even in FrontPage 98's less-than-perfect implementation). Unfortunately, you must manually add the HTML code to link a style sheet to a page.

To link a style sheet to a page, insert the following line into the `<head>` ... `</head>` section of the page:

`<link rel="STYLESHEET" href="styles.css" type="text/css">`
Replace "*styles*.css" with the name and path of your particular style sheet.

Using FrontPage's "Designer HTML"

If you've dug around the FrontPage CD-ROM, you may have noted a folder named Designer HTML in the SDK (Software Development Kit) folder. The small Read Me file in this folder would lead you to believe that the HTML files are going to provide you with wonders beyond your imagination and make your life easier.

Don't believe it for a minute.

ExcellA.htm

This file supposedly makes your life easier by providing a place for the Excel HTML Assistant to drop a table directly into your page. Yes, it works as advertised, but with one major downside: The inserted Excel table is not visible in Normal view, only in Preview mode—all you see in Normal view is the Microsoft Excel Internet Assistant table output area. This makes it nearly impossible to do any editing on the table.

There are two workarounds for this problem.

To insert an Excel table quickly and relatively easily:

1. Open the page in which you want to insert the Excel table.

2. Switch to HTML view and add the following text where you want to insert your table:

   ```
   <!--##Table##-->
   ```

3. Save your page and close Editor. (You can also close Explorer, if you like.)

4. Start Excel and open the spreadsheet you want to include in the page.

5. Highlight the area of the spreadsheet you want to use.

6. Select File ➪ Save as HTML. The Internet Assistant Wizard dialog box (shown in Figure 9-5) opens and displays Step 1 of 4.

7. Confirm that the area you want to export is included in the Ranges list box and click the Next button. The Step 2 of 4 dialog box now opens.

8. Check the Insert the Converted Data into an Existing HTML File radio button and click the next button. The Step 3 of 4 dialog box opens.

9. Check the Open the File Directly radio button.

10. Click the Browse button and locate the page you want to insert your table into, and then click the Open button to return to the Step 3 of 4 dialog box. (Typically your page will be located in a folder contained in the C:\Webshare\Wwwroot\ folder.)

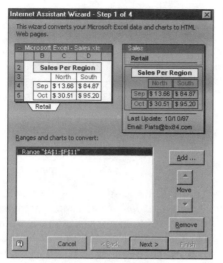

Figure 9-5: Microsoft Excel 97's Internet Assistant Wizard

11. Highlight the filename and path in the Path of the Existing File text box and press Ctrl+C.

12. Click the Next button. The Step 4 of 4 dialog box opens.

13. Check the Save the Result as an HTML File radio button.

14. If you want to replace the existing page, highlight the filename and path in the File Path text box and press Ctrl+V to paste the filename that you copied in step 11.

15. Click the Finish button to export your table into your page. (If you performed the paste in step 14, you will be asked if you want to replace the existing file; click Yes.) The table is now inserted into your page.

16. Close Excel and open the page in Editor. Your table now appears, ready for you to start editing it.

If you insist upon using this piece of "Designer HTML":

1. Open the page in which you want to insert the Excel table.

2. Open the `Designer HTML` folder in Windows Explorer (the "regular" Explorer, not FrontPage Explorer).

3. Click and drag the file `Excel1A.htm` from Explorer to your page. Notice that a vertical line appears to indicate where in your page the file will be inserted.

4. Release the mouse button to drop the file. The words "Microsoft Excel Internet Assistant table output area" now appear at this location.

5. Save your page and close Editor. (You can also close Explorer, if you like.)

6. Follow steps 4 through 16 in the preceding set of instructions. Note that when you view your page in Normal view, it appears just as it did before you inserted the table.

7. Select HTML view and delete the following lines of HTML code:

```
<!--webbot bot="HTMLMarkup" startspan
ALT="&lt;b&gt;Microsoft Excel Internet Assistant table output
area&lt;/b&gt;"-->
```

and

```
<!--webbot
bot="HTMLMarkup" endspan -->
```

8. Save your page and switch to Normal view. *Now* your table appears as a normal Internet table.

Image Map.htm

I'm not quite certain why this file was ever included. From the description in the Read Me file, this directory is supposed to be filled with extra goodies, but as you saw in Chapter 4, creating an image map is quite straightforward. And besides, why would you want a half-completed image map for a company called The Volcano Coffee Company with links that don't work?

That said, if you want to include this image on a page, just open your page in Editor and open the `Designer HTML` folder in Windows Explorer, and then drag the file `Image Map.htm` onto your page.

SpecialSearch.htm

Chapter 6 includes instructions on inserting the Search Form—a component that lets you quickly add text search capabilities to your Web. The `SpecialSearch.htm` page is just the standard Search Form component with the instruction line changed from "Search for:" to "Search for this:", the Start Search button changed to read "Start Searchin'!" and the Reset button changed to "Try Again." I wouldn't bother with this "Designer HTML" file.

The Date.htm

Finally, a truly handy piece of Designer HTML—a small Java script that displays the current time and date when your page is viewed. (I guess this is handy if someone visiting your page doesn't have a watch on.) It would be even handier if it worked.

Two small typographical errors in this script keep it from working. They are easy to fix, though.

To insert the Java script:

1. Open your page in Editor and open the `Designer HTML` folder in Windows Explorer, and then drag the file `The Date.htm` onto your page. If you're in Normal mode with formatting marks turned off, your page won't look any different.

2. Click the Show/Hide (¶) button in the toolbar. The small yellow flag with a *J* in it represents the script.

3. Highlight the flag and switch to HTML view. The entire text of the script is highlighted.

4. Change the capitalization of the *D* and the *W* in the phrase `Document.Write` so that it is entirely lowercase (that is, `document.write`).

5. Save your page and you're set to go.

Tip

Not being able see a piece of JavaScript in Normal mode can be a problem—sometimes you can inadvertently move or delete the script. This also makes it difficult to lay out your page with any accuracy (unless you spend all day switching back and forth between Normal and Preview modes). One easy way to make sure that you don't delete the script is to put a comment before and after it. You can insert a comment by selecting Insert ⇨ FrontPage Component and then picking the Comment component (a.k.a. the PurpleText WebBot). Any text you type using the Comment component appears in Normal view, but not in Preview mode or a browser.

Validating HTML

HTML validation refers to the process of checking the accuracy of your HTML to make sure that you have not made any typographical errors or used tags and their attributes incorrectly. The strictest validation methods parse your HTML against the actual DTD, or document type definition, that defines what elements are legal in various types of HTML.

FrontPage does not include any validation reporting capabilities for your HTML, although you can use FrontPage to verify internal and external links. On the one hand the lack of a validation feature is not a big problem, given that FrontPage is writing most of the HTML itself. On the other hand, the fact that you can still add your own HTML is reason enough to want to check your HTML for accuracy.

Taking the Next Step

This chapter has taken something of a detour into the inner workings of FrontPage. In the process we have learned some simple techniques for viewing and editing HTML in your Web pages. The next chapter introduces FrontPage style sheets. A powerful new feature in FrontPage 98, style sheets let you tell Editor (and consequently your visitors' browsers) exactly what you want your page to look like.

✦　　✦　　✦

Using Style Sheets

When you've designed Web pages with Editor, you've often used styles for such varied tasks as setting up headings, making lists, and what-have-you. While you've had some control over how a page looks, most of these styles are under the control of your visitors' browsers. Using style sheets (a new feature in FrontPage 98), you have more power to tell Editor (and consequently your visitors' browsers) exactly what you want your page to look like. This chapter shows you how to unleash that power.

New in 98

Although FrontPage 98's new style sheet feature gives more power, you still don't have complete control. Many browsers don't understand style sheets at all, while others don't support all of the specifications for style sheets. This is the good news and the bad news all in one.

Discovering Style Sheets

Style sheets are collections of formatting statements that you can link to a number of different pages. Any pages that include a link to a particular style sheet then have access to quick formatting options. These styles can modify existing styles (say, Heading 1), or you can create your own.

Like Web pages, style sheets are simply text files that contain the appropriate formatting codes (see Figure 10-1). Of course these formatting codes aren't the same as HTML code—that would be too easy.

There is a reason that these codes aren't identical: Style sheet formatting is far, far more versatile than standard HTML, and you can use this versatility to make pages that just couldn't be done without styles. Using styles, you can add background images to individual paragraphs, make text an exact size (rather than just the seven logical sizes available to HTML), add borders around text, and even adjust the spacing between lines of text.

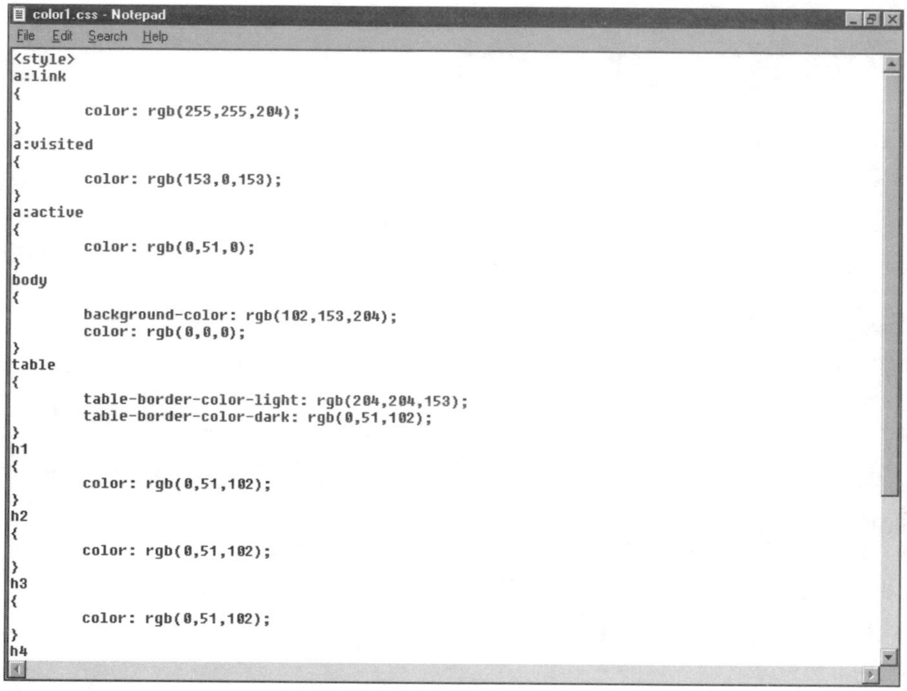

color1.css - Notepad

File Edit Search Help

```
<style>
a:link
{
	color: rgb(255,255,204);
}
a:visited
{
	color: rgb(153,0,153);
}
a:active
{
	color: rgb(0,51,0);
}
body
{
	background-color: rgb(102,153,204);
	color: rgb(0,0,0);
}
table
{
	table-border-color-light: rgb(204,204,153);
	table-border-color-dark: rgb(0,51,102);
}
h1
{

	color: rgb(0,51,102);
}
h2
{

	color: rgb(0,51,102);
}
h3
{

	color: rgb(0,51,102);
}
h4
```

Figure 10-1: A style sheet contains commands for formatting Web pages.

Creating New Style Sheets

A style sheet may look like a confusing jumble when you first look at it, but there is order in the chaos. The beginning and end of the style sheet—`<style>` and `</style>`—merely indicate that it is a style sheet. Each line between these two tags provides the formatting commands. Notice that each line begins with a name (for example, `h1`) followed by a series of phrases separated by semicolons. Referring to the first few lines in Figure 10-1 (after the `<style>` heading):

✦ `h1`—This is the style's *selector*. There's nothing mysterious here. It's just a name for you and your visitors' browsers to identify the particular style. (If you've fiddled with HTML code before, however, you'll notice that this particular name is the code for Heading 1.)

✦ `{ ... }`—These two brackets indicate that everything between them is formatting options. There are many, many options, which are outlined in the next section.

Creating embedded styles

The preceding discussion concentrated on style sheets that are linked to your Web pages. To begin the instructions for creating your own, however, we're looking at style sheets that are embedded within a Web page's HTML code. There is one very important reason why this was done: Although FrontPage doesn't provide any tools for editing linked (also called external) style sheets, Editor comes with a rudimentary dialog box for creating embedded styles. (Also, the next section on creating linked style sheets contains a terribly useful tip that requires your knowledge of this section.)

To create an embedded style sheet:

1. Select Format ⇨ Stylesheet to open the Format Stylesheet dialog box shown in Figure 10-2.

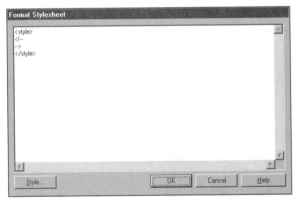

Figure 10-2: Use the Format Stylesheet dialog box to create new embedded styles.

2. Place the cursor at the end of the line <!– and press Enter to create a new line.

3. Type in a selector for your style. There are three types of style selectors:

   • **Style name**—These selectors correspond to standard HTML styles. When you specify styles for style name selectors, you take control of that style name so that every time it's used, the formatting you specify is used. Chapter 9 provides an introduction to editing HTML and the more common styles. In addition, you can add a couple of extras to some style name selectors. (These are called pseudo-elements.)

The anchor HTML style (used when making links) can have up to three different states, showing an unvisited link, a visited link, and an active link (the style displayed when the link is actually being clicked). To specify these three selectors, name them **A:link**, **A:visited**, and **A:active**, respectively.

The paragraph HTML styles have two additional states that can be added and that affect the entire first line of text or the first letter. To specify these additional states, name the selectors *x*:**first-line** and *x*:**first-letter**, respectively, where *x* is the name of the HTML paragraph style.

- **Class**—This type of selector is a modifier. That is, you use this style to modify all or part of text that may already have been formatted with a style. These selectors always begin with a period (.), which identifies them as class selectors. Class selectors appear in both the Change Style drop-down list and the Style dialog box (which is accessible from most formatting dialog boxes). When they have been selected from the Change Style drop-down list, the formatting you have set is applied to an entire paragraph, whereas when they have been selected from the Style dialog box, the formatting is applied only to new text or individual characters that you have highlighted.

- **ID**—Also modifiers, ID selectors are most useful in inline styles. These always begin with a pound sign (#) to identify them.

4. Press the Style button to open the Style dialog box shown in Figure 10-3.

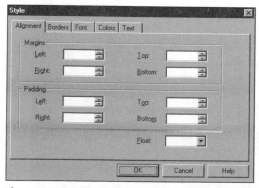

Figure 10-3: The Style dialog box lets you specify the styles for a particular selector.

5. Set the formatting you want associated with the selector and press the OK button. The formats are now displayed between brackets after the name of the selector. Descriptions of all the style options are given just after these instructions.

6. Create new selector/format combinations according to the preceding instructions and press OK when you're done.

Note that if you want to change styles, you must place the cursor between the curly brackets ({ and }) or the new commands will be inserted at the cursor location and not merged with the existing styles.

The Style dialog box contains much more advanced commands for formatting your Web page than the normal Font and Paragraph formatting options available in straight HTML. Each tab of this dialog box handles a different aspect of the formatting. You don't need to set all of the available options—any that you leave blank will use the default HTML formatting. The next sections cover each tab in detail.

All units are not created equal

Many of the options available for styles involve distances (margins, line height, font size, and such). While you may be used to having the units in a Web page forced on you (for example, table borders are always set in pixels), you have many options when you're using style sheets. You can choose from:

✦ *###*px—This specifies the distance in pixels.

✦ *###*ex—This specifies a height based on the height of the current font's capital letter X.

✦ *###*em—This specifies a height based on the height of the current font's lowercase letter m.

✦ *###*in, *###*cm, and *###*mm—These specify distances in inches, centimeters, and millimeters, respectively. Note that the dots-per-inch (dpi) settings on most monitors are different, so the physical distances will be different. A 15-inch monitor and a 17-inch monitor both set to the same resolution have different dpi, which may not correspond to the dpi setting.

✦ *###*pt and *###*pc—These specify distances in points and picas, respectively. Both of these are typesetting measurements (you are probably familiar with setting font sizes in points). The same dpi considerations come into play for point and pica measures as for inches, cm, and mm.

While it may not seem intuitive at first, I would suggest that you always set font sizes in pixels rather than points. In addition, unless absolutely necessary, you should avoid all of the "absolute" measurements (inches, cm, mm, points, and picas) and stick with pixels, ems, and exes. I say this because, as just noted, you have no control over the dpi setting for your visitors' monitors, and text can be displayed in a wildly different size than you intended. By using pixel measurements, you tell the browser exactly what size you want the text. Also, since the ex and em sizes are based on the font size, your display will be an accurate representation of what your visitors see.

Caution

If you produce a page that you intend to be printed, ignore the preceding advice about setting text size in pixels. If you do, then the text will probably print out amazingly small! (On a 300-dpi printer, text 10 pixels high will print out about $\frac{1}{32}$ of an inch high.)

The Alignment tab

The Alignment tab of the Style dialog box determines how portions of your page using the selector interact with other text and graphics:

✦ **Margins**—Settings in this section specify the distance that the text or graphic is offset from other page contents. Note that you can specify all four directions (top, bottom, left, and right) separately.

✦ **Padding**—The settings in this section specify the distance between the text or graphic and the margin. This is especially useful if you use the Colors tab to specify a background color and want to have the background color extend well beyond the text itself.

✦ **Float**—The three settings available in this drop-down list (None, Left, and Right) allow you to specify how text flows around the object using this style. None means that the text doesn't flow, Left places the current object on the left-hand side of the browser window and has text flow to its right, and Right places the object on the right-hand side with text flowing to the left.

The Borders tab

In most word processors, you are able to place lines of varying thickness and appearance around paragraphs and words. The Borders tab lets you do the same thing. Simply pick the style (dashed, dotted, solid, and so on), color, and width from the appropriate drop-down list.

The Font tab

This tab provides more complete control over the font and size used than is available on the formatting toolbar. In addition to being able to pick the font, you can also set the exact size of the text just as you would using a regular word processor. Remember that the point size is based on the dpi (dots per inch) setting of your visitors' computer screens and that specific type sizes will not necessarily look the same. Make sure that you enter a unit (as described in the preceding sidebar) when you specify the font size.

The Secondary Font drop-down list is available for you to set a font to be used if someone visiting your site doesn't have the font set in Primary Font—note that it's usually a good idea to use a generic font (serif, sans serif, cursive, fantasy, or monospace) for this setting to make your pages more universally accessible. In addition, you can use the Font text box to specify more alternative fonts.

Use the Text tab options to set other text attributes.

The Colors tab

Here you can set a background color or image, much as you can with a Web page as a whole or a table—though there are some twists:

✦ **Background Color**—Select a color to use as a background from this drop-down list.

✦ **Foreground Color**—Select a foreground color from this drop-down list. Typically, the foreground color sets the color for text. Note that this setting will override a text color setting you may set in the Text tab.

Tip

The Background Image, Attachment, Repeat, and Vertical and Horizontal Position options provide extra functionality for your page's background image. To use these options for your page's background, create a style selector called **body**.

✦ **Background Image**—Enter the URL of the image you'd like to use as a background in this text box, or press the Browse button and use the Image dialog box. Although they are not grayed out when no image is selected, the following settings are used only for specifying image position.

✦ **Attachment**—The two settings here, Scroll and Fixed, determine whether the background image scrolls with the page or remains stationary. If the background image is fixed, then it remains stationary while the page scrolls. Note that this option only works when the background image is used with the style selector **body** as noted in the preceding tip.

✦ **Repeat**—This option lets you determine how the image will repeat. While a normal page background automatically repeats (tiles) in both the X and Y directions, you can specify that the background image repeat only in one direction or not at all.

✦ **Vertical and Horizontal Position**—These settings specify where the image appears on the page.

The Text tab

Use the Text tab to take more control over the way text is displayed:

✦ **Weight**—This determines whether the text will be bold or not. Note that even though there are 13 settings, typically only two (Normal and Bold) are available to anyone viewing your pages. The others (Bolder, Lighter, and 100 through 900) are settings that are not supported by most typefaces. Until typeface support gets better, I would ignore all settings other than Normal and Bold.

✦ **Style**—Here you can choose from Normal, Italic, and Oblique (*really* Italic). Note that Oblique is not supported by most typefaces and, again, I would ignore this setting.

✦ **Variant**—This setting allows you to specify small caps for the text formatted with this style.

✦ **Transform**—If you hate to use the Shift key, you may like the settings available here (Capitalize, Uppercase, and Lowercase). Capitalize forces the first letter of each word to be capitalized, whereas Upper- and Lowercase force all letters to be the appropriate case.

✦ **Decoration**—This option can be used to add a decorative touch to text. The settings available are: Underline, Overline, Line-Through (strikethrough), and Blink.

✦ **Indent**—This setting allows you to create a hanging indent for a paragraph.

✦ **Line Height**—In typesetting parlance this is called *leading* and is the distance between lines of text.

✦ **Character Spacing**—This is the distance between individual letters and is typically referred to as *kerning*.

✦ **Text Alignment**—Use this option to set the usual Left, Right, or Center alignment; note also the long-awaited Justified setting, which makes each complete line in a paragraph line up on both the left and right margins.

✦ **Vertical Alignment**—In addition to the usual Top, Middle, and Bottom alignments, this option also includes the graphics-related alignment options Baseline, Text-Top, and Text-Bottom. Because of the way text formatted with styles behaves, you can also use these graphics-related options for text! Also included are Sub and Super, which provide subscripted text and superscripted text.

Creating external style sheets

As you saw in the preceding section, a style sheet is "merely" a listing of names (called selectors) and format settings. I put "merely" in quotation marks because this listing can quickly become as intricate as a whole Web page—and just as complicated. Styles use many codes that are quite different from their standard HTML counterparts.

You purchased FrontPage so that you wouldn't have to worry about remembering funky codes and, worse yet, remembering their sometimes arcane syntax. Editor does a wonderful job of insulating you from all of this with its WYSIWYG (what you see is what you get) interface. Unfortunately, FrontPage doesn't include an editor specifically designed for style sheets...or does it?

Let me give you three quick pieces of information about style sheet files before I answer that obviously loaded question:

✦ Style sheets, like HTML files, are just text files and can be edited using Notepad.

✦ Style sheet files use exactly the same codes and syntax as embedded style sheets.

✦ You can use standard copy and paste techniques with Notepad.

I think you see where I'm going with this.

Even though FrontPage doesn't specifically provide a style sheet editor, you can use the Format Stylesheets dialog box to create style sheets to your exact specifications without having to know practically anything about their codes or syntax.

To create a style sheet file:

1. Create a blank page and name it something like Style Sheet Test.

2. Add an embedded style sheet to the page as just outlined, in "Creating embedded styles."

   Tip

   It's a good idea to format your test page using the styles you create so that you can make sure they look as you intend. This also provides immediate feedback if you change a style. The later section "Using styles" shows you how to format your pages using styles.

3. Create all of the formats that you want.

4. Highlight all of the text in the Format Stylesheet dialog box, including the `<style>` and `</style>` lines.

5. Press Ctrl+C to copy this text to the clipboard.

6. Start Notepad.

7. Press Ctrl+V, or select Edit ➪ Paste to paste the style sheet commands from the clipboard.

8. Save the file with the extension `.css`, for cascading style sheet. Make sure that you save this file in the same folder as you did the page in which you built the embedded style sheet—if you don't, any URLs you may have specified (say, for background images) won't work.

9. Link the style sheet to any pages you want using the steps outlined in the later section "Using styles."

You will want to save a copy of your style sheet test page so that you can go back and edit it later if you want. If you do make changes, just follow steps 3 through 8 in the preceding sequence (remembering to highlight all of the text in Notepad before performing step 7), and all your pages will be instantly updated.

Tip

If the system just described doesn't provide you enough power for editing style sheets, we've included StyleMaker on the CD that comes with this book. See Appendix D, "Using the CD-ROM," for more information about this program and how to install it.

For specific information about style sheet codes and syntax, see the World Wide Web Consortium's Guide to Cascading Style Sheets at `http://www.htmlhelp.com/reference/css/` or, for a more user-friendly approach, read *Dynamic HTML For Dummies*, by Michael Hyman (published by IDG Books Worldwide).

Putting Style Sheets to Work

Now that you've created embedded and external style sheets, how do you use them? If you're using embedded styles on a page, then you can skip right to the later section called "Using styles." If, however, you want to use styles stored in an external style sheet, you need to *call* the style sheet as outlined in the next section, "Linking to an external style sheet."

Linking to an external style sheet

While FrontPage has added support for external style sheets, it still has not added any simple way to actually link a page to a style sheet. You have to do this by hand by adding a code to your page's HTML code. Chapter 9 includes a more in-depth discussion of editing HTML code, so the following instructions are very cut and dried:

To link a page to an external style sheet:

1. Open the page in Editor.

2. Click the HTML tab to display the page's HTML code (see Figure 10-4).

3. Create a new line between the <head> and </head> lines on the page.

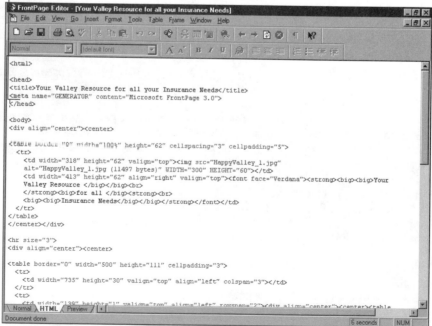

Figure 10-4: A typical page's HTML code

4. Type in the following code, replacing *filename*.css with the path and name of your style sheet file:

```
<LINK REL=stylesheet HREF="filename.css" TYPE=text/css">
```

Caution

If you will be publishing your Web to a UNIX Web server, you must ensure that the filename of your style sheet exactly matches the capitalization of the file. If the capitalization doesn't match, your styles will not be applied once you publish your Web.

5. Click the Preview tab to view your page with the styles added. Note that many styles do not display accurately in Normal view.

Using styles

No matter whether your page uses external or embedded styles, the ways to use them remain exactly the same.

To apply a style to an entire paragraph, place the cursor anywhere within the paragraph and select the style from the Change Style drop-down list. This list shows all of your style name and class selectors.

To apply a style to only a word (or words) or an image:

1. Highlight the text or graphic and press Alt+Enter to open the Properties dialog box appropriate to the object. You can also open any other dialog box that contains a Style button.

2. Press the Style button to open the Style dialog box shown in Figure 10-5. Note that all class selectors in the style sheet are listed on the Class tab.

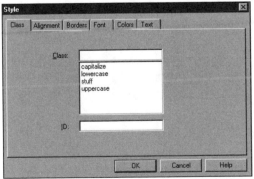

Figure 10-5: A typical set of class selector styles ready for use

3. Select a class selector from the list and press OK to close the Style dialog box and OK again to close the Properties dialog box. The style has now been applied. Press the Preview tab to see the style in action.

Taking control with local styles

Style sheets are all well and good, but what happens when you just want to make a couple of quick adjustments? In that case, you can just use a *local* style.

To apply a local style, open the Style dialog box by pressing the Style button in any appropriate dialog box (Font, Paragraph, Image Properties, and so forth), make the style settings you want, and press OK twice to close the dialog boxes.

The Style dialog box is the same one described earlier in the chapter under "Creating embedded styles" (with the addition of the Class tab).

Note

You need to keep one thing in mind if a page links to an external style sheet and includes embedded and/or local styles: Local styles override embedded styles, and embedded styles override linked styles. This feature gives you maximum flexibility in making adjustments to any particular page.

Taking the Next Step

This chapter culminates the formatting techniques introduced throughout Part III. Now, using styles, you can create Web pages that are freed from the limitations of "old-fashioned" HTML. As you saw, even though FrontPage Editor provides a WYSIWYG environment for creating Web pages, you needed to directly edit HTML code to access an external style sheet. There are some other aspects of your page's construction that Editor doesn't deal with or does not provide complete support for. The previous chapter showed you how to directly write and update your pages' HTML code to extend Editor's capabilities.

The next part of the book launches into the subject of adding interactivity to your Web pages—forms, text searches, discussion forums—and introduces FrontPage components (a.k.a. WebBots).

✦   ✦   ✦

Adding Interactivity

◆ ◆ ◆ ◆

◆ ◆ ◆ ◆

Creating and Implementing Forms

In this chapter we introduce the basics of constructing
forms in FrontPage and describe the various FrontPage
components (WebBots) available for processing form input
and for customizing results pages. We discuss the four steps
of implementing an online form: designing the form, defining
its valid input, adding programming to process form input,
and displaying a results or confirmation page after the data
has been processed. This chapter also serves as the foundation
for later chapters in this and the next part of the book, where
we look at various kinds of programming elements that can be
used to handle forms processing in your FrontPage Web.

Discovering Interactive Forms

Up to this point, the Web pages you have built have had a
limited ability to accept input from users. Some people claim
that the mere fact that a Web page has hyperlinks or image
maps to click makes it interactive, but those people are all in
marketing, so enough said.

Form elements open up a whole new level of interactive
possibilities. Granted, a registration form asking the user to
provide information for my contact database is not exactly the
height of interactivity either. But the same interface elements
used to create that form could be used to build applications
that enable users to access and share information, conduct
business or play games, and perform a variety of complex
tasks. All this is possible because forms provide various
means for users to add their input via a Web page and to
get back information based on that input.

Creating a Form

A Web page form is composed of one or more elements for accepting user input and some means of submitting the input for processing. In general, the simplest form includes a single input field and a button to submit the results for processing.

You have probably seen search engines with a single input and no submit buttons. How is that done? It works because some browsers are designed such that if a form has only one input box, pressing the Enter key performs the same function as clicking a submit button.

Forms can be used as a means of collecting information from users, of requesting feedback, of initiating a database query, or of facilitating a discussion.

To create a form in FrontPage, you first position the form elements on the Web page and adjust the properties of each. In this section we will describe each of the basic form elements and their properties as well as some of the basic properties of forms in general.

Working with Form Templates

FrontPage includes several templates that contain predesigned forms. If you are looking for a fairly standard form type, starting with one of these templates is likely to save you some time. There is also a Form Page Wizard, which we will discuss toward the end of the chapter.

✦ **Feedback form**—This simple form is designed to solicit comments from users on a variety of company-related topics. It uses the Save Results component to process and record feedback.

✦ **Guest Book form**—The Guest Book form is a basic text input form, much like the guest register of a small hotel or bed and breakfast inn, that allows visitors to the site to record a comment. Although it is more a courtesy to users than anything else, a surprising number of people will actually take the time to "sign" your guest book (especially if you let them read what they and others have written). The guest book is linked to the Web Save Results component.

✦ **Search form**—This is a simple one-field text string search form used in conjunction with FrontPage's built-in text search engine. This form, which is part of the Search component, is discussed in detail in Chapter 13.

✦ **User Registration form**—This form enables users to enter a username and password that will gain them access to a designated access-controlled Web. This component is restricted to certain Web servers and must be saved in a root Web. Results are processed by the Web Registration component.

Dealing with Form Elements

All Web forms are composed of a handful of form elements: a one-line text box, a scrolling text box, a check box, a radio button, a drop-down menu, and push buttons. In FrontPage these elements can be inserted into your Web page either by selecting Insert ⇨ Form Field and choosing the desired item or by using the Forms toolbar, which can be accessed by selecting View ⇨ Forms Toolbar. This toolbar is shown in Figure 11-1.

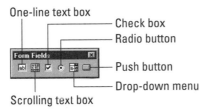

Figure 11-1: The Forms toolbar

If you insert a form field into a location that does not already have a form defined, FrontPage will generate a new form. If you insert a form element into an existing form, the new field will be added to the existing form. A form is represented in Editor's Normal view by a dashed rectangle that is not visible in Preview mode or in a browser. In the next section, we identify all of the major form field types as well as the various options and parameters that each possesses.

Tip

Form fields display differently on different browsers. To keep your form looking nice and neat, you should consider using a table to line things up. After you've inserted your first form field (and created the form container), insert a table within the dashed container box. You can now drag the form items into the appropriate cells in the table. See Chapter 7 for more information about constructing tables.

One-line text boxes

The *one-line text box* is the staple of most online forms. It is suitable for short input, such as is shown in the User Information section of the Product or Event Registration form in Figure 11-2.

To create a one-line text box, select Insert ⇨ Form Field ⇨ One-Line Text Box or press the corresponding icon on the Forms toolbar.

To resize the input box, select it and drag with the mouse from either side of the box. Note that a one-line text box cannot be resized vertically (that is, it can be made longer or shorter but not taller).

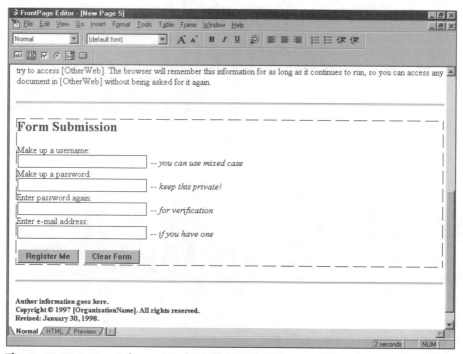

Figure 11-2: A User Information form illustrating the use of one-line text box fields

Text box properties

To edit the text box properties, double-click the input box or click the box with the right mouse button and select Form Field Properties. The Text Box Properties box, shown in Figure 11-3, is displayed. You can edit the following properties:

Figure 11-3: The Text Box Properties dialog box

- ✦ **Name**—This is the name of the form field. This name is used internally when the form is processed. By default, the name of a text field is "T" plus a number corresponding to the number of text fields that have been placed on the form.

- ✦ **Initial Value**—This is the default text that appears when the form is first opened or when it is reset. The initial value is empty by default.

✦ **Width in Characters**—This is the length of the field horizontally. This value is adjusted automatically whenever you resize the form using the mouse, as just described. Note that this number designates the physical size of the text box. It does not limit the amount of text that can be entered in the box. For information on limiting text input, see the later section "Validating text box input."

Caution

You may find that the text input box does not display exactly in FrontPage. (In my experience, the box is one character shorter than the designated width.) However, it does display correctly when previewed in a browser.

✦ **Tab Order**—When filling out a form, your visitors can use the Tab key to switch between fields. By default, your users tab between fields in the order that they appear onscreen. To change this order, enter a number in this text box (remember to give each field a different number, in sequence).

✦ **Password Field**—Generally, the text input box echoes to the screen any characters that the user types into it. If the input box is created as a password field, by choosing the Yes radio button for the password property, you arrange that placeholder characters are echoed instead (see Figure 11-4). This feature provides a modicum of security for user passwords. Recognize, however, that this property only governs the screen display. It does not provide any encryption of the input when it is sent back to the server.

Password fields

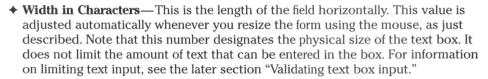

Figure 11-4: A password field showing its masked input

For some reason, HTML has not gotten around to providing formatting properties, such as font style or background color, for text boxes. However, you can format most form items using style sheets (either embedded, inline, or local) as outlined in Chapter 10. To add local styles to, or specify class selectors for, a form field, select the Style button in its Properties dialog box.

Validating text box input

In addition to its basic properties, each form field type in FrontPage can be configured to limit its acceptable inputs using the form field's validation options. You access a form field's Validation dialog box either via the Validate button on the Properties dialog box or by clicking the form field with the right mouse button and selecting Form Field Validation.

Anytime you specify validation options, be sure to alert your user to the presence of those options on the form itself if the restrictions are not obvious ones. A good example would be any fields that you designate as required. Failing to alert your user is likely to reduce the number of people who will complete the form and probably result in some curt messages from users who do not appreciate surprises.

The Text Box Validation dialog box is shown in Figure 11-5. It includes several options for specifying what input will be accepted by the form. By default, the field's accepted Data Type option is set to No Constraints, meaning that any input will be accepted, including no input. Options include Text, Integer, or Number.

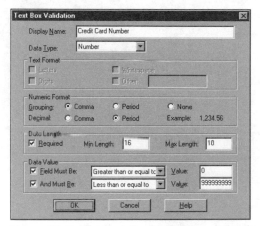

Figure 11-5: The Text Box Validation dialog box

Data Type constraints

Selecting one of the data type constraints will activate additional validation options. Fields limited to the text data type can have the Text Format restricted to text characters, number characters, white space (space, tab, carriage return, and line feed), and/or other. To include one or more of these formats, check the box next to its name. If you select Other, you must also type the other characters you wish to permit, such as a comma, hyphen, dollar sign, or at (@) sign.

Integers

If the field type is set to Integer, that is, to whole numbers, you can also designate how the digits of the number should be grouped. Options are a comma (for instance, 1,234,567), a decimal (for instance, 1.234.567) or no grouping (for instance, 1234567). If you have selected a field type of Number, you can also designate the decimal character in the same way. Note that the grouping character and the decimal character cannot be set to the same character.

Display Name

If you have selected a data type constraint, you can also designate a Display Name for the field. This name is used to identify the field to users in the event that they have not entered valid data into the form field. By default any error message will use the name of the field as specified in the form field properties. Use this field if you are using shorthand field names (such as T1) and would like to include a more recognizable name in any error messages. The best approach is to provide a name that matches the field label on the form itself.

Data Length/Data Value

Even if you do not wish to constrain the data type, you can still constrain the data length and data value. For the data length, you can stipulate that input in the field is required. In addition, you can designate minimum and maximum acceptable lengths in characters for any input.

Tip

You should always designate a maximum length in any text field. This will prevent potential misuse of the form. Give users a reasonable length limit but no more than reasonably necessary.

The Data Value section of the Validation Options dialog box allows you to restrict input to a range of acceptable values. If you have constrained the data type to integers or numbers, FrontPage will check results numerically. If you have constrained the data type to text or have not set any constraints, input will be compared using alphabetic order. Options for limiting data values include: less than, greater than, less than or equal to, greater than or equal to, equal to, and not equal to. Use the second data value check box if you want to designate two range criteria, such as upper and lower range limits.

Scrolling text boxes

A *scrolling text box,* called a *text area* in HTML, is used for data input longer than a few words. Typically it is used when a paragraph of text is called for, such as comments or messages.

To create a scrolling text box, select Insert ➪ Form Field ➪ Scrolling Text Box or press the corresponding icon on the Forms toolbar.

To resize the input box, select it and drag with the mouse from any side or corner of the box. A scrolling text box can be resized horizontally and/or vertically.

Scrolling text box properties

To edit the scrolling text box properties, double-click the input box or click the box with the right mouse button and select Form Field Properties. The Scrolling Text Box Properties dialog box, shown in Figure 11-6, is displayed. You can edit the following properties:

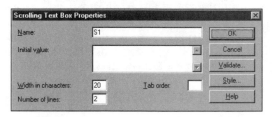

Figure 11-6: The Scrolling Text Box Properties dialog box

✦ **Name** — The name of the text box is used internally when the form is processed. By default, the field name is "S" plus a number corresponding to the number of scrolling text fields that have been placed on the form.

✦ **Initial Value** — This is the default text that appears when the form is first opened or when it is reset. The initial value is empty by default.

✦ **Width in Characters** — The horizontal width of the field is adjusted automatically whenever you resize the form using the mouse, as previously described. Note that this number designates the physical size of the text box. It does not limit the amount of text that can be entered in the box. For information on limiting text input, see the previous section "Validating text box input."

✦ **Number of Lines** — This designates the height of the text box vertically. This value is adjusted automatically whenever you resize the form using the mouse, as previously described. Note that this number designates the physical size of the text box. It does not limit the amount of text that can be entered in the box. For information on limiting text input, see the previous section "Validating text box input."

✦ **Tab Order**—Enter the position number you want this field to have when your visitors use the Tab key to move through the form's fields.

Wrapping text refers to the ability of text to start a new line automatically any time the text approaches the end of the text box. In Internet Explorer scrolling text boxes wrap by default. In Netscape Navigator, they do not. To enable text wrapping in Netscape, open the form page in Editor and select View➪HTML. Locate the `<text area>` tag that corresponds to the scrolling text box. Add the attribute `wrap` inside the tag (that is, so that it reads `<text area wrap>`). See Chapter 9 for help on using the HTML view.

Validating scrolling text box input

To select validation options for a scrolling text box, select the Validate button from the Properties dialog box or click the form field with the right mouse button and select Form Field Validation. Validation options for a scrolling text box are the same as for a one-line text box as described in the previous section.

In addition to using scrolling text boxes for form input, some developers like to use them to display messages to the user. In such cases it would be nice to be able to make the text field so that it could not be edited, since by default users could delete the text from the message box or type in their own. (Note that any changes made by the user would not effect the message for anyone else.) There is currently no way to create fields in HTML that cannot be edited except by recourse to additional programming.

Check boxes

A *check box* allows users to indicate a selection by clicking a small box. Selecting a check box typically marks it with an *x* or check mark. Check boxes are used for simple yes/no input. Although check boxes are often used for a group of options, they are nonexclusive. This means that checking one box does not restrict the user from checking another box in the same grouping. This is the chief difference between check boxes and radio buttons, described later.

To create a check box, select Insert➪Form Field➪Check Box or press the corresponding icon on the Forms toolbar.

Check box properties

To edit the check box properties, double-click the check box or click the box with the right mouse button and select Form Field Properties. The Check Box Properties dialog box, shown in Figure 11-7, is displayed. You can edit the following properties:

✦ **Name**—This is the name of the check box. This name is used internally when the form is processed. By default, the name is "C" plus a number corresponding to the number of check boxes that have been placed on the form.

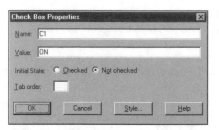

Figure 11-7: The Check Box Properties dialog box

✦ **Value**—This is the value that is sent by the check box if it is checked. By default, the value is ON. This value is used internally, so unless you are writing your own program to process a form, there is probably little reason to change the default. Typically you will want to create a more meaningful value to aid you in interpreting the forms output.

✦ **Initial State**—Selecting the Checked option causes the check box to be checked by default when the form is first accessed or when it is reset.

✦ **Tab Order**—Enter the position number you want this field to have when your visitors use the Tab key to move through the form's fields.

Often when you are creating check boxes, you are creating a list of items that your visitors can select from. For example, you might have a series of check boxes each labeled with a different type of animal, asking your visitors what type of pets they have. To help keep your form reply more manageable, you will find it easier to provide all of the check boxes in this type of series with the same name but different values—for instance, name all of the check boxes "pet" and assign each check box a unique value such as "cat," "dog," or "orangutan."

Validating check box input

There is no mechanism for validating a check box. If you wish to ensure that users check a particular box on a form before proceeding (for example, a check box acknowledging understanding of certain policies or restrictions pertaining to the form), you will need to add some simple scripting to the check box. Scripting languages are discussed in Chapter 15.

Alternatively, you can use a single radio button for this purpose—since it is possible to require a radio button in FrontPage. See the next section for details on validating a radio button.

Radio buttons

A *radio button,* also known as an *option button,* is a hollow circle that contains a smaller, solid black circle when selected. Radio buttons are always used in an exclusive grouping, meaning that only one option in the group can be selected at a time. Selecting a new option automatically deselects any previous selection.

To create a radio button, select Insert ⇨ Form Field ⇨ Radio Button or press the corresponding icon on the Forms toolbar.

Although it is possible to create a single radio button, in practice radio buttons are usually grouped. By default additional radio buttons you create will be grouped with any button that precedes them. To change groupings, use the Properties dialog box as described in the next section.

Radio button properties

To edit the radio button properties, double-click the radio button or click the button with the right mouse button and select Form Field Properties. The Radio Button Properties dialog box, shown in Figure 11-8, is displayed. You can edit the following properties:

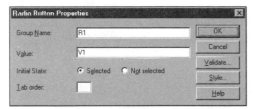

Figure 11-8: The Radio Button Properties dialog box

✦ **Group Name**—This name is shared by all radio buttons in the same group. Users can select only one option from the group. By default, the group name is "R" plus a number corresponding to the number of radio button groups that have been placed on the form.

To create more than one group of radio buttons, create the first radio button of the second group, change its name to differentiate it from the first group, highlight it, press Ctrl+C, and then press Ctrl+V to paste copies of it.

✦ **Value**—This is the value that is sent by the radio button if it is checked. A radio button value needs to be unique within its group in order to distinguish responses. By default, the value is "V" plus a number corresponding to one more than the value of the preceding radio button. Typically you will want to create a more meaningful value to aid you in interpreting the forms output.

✦ **Initial State**—Choosing the Selected option causes the radio button to be selected by default when the form is first accessed or when it is reset. Note that only one radio button in a group can be selected by default. Choosing Selected for a given button will automatically cause any previously selected button to lose its default selection.

✦ **Tab Order**—Enter the position number you want this field to have when your visitors use the Tab key to move through the form's fields.

Validating radio button input

You can use radio button validation to require that users select one of the options from a radio button grouping.

You access a radio button's Validation dialog box either via the Validate button on the Properties dialog box or by clicking one of the radio buttons in a group with the right mouse button and selecting Form Field Validation.

Tip

Radio buttons are typically designed so that a selection is required. Once a button has been selected, it is difficult to deselect all buttons. If one of the options for a set of radio buttons is None, you should include this as an explicit choice and make it the default.

The Radio Button Validation dialog box is shown in Figure 11-9. Check the Data Required check box to require that users select one of the radio buttons in a grouping. Note that checking this option for one of the buttons in a group activates the validation for all buttons in the group. In addition, you can designate a display name to be used if it is necessary to prompt the user to select an option.

Figure 11-9: The Radio Button Validation dialog box

Caution

If you open the Radio Button Properties dialog box and change the group name associated with the radio button, the Validate button is temporarily grayed out. Close the dialog box and reopen it to reactivate the Validate button.

Drop-down menus

To create a drop-down menu list, select Insert ➪ Form Field ➪ Drop-Down Menu or press the corresponding icon on the Forms toolbar. This creates an empty drop-down menu, which is not very useful. To add items to the menu list, edit the drop-down menu properties as described in the following section.

Drop-down menu properties

To edit the drop-down menu properties, double-click the drop-down menu or click the drop-down menu with the right mouse button and select Form Field Properties. The Drop-Down Menu Properties dialog box, shown in Figure 11-10, is displayed. You can edit the following properties:

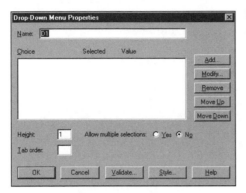

Figure 11-10: The Drop-Down Menu Properties dialog box

✦ **Name**—This is the name of the drop-down menu field. This name is used internally when the form is processed. By default, the name of a drop-down menu is "D" plus a number corresponding to the number of drop-down menus that have been placed on the form.

✦ **Choice**—This is where you create the list of items that appears in the drop-down menu. To add an item, select Add. This opens the Add Choice dialog box as shown in Figure 11-11. Type the list item into the Choice input field. Optionally, check the Specify Value field and type a value to be sent when the form is submitted. Because the value is used internally, there is no need to specify a custom value unless you are writing your own program to handle the form. Select the Selected radio button to have this item selected by default.

Once you have added at least one choice item, use the Modify button to edit an item, Remove to delete an item, or the Move Up and Move Down buttons to change the order of items.

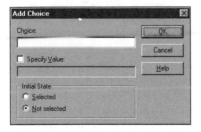

Figure 11-11: Use the Add Choice dialog box to add items to a drop-down menu.

✦ **Height**—By default the height of the drop-down menu is 1. You can edit this number in order to display more items in the list at one time. Using any number greater than 1 will cause the menu list to change from a drop-down menu to a menu list. If the number of items in the list is greater than the height, the menu list will include a vertical scroll bar. If the number of items is less than or equal to the height, the menu list will simply display all items. These three options are illustrated in Figure 11-12. Note that in Normal view, Editor usually displays menu lists of more than one line with an extra line that is not visible in a browser.

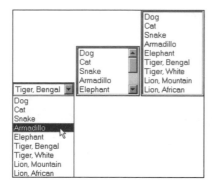

Figure 11-12: Variations on the drop-down menu theme

✦ **Allow Multiple Selections**—If this option is checked, users can select more than one choice using a method appropriate to their browser and operating system. (On a Windows system, hold down the Shift key to select a range of items; hold down the Ctrl key to select noncontiguous items.)

Validating drop-down menu input

You access a drop-down menu's Validation dialog box either via the Validate button on the Properties dialog box or by clicking the drop-down menu with the right mouse button and selecting Form Field Validation.

The drop-down menu has two different validation menus, depending on whether or not the menu has been configured to accept multiple selections. The validation options for menus that allow only single selections is shown in Figure 11-13.

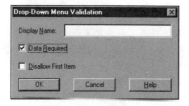

Figure 11-13: A Validation dialog box for a drop-down menu that allows only one selection

Check the Data Required check box to require users to select an option from the menu. Select Disallow First Item if you want to place a direction, such as "Select an Item," as the first item in the list and do not want this to be included as a valid selection. If you have made the menu required, you can optionally designate a name to be used to identify the menu field to users if they fail to make a valid selection.

The Validation dialog box for menus allowing multiple selections has an additional option, as shown in Figure 11-14. In this case, you can stipulate a minimum and maximum number of allowable choices, using the Minimum Items and Maximum Items fields.

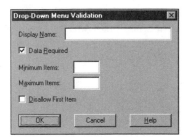

Figure 11-14: A Validation dialog box for a drop-down menu that allows multiple selections

Push buttons

A *push button,* also known as a *form button*, is a special button that initiates some action in relation to a form. When a user fills out a Web-based form, that user is filling out a copy of the form resident on his or her computer. In order for the server to process the form input, it must be sent back to the server. Submitting data for processing is the primary function of a push button. Another function is to reset the form to its default state. Note that when you add the first field to a form, the Submit and Reset buttons are added automatically.

Other buttons can also be defined and associated with custom actions, but this topic is beyond the scope of the present chapter. We come back to these buttons in Chapter 15, when we discuss scripting in FrontPage.

Creating a push button

To create a push button, select Insert ➪ Form Field ➪ Push Button or press the corresponding icon on the Forms toolbar.

Push button properties

By default, push buttons are created as normal buttons, which require scripts to work. To edit the properties of your push button, double-click the button or click the button with the right mouse button and select Form Field Properties. The Push Button Properties dialog box, shown in Figure 11-15, is displayed. You can edit the following button properties:

> ✦ **Name**—This is the name of the button. This name is used internally when the form is processed. By default, the name of a push button is "B" plus a number corresponding to the number of push buttons that have been placed on the form.

> ✦ **Value**—Although it may seem counterintuitive, the value of the button is the descriptive text that appears on the button on the Web page. Type the text that you would like to appear on the button.

Figure 11-15: The Push Button Properties dialog box

Tip

> To center the text on the button and extend the length of the button, insert one or more spaces in front of the text and an equal number of spaces after the text.

✦ **Button Type**—A submit button sends input from the form to the action designated in the Form Properties dialog box (discussed later in this chapter). A reset button restores the form to its default form without sending any data. A normal button performs no inherent action and must be associated with a scripting function in order to be of any other than decorative use. We discuss scripting in Chapter 15.

Images

An image used as a form button sends to the server the location where the user clicked it, but this information is not used by any of the FrontPage components. To make use of this feature requires custom scripting. Form images are linked to the Scripting Wizard, simplifying the task of creating functional buttons and other interactive image elements. We discuss the Scripting Wizard feature in Chapter 15.

To create an image form button, select Insert ➪ Form Field ➪ Image. The image form field is not accessible from the Form toolbar. Images inserted in a form have the same properties as regular images.

Form fields labels

All form fields should be labeled on the Web page form so that users recognize what to input into each field. HTML makes no special provision for form field labels, but for some reason, there is a special menu item for labeling form fields in FrontPage. To add a form field label, create a form field and type in some text adjacent to it. Now highlight both the field and the text and select Insert ➪ Form Field ➪ Label. A small dashed box appears around the text indicating that it is a field label.

Processing Forms

Once you have created your form, you need to connect it to some programming capable of processing the input, storing the results, and returning a confirmation page to the user. In later chapters we examine various ways to build your own custom programming or incorporate off-the-shelf third-party programming. Even if you are not a programming guru, however, you can still create useful forms in FrontPage by connecting your form to one of the available components designed for just this purpose. In this section, we examine the available component options.

The forms properties

To designate the programming option for your form, select the Form Properties dialog box. To do this, click with the right mouse button inside the form box on your Web page (indicated by long dashed lines) and select Form Properties. The Form Properties dialog box is also accessible by double-clicking one of the buttons associated with the form and then clicking the Form button in the Button Properties dialog box.

The Form Properties dialog box, an example of which is shown in Figure 11-16, consists of two principal sections. The first allows you to designate a form handler. This is the programming that will process the form, the details of which we return to momentarily. In addition, you can provide a name for your form and, if you are using frames, the target frame for any results displayed by the handler. Options for the particular form handler you are using are displayed when you click the Options button.

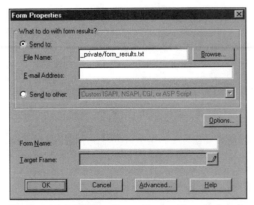

Figure 11-16: The Form Properties dialog box

The second section of the Form Properties dialog box, accessed by clicking the Advanced button, enables you to add hidden fields to the form page. A *hidden field* consists of a name and value pair that is passed along with the other form input to the form handler. To add a hidden field to your form, select the Add button and give the field a name and value. In general, hidden fields are more useful when you are creating custom form handlers.

Although a hidden field is called "hidden," it is just a variation on a standard HTML text input field. That means that anyone who takes the trouble to view the source of your HTML form will be able to see the value of all your hidden fields. So by all means use hidden fields to pass values without troubling the user about them. But don't think that you are keeping any secrets from them!

Form handlers

FrontPage enables you to connect your form to one of several types of form handlers. The various custom scripting formats are discussed in Chapter 15. The Internet Database Connector is discussed in Chapter 17, "Database Connectivity." The other form handlers are all components, which are described here.

The Save Results component

The Save Results component is the most commonly used form handler in FrontPage—this is the default setting (even though its name is not mentioned in the dialog box). It is used to record the data submitted via a Web form in one of several formats, return a confirmation page to the user, and, optionally, save the results to a second format or even send an e-mail message containing the results. In this section, we examine each of these operations in detail.

When you first create a form, the results are by default sent to a file called `form_results.txt`, located in the `_private` folder of your Web. You can change the name and path of this file either in the Form Properties dialog box or by pressing the Options button to open the Options for Saving Results of Form dialog box, which provides more detailed options for this file. This dialog box contains four tabs: File Results, E-mail Results, Confirmation Page, and Saved Fields.

File Results settings

The File Results tab, shown in Figure 11-17, allows you to designate a name and format for the file that records data input from the form. Each time the form is used, the new data is added to the end of the file—at no time does the Save Results component erase your old data.

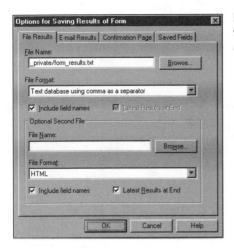

Figure 11-17: File Results options in the Options for Saving Results of Form dialog box

✦ **File Name**—In this field, type the name of the file that will store the form data. Give the file a name that links it to the form (for example, `petsurvy.htm`) and that indicates the format of the file.

✦ **File Format**—The Save Results component is capable of recording form input in any one of a variety of formats. These include several HTML formats suitable for online viewing, a reader-friendly text format, and several varieties of delimited text database formats. If you simply want to look at the results or potentially display them for others, choose one of the HTML options. If you have any plans to synthesize the information or use it for another purpose (for example, as the basis for a future mailing list), then one of the database formats is clearly preferable. These can be imported into any standard database or spreadsheet application.

If your form collects tabular data, you may want to save it in delimited format, even if you eventually want to display it online. This way you can import it into a spreadsheet and then use FrontPage to convert it automatically to a table-based HTML page. In many ways, the delimited formats provide the most flexibility for later use.

By default, the Save Results component saves both the names of fields and the input values. Uncheck the Include Field Names check box to store only data. Saving field names as well as data is more appropriate for the HTML formats than for database formats.

If an HTML format is used, the results of the form can be added at either the top of the file or at the end. Placing the latest values at the beginning of the file makes it easier to scan the newest information first—to set this option, uncheck the Latest Results at End check box. Leaving the check box checked adds new information at the bottom of the file.

These options are also available if you want to save your results to an Optional Second File. To activate this option, simply add a filename in the File Name text box. This option provides increased flexibility—for example, you might have one file in a delimited database format for analysis by a database or spreadsheet program, while leaving the other in HTML format for quick study.

E-mail Results

To find out immediately when a form has been filled out, you can have the results e-mailed to any e-mail address. Be careful when picking an e-mail format: if your e-mail client (or the client being used by the e-mail addressee) is capable of directly displaying HTML (as is Microsoft Outlook), then you might find this the most convenient and readable format. However, if your mail client can't display HTML, an e-mail message sent in this format will arrive as an attachment, a form that is generally not as convenient.

To have the contents of one of the form fields used as the e-mail message's subject line, check the Form Field Name check box next to Subject Line and enter the name of the form field in the text box directly below it.

If you have asked for an e-mail address in the form, an easy way to send a quick e-mail message back to the person who filled out the form is to include that e-mail address in the Reply To line of the form's e-mail. To do this, leave the Form Field Name check box next to Reply-To Line checked and add the name of the field that requests the e-mail address in the text box directly below it. If you don't want to include this, just leave the text box blank.

Note Note that if you use the e-mail option, you will need to configure Personal Web Server to deal with e-mail transmissions if you want to test the form before publishing it. Alternatively, make sure that the server where your Web will be published is set up to deal with component/WebBot e-mail submissions and leave Personal Web Server as is.

Confirmation Page

By default the Save Results component returns an HTML page to users thanking them for their submission and listing the contents of the data they submitted. It also includes a default validation failure message in the event that a user submits data that does not conform to the validation options you have set for the form fields.

Alternatively, you can create your own pages to perform these functions. If you do so, record the URL of these pages here. URLs can be designated using an absolute (for example, `http://www.myserver.com/confirm.htm`) or relative (`confirm.htm`) format. The next section, "Creating a Custom Confirmation Page," details how to set up this page.

Saved Fields

This tab allows you to select some or all of the form fields to be included in the file(s) or e-mail. Since there is no browse feature for selecting the fields, the easiest way to select fields is to press the Save All button and then remove the unwanted fields. To remove an unwanted field, highlight its name and press the Delete key.

In addition to the data input by the user, the Save Results component can optionally store other information pertaining to the user who submitted the forms. These options are:

✦ **Time**—This is the time the form was submitted.

✦ **Date**—This is the date the form was submitted.

✦ **Remote computer name**—This is the Internet host name, if that is available, or an IP address if a name can not be determined.

✦ **User name**—This information is only available if the user has had to enter a username to gain entrance to the form.

✦ **Browser type**—This information can be used to collect data on what types of browsers users are accessing your site with, enabling you to make better decisions about which browsers your Web needs to support.

Other form handlers

The Form Properties dialog box also allows you to select alternative form handlers for your results. These are selected by checking the Send To Other radio button in the Form Properties dialog box and picking the appropriate handler from the list.

The Registration component

This component serves the more specialized purpose of allowing users to register with a username and password to enable them to access password-protected Webs. Forms that make use of the Registration component must be saved to the root Web of a FrontPage Web server. The Registration component can also save additional information from a form in the same manner as the Save Results component. Examples of the Registration component are given in Chapter 14, "Discussion Forums," and Chapter 18, "Managing and Publishing Your Web Project."

The Discussion component

The Discussion component is also a specialized form handler, designed to store message input from a discussion form. The Discussion component stores each message as an HTML page and adds the page to a discussion table of contents, arranged according to messages and their responses. This component is discussed in detail in Chapter 14, "Discussion Forums."

Custom scripts

These scripts, or programs, run on the Web server and can utilize form data in any number of ways (including replicating the actions of the Save Results, Registration, and Discussion components for systems not running the FrontPage extensions). Examples and instructions for implementing these types of scripts are given in Chapter 15.

Creating a Custom Confirmation Page

If you would like to create a custom confirmation page for your form, you can do so using the Confirmation Form template or by creating your own page.

In addition to adding a generic confirmation message, you can also add custom information from the form itself, using the Confirmation Field component. An example of a custom confirmation page is shown in Figure 11-18. The bracketed text ([Firstname]) represents a Confirmation Field component for the name of the pet owner that the user input in the Pet Survey form. When the user sees the confirmation form, the bracketed text is replaced with the custom data that he or she has input.

Form field names

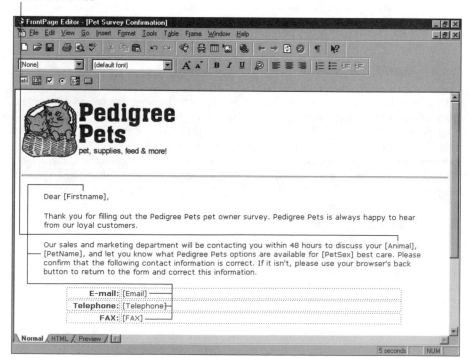

Figure 11-18: A typical confirmation page showing confirmation fields in brackets

To add a Confirmation Field component to your confirmation page, place the cursor in the location where you want the field to appear. Select Insert ➪ FrontPage Components, and choose Confirmation Field. In the Confirmation Field Properties dialog box (see Figure 11-19), type the name of the field whose value you wish to appear on the page.

Figure 11-19: The Confirmation Field Properties dialog box

Once you have created a custom confirmation page, you need to configure the Save Results component to recognize this page. To do this, open the form page and click with the right mouse button in the form. Select Form Properties and click the Options button. Click the Confirmation Page tab and type the URL of the custom confirmation page in the appropriate field, or use the Browse button to locate the file in the current Web. Click OK to close the Properties dialog box. Click OK again to close the Form Properties dialog box. Save your work.

Using the Form Page Wizard

In addition to the form templates described earlier in this chapter, FrontPage also includes a Form Page Wizard that can help you construct a sophisticated form quickly. By way of illustrating the use of this wizard, we will return to the Pill Quiz image map Web page we created for Happy Valley Health in Chapter 5. Using the Form Page Wizard, we add the quiz questions.

Note

To follow along with this exercise, open the `Examples/ch11` folder on the CD and select `pillquiz.htm`.

The Pill Quiz image map consists of a large graphical image with eight colorful pills scattered about on it. The goal is to link each pill to a quiz question. When users have answered each question, they click the Submit Quiz button to have their answers scored.

In order to use the Form Page Wizard, we first create a new quiz page that contains the questions. Afterward, we reintroduce the images from the original page.

To create the form page using the Form Page Wizard, select File ➪ New, and choose the Form Page Wizard from the New File template list. You are greeted with the first screen of the wizard as shown in Figure 11-20. Click Next to continue.

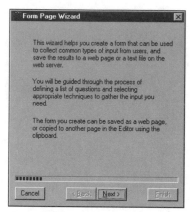

Figure 11-20: The opening screen of the Form Page Wizard

Name the form

In the next dialog box, shown in Figure 11-21, give the page the URL **pillquiz.htm** and name it **Happy Valley Health Pill Quiz**. Click Next to continue.

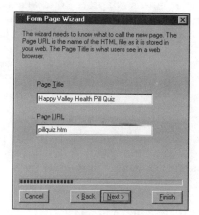

Figure 11-21: Naming your form using the Form Page Wizard

Form input types

The next page is the main selection page of the wizard. From this page you can add as many different questions of as many types as you like to your form. There are many options to choose from:

✦ **Contact Information**—This builds form fields to capture name, affiliation, address, and phone number.

✦ **Account Information**—This prompts for username and password.

✦ **Product Information**—This asks for a product name, model, version, and serial number.

✦ **Ordering Information**—This produces a form to take a sales order, including a list of products to order and billing and shipping information.

✦ **Personal Information**—This is a form to collect information such as a user's name, age, and other personal characteristics.

✦ **One of Several Options**—This is a form item that requires users to pick exactly one option.

✦ **Any of Several Options**—This is a form item that allows users to pick zero or more options.

✦ **Boolean**—This prompts users to input a yes/no or true/false question.

✦ **Date**—This prompts users to input a date format.

✦ **Time**—This prompts users to input a time format.

✦ **Range**—This creates a rating scale from 1 to 5.

✦ **Number**—This creates an input box for a number.

✦ **String**—This creates a one-line text box.

✦ **Paragraph**—This creates a scrolling text box.

Adding an input type

We would like to start the quiz by asking for some basic personal information. This will help us learn something about who is using the quiz page and how much they know about pills.

Select the personal information type and change its prompt to read "**Before you take the quiz, please tell us a little bit about yourself by answering the following brief questions:**". Click Next to continue.

The next page gives you options for what kinds of personal questions to include. We are interested in name, age in years, and sex. These three items are all checked by default. Select the Years Old radio button for the Age item and change the group name to **PersonalInfo** as shown in Figure 11-22. Click Next to continue.

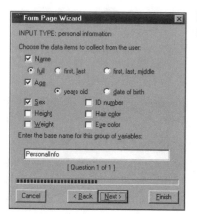

Figure 11-22: Adding questions to a form using the Form Page Wizard

Additional input types

The next screen shows the first section of our form completed. From here we can continue to add form input types. Click the Add button to return to the input types selection screen.

Ideally we would need to create a question for each pill in the image map. For purposes of our example, we walk through the creation of two more questions, a Boolean true/false question and a multiple-choice question.

Creating a true/false question

To create a true/false question, select the Boolean option from the Input Types list. In the Prompt Input box, type the question, **"This pill is an aspirin. True or false, taking aspirin can decrease the risk of high blood pressure?"** Click Next to continue.

In the Boolean Input Type dialog box, select True/False radio buttons and type the word **aspirin** for the variable name. Click Next to return to the list of input questions. Click the Add button to add another question.

Creating a multiple-choice question

To create a multiple-choice question, select the One of Several Options item from the Input Types list. In the Prompt Input box, type the question, **"This pill is used to thicken the blood. It is a(n):"** Click Next to continue.

In the One of Several Options dialog box, type the following option labels as shown in Figure 11-23:

```
Amphetamine
Coagulant
Vitamin
Antibiotic
Placebo
```

Select the Radio Buttons option in answer to the question, "How should the user choose an answer?" For the variable name, type **mc1** (for multiple choice). Click Next to continue.

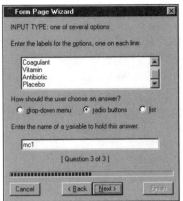

Figure 11-23: Adding multiple-choice options to a drop-down menu item in the Form Page Wizard

Presentation options

We now have three questions in the Form Page Wizard list. It is time to go on, so click the Next button to go on to the Presentation Options dialog box, pictured in Figure 11-24. The dialog box enables us to control how the questions appear on the form page. We will leave all options here set to their default values. The option to create the form items in a table is an especially nice feature, providing our form with a cleaner, more structured look. Click Next to continue.

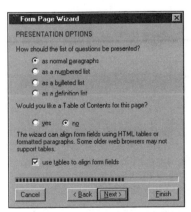

Figure 11-24: Selecting presentation options for your form

Output options

The next dialog box involves choices about how to process the form and what to do with the output. We opt to save the results to a text file, named `pillquiz.txt`. Select the Save Results to a Text File radio button, and type **pillquiz** into the input box. The wizard adds the `.txt` extension automatically. Click Finish to have the wizard create our quiz form, the results of which are shown in Figure 11-25. Check the format of the text file where the results are stored. Ultimately it would be nice to score the results, but that will have to wait until we can add some custom programming.

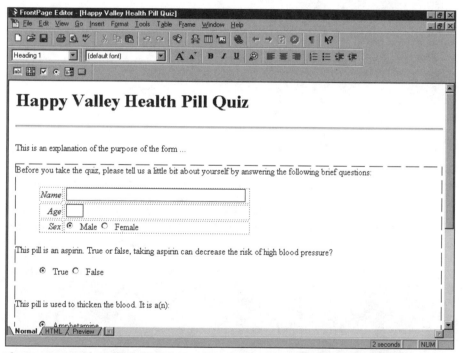

Figure 11-25: The Pill Quiz form as generated by the Form Page Wizard

To add the appropriate image for each question, open the pill quiz image in Image Composer (this image is named `PillQuiz.gif` and is located in the `Contents/ch11` folder on the CD-ROM that comes with this book). Use the cutout tool to cut out two of the pills and then drag them (or copy and paste them) from Image Composer into the form page as shown in Figure 11-26. To neaten up the appearance of the form, both images use Left Float, and a line break to clear both margins (Insert ➪ Break) was inserted between the first and second pill questions. Chapter 5 details the use of Image Composer.

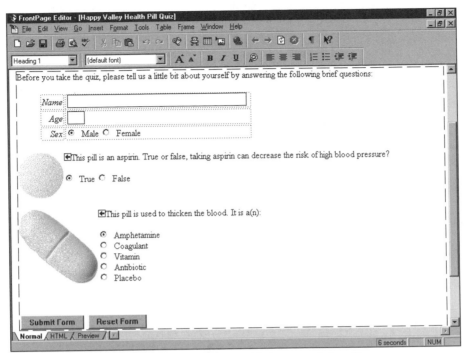

Figure 11-26: The final pill quiz, complete with images of the pills

Note

My apologies to those members of the health care profession for my probable errors as to the types of pills located next to the questions in the preceding image.

Taking the Next Step

FrontPage has well-developed facilities for creating and implementing forms. This chapter has covered the basic details of form building and the options for saving results and returning customized confirmations. In the next three chapters, we examine the components (WebBots) that are included with FrontPage, including two of the most sophisticated: the Text Search component and the Discussion component.

✦ ✦ ✦

FrontPage Components

This chapter introduces FrontPage *components,* the ready-to-use programs that are an integral part of FrontPage's operation. Using these components, you can easily add interactive functionality to your site, without taking a course in computer programming. This chapter provides an overview of the components that come with FrontPage. In the remaining chapters in Part IV, you will get a detailed look at using components in conjunction with online forms, text searching, and discussion forums.

New in 98

For some reason, what used to be called WebBots are now referred to as components in FrontPage 98. Their HTML codes and names are identical. In fact, if you look at the HTML code for a component, it is referred to as a WebBot. So if you're familiar with the WebBot feature of previous releases of FrontPage, you're already familiar with components.

Defining and Using Components

Component refers to prebuilt programming modules you can customize and insert into your Web pages. Some of the components, like the Comment component we encountered briefly in Chapter 2, perform administrative functions. Others enable you to include customized content in your Web pages. Still others, such as the Text Search component and the Discussion component, provide your Web with added functionality for users.

Because the components work in conjunction with your Web server, they only work with Web servers that have had the FrontPage server extensions installed. Server extensions are available from Microsoft for several varieties of Windows and UNIX Web servers. See Appendix C, "FrontPage Server Extensions," for more detail.

How they work

When you add a component to your Web page, FrontPage inserts HTML tags that reference it, much as HTML is used to reference a graphic, a sound file, or a Java applet. Customization of components is done through HTML attributes in the component tag. Figure 12-1 shows an example of the HTML used to point to a component, in this case, the Comment component we discussed briefly in Chapter 2.

Comment component

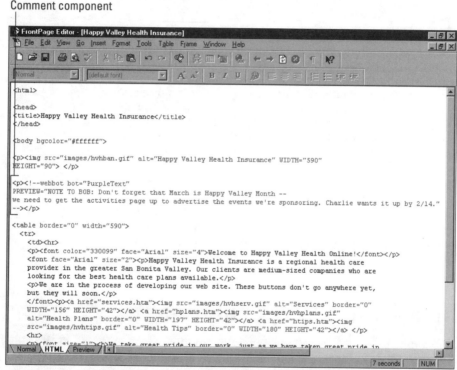

Fig 12-1: The Comment component, showing a comment and the HTML that produces it

When a user requests a Web page containing an embedded component, the server must activate the appropriate component, enabling it to perform its magic before the page is sent. Components are closely tied to the operation of the server. This is why components only work on FrontPage-enabled Web servers. No special additions are required at the user's end. A Netscape browser will display components as well as Microsoft's browser.

Note

The component comment is embedded using a variant on a standard comment tag. This "hijacking" of HTML's comment tag is part of the reason that FrontPage does not support standard HTML comments.

Because they require FrontPage-enabled servers, components are less portable than standard CGI applications or Java applets and more akin to other Microsoft technologies, such as their Active Server Pages, that are limited to servers supported by Microsoft. But if you have access to a FrontPage-enabled Web server, the ease with which you can add components makes them hard to resist.

Note

If you do not have access to a FrontPage server, you may want to jump ahead to Part V, where we introduce other programming components that you can use to create many of the same functions, with perhaps a wee bit more labor on your part.

Inserting components

You have two principal ways to add a component to your Web page. The primary method is to insert the component directly into your Web page. The secondary method is to use one of the many Web page templates and wizards that come with preconfigured components. This section describes the general method for inserting components. In the next section we describe each of the components that come with FrontPage and identify any predefined templates that utilize a given component.

To insert a component, first open your Web page in Editor and position the cursor where you want the component to appear. Select Insert ⇨ FrontPage Component or click the Insert FrontPage Component icon in the toolbar. The list of available components, as shown in Figure 12-2, is displayed.

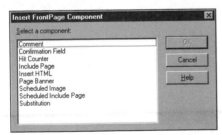

Figure 12-2: The FrontPage component list

After you have selected the component, additional dialog boxes may appear, allowing you to customize the component's properties. Once added to your Web page, a component can be distinguished by the robot cursor that appears any time the cursor passes over it. As you might suspect, double-clicking the component allows you to edit its properties. Alternatively, click with the right mouse button and select (Component's Name) Properties from the pop-down menu or select the component and select Edit ⇨ FrontPage Component Properties.

Exploring FrontPage Components

In this section we briefly examine the operation of all of the components that come packaged with FrontPage. Some receive extended treatment in this chapter. Others will be discussed in more detail in Chapters 13 and 14.

The Comment component

To add a comment, first position the cursor where you would like the comment to appear in the Web page. Then select Insert ↔ FrontPage Component, highlight Comment in the list, and click OK. The dialog box shown in Figure 12-3 appears, allowing you to enter the text of your comment.

Figure 12-3: The Comment dialog box

Comments show up in FrontPage in the visited link color, purple by default (in fact the actual name of this component is *PurpleText*, as you can see if you look closely at the HTML back in Figure 12-1). Comment text does not appear when the page is viewed by a Web browser, since the entire component is enclosed in a standard HTML comment tag.

The comment may not appear on the Web page, but it is still there in the HTML, viewable by anyone who decides to view the HTML source of the page. As a result, use of the Comment component to record your trade secrets or the combination of your safety deposit box is, as they say, discouraged.

The Comment component is used in almost every template to instruct you in the purpose of the template or how to customize it.

The Confirmation Field component

When a user completes an online form and submits some information, it is customary (and a generally good idea) to provide a confirmation message to assure the user that the information was submitted successfully—not, mind you, that anything ever fails to work as anticipated on the Web. A confirmation page can also be used to provide the user with further steps to take once a form has been submitted.

The Confirmation Field component allows you to insert the input from designated fields in the form into a confirmation page. For example, having asked users to input their names, you could use the Confirmation Field component to insert their names into the confirmation page. Another possible use would be to show users all of the information they input and ask them to confirm that this is the data they want to send before submitting it. If they've made a mistake, instruct them to use their browsers' Back button to return to the form and fix the error—in general, the information will still appear in the form using this method.

To use the Confirmation Field component, you should first have created a form. Creating forms is the topic of Chapter 11. Record the names of all the fields in your form that you would like to use in the confirmation page. Next create a normal HTML page that includes any standard message you would like to give the user. If you like, you can use the Confirmation Page template, which already contains several basic confirmation fields, to get you started.

To add a confirmation field, position the cursor where you want the field input to appear. Select Insert ⇨ FrontPage Component and choose Confirmation Field from the list of available components. This activates the dialog box shown in Figure 12-4.

Figure 12-4: The dialog box for the Confirmation Field component

Enter the name of the field whose input you want to appear. Click OK to insert the component. (Unfortunately, FrontPage doesn't give you a list of available fields from the form—FrontPage 99 may.) FrontPage inserts the field name in brackets (for instance, [username]) as a placeholder to indicate the presence of the component. When the confirmation page is displayed, this placeholder will be replaced with the actual input from the field.

See Chapter 11 for a more in-depth example of how to create a confirmation page.

The Include component

This component allows you to insert the contents of another file into your Web page. This feature is particularly useful as a means of including elements that are common to many pages, for example headers, footers, and page style information. By including these elements in a separate Web page, you can edit the included page and the changes will be reflected on all pages.

When FrontPage first creates a new Web, it creates a folder named _private. Contents of this folder are not directly accessible to visitors to the Web site, but it can be used to store objects that are part of the Web. This is a good place to put files that you want to include using the Include component.

Creating a footer

To illustrate use of the Include component, we create a footer file and add it to the pages of the Happy Valley Web.

The first step is to create the footer file that contains copyright information and an e-mail address for comments regarding the Web site:

1. Create a new page by selecting File ⇨ New and choosing the Normal template or by clicking the New File icon in the toolbar.

   When you include a file using the Include component, it only includes the contents of the page (that is, everything between the <body> tags). Properties such as the page title, style sheet, and page background are not included.

2. Select Insert ⇨ Horizontal Line to insert a ruled line that will mark the beginning of the footer.

3. Type the text of the footer as illustrated in Figure 12-5. Format the text using the Heading 6 style (for this illustration, the Heading 3 style has been used so you can read it). Note the line break (represented in Editor by an arrow symbol pointing down and to the left) inserted after the copyright statement to force the text onto two lines.

4. Insert a copyright symbol at the beginning of the first line. You could do this by selecting Insert ⇨ Symbol and choosing the copyright symbol. As mentioned in Chapter 9, however, FrontPage does not insert this symbol using the standard HTML format. Consequently, we have chosen to insert the symbol using the HTML Markup command (use of this feature is detailed in Chapter 9). Select Insert ⇨ HTML Markup. In the dialog box, type **©**, the entity reference for the copyright symbol in HTML. Click OK. Editor displays the HTML markup question mark seen in Figure 12-5. Web browsers will display the correct symbol, however.

5. To add a little visual interest to the bottom of the page and to tie it thematically to the top, we have added a variation of the Happy Valley logo that appears at the top of the page. To add this image to your footer page, position the cursor in front of the footer text. Select Insert ⇨ Image and locate the image, hvhfoot. gif, on the CD-ROM in the Contents/ch12 folder. Click OK to add the image to the Web page.

   Select the image and open the Image Properties dialog box. In the Alternative Representations section, type **Happy Valley Health Logo** into the Text field. Click the Appearance tab. Change the Alignment to Left and Horizontal spacing to 10. Click OK to accept these changes and return to the Web page.

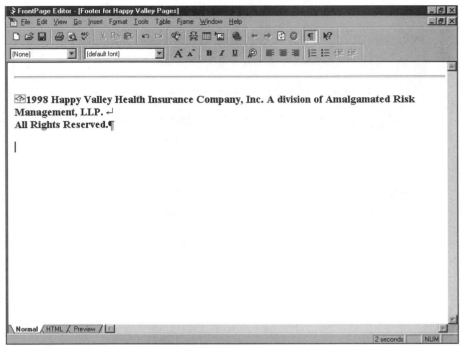

Figure 12-5: The footer page for the Happy Valley Web as seen in Editor

6. Save the footer as hvhfoot.htm in the _private folder of the current Web. Save the image to your Web when prompted to do so.

Adding the footer to the Happy Valley home page

Now we can add this footer to the Happy Valley home page we created back in Chapter 3. Open the Happy Valley home page, default.htm, located on the CD-ROM in Examples/ch03. Position the cursor at the bottom of the page. Select Insert ⇨ FrontPage Component and choose the Include component. In the dialog box shown in Figure 12-6, click the Browse button and locate the hvhfoot.htm footer file. Click OK to include this file in the current Web page. The results should resemble Figure 12-7.

Figure 12-6: Selecting a file to include with the Include component

Included page

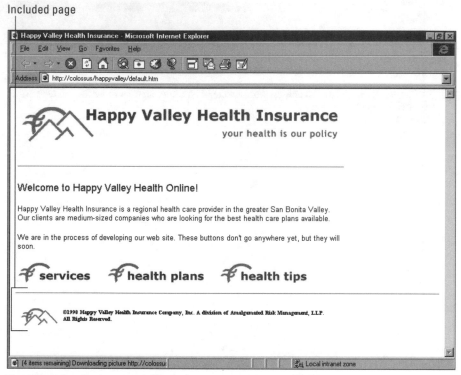

Figure 12-7: The Happy Valley home page with included footer

The Scheduled Image and Scheduled Include components

The Scheduled Image and Scheduled Include components are both variations on the Include component just described. The difference is that the two scheduled components enable you to designate a particular time period during which a given image or other Web content will be displayed. The time interval is indicated with a begin time and an end time. The time range can be from one second to several years, with minutes, hours, days, and months as options in between.

By default nothing will be displayed by the component until the scheduled begin time. Alternatively, you can include an alternative, default image to display before and after the time interval.

To add a Scheduled Image component to your Web page, position the cursor on the Web page where you want the image to appear. Select Insert ⇨ FrontPage Component and choose the Scheduled Image component. In the dialog box (see Figure 12-8), indicate the image to include, the begin and end times to display the image, and, optionally, an image to display before and after the scheduled time frame. Note that browsing for the image to include is limited to the current Web or the World Wide Web. Consequently, you will want to import the desired image into your Web prior to configuring the component. Click OK to add the image to the current Web page.

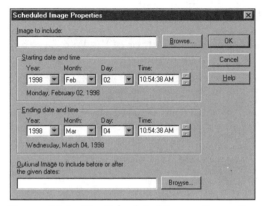

Figure 12-8: The Scheduled Image Properties dialog box

If the current time is within the range of the scheduled image time, the selected image displays in Editor. If not, it displays a bracketed message: "[Expired Scheduled Image]." This message is displayed even if the begin time for the scheduled image has not been reached yet. Otherwise, if you have opted to include an alternative image, this image displays in lieu of the bracketed message.

You add a Scheduled Include using the same technique. The only difference is that instead of specifying an image, you specify the URL of the page you wish to use for the Scheduled Include. You can designate an alternative URL to display before and after the scheduled time.

As currently configured, the Scheduled Image component is a useful way to provide information about one-time-only events, such as product promotions, sales, and contests.

The Search component

The Search component is used to add a text search component to your Web page. The Search component enables users to search all or part of your Web for pages containing one or more text strings. Results of a search are displayed by listing the titles of matching pages hyperlinked to the actual page. Details of the results page can also be controlled via the component. If you have a content-rich Web and are looking for a relatively simple way to enhance the usability of your Web site, the Search component could be just the thing. (The Search component is discussed in detail in Chapter 13.)

The Substitution component

The Substitution component enables you to insert information contained in the configuration variables that are defined for your Web. By default, your Web's standard configuration consists of the following predefined items, all of which are reported in the Web Properties dialog box in Explorer. To view the Web properties, open your Web in Explorer and select Edit ➪ Properties.

> ✦ **Author**—This variable identifies the original author of the Web page as indicated by the Created By field in the Web Properties dialog box. The author's name is given by the FrontPage Username, if one is necessary to access the Web. Otherwise, the Windows' logon Username is used.
>
> ✦ **Modified By**—This variable identifies the author of the most recent changes to the Web page, as indicated by the Modified By field in the Web Properties dialog box.
>
> ✦ **Description**—This variable is replaced with the contents of the Comments field of the Web Properties dialog box. By default this field is empty, so before using the Description substitution, you should input the description you want in this field.
>
> ✦ **Page-URL**—This variable is replaced with the location of the file, using the full URL including the protocol and domain name.

You can add these predefined configuration variables to your page, and you can also add your own variables.

To create a new configuration variable, open your Web in Explorer, select Tools ➪ Web Settings, and choose the Parameters tab. Any existing user-defined variables will be listed in this dialog box, shown in Figure 12-9. Select Add and input the name of the parameter and its value. The parameter name will be added to the list of available configuration variables in the Substitution dialog box pull-down menu.

Figure 12-9: Use the Parameters tab of the Web Settings dialog box in Explorer to configure variables for use with the Substitution component.

Once you have defined a substitution parameter, you can easily insert its value into any Web page in the Web. To do so, open the page in Editor and position the cursor where you want the substitution to occur. Select Insert⇨FrontPage Component and choose the Substitution component. This opens the Substitution Component Properties dialog box shown in Figure 12-10. Select a variable from the pop-up menu list. The value corresponding to the variable name will be inserted at the cursor.

Figure 12-10: Select a variable from the Substitution Component Properties dialog box to insert the text associated with it.

The Table of Contents component

It is frequently useful to create a list of the contents of your Web or of a certain portion of your Web so that visitors can see what you have to offer and also so that they can navigate easily from place to place. Maintaining a table of contents can be tiresome, however, if you have content that changes with any frequency. The FrontPage Table of Contents component generates its table of contents automatically and updates it every time you save the page.

Using the Table of Contents template

There are numerous ways to generate a table of contents. The quickest way is to use the Table of Contents template to create a separate table of contents page. To use this template to create a list of pages in the Pedigree Pets Web, first open Editor and then select File⇨New and choose the Table of Contents template. This opens a new template as seen in Figure 12-11. (Note the use of the Timestamp component—which is detailed later in this chapter—at the bottom of the page.)

The Table of Contents component inserts a placeholder list of names like that seen in Figure 12-11. The actual content of the file list only appears when you view the page in your browser.

To edit the component properties, click the component once to select it and select Edit⇨FrontPage Component Properties. Alternatively, click with the right mouse button on the component. Either way, the Table of Contents Properties dialog box appears, as shown in Figure 12-12.

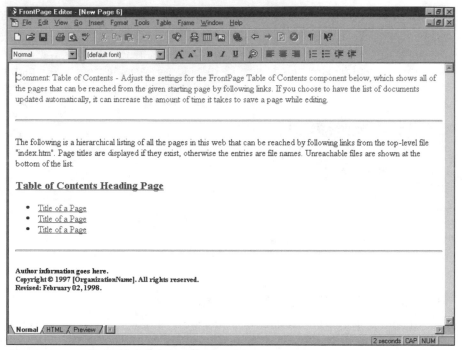

Figure 12-11: The Table of Contents template page

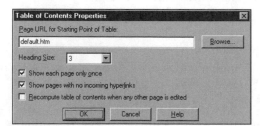

Figure 12-12: The Table of Contents Properties
dialog box

This dialog box contains several options. The most important is to choose the
start page for the table of contents. This page serves as the starting point for the
component. It appears in the header of the Table of Contents unless you specify
None for the heading size.

The heading size refers to the size of the initial link, the title of which can serve as the main header for the list. Select the desired start file. The title of this Web page will appear in the header location.

If you are developing your Web locally on a Windows system and publishing to a UNIX server with FrontPage extensions, FrontPage may automatically convert the filename of your home page from `Default.htm` to `index.html`. It does not, however, reflect this change in your table of contents. One solution is to change the name of the home page from `Default.htm` to `index.html` in your local server.

The check box options are as follows: Show Each Page Only Once is usually a good idea, unless you really want to display the full hierarchy of your Web pages. Show Pages with No Incoming Hyperlinks is designed to weed out pages that are no longer referred to by other pages in the Web. However, it also effectively means that the table of contents cannot be used to generate the main navigation of the site. It can really only support sites with a complete navigation system already intact. Recompute Table of Contents When Any Page Is Edited may be worth the extra time it adds if you make frequent changes to the content.

The Table of Contents also makes excellent use of shared borders (or navigation bars) and Explorer's Navigation view. If you use navigation bars, the Table of Contents becomes a hierarchical list with the different levels of your Web indented to show its organization. Shared borders and navigation bars are explained in Chapter 8, and Explorer is explained in Chapter 3.

Inserting the Table of Contents component

Alternatively, you can insert the Table of Contents component directly into a new or existing Web page. To insert the component, open in Editor the page where you want the component to appear. Select Insert ⇨ Table of Contents option. The component will insert the same placeholder list you saw in the template. Note that you cannot edit this text. It is only there as a reminder to you that the component is present. Edit the component properties as described in the previous section.

If you want to use the Navigation view tip from the previous section, you must do some HTML editing to add the following codes to the component. Editing HTML code is detailed in Chapter 9.

```
min-ul-levels="0"
i-ul-levels="1"
max-heading="6"
min-heading="0"
```

Table of contents challenges

The Table of Contents component is useful, but it can create some challenges to implement. The component works by reading the links from the start page, and following each of those to the next page, and so on. The component works well when you want to display the structure of links on your pages. This produces a list of Web pages in order of how they are linked to one another, which is not typically the way you organize Web pages to present to visitors.

Here are a few challenges you may encounter:

✦ If you change the filename of a file on the local copy of your Web and then publish the Web to a remote server, FrontPage adds a new file with the updated name but does not delete the previous version of the file. Under normal circumstances this adds some clutter to your file system but is not a problem for users. However, if you have included a Table of Contents component, you should be sure to uncheck the component option Show Pages with No Incoming Links. Otherwise your table of contents will show all of the unlinked pages.

✦ Another challenging situation involves the use of the Table of Contents component to generate a separate page. If you are using this table of contents as the sole navigational element, the other pages will not be linked. If they are not linked, you cannot check the No Orphans check box.

✦ In addition, the Table of Contents page does not work especially well with frames, since it will generate links to both frame set documents and individual component pages.

Inserting a Timestamp

The Timestamp component displays the modification time and date of the Web page on which the component resides. Including a last modified date on your Web pages is a courtesy to visitors, since it will help them judge whether or not the information on your site is up to date. On the other hand, you may decide that you would rather not have such an obvious indication of pages that have not been updated recently.

Tip

Of course, one way to get around the problem of pages that are not modified regularly is to resave the pages from time to time in order to update their file modification date. This may seem like cheating to some people, but look at it this way: The point of publicizing the modification date is to demonstrate that someone is actively maintaining the pages as much as it is to show when content was last changed. (Anyway, there are better ways to alert people to recently updated content on the page, such as the now-ubiquitous New! icon.) Manually updating the modification date is just a way of indicating that you *are* maintaining the page, even if the content has not changed recently.

To add a timestamp, position the cursor at the location where you would like the component to appear. Select Insert⇨Timestamp. The Timestamp component displays a dialog box as shown in Figure 12-13. You can select from the following options:

✦ **Display**—You can choose to display the date the page was last edited directly or the last time it was updated automatically, if it is a page like the table of contents that is subject to automatic updates.

✦ **Date Format**—Select from a variety of date formats listed in the drop-down menu.

✦ **Time Format**—Likewise, select from a variety of time formats listed in the drop-down menu.

After you have made your selections, click OK to insert the timestamp in your page. The timestamp will appear just as it will look in the Web page. Only the tell-tale wizard cursor that appears when you move the mouse over the timestamp will remind you that this is no ordinary text.

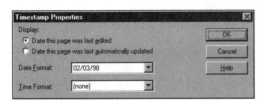

Figure 12-13: The Timestamp Properties dialog box

Activating a Hit Counter

The Hit Counter component displays the number of times a particular page has been accessed, or "hit." To insert a Hit Counter, select Insert⇨FrontPage Component and pick Hit Counter. Then select the options you want for the display and click OK. A small placeholder indicates where the counter will be displayed on your page. Chapter 6 includes complete details for adding and customizing the Hit Counter.

Working with Components in Forms

In addition to the several components accessible from the Insert menu, three components are used exclusively in conjunction with forms processing, a topic we delve into in the next chapter.

In order to do anything useful, a form needs to be connected to programming that is capable of processing the data that the user inputs into the form. This programming can take many forms; the more common programming options are described in Part V of this book.

If you are not a programming guru (or even if you are), the simplest way to add programming to your forms is to link them to one of the components that are designed specifically to deal with forms input. These are described briefly here to complete our list of available components. Each is described in more detail elsewhere in the book.

✦ **Discussion component**—This component processes input from forms designed for use in a discussion Web.

✦ **Registration component**—This component is designed for use in registering users with a password in order to access password-protected Webs.

✦ **Save Results component**—This is the most general-purpose forms-processing component that comes with FrontPage. Input can be saved in a variety of formats, and several options deal with how to treat confirmation messages returned to the user.

Using Components Wizards and Templates

In our discussion of the components accessible from the Insert menu item, we have mentioned any time a component is used in one of the templates or wizards that accompany FrontPage. We list the templates and wizards that include components here as well, for your convenience. Note that we have not mentioned the several templates that use the Comment component or the Timestamp component:

✦ **Confirmation form**—uses Confirmation Field components

✦ **Feedback form**—uses the Save Results component (Chapter 11)

✦ **Guest Book**—uses the Save Results component (Chapter 11)

✦ **Search Page**—uses the Search component (Chapter 13)

✦ **Table of Contents**—uses the Table of Contents component

✦ **User Registration**—uses the Registration component (Chapter 14)

✦ **Discussion Web Wizard (in Explorer)**—uses the Discussion component (Chapter 14)

Taking the Next Step

This chapter introduced you to the components (formerly known as WebBots) included with FrontPage and demonstrated how some of the simpler examples work. By far the most commonly used major components are the ones associated with online forms. How to create a form in FrontPage and how to link it to the necessary component programming are the topics of the previous chapter. Chapters describing the Text Search and Discussion components in more detail follow this one.

✦   ✦   ✦

Text Searching

This chapter describes several ways to use the Text Search component (WebBot) that comes with FrontPage. The chapter begins with an overview of how text searches generally operate. We build a simple text search form and learn how to create and maintain the search index for your Web. The latter part of the chapter presents several interesting variations on the standard text search interface.

New in 98

As we pointed out the last chapter, what used to be called WebBots are now referred to as components in FrontPage 98. If you're familiar with the WebBot feature of previous releases of FrontPage, you're already familiar with components.

Searching the Great Web

The World Wide Web has made it relatively easy for individuals and institutions to place online a vast amount of text-based information. Having this much information at our fingertips is marvelous, but finding the information you need can be quite time consuming. One of the largest challenges that the Web as an information delivery system faces is how to help people find information quickly.

Text search engines are one solution to the problem of information overload. From the user's perspective, the concept of conducting a search is quite simple. The user enters one or more keywords related to the subject he or she wants information on and is given a list of items that match these keywords. The user then selects pertinent items from the list in order to retrieve the information.

This relatively simple model has several distinct parts:

1. **Search form**—an interface that enables users to indicate what they want

2. **Search engine**—a mechanism for matching requests with the available information

3. **Drill-down list**—a list interface that helps users decide which items they want to know more about

The FrontPage Text Search component provides a built-in search engine. It also provides assistance in generating user interfaces for both conducting searches and displaying the results. This chapter describes each of these steps in detail.

Learning about Search Engines

FrontPage takes care of conducting searches automatically, but it pays to understand the process it uses to do this.

The FrontPage search engine is composed of two parts: one that is responsible for indexing the content of your Web pages and one that actually conducts the searches. The indexing portion of the search engine builds a dictionary of all the words in all of the documents that you include in your text searches. This dictionary keys every word in its list to every instance of that word in your documents. That way, when a user searches for a keyword, the search engine goes to this dictionary to locate matches quickly.

In addition to the simple process of matching keywords to instances of those words in your documents, the FrontPage search engine, like any good search engine, has two additional capabilities. It provides for a simple syntax that allows users to build a search request that involves multiple words. It also incorporates a system for deciding which documents are most likely to be relevant to the user and a method of reporting relevancy information to the user. We examine how these mechanisms work in FrontPage later in the chapter.

At this point it is time to see just how easy building a text search mechanism is in FrontPage. We explore several variations on text searches in this chapter. For all of those examples we use a small set of documents (nine, to be exact) intended to represent a collection of advice on health-care-related topics. These are intended as examples only. The content should not to be mistaken for real advice (I had to say that). More important, you should recognize that you would probably not bother to build a search engine for five pages. In this case, a single table of contents describing each page would better serve your users. So while you are reading this chapter and following the exercises, pretend that the five pages are really five hundred; this will help you imagine a really useful context for a search engine.

Note

The text search examples are included on the CD-ROM that accompanies this book. They are found in the Examples/ch13 folder on the disc.

Does your site need a search engine?

FrontPage makes it so easy to add a search engine to your site that in some respects you may as well include one, even if it is not absolutely necessary. If you have a small site, however, don't use the search engine as the primary method of navigation through the site. You can index all of your pages and offer a minimal keyword search capability as an additional way to find information, but you should also use a table of contents or other navigation device to identify the content areas of your site. Provide a search interface on your home page.

If you have a large site, particularly if you have one or more collections of documents online, you should definitely include a search engine. In this case, you may want to consider a more specialized approach to using the search engine. Possibilities discussed later in this chapter include:

✦ Building separate searches for particular subsections of your site

✦ Generating a set list of keywords to search for

✦ Making the search accessible from multiple locations

Adding a Search Form

In our first example, we insert a simple Search form into the Happy Valley Health Insurance home page. This method works best for administrators of small sites who wish to index the entire contents of their site (see the sidebar for more information).

To begin, open the Happy Valley Health home page (`default.htm`) in Editor. Position the cursor between the main paragraph of text and the navigation buttons. Select Insert ➪ Active Elements ➪ Search Form.

The dialog box shown in Figure 13-1 is displayed, enabling you to customize several aspects of the text search input and results.

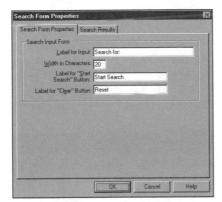

Figure 13-1: The Search Form Properties dialog box

Search input form properties

The search input form is the form where users enter their search requests. The default Search form, which you get if you click OK without changing any of the input form properties, is shown in Figure 13-2.

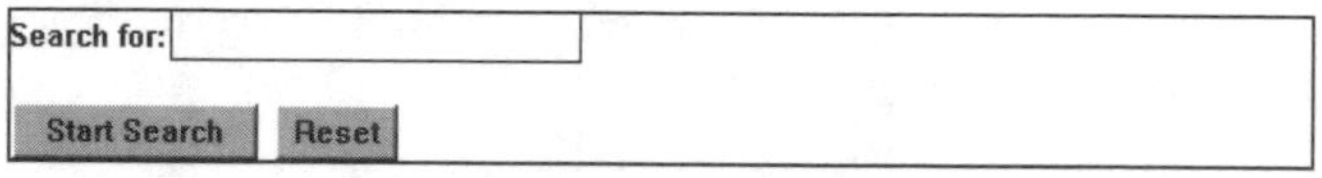

Search for: [   ]

[Start Search] [Reset]

Figure 13-2: The plain vanilla version of the Search Component input form

To customize the Search form, change the Label for Input text from "Search for" to "Search the Happy Valley Web site for" (this text, which precedes the input form, provides a brief indication of the purpose of the Search form). Web users, particularly novice users, are often confused by the multiplicity of search options on the Web. It can be unclear whether they are conducting a search of a single page, a Web site, or the entire Internet. Our label indicates both the function of the form and the scope of the search.

The remaining options concern the appearance of the form components:

✦ **Width in Characters**—This determines the width of the text field input box. The default is 20. Let's make ours a bit wider by changing the value of this property to 40.

✦ **Label for "Start Search" Button**—This is the text that appears on the Submit Form button. You can leave this as is for now.

✦ **Label for "Clear" Button**—This is the text that appears on the Reset Form button. You can leave this as is.

Search results properties

The options in the Search Results tab of the Search Form Properties dialog box concern how matches are displayed to the user.

The first option is the Word List to Search. We return to the ability to designate multiple word lists in a later example. For now, the default "All" is the appropriate response, indicating that the search should encompass every page on the Web site.

The remaining options consist of three check boxes, all unchecked by default:

✦ **Score (Closeness of Match)**—Checking this box causes the component to display a score for each match in its results page. Whether this box is checked or not, the component still uses the score to determine the order in which matches are displayed. This option only affects whether or not the score is displayed.

✦ **File Date**—This displays modification date information for the matched file. It is useful if you are displaying time-sensitive information or if you maintain multiple versions of the same documents. Unfortunately, you cannot sort the results by date.

✦ **File Size (in K Bytes)**—This displays the size of the file in kilobytes. This is probably only useful if you have abnormally large text files. Note that this lists only the size of the HTML page file, not those of any graphics that are linked to the page.

For now, check all boxes so that we can see how these options are displayed. Click OK to record the changes and exit the dialog box. The Form Input dialog box is inserted into the Happy Valley home page as shown in Figure 13-3. Save your work.

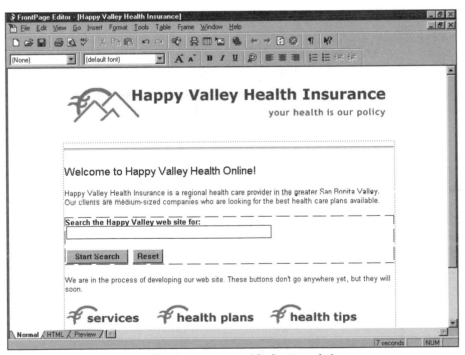

Figure 13-3: The Happy Valley home page with the Search form

Using a Search Form

When you add the Search component, FrontPage automatically builds the indexes necessary to perform searches. The index files are stored in a subfolder of the _vti_txt directory. (You cannot see this folder in FrontPage Explorer, but it is visible in standard Windows Explorer.) To test your Search form, first make sure that you have saved the Search form in the Happy Valley home page. If you would like to follow the examples that follow, you need to have the home page saved to a Web that also includes the other content files contained in the Examples/ch13 folder of the CD-ROM.

Note
In order for the Search component to work, you must preview the Web on a Web server that has the FrontPage extensions installed. For information on installing these extensions, see Appendix C, "Installing FrontPage Server Extensions."

With the Happy Valley home page open in Editor, select File ➪ Preview in Browser. With the home page in your browser, locate the Search form, scrolling down the page if necessary. Type the word **work** into the keyword input form and press the Start Search button.

The component returns results similar to the ones shown in Figure 13-4, showing the results score, file size, and date fields we requested in addition to the document title hyperlinked to its respective Web page.

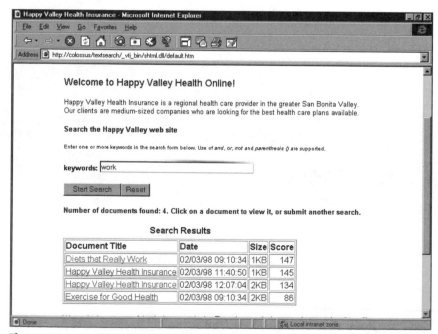

Figure 13-4: Looking for work? The Search component results list Web pages that contain the word "work."

The results page display

Several things are worth noting about how the Search component displays search matches.

The first thing

Results are shown right in the initial page rather than on a separate page. This is OK for a short list of results like the one we are working with in this chapter, but if you have one hundred documents indexed, it might be inconvenient to dump the results back into the home page (or any other page, for that matter). It is also possible that the results would not be visible on the page, causing the user to wonder if the search had worked correctly. Given this, you may find it most useful to build your search page as a separate page and provide a link to it from your other pages. An example of this technique is coming up later in the chapter.

Do you really want search results on a separate page?

I know. I said that FrontPage does not allow you to display the search results on a separate page. And that is true. However, there is a way around FrontPage's unabashedly autocratic behavior. It is not a particularly convenient workaround, but it works. So I'll tell you once and then for the remainder of the chapter go back to claiming that it can't be done.

The workaround depends on the fact that between the HTML that FrontPage displays in its internal editor and the HTML that it saves to the file, FrontPage silently makes some changes. In the case of the Search component, one of those changes happens to be the `form` tag action attribute. If you peek at the Search component in the FrontPage HTML editor, you will notice that the `form` tag is blank. It simply says `<form>`. If you try to edit it, FrontPage complains and restores the page to its former state.

However, if you open the search page HTML in an external text editor such as Notepad, you will notice that FrontPage has inserted the action attribute, which will look like `action="_vti_bin/shtml.dll/"` plus the filename of the Search form page. To have the search results display in a separate page, you need to do the following:

1. Create a new search results page in Editor.

2. Copy the Search component into the form (as far as I know, there is no avoiding this, although you can change the Search form properties).

3. Put whatever other content you want in this file and save it to the current Web.

4. Open the original Search form page in a text editor and change the filename in the `form` tag's action URL to the name of this new file. Save the file.

Now when you do an initial search, the results are displayed using the new file. Of course any subsequent searches continue to display in this file, unless of course you repeat the process just described for this file, too.

(continued)

(continued)

The catch? Don't ever edit the page in FrontPage Editor again. If you do and try to save your changes, FrontPage warns you that you are about to overwrite a more recent version of the file. If you fail to heed this warning and save the file, it will restore the action URL to its default. Bummer.

The second thing

We cannot control several characteristics of the display. For example, results are displayed in a simple table with visible borders. This is all right in the present case, when the table consists of multiple columns (if you happen to like visible borders), but results are displayed the same way even if only the title is returned (see Figure 13-5). In this case the table borders are certainly superfluous. It would also be nice to have some options for column order, not to mention the sort order of the items returned. Currently items are returned in order of their score, with the highest score first.

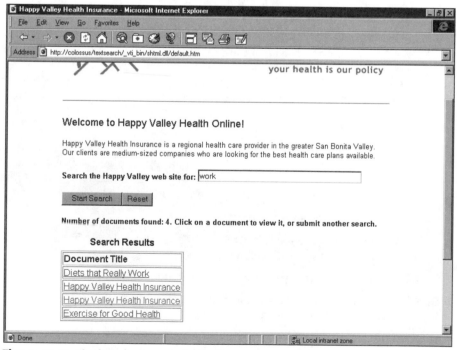

Figure 13-5: Single-column search results

The third thing

Speaking of the scores, you may be wondering what a score of 157 means in this context. Good question. Well, it means that it is a higher score than 147, which is higher than 87. To be a little more precise, although it is hard to say for sure how FrontPage calculates this number, typically the score takes into account the number of pages in the index, the number of matching pages, and the number of matches found on the page. In the case of Boolean queries, the score also takes into account how many of the words were matched.

The fourth (and last) thing

You may have noticed that the home page appears to have been indexed twice, because its title shows up twice in the list (check Figure 13-5 again if you didn't notice). In fact, FrontPage indexed an earlier draft of the home page that happened to be left in the Web. This is a common problem, since it is fairly typical for people to leave outdated versions of their Web pages lying around on the Web server. With the Search component, as with the Table of Contents component described in Chapter 12, this can create a mess. In a moment, we remedy this problem.

Search options

When you search on a single word, FrontPage looks for matches of that word. It returns results on complete word matches only. For example, searching on the word "mat" would not match the word "match" or the word "mattress." However, the search engine is apparently smart enough to know something about word endings (or smart enough to ignore them). This means that searching on the word "mat" would match instances of "mats," "matting," or "matted."

The FrontPage component provides several options (technically called Boolean operators) for searching on combinations of words. These include:

✦ **"and"**—Use the word "and" between search words to indicate that both words must be present in order for a match to occur. For example, "car and mat" returns only pages that include "car" and "mat" somewhere on the page, not necessarily together. There is no documented way to return words in a phrase, such as "car mat."

✦ **"or"**—Use "or" between search words to indicate that at least one of the words must be present on the page in order to constitute a match. For example, the search "car or mat" returns all pages that contain one or the other or both words. A list of words with no operation indicated (for instance, "car mat" or "car, mat") generates an implicit "or" search. Note that there is no way to know which word or words are matched.

✦ **"not"**—You can use "not" to exclude any pages that contain a designated word. For example, "auto not car" returns all pages that contain the word "auto" but not the word "car." Note that, as is true with the other Boolean operators, you cannot use "not" with a single-word request. In other words, "not car" will not return all documents that do not contain the word "car."

✦ **Parentheses "()"**—You can use parentheses to group complicated search requests. For example, "(auto not car) or vehicle" will match any pages with the word "auto" but not the word "car" or the word "vehicle" (with or without the word "car"), whereas "auto not (car or vehicle)" will match pages that contain the word "auto" but not pages containing either the word "car" or the word "vehicle."

✦ **Wildcard ("*")**—Use of the asterisk (*) or star character as a wildcard appears to work, albeit only at the end of words. For example, a search on "mat*" will match "match" and "mattress" as well as all the forms of "mat" previously described.

If you include a wildcard in your search, FrontPage appears to ignore any additional characters. This means that searching on "mat*" is functionally equivalent to searching on "mat*xyz," which is not exactly what one would expect (or want).

Editing the Search component

Now let's return to our Search form and make a few revisions. First we edit the Search form itself to alert people to the various search options available to them. Because we cannot insert text into the component form itself, we create a heading for the Search form and add our directions there. Then we simplify the form label and remove some of the information from the results display. Here are the steps:

1. Open the `Default.htm` page for the Happy Valley Web in Editor as described earlier in the chapter.

2. Scroll down to the Search form. Add the text "**Search the Happy Valley Web site**" above the dotted line indicating the top of the component form. Change the style of this to Heading 2 by selecting this style in the Change Style drop-down menu list on the left side of the toolbar.

3. With the cursor at the end of the heading, press Enter to start a new line. Type the directions, "**Enter one or more keywords in the search form below. Use of *and, or, not* and *parenthesis ()* are supported.**" If you feel that this is too cryptic, you might want to link the directions to a separate page that explains the operation of these elements in more detail.

4. To edit the component itself, double-click the form (the cursor turns to the robot cursor when it is positioned over the component). This opens the Search Component Properties dialog box. Revise the label text to say simply "**keyword(s):**" Uncheck the Date and File Size check boxes in the Search Results options section.

5. Click OK to accept the changes and return to the Web page in Editor.

Preview the results. They should resemble Figure 13-6, which shows the revised home page in Netscape Navigator.

Removing extra pages

If you, like so many of us, keep out-of-date pages littering your Web, you will probably find that running a search returns pages that you really don't want people to see any more. Rather than delete these pages or move them outside of your Web, you just need to move them to a hidden folder so that the search engine doesn't catalog them. I like to add and use a folder called _out_of_date (remember to include the underscore at the beginning of the folder name to let FrontPage know that this is a hidden folder).

You'll have to reindex your site to update the search engine and exclude the page(s). The next section, "Updating the search index," tells you how to do this.

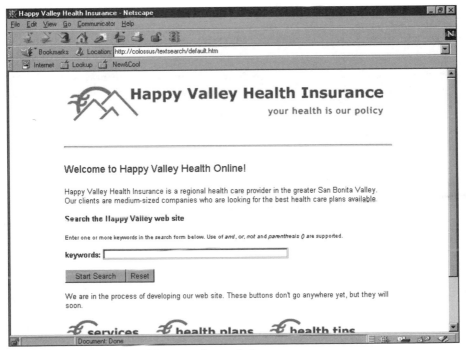

Figure 13-6: The new and improved Search form page

Updating the search index

The search index is the master dictionary of words in your site and the record of which pages include which words. Every time you save a page, FrontPage automatically updates your index with any new words that it finds in that page. However, it does not remove references to words that have changed or that no longer exist. In order to ensure that your index reflects the current state of your Web, it is best to manually update the index every time you modify your pages.

To update the search index:

1. Open the Web in Explorer.

2. Select Tools ➪ Recalculate Hyperlinks.

3. When prompted that this could take some time, click Yes.

Although the action specifies that FrontPage is recalculating hypertext links, it also updates other system information at this time, including the search index.

Using a Search Template

In the previous section we demonstrated how you can insert a Search component directly into your Web page. The main drawback to this method is the fact that the Search component inserts the results on the same page. This could actually be useful if you could also define which files to include in the search, but unfortunately you can't, except in the special case of a discussion Web. (Discussion Webs are the topic of Chapter 14.)

For the moment, then, you are likely to create a separate search page and create a hyperlink to it, typically from the home page and possibly from additional pages if you have a Web large enough to warrant it.

To create a new search page in Editor, select File ➪ New and choose the Search Page option from the list of templates. FrontPage generates your search page, a portion of which is shown in Figure 13-7.

If you like this page as is, you are done. You may want to scroll to the bottom of the page and change the "Your Company Name" text to something more interesting, but the point is that the search engine works without your having to configure anything. There is nothing special about this page or the Search component included on it — you can format the component exactly as outlined earlier in this chapter.

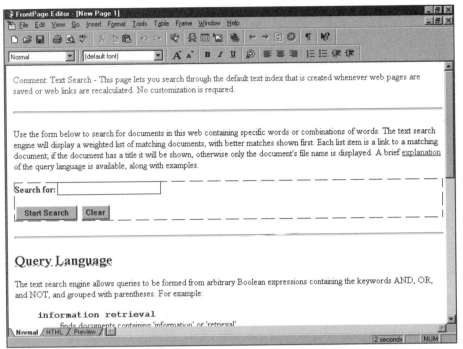

Figure 13-7: The default Search template showing the query language directions included on the page

Working with Frames

So far in this chapter we have looked at two methods of introducing a Search form into your Web site: by placing the form directly onto an existing page, such as your home page, or by creating a separate Search form page and linking to it. A third alternative, especially if you are already contemplating using frames, is to build the Search form into a frame document that is visible at all times. In this way, users can conduct a search without first having to locate your Search form.

All that's required is to set the target frame for the search frame (otherwise the results of the search will be displayed in the search frame). Chapter 8 contains complete instructions for creating and implementing frames in FrontPage. Figures 13-8 and 13-9 show a frame-based Web search before a search is conducted and after. (Notice that the search frame page contains a single cell table set to 100% width and 100% height to frame the search and make it appear to be separated from the rest of the frame set without having to use frame borders.)

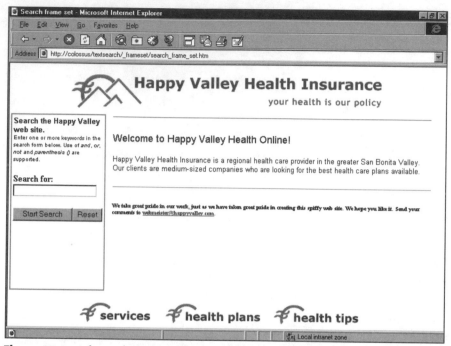

Figure 13-8: A frame-based Web incorporating a search page

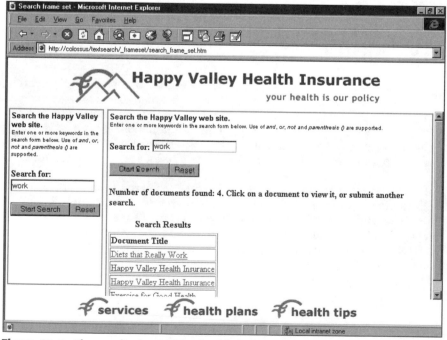

Figure 13-9: The result of searching in this frame set

Note The frame set shown in Figures 13-8 and 13-9 is located in the _frameset folder in the Examples/ch13 folder on the CD-ROM.

Note that the Search form is repeated in the main frame after the search is conducted. This is something of an annoyance, but unavoidable.

Tip Another potential drawback of using frames with the Search component is that it will include each of the frame documents in its index. The word "Search" does appear on the Search form page, however, and it would show up in a search on "search." If this is an issue, you can always store the frame documents in the _private folder, as described earlier. FrontPage can still locate them, even though they are inaccessible to the user.

Exploring Some Alternatives

In this chapter, we have examined three ways of incorporating the Search component into your Web. We have discovered how easy it is to configure the Search component, but we have also run up against the limitations that are built into this feature. For basic text searching needs, the component is probably adequate. For anything more than basic needs, you may want to shop for an alternative. This section briefly identifies some of the leading alternatives.

✦ If your Web server is a UNIX system and you have access to a compiler, there are several decent freeware search engines available for you:

- SWISH

- FreeWAIS

- Harvest (Glimpse)

✦ If you are using Microsoft's Internet Information Server (IIS) on Windows NT, you can use the Microsoft Index Server.

✦ If you are running O'Reilly's WebSite Web server on either Windows NT or 95, it comes with a version of the SWISH search engine ported to Windows.

✦ If you are running a Windows NT Web server, you can download a free version of Excite for Web Servers, an early but quite serviceable version of the Excite search engine.

✦ If you have a generous budget, several excellent commercial search engines are available, such as:

- Verity

- OpenText

Taking the Next Step

This chapter has provided several working implementations of the FrontPage Text Search component. We have addressed both its strengths and, where appropriate, some of its shortcomings. For a small to medium-sized Web and relatively little hassle, the FrontPage text search engine is more than adequate. In the next chapter, we take on the Discussion Web Wizard, subjecting it to similar treatment, with very similar results. We describe the steps required to create a Web-based discussion in FrontPage, demonstrate a number of ways to customize the appearance of your forum, and access the means at hand for administering a discussion Web.

✦   ✦   ✦

Creating a Discussion Forum

T he previous chapter focused on the issues of adding text searching capabilities to your Web. This chapter takes an equally practical look at implementing discussion forums. Our focus is the multifaceted Discussion Web Wizard. Using this wizard, you can create a discussion forum with an automatically updating table of contents, threaded messages, custom confirmations, and a search engine. This chapter walks through each step in the creation of a discussion Web. Its real focus, though, is how you can customize your forum (and how you can't).

New in 98

What used to be called WebBots in FrontPage 97 are referred to as components in FrontPage 98. If you're familiar with the WebBot feature of previous releases of FrontPage, components are something you're already familiar with.

Exploring Modes of Discussion

Discussion forums in a variety of modes have existed on the Internet for almost as long as the Internet has been in existence, much longer, certainly, than the upstart World Wide Web, which has really only been with us since the early 1990s. Most of these began as separate Internet services, just as the Web is one Internet service. So each method of communicating has its own set of protocols and standards, as well as its own set of client applications (that is, the programs you use to interact with the particular service).

The early modes of Internet discussion break down into two categories: asynchronous or non–real time message systems (such as e-mail, mail lists, and newsgroups) and text-based synchronous communication systems, such as Internet Relay Chat, or IRC.

With the boom in Web popularity, there was an initial push to consolidate all Internet services in the browser. Web-based discussion forums, such as the one included with FrontPage, are one by-product of this phenomenon. Another by-product has been the intensive drive to consolidate multiple services under the umbrella of a single application (or at least a single brand name)—witness the transformation of Netscape's Navigator product into the current Communicator suite, and Microsoft's similarly aggressive production of Net applications. A third driving force has been to create multimedia real-time communication: Internet phone, video conferencing, as well as 3-D chat environments.

All of which is, of course, beyond the ken of the humble FrontPage Web Discussion Wizard. In the meantime, we can create a very useful discussion forum that combines the convenience of a newsgroup with the Web's ease of use.

Discovering the Discussion Web Wizard

The Discussion Web Wizard is FrontPage's most full-featured wizard. In a matter of minutes, it can generate a fully functioning Web-based discussion forum, complete with:

✦ **Threaded messages and replies**—In the world of electronic messaging, a "thread" refers to a given message and any replies generated from that message. In general, it is easier to read a group of messages that have a common thread than simply to read messages in the order that they are posted to the forum, which is fairly haphazard. Organizing messages by threads is an optional feature of the discussion Web.

✦ **Table of contents**—The virtue of the discussion Web table of contents is that it updates automatically. From a management perspective, that is a godsend. (Imagine having to update the table of contents by hand!) From the user's standpoint the only drawback is that, thanks to your Web browser's ability to cache Web pages, it is sometimes necessary to refresh the page in order to see new content.

In Web browser lingo, as in computer lingo generally, a cache consists of files that the application stores close at hand in anticipation of needing them again. Each time you access a Web page, your browser stores a copy of the HTML file and any subsidiary files in its local cache on your hard drive. Then if you return to the page, that tricky browser draws it from its cache, providing you with the momentary illusion of speed on the Internet.

✦ **Customizable submission form**—The Web Discussion Wizard offers you limited options for the discussion's submission form. Afterward, however, you can add as many fields as you like and as your users will tolerate.

✦ **Confirmation pages with Confirmation Field components**—As with other FrontPage forms, you can return a custom confirmation page to anyone who submits a message. Using the Confirmation Field component, described back in Chapter 11, the confirmation page can display any and all data submitted.

✦ **Searchable index**—A FrontPage discussion Web can include the same text search engine we discussed in the previous chapter. In this case, however, searching is confined to the posted messages.

Although it has many steps, the Discussion Web Wizard is actually quite easy to complete. Many of the steps involve little more than including or excluding certain features. Because it is so easy, however, it is good to know what you are getting yourself into. Some features are worthwhile to include when you first create the discussion forum. Others, such as frames, may be implemented more easily and more flexibly later, should you so choose, using the Frames Wizard.

Creating a Discussion Web

Creating your discussion Web is the easy part (easier than maintaining the discussion forum, for instance), because the wizard does all the hard work. It is a good idea to plan what you want ahead of time, though. The Discussion Web Wizard is the most sophisticated of the wizards that accompany FrontPage. Here are the issues to think about before you start:

✦ Will your forum be large enough to warrant a search engine in the beginning? (There is nothing sadder than a search that returns zero matches).

✦ Will your users benefit from using a frames environment to display the table of contents and messages simultaneously? (Or will they burn you in effigy for even thinking such a thought?)

✦ Does your discussion Web need to have multiple discussion areas, or will a single forum suffice?

✦ Can anyone add messages to your forum, or do you need to restrict access with a registration form?

These are some of the major design-related questions you may want to ponder before diving into the creation of your discussion forum.

Do you really want to do this?

There is one other question, easy to overlook, that you should also ponder before going any farther: Do you really have the time and resources to manage an active discussion forum? Even though FrontPage makes it easy to create your Web, it is going to require work to maintain.

The table of contents is going to swell to ungainly proportions, the search index is going to take longer and longer to perform its updates, messages are going to get corrupted and require attention. Am I scaring you sufficiently yet? The point is not to dissuade you from forging ahead—hey, there's a whole chapter to go here!—but do not make the decision to create a discussion Web casually. Enough said.

Opening the Discussion Web Wizard

To create your discussion Web, open Explorer, select File➪New, and choose the Discussion Web Wizard from the New FrontPage Web dialog box. In the first Discussion Web Wizard dialog box, identify the Web server or file location of your discussion Web and give it a name. Like other Web names, this one is only used internally, so it can be short and simple. If you are following the example, call the Web "pettalk," as shown in Figure 14-1. Click OK to continue.

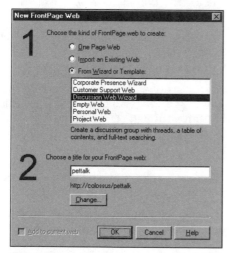

Figure 14-1: Naming your discussion Web is the first step toward creating it.

The first wizard screen describes the purpose of the Discussion Web Wizard and gives an overview of the process. All very charming. Click Next to get on with it.

Selecting discussion Web features

The next wizard screen asks you to select the features you want to include in your Web. Your answers here determine what additional questions the wizard will need to ask. As illustrated in Figure 14-2, the options include:

✦ **Submission Form**—The submission form is used by folks who want to post a message to the discussion. Since a discussion Web without any way to contribute is not very useful, this one is a required option (kind of oxymoronic, no?).

✦ **Table of Contents**—The table of contents lists all messages and their respective responses. This page is updated each time a new message is posted to the Web.

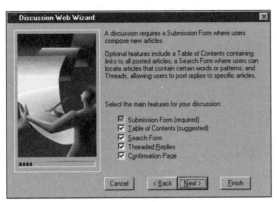

Figure 14-2: So many discussion features to choose from!

✦ **Search Form**—This is the same search engine we explored in the previous chapter, but here it is applied to the discussion messages.

✦ **Threaded Replies**—A thread refers to a message and all of its replies. Threaded messages are linked hierarchically, so that it is possible to read messages as part of a conversation, rather than haphazardly in the order they happened to be posted.

Note

Personally, I have mixed feelings about the virtues of threaded forums as they are implemented in FrontPage. The discussion Web takes any reply to be a new subthread under the original message. That means that if person A posts a message, person B replies, person A replies to the reply, and person B replies to that reply, the messages will look like a series of nested threads, when in fact what most likely took place was a conversation sparked by the initial post. If your discussion Web is fairly free-form, this may be OK. If you are planning a more topical discussion Web, you may prefer to leave the messages unthreaded.

✦ **Confirmation Page**—After a person submits a message, it is nice to respond with a confirmation page that reassures that person that the submission has not simply been swallowed up in the virtual void.

For the purposes of this demonstration, we have selected all of the options. Why not have it all, it's so easy! When you are happy with your choices, click Next to continue.

Naming the Web

The next screen asks you for the title of the Web. This is the information that visitors see at the top of each discussion page. The title should be descriptive without being overly long. Our Web discussion for Pedigree Pets is entitled "Pet Talk."

The second item of information requested in this screen is the name of the folder where discussion messages are kept. The folder is not directly visible to people who access your site. It is only accessed indirectly, typically via the table of contents. This is why the folder name begins with the underscore character, FrontPage's way of marking private system folders. We have named our folder in accordance with the title, "_pettalk." Click OK to continue.

Selecting input fields

In this screen, you select the fields you wish to include in the submission form. These are the fields completed by anyone posting a message. At a minimum, you should have a subject field and a comment field. In addition, you can include a category or product list to select from. As shown in Figure 14-3, we have opted for the basics: subject and comment.

The problem with the category and product lists is that they have no impact on how messages are organized. The person's selection is simply recorded along with the rest of the message. If you really want to organize your discussion by categories or products, consider creating multiple discussion Webs, one for each topic.

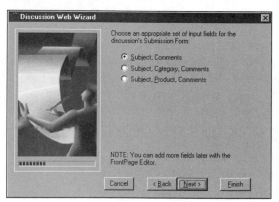

Figure 14-3: Selecting input fields for the discussion Web submission form

This is a fairly meager set of options. Fortunately, you can customize the submission form later; any additional fields you add are saved along with the default fields. Click Next when you have made your choice.

Choosing protected versus open discussions

The next screen asks whether you want to require users to be registered before they can participate in a discussion. Registration can be enforced in one of two ways:

✦ **Pre-registration**—Only those users who are already registered can use the discussion forum. In this case, users need some way to request that they be added to the list of registered users.

✦ **Self-registration**—In this scenario, users must still be registered to participate in the discussion, but they can register themselves. This way, there is no time lag between requesting admittance and gaining it. There is also no chance to reject registrants. You fill out the form and you can post.

Adding a Registration component to a discussion forum is described later in the chapter. For now, let's stick to basics. Select "No, anyone can post articles" (see Figure 14-4) and click Next.

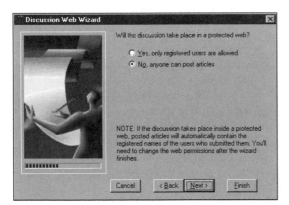

Figure 14-4: To register or not to register, that is the question!

Selecting the message sort order

The next screen poses a simple option. Do you want messages to appear with the oldest first (that is, at the top of the page) or with the newest first? Putting the newest messages first is convenient for those users who just want current information without scrolling through last month's messages. If messages are not threaded, however, this can frequently result in reading replies to messages before you have read the message itself. Since our current Web is threaded, we select the Newest to Oldest option, as you can see from Figure 14-5. Click Next to forge ahead.

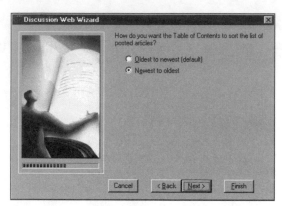

Figure 14-5: Which comes first, the new or the old?

Clever news and messaging applications sometimes solve this problem by showing you only unread messages by default.

Choosing the table of contents as the home page

This is what we like, a simple yes-or-no question: Do you want the table of contents to be the home page? It is possible to add a discussion Web to an existing Web, but in this case we are creating a new Web around the Discussion component. Even so, we want to have an introductory page for our Web that leads to the table of contents. So we just say "No" to a home page table of contents (see Figure 14-6). Click Next to proceed.

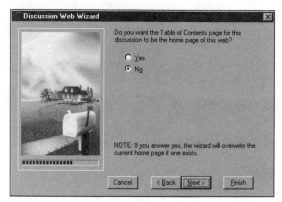

Figure 14-6: Opting not to make the table of contents our Web's home page

Selecting the Search form information

This screen sets the display options for the discussion Web search results. If you recall from Chapter 13, the search results page is capable of displaying some combination of the subject, the match's score, the file size, and the file date. Inexplicably, the wizard limits the choice of these options to four possible combinations, three of which insist on the file size, which strikes me as not particularly useful in the context of discussion messages.

Is this just one that slipped past quality assurance? Or is it some nefarious plot secretly sponsored by the owners of the code that generates system file sizes? Details at 11.... (Of course, knowing the file size does let you avoid overly wordy messages, but you, as the administrator, should set some limits as noted later in this chapter.)

Fortunately, you can edit the Search component later. For now, just select Subject, as shown in Figure 14-7. Click Next to move along.

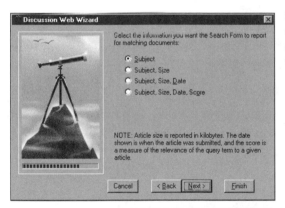

Figure 14-7: You can select some of the possible options for the Search component here. Later you can edit the component properties.

Choosing Web themes

To take advantage of FrontPage's themes, you can click the Choose Web Theme button on the next screen. This brings up the standard Choose Theme dialog box shown in Figure 14-8. Chapter 4 has a complete discussion of themes.

At the moment we are too eager to finish our Web to think about interior decorating. We plan to customize this page later. Click Next to keep moving forward. If you happened to click the Choose Web Theme button, FrontPage assumes you want a theme and assigns one. Just check the This Web Does Not Use Themes radio button and click OK to close the Choose Theme dialog box, and then click Next to continue.

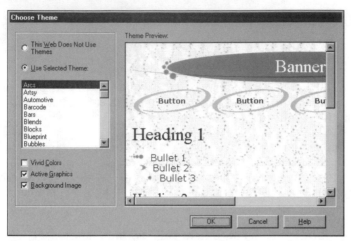

Figure 14-8: Dress up your Web using the Choose Theme dialog box.

Framing your discussion

The next screen offers the choice of a variety of frame and nonframe versions of the discussion Web. The available options are:

✦ **No Frames**—This is just what it says.

✦ **Dual Interface**—This uses a simple two-frame set combined with a no-frames option.

✦ **Contents above Current Article**—This is the same as the two-frame set in the dual interface, with the addition of a banner frame and no option for no frames.

✦ **Contents beside Current Article**—This puts the table of contents in a vertical column on the left side of the frame set and content on the right. It includes a banner frame at the top but offers no option for no frames.

To see how each of these is laid out, click its radio button. The window on the left changes to reflect the currently selected arrangement (see Figure 14-9).

If you select the dual interface, the Web Discussion Wizard builds two versions of the table of contents, one designed for use in a frames environment, the other as a stand-alone page. For the moment, we are going to elect No Frames. Later in the chapter we discuss some of the advantages and disadvantages of using frames for your discussion Web. For a more complete treatment of using frames in FrontPage, see Chapter 8, "Working with Frames."

You could also wait and at a later date convert your discussion Web into a frame-based Web using the Frames Wizard. This is probably a good idea only if you want to create a custom frame set that is not among the four options that the Discussion Web Wizard offers.

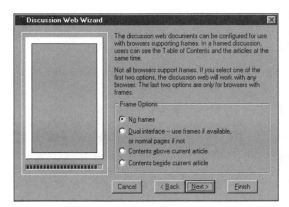

Figure 14-9: The Frames Selection dialog box of the Discussion Web Wizard

Click Next to continue on to the final screen, which repeats what you selected for your table of contents page and the submission form. (What about those other pages, you may be wondering?) Click Finish, and your Web is created. Figure 14-10 shows the Hyperlinks view of the newly created Web for Pet Talk. In the next section we explore what we have created.

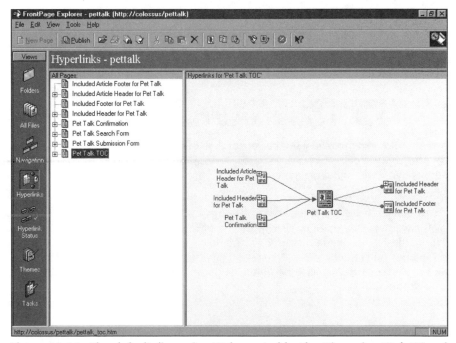

Figure 14-10: The default discussion Web created by the Discussion Web Wizard

Note   To view the Web generated by this series of choices, open the `pettalk1` Web in the `Examples/ch14` folder on the CD-ROM.

Customizing Your Discussion Web

In this section, we explore our newly created Pet Talk Web to find out what's there and how it works. Once we have familiarized ourselves with the terrain, we proceed to perform some home improvement. In the next several sections, we discuss each of the Web Discussion components in a fair amount of detail, with an emphasis on customizing the forum to your needs. If you are impatient, you can experiment with your Web right now—it is basically functional, if not glamorous. You might want to skip on ahead to the section "Working with the Discussion Web," where we put our forum through its paces. Keep your thumb here, though, so you can find your spot again when you are ready to customize.

Before you can readily customize your discussion Web or make changes to it for maintenance purposes, you need to know where its files are. This section provides a map of the most important files in the discussion Web, both system files and public HTML files.

Note   You can follow along with the examples in this section by opening the `pettalk1` Web in `Examples/ch14` on the CD-ROM. If you prefer to see the completed results, open `pettalk2`.

What goes on behind the curtain?

Magicians are told never to reveal the secrets of their black art. The FrontPage wizards seem to live by the same creed. They are very easy to use, but it is difficult to figure out what exactly they have done and where they put it.

Why are wizards so secretive? Partly, I suspect, it is the Wizard of Oz syndrome: "Pay no attention to that man behind the curtain." The more mystery you can maintain, the more power you have over the mystified. Partly, too, FrontPage is not eager to have you mucking around in its files, since the less you know, the less likely you are to mess something up and then blame the creators of the application. Shame on you! On the other hand, knowing how the discussion Web is assembled helps immensely should you need to troubleshoot a problem.

Support files

A FrontPage discussion Web is created with four supporting HTML files—the included header, the included footer, the included article header, and the included article footer—which are stored in the private folder of the discussion Web and which are used as includes on the main pages. This section describes how each of these functions.

The included header

The included header file provides a consistent header for each of the main Web pages. The header file is located in the _private folder. It is named *yourweb_ head.htm*, and its complete title is "Included Header for *YourWebTitle*," where *yourweb* represents the name you gave your discussion Web when you created it in the Web Discussion Wizard and *YourWebTitle* represents its title.

Open the Web header file from the pettalk1 Web in FrontPage Editor. In this case, the default header consists of four text hyperlinks (the actual number of links may be less depending on the selections you make in the Web Discussion Wizard).

We want to replace the text hyperlinks with graphical buttons. This requires some care, however, in order to retain the links as they have been created. The process we use is to add the graphics above the text links and then edit the links using the View HTML feature in Editor. In the next section we move the text links from the header to the footer.

Tip

If you want your Web to be available to the widest possible audience, always provide a text link version of all site navigation. Not all Web browsers are graphical browsers, and some users who have browsers capable of viewing images choose to turn off the images to speed the loading of pages.

Adding graphics

With the included header file open in Editor, select the text headline, "Pet Talk," and delete it using the Delete key or by selecting Edit ➪ Delete. Position the cursor at the top of the page and select Insert ➪ Image. Locate the images folder for this chapter on the CD-ROM in Examples/ch14/pettalk1. Select the Pet Talk banner, ptbanner.gif. Click OK to add the banner to the page.

Next insert the four graphical buttons for Home, Contents, Search, and Post. These images are located in the same folder as the banner graphic. They are named pthome.gif, pttoc.gif, ptsearch.gif, and ptpost.gif respectively. To insert the images, first position the cursor on the line below the banner (press Enter to create a new line if necessary). For each graphic, select Insert ➪ Image, locate the image, and click OK. You may want to insert a space between each image (remember that multiple spaces are ignored). The results should resemble Figure 14-11.

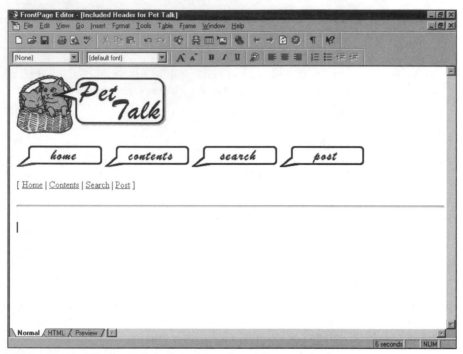

Figure 14-11: The Pet Talk included header with a new look

Editing graphic properties

For each of the newly inserted images, you should edit the image properties to add a text alternative and to remove the border outline. To accomplish this, for each image:

1. Select the image by clicking it once.

2. Select Edit ⇨ Image Properties.

3. In the General tab, add an appropriate text equivalent for the image in the Text Input field of the Alternative Representations section.

4. In the Appearance tab, set the Border Thickness to zero (0).

5. Click OK to apply the changes.

Editing links

It would be possible to add static hyperlinks to these graphics using the standard method (select the image, select Edit ⇨ Image Properties, and add the link to the Default Hyperlink field of the General tab). The dilemma, however, is that one of the default links includes component information. Rather than lose something important, therefore, we use the HTML editor to copy the hyperlink information to the images.

With the included header file open in Editor, select the HTML tab. The page should resemble Figure 14-12.

Text with hyperlinks   Images

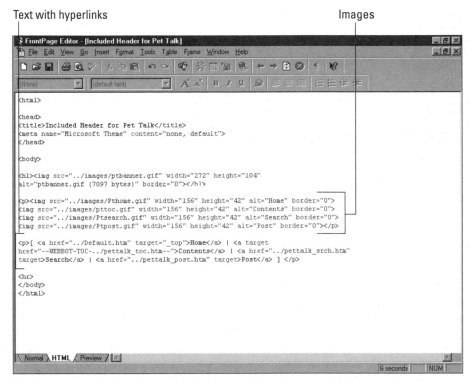

Figure 14-12: The HTML text for the included header page before copying the hyperlinks to the images

Two sections, as indicated in the figure, are of particular interest to us. The first is composed of a series of four `<img>` tags. These are the buttons. The second section consists of the text links for Home, Contents, Search, and Post. Our mission is to copy the `<a href>` information from the text links to the buttons. The procedure is the same for all four buttons. For each:

1. Locate the text corresponding to the button. For example, for the first button, locate the "Home" text.

2. Select the `<a href=...>` tag immediately preceding this text. Select everything between the `<>` brackets (including the brackets).

3. Use the keyboard shortcut Ctrl+C to copy this tag to the clipboard.

4. Position the cursor immediately before the corresponding image tag (for example, `<img src="pthome.gif">`).

5. Use the keyboard shortcut Ctrl+V to paste the hyperlink tag in front of the image tag.

6. Position the cursor immediately after the image tag and type `</a>` to end the hyperlink tag. (Note that you could copy and paste this as well, if you prefer).

Repeat this for each of the four buttons. When you are finished, the HTML should resemble Figure 14-13. You can also check that the information was copied correctly by using either of two other methods:

Images with hyperlinks

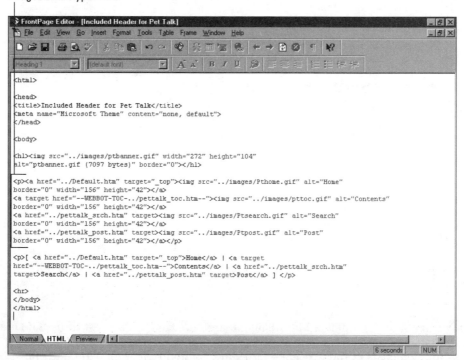

Figure 14-13: The revised header file HTML (with a little extra spacing for readability)

✦ Pass the mouse cursor over each image. The hyperlinked URL should appear in the status bar at the bottom of the Editor window.

✦ Open the Image Properties dialog box. The correct hyperlink should appear in the Default Hyperlink field.

Caution If you edit the HTML in anything other than FrontPage's built-in HTML editor, be aware that the various components used in the discussion Web add information to the file that is not seen in the FrontPage HTML editor. Consequently, the HTML you see in an external text editor looks slightly different.

If you are satisfied with the results (which you should be if you've followed the directions), save your changes.

The included footer

The included footer file provides a consistent header for each of the main Web pages. The footer file is located in the _private folder. It is named *yourweb_ foot.htm,* and its complete title is "Included Footer for *YourWebTitle,*" where *yourweb* represents the name you gave your discussion Web when you created it in the Web Discussion Wizard and *YourWebTitle* represents its title.

Open the Web footer file from the pettalkl Web in FrontPage Editor. The default footer consists of a simple horizontal rule with the Timestamp component underneath it.

We make two changes to this file. First we move the text navigation from the header file to the footer. Then we add some additional identifying information to the end of the footer. The steps are as follows:

1. To move the text navigation, first open both the header and footer files in Editor. Switch to the header file using the Window menu. Select the text navigation row. Select Edit ⇨ Cut or use the keyboard shortcut Ctrl+X to cut the navigation from the header file and place it in the clipboard. Switch back to the footer file. Position the cursor above the horizontal rule. Select Edit ⇨ Paste or use the keyboard shortcut Ctrl+V to paste the text navigation, including hyperlinks, into the footer. Save your changes.

Tip Sometimes horizontal rules in FrontPage can be ornery about letting you insert the cursor in front of them. If you have trouble, try the following: Click the horizontal rule to select it so that it has a large dark rectangle around it. Press the left arrow key. The cursor moves one space before the horizontal rule.

2. Adding additional text is simply a matter of typing the text you want. We have added a line identifying the owner of the discussion Web as well as a disclaimer (which probably has no legal validity but at least sounds official). Figure 14-14 shows the completed footer with the text we have added. Save your changes.

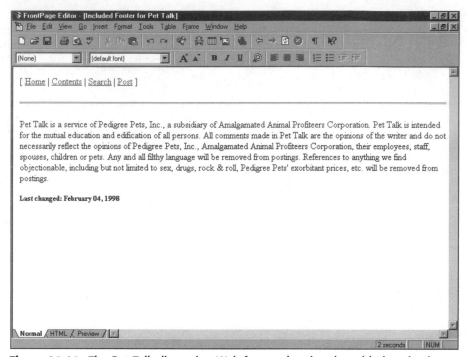

Figure 14-14: The Pet Talk discussion Web footer, showing the added navigation and revised text

The included article header

The included article header file provides a consistent header for messages posted to the discussion Web. Located in the `_private` folder like the main included header, this article header is named *yourweb_ahdr.htm*, and its complete title is "Included Article Header for *YourWebTitle*," where *yourweb* represents the name you gave your discussion Web when you created it in the Web Discussion Wizard and *YourWebTitle* represents its title.

This header is very similar to the general header with the addition of four new buttons:

✦ **Reply**—This opens a submission form with a standard "Re: *the original subject*" line placed in the subject header. Reply messages are listed directly under the original in the table of contents.

✦ **Next**—This jumps to the next message in the same thread (that is, to the same level of indentation in the table of contents).

✦ **Previous**—This jumps to the previous message in the same thread.

✦ **Up**—This jumps to the "parent" of the current message (that is, to the original message to which the current message is related).

Our goal is to make the article header look like the general one. To do that, you can follow the earlier directions to (1) add the graphical banner and navigational buttons, (2) edit the properties of each graphic to add a text alternative and eliminate the border, and (3) copy the text hyperlinks to the buttons.

To add the Reply button, use ptreply.gif; for the Next button, use ptnext.gif; for Previous, use ptprev.gif; for Up, use ptup.gif. Do not delete the text navigation links, as we copy those to the article footer in the next section. Compare your results with Figure 14-15.

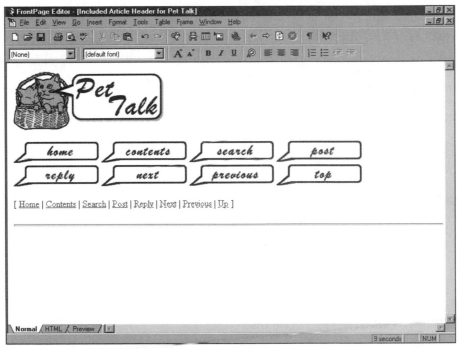

Figure 14-15: The article header with a multitude of buttons

The included article footer

The default article footer, also located in the _private folder, is named *yourweb_aftr.htm*, and its complete title is "Included Article Footer for *YourWebTitle*," where *yourweb* represents the name you gave your discussion Web when you created it in the Web Discussion Wizard and *YourWebTitle* represents its title.

Open the Web footer file from the pettalk1 Web in FrontPage Editor. The default article footer looks exactly like the default Web footer. We want to add the same copy we previously added to the Web footer. We also move the article text navigation to this footer.

By now, if you have followed the earlier steps, you should be able to make these changes unprompted, but just in case, here are the basics:

1. To move the text navigation, first open both the article header and article footer files in Editor. Cut the navigation from the article header file. Switch back to the footer file and paste the text navigation, including hyperlinks, into the footer. Save your changes.

2. To copy the footer text, open both the general footer and article footer files in Editor. Copy the text. Switch back to the footer file and paste the text into the footer. Save your changes.

The main pages

Once you have edited the various included pages of your discussion Web, you are practically ready to launch your forum. There is very little more you need to do to make your Web functional. In fact there is very little more you can do, even if you want to, since FrontPage handles just about everything. In this section we examine the main pages of your discussion Web and ready them for a test run.

A FrontPage discussion Web created with all available features has four main pages:

✦ A table of contents for listing messages

✦ A submission form for posting messages

✦ A confirmation page for responding to submissions

✦ A search form for locating messages

In addition, you need one additional page, if you have indicated, as we have done, that the table of contents page is not the home page of this Web. As you may have noticed when we were editing the included header files, the Web Discussion Wizard has assumed that we have a home page, `Default.htm`, so we have added one.

The table of contents

The table of contents page is named *yourweb*_toc.htm, where *yourweb* represents the name you gave your discussion Web when you created it in the Web Discussion Wizard. It is located in the main folder of your discussion Web. The Web Discussion Wizard "suggests" but does not require that you include a table of contents in your discussion Web.

As you can see from Figure 14-16, the default table of contents page is not much to look at even with the included graphics, since we do not yet have any articles listed. FrontPage maintains this page automatically, so in principle you never need worry about it.

If you have configured your discussion as a threaded forum, messages are arranged in outline fashion, with replies indented underneath the messages that prompted them. Figure 14-17 shows what the table of contents looks like once the forum is active.

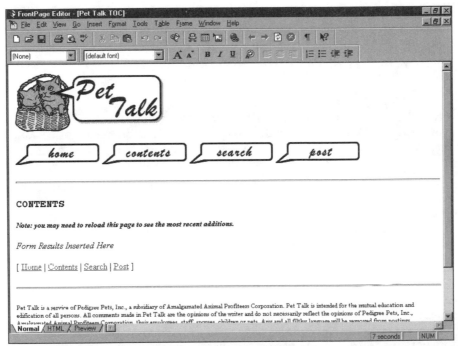

Figure 14-16: The table of contents as it looks before there are any contents to table

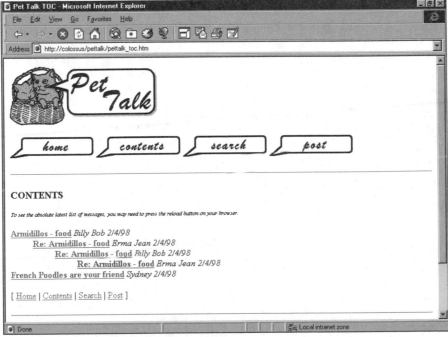

Figure 14-17: The table of contents once the forum is in use

Introducing toc.htm and tocproto.htm

In addition to the included files and the main pages we focus on in this section, the Web Discussion Wizard also creates two crucial files, `toc.htm` and `tocproto.htm`, that it places in the _yourweb_ folder, where _yourweb_ represents the name you assigned to the discussion Web.

These two files are used by FrontPage to build the table of contents. The `tocproto.htm` file is included in both `toc.htm` and the table of contents file for the discussion Web. We return to the function of these two files in the section "Managing Your Discussion Web." In general it is best to leave these files alone unless absolutely necessary.

Note that the _yourweb_ folder is initially hidden so that you cannot see these pages. To view and edit these pages, you need to allow viewing of hidden folders: Open the FrontPage Web Settings dialog box in Explorer (select Tools⇨Web Settings) and check the Show Documents in Hidden Directories check box located on the Advanced tab.

You can make changes to the table of contents by adding, deleting, or modifying text between the headline, "CONTENTS," and the directions, "Note: you may need to reload this page to see the most recent additions." Figure 14-18 shows some changes we have made to the copy on this page in an effort to make the page sound a bit more personable (although not much, frankly). The only formatting change was to remove the Courier font (in the guise of the `<tt>` tag) from the CONTENTS headline.

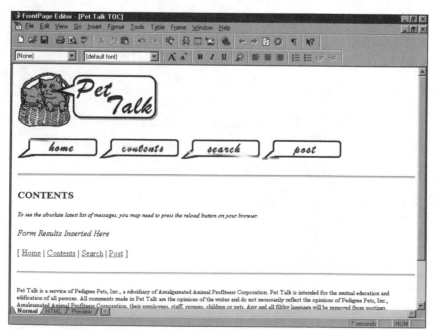

Figure 14-18: The table of contents with revised copy

The submission form

The submission page is named *yourweb*_post.htm, where *yourweb* represents the name you gave your discussion Web when you created it in the Web Discussion Wizard. It is located in the main folder of your discussion Web. The submission form is required, so, like it or not, your Web has one. The submission form uses the Web Discussion component to process all information submitted.

What fields appear in your submission form by default depends on the choices you indicated when you completed the Web Discussion Wizard. We elected to include only a Subject and Comments. The only other field included is the From field. This field is included by default unless you have created a form that requires registration. In this case, the Discussion component automatically includes the username in the From input field and does not prompt for it in this form. Had we opted to include either a Category field or a Products field, an empty drop-down menu would have been included, enabling us to create a list of available categories or products.

Editing the submission page

You can edit this page in two places. The first is the main copy, in which there is only a headline by default. This would be a good place to put some directions. Be careful, however, because this same page is used to build the Reply form (you have no doubt noticed that there is no separate page for this). Any copy you include here should be as applicable to a reply message as to a general, posted message. The solution used here is to provide directions for both cases. Not the most elegant method, but perhaps slightly better than nothing at all.

Editing and validating form fields

You can also edit the form itself. You can edit any of the existing field properties: labels, sizes, names, and so on. For the most part these amount to cosmetic changes. For example, as illustrated later in Figure 14-20, we have changed the name of the main text area from "Article" to "Message." We have also lengthened the fields to better match the graphic buttons.

One important change you can make to the submission form is to provide validation requirements for the form fields. This may not prevent people from dumping junk into your forum, but it will at least put a cap on how much junk they can dump at one time. You can also use validation to require certain fields, so that you don't end up with a table of contents with an empty row, or even worse, messages with no text.

At the very least, we recommend that you institute some limits on the length of messages. Figure 14-19 shows the Text Box Validation dialog box for the Message form field. We have indicated that this field is required and that it has a limit of 1,000 characters. Even if you do not require a field, however, it is good practice to limit its maximum length to a reasonable quantity.

Note   The Form Field Validation dialog box is accessible in one of two ways: by clicking the form field with the right mouse button and selecting Form Field Validation, or by selecting Edit ⇨ Form Field Properties and clicking the Validate button in the Properties dialog box. For more information on form field validation properties, review Chapter 11, "Creating and Implementing Forms."

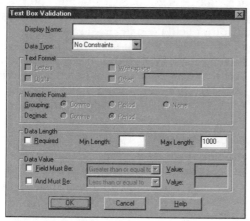

Figure 14-19: The Text Box Validation dialog box, showing validation parameters for the message text box

Adding fields to the submission form

In addition to editing the existing form fields, you can also add custom fields to the submission form. Input from these fields is added to the top of the message page, with the following format (where *FieldName* represents the Name property of the form field and *InputValue* represents whatever the user submits in the field):

```
FieldName: InputValue
```

To illustrate this, we have added an e-mail field to the form, enabling users to include an e-mail address if they would like to receive personal responses directly. To add this field, position the cursor in front of the Comments box label and press Enter to create some space. In the line immediately below the From field, type **Email:** and insert a line break by pressing Shift+Enter. Select Insert ⇨ Form Field ⇨ One Line Text Box. Adjust the size and other properties of the Email field to your liking. Be sure to change the default field name (something like "T1") to "E-mail."

Our completed submission form page is shown in Figure 14-20.

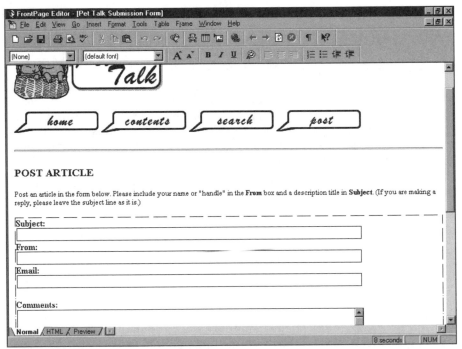

Figure 14-20: The heart of the revised version of the Pet Talk submission form

Editing submission form handler settings

Every Web form has a handler, a program that processes and responds to the input from the form. (If this is news to you, you many want to review Chapter 11, "Creating and Implementing Forms.") The form handler for the discussion Web submission form is, surprise, surprise, the Web Discussion component. It is automatically associated with this form when you create your discussion Web. It does have some optional settings that you can configure to your liking.

To access the form handler settings, click with the right mouse button inside the dotted-line box that surrounds the form element. Select Form Properties. The dialog box indicates that the Web Discussion component is, indeed, the selected Form Handler. Click the Options button below the form handler drop-down menu list. The Settings for Discussion Form Handler dialog box appears, with three tabs. Here are the options you can adjust on these three tabs:

Somehow the Web Discussion Wizard forgets to mention the fact that discussion folder names can be no more than eight characters, including the underscore (see the FrontPage Help entry for the Discussion tab of the Settings for Discussion Form Handler dialog box. I learned this one the hard way, when I tried to change the folder name manually (you don't want to know...) and it insisted on changing it back.

✦ **Discussion tab**—Here you can identify the title of the discussion Web, the directory where the discussion articles are stored, and the optional name of a styles page. These are all set by the Web Discussion Wizard. The more interesting options are in the section titled Table of Contents Layout. Here you can indicate what fields to display for each record in the table of contents. These can consist of any of the fields in the submission form as well as the Time, Date, Remote Computer Name, or User Name fields, which are added to articles automatically. You can also select the order of the table of contents entries from this tab. Check the Order Newest to Oldest check box to display entries in reverse chronological order. Leave it unchecked to display entries chronologically.

Of course, if you change the Table of Contents Layout options after your table of contents already has contents, the new options take effect only at that point. They are not applied retroactively.

✦ **Article tab**—Use the Article tab to change the default name of the header and footer files to include on the article page. More important, you can select what automatic information to display for each article. Options are: Time, Date, Remote Computer Name (or IP number if no name is available), and User Name (if the Web has a Registration component).

✦ **Confirm tab**—This tab has options to identify the URL of a confirmation page as well as a validation failure page. The confirmation page is created automatically if you requested that option in the Web Discussion Wizard. The validation failure page you have to create on your own, although FrontPage provides a default error page.

The confirmation page

The confirmation page displays a message to anyone who submits a message to the discussion Web. It is located in the main folder of your Web and named `yourweb_cfm.htm`, where `yourweb` represents the name you gave your discussion Web when you created it in the Web Discussion Wizard. The confirmation form is optional but fairly conventional.

This confirmation page works like all form confirmations in FrontPage. The page consists of a general-purpose message with embedded Confirmation Field components. In the default version of the confirmation page, the only field inserted in this fashion is the Subject. In general it is a good idea to limit the confirmation fields to those fields you know the user has submitted. Alternatively, you might use the confirmation page to parrot the information that the user has just submitted.

The Pet Talk confirmation page, with some minor cosmetic revision, is shown in Figure 14-21.

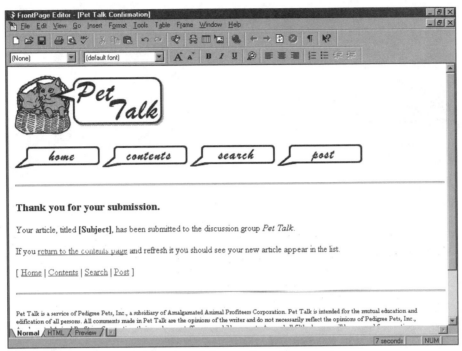

Figure 14-21: The revised version of the confirmation page

The Search form

The discussion Web uses the same Search component that is used to index general-purpose Webs. The index for this search, however, is limited to the files contained in the _yourweb_ folder. The Search form page is named *yourweb_ srch.htm* and is located in the main folder of the discussion Web.

The Pet Talk Search form page, with minor revisions, is shown in Figure 14-22. The principle innovation we have introduced is the link to a Search Options page (described in the previous chapter). Functionally, the discussion search engine is exactly the same as the general-purpose search engine. For more information on the search function, see the preceding chapter, "Text Searching."

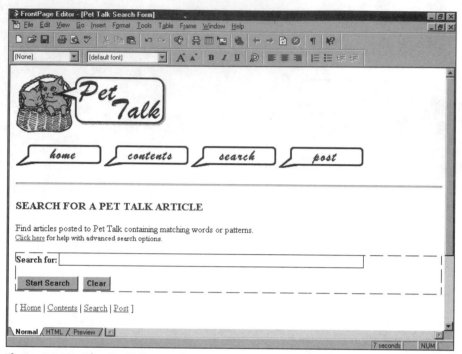

Figure 14-22: The Pet Talk search page

Working with the Discussion Web

At last, it is time to put it all together. If you have been following along thus far, you should import into your Web the Default.htm page from pettalk2 on the CD-ROM. This is the home page we created while you weren't looking to put in front of our discussion Web (see Figure 14-23).

Although the copy on this page, as illustrated in Figure 14-23, is somewhat facetious, this home page illustrates some principles you might want to imitate when you set up your Web discussion.

✦ First, it states the purpose of the discussion forum, clearly identifying what is and isn't permissible. This will not keep people on topic, but it gives you a basis for removing content if that should ever be necessary.

✦ Second, like the footer text mentioned earlier, it explains the limits of liability assumed by the operators of the discussion forum and also emphasizes their conscientious efforts to make the forum an environment conducive to open discussion.

♦ Finally, it provides a feedback mechanism, so that users can contact the operators directly if they choose.

The discussion forum is not rocket science. One of its virtues is the fact that it is fairly intuitive to use. In case you don't have the forum in front of you, however, this section takes a quick tour of its main operations.

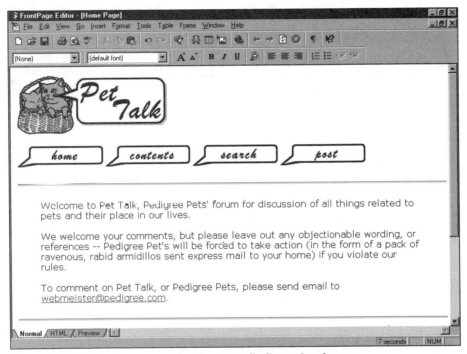

Figure 14-23: The home page for the Pet Talk discussion forum

Submitting a message

To add a message to the forum, simply click the Post button from any page. Note that clicking the Post button always creates a message at the top level of the message hierarchy. This is easy to forget when you are three levels down reading a message and click the Post button, thinking that you are responding to the message you have been reading. Figure 14-24 shows a message in the process of creation. (Note that the first time you use your forum, you can't go to the table of contents because one hasn't been built yet.)

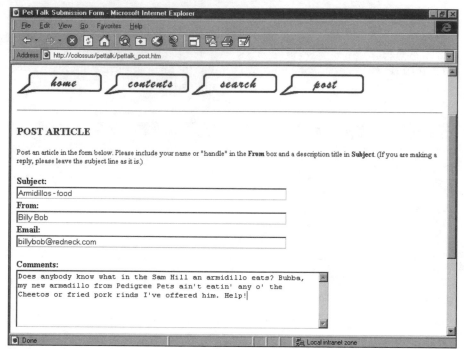

Figures 14-24: A discussion Web message in the process of creation

Replying to messages

You reply to a message when you have accessed its page. Clicking the Reply button takes you to a version of the submission form but loads a default "RE: *the-original-subject*" line in the subject header. Of course, this can lead to endless repetitions of this in the table of contents.

Navigating

Sending and replying to messages is the main activity of the Web. Before you can reply to a message, however, you have to find an interesting one. Either you can browse through messages, using the Next, Previous, and Up buttons as described earlier in the chapter, or you can go straight to the Search feature.

Note

One for the wish list: It would be nice if each message had a list of its replies on the same page with it. For what it's worth, I have tried to figure out if that is what the otherwise mysterious (to me anyway) `toc.htm` file could be for, but I have not found any way to coax it into action.

Of course, searching for articles may cause you to lose the thread of a conversation. Once you have found an interesting article, you can use the navigation buttons to get a better sense of the message's context.

It appears that the discussion Web is designed so that if you are reading message number 3001 and you jump back to the table of contents, it takes you to that message. However, I have had difficulty getting this to work, if that is its intent.

Adding Frames to Your Forum

When we created our first discussion Web, we chose not to build our Web using frames. If you do not use frames, your discussion Web will be accessible to more users. However, you may notice that jumping back and forth from the table of contents to articles can become tiresome if you are trying to catch up on discussion postings. Using the Next, Previous, and Up navigation buttons can help, but there you are operating on faith, since you can't see what you will get until you get there.

The chief advantage of using frames for your discussion is that users can view the table of contents while they read articles. Since we cover the techniques for creating frames elsewhere in the book (see Chapter 8, "Working with Frames"), this section provides a brief overview of the frame options available in the Web Discussion Wizard. These include frame sets with a vertical orientation of the table of contents and a horizontal orientation.

A vertical table of contents

A frame set with the table of contents located in a vertical column on the left is easily the most popular frame structure currently on the Web. If you use the Web Discussion Wizard, you can create a three-frame set that uses this structure and includes a banner frame at the top, as shown in Figure 14-25.

This option may have the advantage of convention, but it can run into a small snag, if you happen to have a deeply nested thread like the one pictured in Figure 14-26. You can minimize the problem by making the frames resizable (the default when you create them in the Web Discussion Wizard) so that users can expand the size of the contents window if they need to. Or you can use a frame set with a horizontal orientation.

Keep in mind that if you create the vertical table of contents frame set using the Web Discussion Wizard, you will need to edit the frame set to add a provision for nonframes browsers.

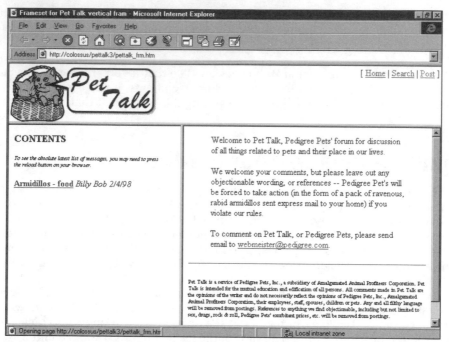

Figure 14-25: A vertical frame version of Pet Talk

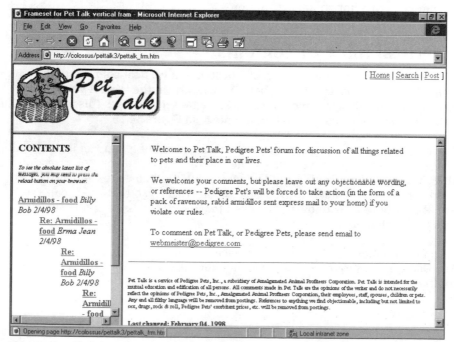

Figure 14-26: A heavily nested table of contents in a vertical frame opens a can of worms.

A horizontal table of contents

The Web Wizard offers two variations on the horizontal table of contents: a two-frame version that includes provision for nonframes browsers, and a three-frame version that adds a banner frame but does not provide an alternative for nonframes browsers.

An example of the three-frame version is shown in Figure 14-27, with the same table of contents that created problems for the vertical orientation described in the previous section. This is clearly a more readable table of contents, although it is somewhat more difficult in this version to see the entire article (unless you happen to have a large monitor at high resolution). Again, making the frames resizable can help.

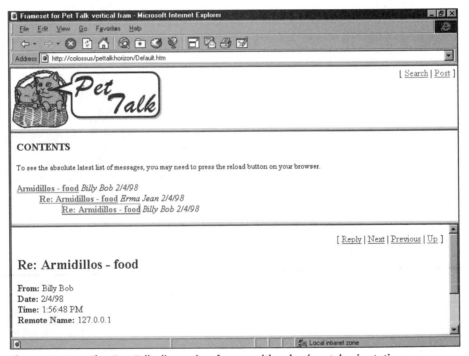

Figure 14-27: The Pet Talk discussion forum with a horizontal orientation

Managing Your Discussion Web

The FrontPage Discussion Web was designed to be configured once and then left alone. There is no provision for editing the list of messages in any way. In fact, the official documentation advises you not to touch the message files.

The official advice

For what it is worth, the official advice on managing content is this: If you need to delete or edit the content of the message, simply replace the content with a generic phrase (for instance, "[Deleted Article]," although personally, I think "Expletive Deleted" is a bit more colorful), but leave the message file intact. This way, you will not interfere with the component's methods of keeping track of how many messages there are and how they are related. Plus, everyone will be able to see what a censorious administrator you are.

The bottom line is, make any changes at your own risk. If you try to create any kind of serious discussion forum, however, you are likely to discover that the risk is unavoidable.

Not being able to edit the forum can be a rather major shortcoming, particularly if you happen to have a popular discussion forum. In this case, you may want to consider some method of archiving content.

A sobering tale from real life, with expletives deleted

The following is a true story (mostly). Never being one to take my own warnings too seriously, when I encountered a glitch due to changing filenames (see the tip earlier in this chapter), I decided to attempt to repair the damage by boldly editing the Pet Talk table of contents and message folder. I was able to move the files around and renumber them. By editing `tocproto.htm`, I managed to get the messages to show up in the correct place in the table of contents. I reset the article counter in the `service.cnf` file. I even got the messages linked to one another by changing a line in the `_vti_cnf` folder entry for each message file. But only after a very, very long time of messing around (and I only had *three* messages at the time). And even then, I was not convinced all was as it should be. In the end, even though it was sort of working, I decided it would be safer and faster to redo the whole thing. So I did.

Conclusion? I cannot recommend attempting to edit anything having to do with the messages or the table of contents. Nor would I recommend manually changing the names of any of the files or folders created. FrontPage scatters information about these files all over the place, and it is easy to overlook one vital place where the information needs to be changed. Maybe someday a braver soul than I will document the way.

Implementing Multiple Discussions

One way to forestall the need to archive your discussion Web would be to create multiple discussion Webs. For example, if your original discussion Web focuses on pets, you might create spin-off specialized discussion Webs for the pets most often talked about, for instance, cats and dogs.

If you have the ability to create multiple sub-Webs, this is probably the safest route, and it has the advantage of making it easier to upload changes to one discussion at a time. Alternatively, you can add additional discussion Webs to your original Web. The method for doing this is essentially the same as that for creating your initial discussion Web. The crucial difference comes right at the beginning. With the current discussion Web open in Explorer, select New ⇨ FrontPage Web. Select the Web Discussion Wizard and check the Add to the Current Web check box below the selection window. Besides this difference, just make sure to give the new discussion Web a different title and folder name.

Note   For better or worse, each discussion Web has its own search index, so cross-discussion searching is not possible.

Customizing the discussion Web template files

If you are planning to create a number of discussion Webs with a similar appearance, you may want to give some thought to customizing the template files that the Discussion Web Wizard uses when it creates the default versions of the discussion Web pages.

A full discussion of how to do this is beyond the scope of this chapter. The Web Discussion Wizard uses a number of .htx files as its templates for the various pages it creates. These files are found in the vtdisc.wiz subfolder of the Webs folder wherever you installed FrontPage (by default in Program Files\Microsoft FrontPage). By editing these files, you can change the way that the wizard builds its default Webs.

Note: Before making any changes to the wizard files, be sure to save a backup copy of the folder in a safe place.

Adding Registration to Your Discussion

When you use the Web Discussion Wizard to create your forum, among other things, it asks you, "Will the discussion take place in a protected Web?" This is the wizard's gentle way of asking if users need to register with a username and password in order to use the forum. If you answer, "Yes, only registered users can post articles," the wizard creates a default registration form, which enables users to register themselves to use your discussion Web. From there you are on your own.

Note

What is the purpose of requiring a password if you then allow anyone to create one? Typically for marketing purposes, that is, because you want to force users to hand over some information about themselves. If you want to use passwords strictly for security, you should come up with another way of enabling users to receive a password—after you or someone else has qualified them. We return to the topic of registration and security in Chapter 19.

Before you blithely answer yes to this question, thinking that a protected discussion is probably a good idea, you need to ascertain that you, in fact, have the authority to implement the registration feature. What it takes and how to do it are the topics of the next section.

So that you better understand what you are doing, let's first examine how the registration system works from the user's perspective. When users come to your discussion Web, they are prompted to enter their usernames and passwords.

Do you have what it takes?

Before you can add a Registration component to your Web (discussion or otherwise), you need to have an appropriate system and an appropriate level of authority within FrontPage. Setting up a Registration component has the following minimum requirements:

✦ You must have access to an NT or UNIX Web server that is capable of maintaining Web passwords and that is running the FrontPage extensions (which are necessary for the discussion Web anyway).

✦ You must have the ability to add Web pages to the root FrontPage Web, which is where the registration form must reside.

✦ You must have administrator-level authority within your own Web.

If you are in one of the following situations, you can forget about registering users via the FrontPage Registration component:

✦ You are using either Microsoft's Internet Information Server for Windows NT or Personal Web Server for Windows 95.

✦ You use a FrontPage hosting service that provides you with access to a sub-Web but not access to the root Web of the system.

✦ You use a hosting service that does not permit customers to implement passwords on their Webs, which is not uncommon.

✦ You are only a FrontPage author without administrator permissions.

Note

You may feel that these exclusions rule out a fair number of circumstances. Indeed it would seem to leave only non–Microsoft Windows or UNIX servers for which Microsoft has published server extensions. For a list of available extensions, see Appendix C.

The registration page

If you have indicated that you plan to have a password-protected discussion forum, the Web Discussion Wizard automatically creates for you a general-purpose registration form. In order to use the registration page, you need to perform two steps:

1. Move the registration form to the root Web of your Web server.

2. Adjust the permissions for the discussion Web to require user registration.

You can also customize the registration page. This topic is discussed in more detail when we return to the registration process in Chapter 19.

Moving the registration page

If you have indicated that you want users to register to use your discussion forum, FrontPage automatically opens the registration page in Editor after it has created your new Web. At the top of the page is a long comment field that repeats the directions here (although in reverse order).

To save the registration page in the root Web, switch to Explorer and close the current Web. Open the root Web in the usual manner. Switch back to Editor and select File⇨Save. The Save As dialog box opens, allowing you to save the registration page to the root Web with the default name of Web_selfregistration_form.htm (or you can change the name to anything else you want).

Setting access permissions

Once you have saved the registration page to the root Web, you need to change the permissions on the Web so that users are required to provide a username and password before entering. This is covered in Chapter 19.

Notice that it is quite possible to set up limited access without providing a registration page that enables user to self-register.

How registration works

First, let's be sure one concept is clear. The registration page is used by currently unregistered visitors to create a new username and password for themselves. This page is not the "logon" page for users who already have a valid username and password. They should proceed directly to the protected Web.

When users go to your protected Web, they are confronted with a standard Web password dialog box, such as the one shown in Figure 14-28.

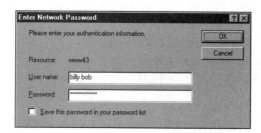

Figure 14-28: An example of the password dialog box the user is prompted with on a protected Web

If users have already created a username and password, they can enter it and proceed on to the page they had requested. If they do not have a username, they receive a message indicating that their authorization has failed.

Some Web servers allow custom pages to be associated with failed authorization. If you have such an option, you can use it to send users directly to the registration form, if they fail to enter a valid username/password combination.

Visitors who do not yet have a username/password combination must proceed to the registration page to make themselves one. Once they have completed the form, they receive a confirmation message, either the default or a custom one of your design. For more on the Registration component and on security measures in general, see Chapter 19.

How do new visitors know that they need to register? Typically, one would create the home page in a nonprotected area—the root Web, or some other Web—and direct users to that page. From there, you can create links to the protected discussion area for registered users and to the registration page for new users. The one catch in FrontPage is that password protection is Web-specific. You cannot create a protected area within a nonprotected Web, or vice versa. So any initial pages need to be in a separate Web.

Taking the Next Step

In this chapter, we explored the many components and features of the FrontPage Web Discussion component, and with that we wrap up our tour of FrontPage's components. In Part V, we raise the bar a notch higher to examine the various ways in which FrontPage can work with programming languages to provide both simple and complex forms of interactivity. If you are not a programmer, don't panic. These chapters do not try to turn you into a code jockey in five easy lessons. Our focus is rather on providing an understanding of the various (no, I did not say "nefarious"!) technologies that FrontPage is capable of working with, peppered with numerous examples you can really use.

✦   ✦   ✦

Programming Elements

Scripting (VBScript and JavaScript)

Using a scripting language such as JavaScript or VBScript, you can add interactive pizzazz to your FrontPage Webs quickly and easily. This chapter provides a basic understanding of how scripting languages work, what they can do, and how they differ. It also offers several examples of JavaScript and VBScript programs you can adapt and use without becoming a programming guru.

Discovering Client-Side Scripting

On the Web, all communication takes place between the Web browser you use to access Web pages and one or more Web servers. Each time you request a new page, your Web browser sends that request to a server, and the server responds. If you submit a form, your browser passes along the information to the server, which is responsible for processing and responding to your input, typically using a CGI program (for more information on the use of CGI, see the discussion later in this chapter).

In many cases, having the server do all processing works very well, and it ensures that the developer does not have to worry about what particular browser you are using. However, sometimes it would be convenient to process a request the user has made, or input submitted, without having to send the information all the way back to the server. *Client-side* scripting languages were created to address this need.

When you use a client-side scripting language, you embed programming directly into your Web page. When a user requests this page, the scripting is sent along with the rest of the page. The browser has to be savvy enough to interpret the scripting language and respond appropriately.

Using a client-side scripting language, you can increase the interactive character of your Web page without forcing the Web browser to send a request to the server and reload the page with a response. With scripting, for example, you can have images on the page change when the user positions the mouse over them, you can perform calculations and automatically update form field information, you can pop up a message if the user enters invalid information into a form field, or you can design your Web page to display different information to the user, depending on the type of browser that users have.

Best of all, client-side scripting languages are easy to learn and use. Of course it helps if you have some experience with other programming languages, but even if you don't, you should be able to follow the example scripts provided in this chapter and adapt them to your own use. Scripting languages are not suited to large-scale applications, but they provide a quick way to increase the flexibility and interactivity of your Web pages.

Previewing an Example

Let's imagine that you have created a form that asks users to supply their name and e-mail address. You realize that a fair number of people are likely to input their e-mail address incorrectly. You would like to have a simple way to catch those who unintentionally mistype their e-mail address.

You could build this function using CGI, but you have two main reasons for not doing so. First, a fair amount of programming overhead is involved in building any CGI application, more overhead than you want for such a simple function. Second, your users are likely to find this function mildly distracting, if not annoying, particularly if they need to correct their e-mail address.

Why you need a scripting language

Using the Common Gateway Interface (CGI) programming specification, you can extend the interactive capabilities of your Web site by linking Web page forms to CGI applications that can process user input and/or generate Web pages dynamically. The CGI specification provides programmers with a great deal of flexibility. Because the CGI specification is recognized by most browsers and because CGI applications reside on the Web server, they can be written in just about any available programming language.

If you have worked with CGI applications, however, you may have noticed that they have one characteristic that is sometimes a drawback. They are relatively slow. Because they reside on the Web server, CGI programs need input sent from the user, typically via the submit button on a form, and after they have done their work, they return a new page with any results or response. Sometimes you would prefer to have the interaction between the user and your program be more immediate. Hence the need for a scripting language.

The fact that CGI programs live on the Web server can sometimes be an advantage, however, particularly when you want to protect your investment in proprietary code.

Using a CGI application, the user must first submit the form to the server. The CGI application then reads the input e-mail address and composes a reply message prompting the user to confirm his or her e-mail address. The user then either confirms the address, in which case the form is resubmitted, or edits the address, in which case the original form must be reloaded with the existing data and the whole process repeated until the user gets the address right.

Now imagine that instead of using a CGI program, you could simply pop up a message box with the same confirmation request when the form was about to be submitted. In this case, if the user makes a mistake, the user is prompted to try again. No information is ever submitted until it is correct. This method is easy on the Web server and easy on the user. Plus, because no connections are made across the Internet, the confirmation process is blazingly fast, even on the slowest dial-up connection.

In order to effect this enhanced behavior, you need some way to create a "smart" Web page, one that can perform this simple function without intervention from the server after it has been sent to the user's Web browser. This approach involves using client-side scripting.

To create this script requires three simple steps:

1. First, create the form (see Chapter 11 for details on building forms in FrontPage). If necessary, change the form field properties of the push button described there so that it is a normal button and not a Submit button. (This is necessary to keep the form from being automatically submitted.) Our form is shown in Figure 15-1.

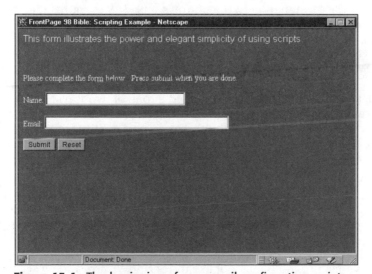

Figure 15-1: The beginning of our e-mail confirmation script

2. Use the Script Wizard to insert the custom script function necessary to perform the confirmation. Later in the chapter we learn how this scripting works. For now, just follow along. The script in question has a single function, called `confirmEmail`. It looks like this:

```
<script LANGUAGE="JavaScript">
//<!--
function confirmEmail(name,email)
{
var confirmedEmail = window.prompt(name + ", Please retype your
email to confirm:","");
        if (confirmedEmail != null && confirmedEmail !="") {
            if (email==confirmedEmail) {
                document.ex1.submit();
                return true;
            }
            else {
                window.alert("First address ("+email+") does not
match confirmation ("+confirmedEmail+"). Please try again.");
                document.ex1.Email.value="";
                return false;
            }
        }
        else {
            return false;
        }
}
//-->
        </script>
```

3. After you have constructed your function, use the Script Wizard to bind the `confirmEmail()` function to the button's `onClick` event handler. When the user clicks the button, it executes the script, causing the `confirmEmail` function to spring into action, as shown in Figure 15-2. To see how this script works, check out `Examples/ch15/example1.htm` for Chapter 15 on the CD-ROM.

Note

The examples in this chapter can be accessed in one of two ways. As always, they can be located directly on the CD-ROM in the appropriate chapter directory within the `Examples` directory. This chapter also has a special interface that is both an example and a means of exploring the other examples. To use this interface, load the `/Examples/ch15/gui/guimain.htm` file from the CD-ROM into your browser.

When to use a script

From this example, you should notice that a scripting language gives you some powerful tools for adding functionality to your Web page. You can manipulate the properties of page objects, such as the value of a form field, based on user-initiated actions. And with a programming tool like the Script Wizard, adding scripts is relatively simple.

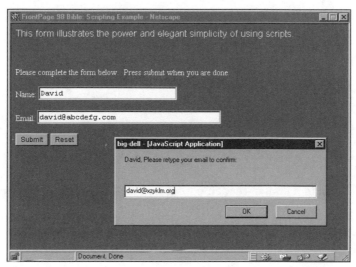

Figure 15-2: The `confirmEmail` script in action—no CGI required!

Anytime you want to add simple functionality to your Web pages, you may want to consider using a scripting language. Remember that if you create script-based functionality that is essential to the operation of the page, you need to find a way to accommodate users with browsers that are not compatible with scripting languages. The following are some of the tasks that scripting languages are well-suited to:

✦ Calculations

✦ Simple animation

✦ Window and frame control

✦ Pop-up messages

✦ Form field updating

✦ Form field validation

✦ Dynamic page control

✦ Browser detection

When not to use a script

Scripting languages are useful, fun, and easy to use (if you like that sort of thing), but they are not suited to every task. For one thing, scripts are uncompiled, which makes them easy to appropriate. Another drawback of scripting languages is that they have tended to be browser dependent, thus complicating the choice of which browser to use when. (But see the discussion of ECMAScript in the next section to hear good news on this front.) These, then, are counterindications for scripts:

✦ If you need to access or process data

✦ If you need to record user input

✦ If you have a big project on a short time frame

✦ If you need to protect your proprietary code

✦ If you need to support a lowest-common-denominator browser

Measuring JavaScript against VBScript

Scripts are written in a human-readable form and embedded into a Web page. When a Web browser receives a Web page containing a client-side script, the browser must be able to interpret the script. This means that a given Web browser must be able to translate and execute the script directly, making the scripting language very much browser dependent.

Because scripts are embedded into Web pages, it is very difficult to protect your code from others. This is another reason that scripts tend to be relatively simple. It also means that most script developers are willing to allow others to use their scripts.

If you are going to use a scripting language, you need to know which browsers support which languages. You also need to know how to deal appropriately with browsers that do not support your scripts.

The first scripting language to hit the Web development world was Netscape's JavaScript. Contrary to what many people assume, Netscape's JavaScript, although it has some similarities in syntax to Java, is not directly related to the popular programming language developed at Sun Microsystems. JavaScript, as of this writing currently in version 1.2, is also the basis of the recently defined standards-based scripting language, ECMA-262, also known as ECMAScript. ECMAScript is the work of ECMA (European Computer Manufacturers' Association), an international standards body. Both Microsoft and Netscape have announced their support for this standard, although both continue to support functionality not contained in the standard. One way to ensure compatibility is to develop using only the standard functionality, although this is somewhat difficult at the moment, given a lack of ECMAScript-aware development tools.

Originally, JavaScript was known as LiveScript. The name was changed partly to signify that JavaScript syntax bore some similarity to Java, but mainly, one suspects, to capitalize on the rising popularity of the hot new programming language. Microsoft, on the other hand, while supporting JavaScript, calls their version JScript, for obvious reasons avoiding any clear associations with the Java name.

Microsoft, in its Internet Explorer browser, has developed support for a JavaScript-like language, which Microsoft refers to as JScript. Because of its support for JScript, Internet Explorer works correctly with many JavaScript scripts. Microsoft has announced 100 percent compliance with the ECMA standard for JScript 3.0. It is important to test any scripts you develop in both Netscape and Microsoft browsers, however, to ensure correct functionality in both environments.

Tip

It is possible to create support for VBScript in Netscape's browser by adding the NCompass ScriptActive plug-in.

In addition to its support for JScript, Microsoft has also developed a second scripting language called VBScript. VBScript, the full name of which is Microsoft Visual Basic Scripting Edition, is a subset of Microsoft's popular programming languages, Visual Basic and Visual Basic for Applications (VBA). If you already know how to program in Visual Basic, learning VBScript is a snap. Also, if you are planning to develop a Microsoft-based Web solution using ActiveX technologies, you may find some advantages to using VBScript. See Chapter 16 for a discussion of ActiveX. Keep in mind, however, that only Internet Explorer contains support for VBScript. You need either to know that your users have this browser or to be prepared to deal with those who do not. For this reason, VBScript can be an appropriate choice for intranet developers, when their company has standardized on the Internet Explorer browser.

Note

Both scripting languages now have server-side versions, so you can use the same programming environment to write scripts for server- and client-side functionality.

Where to find scripts

Even if you have no plans to develop your own scripts, you can still make use of a scripting language by adapting existing scripts to your Web pages. Later in this chapter we present a variety of scripting examples, intended to spur you on to bigger and better things as well as to give you some initial scripts to adapt to your own use.

In addition, you may have already added scripts to your Web page without knowing it. For example, if you have used FrontPage to add form validation rules to your form fields, FrontPage automatically creates JavaScript or VBScript code to perform the validation functions.

You can also adapt preexisting scripts to use in your Web pages. Partly because scripts are easy to create and partly because they are difficult to protect, there are many sources of freely available scripts that you can use. And remember, although by no means a requirement, it is always courteous to credit the source of any scripts you borrow or adapt.

One of the best places to look for scripting examples is the Gamelan site, at http://www.developer.com. For VBScripts, also check out Microsoft's sites, http://www.microsoft.com/vbscript and http://www.vbscripts.com.

Inserting Scripts in FrontPage

The next section of this chapter walks through the process of using FrontPage to add scripts to your Web pages. We do not attempt to give you a crash course in programming. Instead we focus on things you can do even without programming skills, although of course a little understanding of how to write scripts may just sink into your grey matter. You have been warned.

Let's begin by inserting a simple existing script into a Web page. To follow along with this example, you can create your own Web page or use the sample page, `Examples/ch15/example2.htm`, found in `ch15` folder on the CD-ROM. Later, when we look at some scripting examples, we see a more developed version of the time zone script.

The script we use displays a configurable time at the place where it is called. This script illustrates several basic elements of client-side scripts. FrontPage distinguishes between two kinds of scripts: *inline scripts,* which are placed within the body of the HTML page and run when the page is first loaded in the browser, and *event scripts,* which are triggered when the user interacts with an object on the page, such as a form button. One of the main differences between the two types of scripts is that inline scripts are interpreted before they are displayed by the browser. This means that the code used to generate the inline script does not appear when users view the HTML source. This example is an inline script. Inline scripts are best written using the Script Editor.

Inserting the current time

The script consists of two components, the *script function* and a *trigger* that causes the script to execute.

We start with a Web page, such as the one illustrated in Figure 15-3. To insert the current time after the text "At the tone...the time will be," first position the cursor where you want the time to appear (don't forget to insert a space at the end of the text!), and then select Insert ➪ Advanced ➪ Script, or select the Script icon from the Advanced toolbar.

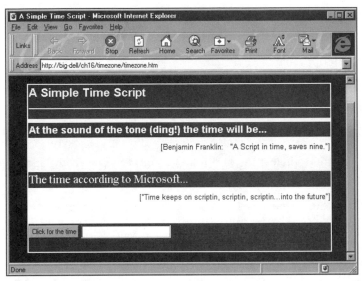

Figure 15-3: Your Web page before inserting the current time script

This opens the FrontPage Script Editor as shown in Figure 15-4. The editor has a simple interface that allows you to select the type of script you want to insert and a bare-bones editing window where you insert the script itself.

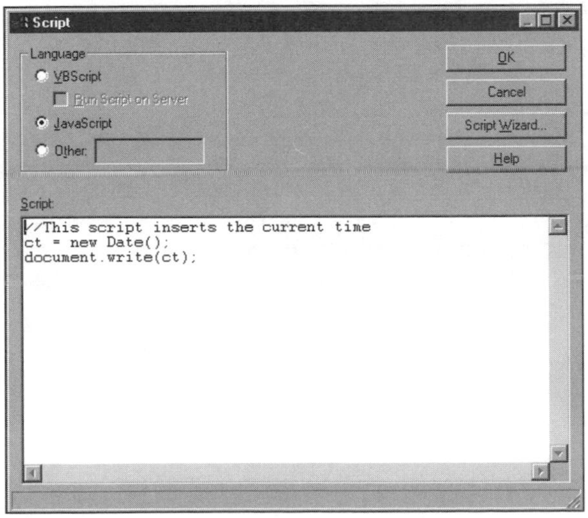

Figure 15-4: The FrontPage Script Editor

To insert JavaScript code

Use the following steps to insert JavaScript code:

1. Select the JavaScript Language option.

2. Type the following code into the Script box:

```
//This script inserts the current time
ct = new Date();
document.write(ct);
```

3. Click the OK button to insert the script and return to your FrontPage document.

If you have turned on the Format Marks, you should see the JavaScript *J* icon displayed where you inserted the script. (To turn on Format Marks, select View ➪ Format Marks. Select this item again to turn off Format Marks.)

In order to view the results of your handiwork, you need to preview the document. You can do this either by selecting the Preview tab in FrontPage Editor or by selecting File ➪ Preview in Browser and loading the page into your favorite browser.

To see how your script looks in your HTML, select the HTML tab. Your page should resemble Figure 15-5. Note that in addition to inserting your code, the Script Editor has added a `<script>` tag and wrapped your code in comment tags.

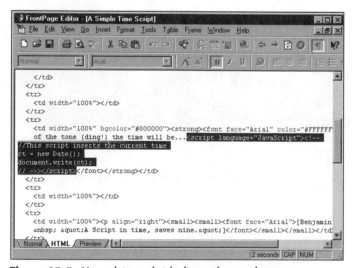

Figure 15-5: Your date script in its native environment

If you have looked at your script page in your browser, try viewing the source. Note that the source has already replaced your JavaScript with the HTML text that appears in the page.

To insert VBScript code

To insert VBScript code, use the following steps:

1. Select Insert ⇨ Advanced ⇨ Script or select the Script icon from the Advanced toolbar to open the Script Editor (see the preceding figure).

2. Select VBScript from the Language option in the Script Editor. Make certain that the Run Script on Server option is not checked. (This option can be used to generate VBScript for Active Server Pages [ASP]. ASP is discussed in more detail in Chapter 17.)

3. Type the following code into the Script box:

```
REM This script inserts the current time
DIM ct
ct=Time()
document.write(ct)
```

4. Click the OK button to insert the script and close the Script Editor.

If you have Format Marks turned on, you should see the VBScript icon where you inserted your script. You can view the results of both scripts by selecting the Preview tab in FrontPage Editor, or by selecting File ⇨ Preview and opening the page in Internet Explorer 3.x or higher. The results are shown in Figure 15-6.

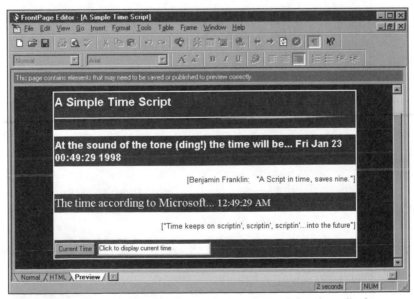

Figure 15-6: The JavaScript and VBScript versions of the time display

Editing an existing script

You can open an existing script in the Script Editor by double-clicking the Script icon inserted into your page. Return to the preceding JavaScript example. Select View⇨Format Marks to turn on format marks if they are not already on. Double-click the JavaScript icon. You can now make any changes you like to your script. Try amending the final line of the script to read:

```
document.write(ct.toGMTString());
```

Click the OK button to save your changes and exit the Script Editor. Now preview the effects of your changes. Now you should see the time in Greenwich Mean Time format, rather than your default system time.

Error trapping

The scripts we have experimented with so far are fairly straightforward, so you probably encountered little difficulty making the script work correctly. But what if you had made an error in the code you entered?

The Script Editor provided with FrontPage 98 has no error-checking facility. It will happily allow you to enter any outrageous code you like. You will not know what happened until you test your script.

To demonstrate this, return to the JavaScript you created earlier. Open the JavaScript by double-clicking its icon embedded in the Web page (refer to the previous section for instructions on editing an existing script).

In the Script Editor Script box, replace the last line of code with the following:

```
document.write(x)
```

Note that the variable "x" has replaced the previous variable "ct." The JavaScript, however, has not defined a value for "x." This will not be well-received when the browser parses the script.

Note

If you try this with the VBScript version, you do not receive an error message. As far as VBScript is concerned, you have just created a new variable. You won't get the time, but you won't get an error message either.

Click the OK button to save your misguided change and return to the Web page. Note that the Script Editor shows no sign of distress or alarm. Now, select the Preview tab in FrontPage Editor. When the preview page attempts to interpret your script, it generates an error message, as shown in Figure 15-7. This is a decent way to catch errors in simple scripts.

If you plan to do more advanced scripting, you should consider a development environment that includes better debugging features. Unfortunately the pickings are lean in this department. You can use a full-blown version of the Visual Basic development environment, of course, but this is probably overkill. Microsoft also has made available (on an off-and-on basis) a debugging tool for scripting languages, although it is less than 100 percent reliable. Netscape also has a visual editing tool for JavaScript. In general, though, the lack of a solid development tool is one of the reasons it is difficult to support an extensive script-based project. (Or perhaps it is the other way around?)

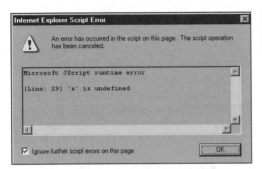

Figure 15-7: A JScript (a.k.a JavaScript) error message generated by FrontPage's Preview mode

Learning Scripting Basics

In the previous section you began to get a feel for how scripting works in FrontPage. In this section we look at some of the basic issues surrounding the use of scripts in your Web pages. After that, we explain how to use the FrontPage Script Wizard, and in the last half of the chapter, we look at a number of sample scripts. You may never have to worry about these issues directly, if you use FrontPage to assist you in creating scripts. The point of this section is to help you understand what FrontPage is doing (and why, when that is possible to infer) so that you can better determine what you want to have it do.

Browser compatibility issues

As mentioned at the beginning of this chapter, one of the downsides of using client-side scripts is the lack of consistent browser support for various scripting languages. If you have more than one browser, try viewing the scripts in various browsers. Note that although JavaScript works in both Internet Explorer and Netscape Navigator, VBScript works only in Internet Explorer.

You have two issues to consider when trying to make your pages useable by as many browsers as possible: (1) how to deal with browsers that do not support scripts at all, and (2) how to deal with browsers that support one or the other type of script.

The no-script alternative

Believe it or not, not everyone uses the latest version of either Netscape's or Microsoft's browser (a pill that is very difficult for most developers to swallow). And even if they do so, some users turn off their browser's support for active elements, such as Java, ActiveX, and scripting, primarily for security reasons.

You can prevent such users' browsers from displaying a script as if it were normal text. You can also define an alternative to the scripting functions you include in your page.

Hiding scripts from old browsers

You can hide your scripts from older browsers by enclosing the script itself in a slightly modified comment tag. A comment tag begins with an exclamation point followed by two hyphens (`<!--`). It is closed with two hyphens (`-->`).

If you look back at the HTML created by the Script Editor in our first two example scripts, you see that the Script Editor automatically wraps your script in comment tags. In the JavaScript version, the end tag is preceded with a double slash (`//`), the JavaScript comment indicator. If your user's browser does not support scripting or if scripting is turned off, the browser will interpret the script as a comment and ignore it. You should use a similar syntax anytime you insert a script manually. Note that the comment tag is placed inside the script tag—otherwise, even script-enabled browsers would ignore the scripts.

Alternatives for nonscripting browsers

Wrapping your scripts in comment tags ensures that noncompatible browsers will not dump your code into your Web page, but this still leaves these users with a blank spot where useful information is meant to appear.

In most cases, you cannot provide these users with the same information. (Otherwise, why are you using scripts at all?) You can, however, inform these users that they are missing out on something. To include a message for nonscripting browsers, place the message in a `<noscript>` tag.

Unfortunately, although both Netscape Navigator and Microsoft Internet Explorer support the `noscript` syntax, FrontPage does not. Consequently, you will have to insert this tag manually.

Return to the JavaScript example earlier in this chapter. Select the HTML tab to view the document source. Insert the following immediately following the end of the `script` tag:

```
<NOSCRIPT>
<H6>Current time display requires a JavaScript compatible
browser with JavaScript currently enabled.</H6>
</NOSCRIPT>
```

Select the Normal tab to return to the WYSIWYG mode. Notice that FrontPage displays the comment tag icon around the inserted text, indicating that it does not recognize this `noscript` tag. Not to worry. Select the Preview tab, and you should see the appropriate display for a JavaScript-enabled browser.

To see the `noscript` text displayed, select File ➪ Preview in Browser and select your favorite browser. Assuming that you have a JavaScript-compatible browser, you should see the current time displayed correctly.

To view the `noscript` text in Internet Explorer, select View ➪ Options. In the Options property window, select the Security tab, and uncheck the Run ActiveX Scripts check box. Return to the Web page and reload it by clicking the Refresh button or selecting View ➪ Refresh. The current time should no longer be displayed. In its place is the alternative message.

To view the `noscript` text in Netscape Navigator 4.*x*, select Edit ➪ Preferences, select the Advanced item, and uncheck the Enable JavaScript check box. Return to the Web page and reload the page by clicking the Reload button or by selecting View ➪ Reload. In Netscape Navigator 3.*x*, select Options ➪ Network Preferences, and then select the Languages tab and uncheck the Enable JavaScript check box. Return to the page and reload as for Netscape Navigator 4.*x*.

The Document Object Model

Both VBScript and JavaScript have their share of basic built-in programming operators, functions, and control statements. You can perform all of the standard math operations, access date and time objects, create variables and arrays, manipulate text strings, and perform conditional and looping statements. The real power of scripting languages, however, lies in their access to the objects that make up the browser, its components, and particularly the Web page documents loaded in the browser. Early versions of JavaScript had limited support for control over these elements. Microsoft was the first to expose all document objects to scripting control. Netscape has followed suit. The result is work on a standard model for this control. Called the Document Object Model (DOM), this standard is the real basis of the next generation of scripting, which has come to be known as DHTML, Dynamic HTML.

Scriptlets

Another trend in the scripting world, this one promulgated first by Microsoft, is the concept of scriptlets. A *scriptlet* is a reusable chunk of scripting code, which can be stored in one place and referenced by multiple Web page scripts. This is an old programming technique, which Microsoft is applying to this new environment. If the past is any predictor of the future, scriptlets are bound to be an important part of the next generation of scripting as well.

Using the Script Wizard

The FrontPage Script Wizard is designed to help you compose simple scripts. It provides a visual list of the available document objects, as well as object properties, methods, and event handlers you can reference. It also allows you to add procedures (called functions in the JavaScript world) and global variables. The Script Wizard hides from you the actual placement of the scripting code in the HTML page (although of course you can always view and edit it in the HTML tab). It is a convenient feature and a nice tool for exploring the composition of scripting objects. It is not by any stretch of the imagination a fully integrated development environment.

The Script Wizard is accessible only in roundabout ways, another sign that Microsoft is not trying to call too much attention to this utility. To open the Script Wizard, you have to go through the Script Editor. Call the Script Editor by clicking the icon representing an existing inline script, by selecting Insert ➪ Advanced ➪ Script, or by clicking the Script icon on the Advanced toolbar. Once in the Script Editor, open the Script Wizard by clicking the button of the same name.

Anatomy of the Script Wizard

The Script Wizard (shown in Figure 15-8), like Gaul, is composed of three parts. The upper-left section is known as the Event pane. It lists any form components or ActiveX controls that have events associated with them. Clicking a component's event (represented by a hollow diamond) activates the Script pane in the bottom half of the wizard, enabling you to associate a script with an event. Once you have done so, the Diamond icon fills in to alert you to the fact that this event is taken.

The upper-right section of the wizard is called the Action pane. It lists the available actions that you can associate with an event. Actions are indicated with an exclamation icon. To associate an action with a particular event, first click the event in question and then double-click the action to add it to the script for that event in the Script pane. At that point you can add to or edit the script as you wish in the Script pane.

The Action pane also lists global variables and procedures, essentially any custom code that you have added to the page. To add a new procedure or variable, right-click the Action pane and select the task you wish to perform from the pop-up menu. If you are creating a new variable, the wizard displays a simple dialog box where you can type the name of the variable. If you are adding a procedure, the wizard starts a new procedure in the Script pane. Once you create the item, it is added to the list of available objects in the Action pane. To edit or delete an existing variable or procedure, right-click it and select your choice from the pop-up menu.

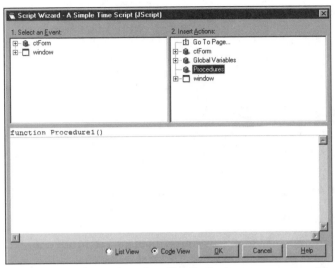

Figure 15-8: The Script Wizard's principal parts, no assembly required

Creating an event-driven script

In the previous section, we created simple inline scripts using JavaScript and VBScript. These scripts are processed when the Web page loads into the browser. In this section, we look at an event-driven version of the same script to display the current time.

An event-driven script is triggered by some element on the Web page, typically, but not necessarily, a button. In FrontPage 98, you can use the Script Wizard to help you build your script. The following examples demonstrate the event-driven model for both JavaScript and VBScript.

Preparing the big event

To create the event-driven script, first create a simple form, using the following steps (for more information on creating forms in FrontPage 98, see Chapter 11):

1. First add a button. Using the Forms toolbar, select the Button icon. Alternatively, select Insert ➪ Form Field ➪ Push Button.

2. Edit the button properties by double-clicking the button or by right-clicking the button element and selecting Form Field Properties. Alternatively, click the button once to select it, and then select Edit ➪ Form Field Properties.

3. In the Push Button Properties dialog box, set the Name element to "ctButton." Set the value of the button to "Current Time" (see Figure 15-9). Click OK to record your changes and return to the HTML page.

Figure 15-9: Creating the button that triggers the event that runs the script that tells the time

4. Position the cursor within the dashed lines of the form element and after the button. Insert a Text field either by using the Form toolbar or by selecting Insert ⇨ Form Field ⇨ One Line Text Box.

5. Edit the text box properties, using one of the methods described in step 2. Set the name to "ctText." Set the value of the text box to "Click to display current time." Set the width of the field to 40. Click OK to record your changes and return to the HTML page.

6. Finally, set the name of the form itself to "ctForm." Access the form properties by right-clicking within the dashed lines of the form element. Click OK to record your change and return to the HTML page. Note: FrontPage 98 may warn you that the form may not work correctly because the settings are invalid. If you receive this warning message, click "No" to indicate that you do not wish to edit the settings (for this example, it does not matter that the button does not correctly submit results back to the server).

7. Save your work by clicking the Save icon in the main toolbar or by selecting File ⇨ Save.

Adding an event-driven script

To add the script to this form, we use the Script Wizard. You can access the Script Wizard in one of two ways. Select Insert ⇨ Advanced ⇨ Script to open the Script Editor, and click the Script Wizard button. Alternatively, click with the right mouse button anywhere inside the form element and select the Script Wizard option in the drop-down menu. The Script Wizard is accessible in this way from any scriptable object, that is, any element of the page that is capable of triggering an event, such as a button click.

The Script Wizard opens (as seen earlier in Figure 15-8). The Script Wizard, described earlier in the chapter, provides point-and-click access to the Web page document objects and their methods.

To use the Script Wizard, first select from the left-hand column the element you wish to work with:

1. Click the plus sign next to the ctForm element. It expands to show the two form elements contained in this form: ctButton and ctText. These elements are shown with the blue object icon.

2. Expand the ctButton object to show its onClick method, indicated with a hollow diamond icon.

3. Select the onClick method. When you do this, the bottom portion of the wizard is activated, enabling you to associate an action with the selected event.

4. For our first experiment, make sure that the Script Wizard is in List view. Click the List View option button to switch to this mode, if it is not already selected.

5. Select an object on which to perform the action. In the right-hand column, expand the ctForm and ctText objects. Double-click the ctText value property. A dialog box appears, as illustrated in Figure 15-10, prompting you to enter a text string. Enter **This is a test** and click OK to return to the Script Wizard. The wizard places the appropriate information in the list of actions to perform. Click OK to return to FrontPage Editor.

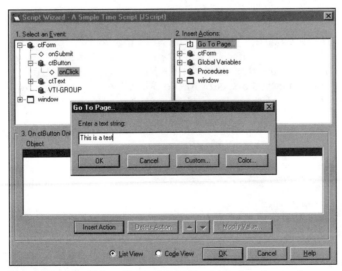

Figure 15-10: Using the Script Editor List view to create a simple script

6. To test the operation of the button, switch to Preview mode. Click the Current Time button. The string "This is a test" should appear in the text field.

Setting the default scripting language

How does FrontPage know what language to use to create scripts when you use the Script Wizard? If the current Web page contains script code already, it uses the language already in effect. If there is no scripting in the page yet, FrontPage uses the default scripting language. If you want to change the scripting language for a page, first open the Script Editor and select the default language for that page by clicking either the JavaScript or VBScript option button.

Note

FrontPage Script Wizard does not support multiple scripting languages in the same page. If you need to use both scripting languages, you must build your scripts by hand, using the Script Editor. If your page contains multiple languages and you open the Script Wizard, it complains.

Inserting custom code

Being able to insert a message such as "This is a test" into a text field is all well and good, but what we really wanted to accomplish was the ability to insert the current time into the field when the user clicks the button. To do this, it is necessary to return to the Script Wizard and insert a very small amount of custom code.

To return to the Script Wizard, click with the right mouse button on either of the form elements in the Web page used earlier. Select Script Wizard. In the left-hand column, expand the ctForm and ctButton objects. Select the ctButton onClick event. The action you inserted appears in the bottom of the wizard. Switch to Code view by selecting the Code View option button at the bottom of the wizard.

In Code view, you can edit the source code of your script directly. Replace the current line of code with the following VBScript:

```
ctForm.ctText.value = Time()
```

or the equivalent JavaScript:

```
ctForm.ctText.value = Date();
```

Notice that if you switch back to List view at this point, you can no longer use List view to edit your script. Click OK to update the script. Switch to Preview mode by clicking the Preview tab. Click the Current Time button. Voila! The current time (see Figure 15-11). Each time you click the button, the field is updated with the latest time. Very handy, I am sure, for those who have nothing else to do all day but click a button and check the time. In the next section we examine some sample scripts that purport to have a bit more practical value (or at least to be more entertaining).

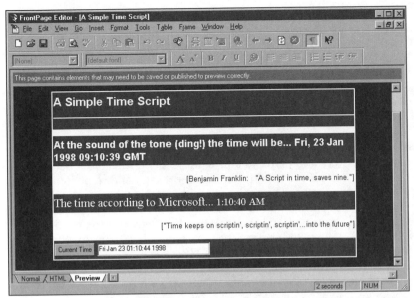

Figure 15-11: My, look how time flies when you are happily scripting!

Working with More Examples

The remainder of this chapter is devoted to an examination of several scripting examples, which illustrate a range of the possible applications of client-side JavaScript and VBScript. The examples are meant to be useable as well as instructive. You can find the completed scripts in the `Examples/ch15` directory on the CD-ROM that accompanies this book. We discuss the first example in some detail, in order to give you a good overview of the range of control possible with a scripting language. The remainder of the examples are described briefly and then left to your perusal.

Interface controls (JavaScript)

The first script example we examine serves as the interface for browsing the others on the CD-ROM. It is a frames-based JavaScript application that controls various aspects of the user interface. It is made up of four files, located in the `Examples/ch15/gui` subfolder of the examples for Chapter 15. The main frame set file, `guimain.htm`, defines a three-frame interface. The top frame, `guibanner.htm`, displays a banner graphic. The main frame, whose start page is `guicontent.htm`, is used to display introductory descriptions of each of the other example scripts in this chapter. Each description page also has a button to launch the example.

If possible, you should view this example in Navigator or Internet Explorer 4.0, because its most prominent feature, the control of images, is not supported in Internet Explorer 3.

What it does

An important element of a good interface design is that it provides contextual feedback to users to help them understand what they are doing. Providing these kinds of visual clues has been a staple feature of multimedia development, but it has been traditionally hard to accomplish in a Web page environment. The script presented here provides some simple ways to overcome that. It also illustrates ways you can use a script to get beyond the one-page-after-another mentality of the Web browser.

When the user moves the mouse over one of the buttons in the left-hand frame, the button changes its state and displays a brief message in the status bar of the window. Clicking a button causes it to remain depressed and to become highlighted, indicating which page the user has selected. The button click also loads new pages into both other frames simultaneously. Each of the main content pages provides a brief description of the associated script. When the Demo button is clicked, it launches the script in its own browser window, which has been stripped of all of the standard browser trappings. Figure 15-12 shows this script in action.

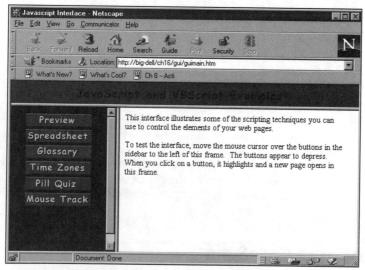

Figure 15-12: The scripting example interface

How it works

Let's look at some of the main features of this JavaScript example and how they work.

Browser detection

We have mentioned that one of the main challenges of using scripts in your Web pages is ensuring that the pages are well-behaved in whatever browsers your site needs to support. In many cases, you can handle browser differences simply by providing an alternative page for those browsers that do not support scripting at all. This script, however, uses a method of altering the display of images that is not supported in Microsoft's Internet Explorer 3, even though IE 3 is capable of recognizing client-side scripts. For that reason, this script contains a function, BrowserCheck, the purpose of which is to prevent IE 3 from running the portion of the script that it would not interpret correctly.

To see the BrowserCheck function, open the main file of the example, guimain.htm, in Editor, and click the left-hand frame containing the buttons to select it. You should notice that this frame has a blue border, indicating that it is the selected frame. Select Insert ➪ Advanced ➪ Script from the menu bar, or click the Script icon in the Advanced toolbar, to bring up the Script Editor. Click the Script Wizard. Using the Script Wizard, you can browse through the scripting procedures and variables used in each example.

Note

Having introduced the technique for browsing through the example scripts, we will not repeat it in subsequent scripts. For more information on using the Script Wizard, see the section on this topic earlier in the chapter.

To display the list of procedures used in this frame, first make sure that you have selected the Code View option at the bottom of the Script Wizard window. Click the plus sign next to the Procedures in the right-hand frame of the Script Wizard (the one labeled Insert Actions). Click with the right mouse button on the first procedure listed, named browserCheck(), and select Edit from the pop-up menu list. The browserCheck() function loads into the bottom frame of the Script Wizard window:

```
function browserCheck()
{
      if (document.images) {
         doIt = true;
      }
      else{
         doIt = false;
      }
}
```

This function has a simple purpose. It checks for the existence of an array of images; if it finds one, it sets a flag variable, doIt. This array is simply the collection of images loaded on the Web page. Because IE 3 does not support this object, it fails to set the tag. The key to using BrowserCheck() is to first check for this flag in any other function that involves the use of the image object. So for example, the next function to run, initButtons(), first checks for the presence of doIt before building the array of Button objects, the purpose of which is described later in this chapter.

Note

If you run this example in Internet Explorer 3.0, it functions correctly. You just miss the cool animated button feature.

Image control

The most prominent effect produced by this interface is its animated buttons.
When you run the mouse over a button, it appears to depress. When you move the
mouse away, it returns to its original state. If you click the button, it remains
depressed and the text is highlighted.

These effects are produced by manipulating the type property of the image object
for each button. Each button is defined by a set of three separate GIF images, one
for each possible state of the button. Any time the user triggers a change in the
state of the button, the appropriate image is loaded into the image's type property.
This is an excellent example of the flexibility achieved by being able to control
elements of the page. The next section describes the key functions that control
the state of the image objects.

Note

If you are used to the slow download times typical for images, you may be
wondering how this script loads the images instantaneously. The answer is that all
of the images for each button download when the page first opens, even though
only one image per button is visible. Thus when the image changes, it is drawn
from the local cache. Note that using this technique does add to the initial
download time of the page, so you should plan your images carefully.

Event handling

The image effects described in the previous section are controlled by means of a
set of event handlers for images that are part of the JavaScripting language. These
handlers include:

✦ onMouseOver—Triggers an event when the mouse cursor is over the object.

✦ onMouseOut—Triggers an event when the mouse cursor leaves the object.

✦ onClick—Triggers an event when the mouse is clicked on the object.

These event handlers are added to the hyperlink tag for each image, as in this
example, which has been broken into multiple lines for easier reading:

```
<a
 href="../talk.htm"
 target="main"
 onMouseOver="mouseOverButton(0);
  window.status=buttons[0].msg;
  return true"
 onMouseOut="mouseOffButton(0)"
 onClick="mouseClicked(0)">
<img
 NAME="0"
 src="../images/gui/preview_up.gif"
 border="0"
 alt="Preview"
 WIDTH="120"
 HEIGHT="25">
</a>
```

This example is associated with a set of custom functions: `Mouseclicked()`, `MouseOffButton()`, `MouseOverButton()`, and `MouseOnButton()`, which are responsible for doing the work of keeping track of the button states and displaying the appropriate images.

The onLoad handler

In addition to the mouse-related event handlers, this script makes use of one other useful handler: `onLoad()`. This method is called from the body tag (as is its cousin, `onUnload()`, which is not used in this script):

```
<body bgcolor="#000000" onLoad="initPage()">
```

Any functions associated with this method are run when the page is first loaded into the browser. In this script, the `onLoad()` method is used to call `browserCheck()` and to initialize the Button objects, described later in this chapter.

Status bar messages

We have called attention to the fact that the buttons in this script change when you move the mouse over them. They are not the only things that change, however. Watch carefully what happens to the text message at the bottom of your browser. The message there should change to match the button your cursor is over.

This message area is called the status line, and it is another window object that you can control. (You may have encountered one of those charming sites that put interminably scrolling text messages in your status bar.) To see how this is done, look back at the code associated with the `onMouseOver` handler described previously.

User-defined objects

The heart of this script is encapsulated in its array of Button objects. Button is a user-defined object that can be used just like the predefined JavaScript objects. The Button object consists of a constructor function that defines the object and a series of instantiations of Button objects, created using the New function. The Button constructor looks just like a regular JavaScript function:

```
function Button(w, h, offsrc, oversrc, onsrc, msg) {
        this.w=w;
        this.h=h;
        this.offImage= new Image(w,h);
        this.overImage = new Image(w,h);
        this.onImage= new Image(w,h);
        this.offImage.src=offsrc;
        this.overImage.src=oversrc;
        this.onImage.src=onsrc;
        this.state=0;
        this.msg = msg;
}
```

The purpose of the constructor function is to define the properties of the Button object. Each Button object has its own associated images and messages. When the button event handler is triggered, any of that button's properties can be identified and used, simply by knowing which button was affected.

To create a new Button object, an array is defined, and then each element of the array is instantiated as a new Button object. Here is one example from the initButtons() function, which creates the Button objects:

```
Button(120,25,"../images/gui/preview_up.gif","../images/gui/pre
view_over.gif","../images/gui/preview_down.gif", "Preview");
```

Using custom-defined objects is an excellent way to keep track of multiple properties in your script. In this example, the Button objects also help manage what happens in the other frames when a button is clicked.

Frame control

Invariably, if you make use of frames in your Web pages, the time will come when you realize that you need to change the content of two or more frames when a single event, such as a user clicking a button, occurs. JavaScripting is the only way to make this happen.

When the user clicks one of the buttons with the mouse, the normal href hyperlink goes into effect. This is what loads the new page into the main window of the frame set. In addition, as part of the function called by the onClick method, this line of JavaScript is executed:

```
window.parent.banner.location.href=buttons[i].bannerpage;
```

This line reads in the bannerpage property of the clicked button and loads that page into the URL of the banner frame. Using a similar method, you can control as many simultaneous frame changes as you like (and your user can tolerate).

Window control

Using JavaScript, you can also control the creation of new browser windows, using the window.open() method. This method is called in a function called NewWindow() that is stored in the frame set document. It is a simple function that takes one parameter, the text string name of the URL to open in the new window. The function is listed here:

```
function newWindow(url)
{
 window.open(url,"new","resizable=no,width=600,height=400,
status=yes");
}
```

Using the open method, you can dictate the size of the new window as well as whether or not the window is resizable. In addition you can show or hide a number of window components, including:

✦ Toolbar—the row of buttons, including Back, Forward, Stop

✦ Location—the field for typing in new URLs

✦ Directories—the row of buttons beneath the toolbar

✦ Status—the status bar at the bottom of the browser window

✦ Menu bar

✦ Scroll bars

By default these items are hidden unless specified in the open method. To include one of these features, add a *[feature]*=yes item to the parameter list, as in the example of the status bar in the preceding example.

We have looked at the interface script in some detail, partly to give you some practice exploring scripts. The remainder of the scripts are for your enjoyment. You can experiment with them in the scripting interface or look under the hood using the FrontPage Script Wizard and Editor's HTML Source tab.

An investment calculator (JavaScript)

The investment calculator illustrates the ability to create a working spreadsheet in a single Web page form, without recourse to CGI. The idea behind this investment calculator is that you want to know what the overall percentage of your investments is given different investment ratios. (In case it is not obvious, the values indicated for the various types of investments are entirely fictional. I don't advise making any investments based on this calculator.)

To see how this calculator works, try inserting different values into the percentages for the various investment types. When you have allocated 100 percent of your assets, click the Calculate button. The calculator tells you what your overall return will be with this asset allocation. If by chance you tried to evaluate more or less than 100 percent of your assets, the calculator does some simple error trapping and chides you to check your math (see Figure 15-13).

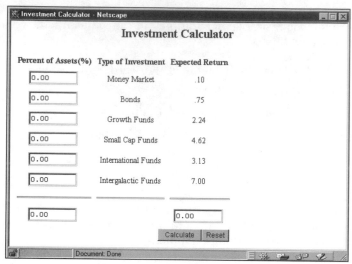

Figure 15-13: The investment calculator

A glossary (JavaScript)

The glossary script shown in Figure 15-14 illustrates two useful principles: the ability to update form input boxes without clicking a Submit button, and the ability to perform the equivalent of simple database functions within a Web page script.

To use the glossary, first scroll through the list of terms. When you select a term, as illustrated in the figure, the definition of the term appears in the text area box on the right-hand side of the page. Alternatively, type the name of a keyword into the Find input box. When you click the Find button, it jumps to that term and displays its definition.

Caution   There is a bug in the way Netscape Navigator handles the Find feature in the current implementation of the script (Internet Explorer handles it correctly). When you click the Find button in Netscape Navigator, the term is selected and its definition appears, but if the term happens to be out of view, the scrolling list does not scroll the term into view.

Displaying time zone information (JavaScript)

The time zone script uses some of the same techniques used by the glossary to automatically update fields when an item is selected. In addition, this script shows off some of the capabilities of scripts to work with time and date information and to update a page continuously. (It also shows some of the limitations of these techniques, since a client-side script depends for its information on the client-side system, not always a reliable source of time and date information).

To use this script, simply select one of the cities from the list by clicking its radio button. The current date and time as well as the city name are displayed in the text boxes (see Figure 15-15).

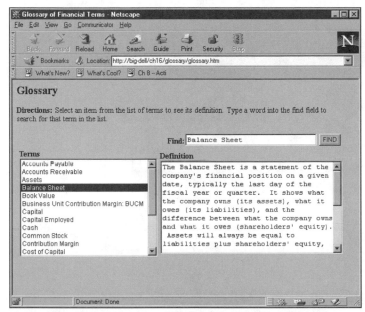

Figure 15-14: The glossary script provides a high-quality, interactive learning experience.

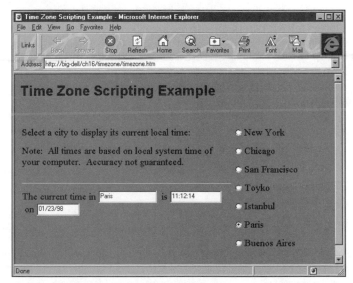

Figure 15-15: You can use the time zone script to find the time in faraway places.

Pill quiz (JavaScript)

This script, shown in Figure 15-16, is an example of a hypothetical online training exercise. Mainly, though, it is intended to illustrate the variety of message boxes available to you in a scripting language. It also demonstrates a simple way of keeping track of user state information.

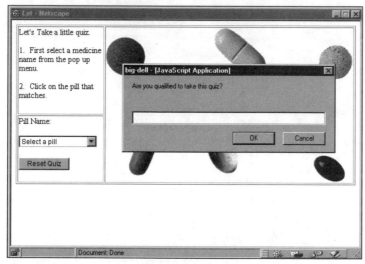

Figure 15-16: Pit your wits against the Pill Quiz challenge!

To take the quiz, first answer the initial question posed by the quiz. (The correct and only acceptable answer, by the way, is "Yes." Answer anything else, and you will not be permitted to take the quiz.) This authorizing question is posed via a Prompt box (called an InputBox in VBScript), which can capture and respond to user input.

Next select a "pill" name from the list of available options. Then guess which pill in the illustration corresponds to the name. Click the illustration you think matches the name—if you are correct, you are congratulated. If wrong, you are exhorted to try again—up to a point. The messages are displayed in Alert boxes (called MsgBox in VBScript).

Mouse tracking (VBScript)

This script, written in VBScript—which means that it can only be run on Internet Explorer—is intended as a simple game. Like most games it is totally useless, and oddly absorbing. It does have the virtue of illustrating some additional capabilities of scripting languages, namely:

✦ Random number generation

✦ Timing

✦ Automatic HTML generation

Note This game is done using frames because of the limited ability of early versions of scripting languages to update a page's content. With the introduction of Dynamic HTML, this methodology is no longer necessary.

The object of the game is to locate the hidden "mouse" (use your imagination) somewhere in the green field. If you think you have found it, click the spot, but don't dawdle, because you only have a limited amount of time to conduct your search. Figure 15-17 shows what happens if you are too slow.

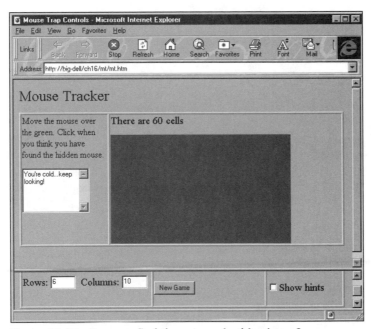

Figure 15-17: Can you find the mouse in this picture?

There are several ways to improve your odds of winning this game. First of all, you can control the size of the playing field. Also, if you pass the mouse cursor over the field, the message area alerts you if you are getting warm. But there is a catch —it is actually this cursor movement that advances the clock that keeps time in this game. The more you move the mouse around, the sooner the game is over. (In addition, the length of time allotted to you is proportionate to the size of the field —the smaller the field, the less time you get.) Finally, if you are really frustrated, you can check the Show Hints option. When you restart the game, it will tell you which square the mouse is in.

Taking the Next Step

This chapter introduced you to the concept of client-side scripting and demonstrated how to use FrontPage to create and edit simple scripts. It called attention to some of the pros and cons of scripting use and provided a head's-up on what to expect from scripting in the near future. Most important, it offered you a number of fascinating scripts for your amusement and edification. If you can break away from mouse tracking long enough, head on to the next chapter, where we explore the big guns of the Web programming world: Java and ActiveX.

✦   ✦   ✦

Advanced Programming Elements

This chapter discusses plug-ins, ActiveX, and Java— advanced programming techniques that enable Web developers to insert interactive functionality into a Web page. This chapter introduces you to each of these elements, explains how they interact with a Web page, and then demonstrates how to add them to your page using FrontPage. The chapter provides a general introduction to each of these technologies and plenty of examples to help you understand the particular strengths and weakness of each approach.

Searching for Active Content

When the HTML standard was first defined, it was fairly limited in terms of the kinds of content that could be incorporated into a Web page. In fact, the only provision was for inline GIF images. In order to allow for the inclusion of other kinds of content, browsers were designed to work with "helper applications," separate programs designed to display certain kinds of nontext content.

The helper application scenario worked like this: Suppose you wanted to allow visitors to your site to listen to an audio recording of your garage band. You could save the audio file in a more or less standard format, such as AU format. You would name the file with an extension that indicated its format, such as gband.au. Then you would simply point to it with a standard HTML hyperlink reference. In order for the browser to correctly identify and deal with this file, however, another step was necessary. The file extension had to be mapped to a content type. This is done using a standard known as MIME, for Multipurpose Internet Mail Extensions.

MIME types

The MIME type specification was first devised to address another problem, namely how to transmit binary (that is, nontext) data via e-mail, a transport mechanism that was designed only to transfer text characters.

Note

From time to time, depending on what e-mail circles you travel in, you may encounter e-mail attachments that have been sent to you MIME-encoded.

MIME types also turn out to be a convenient way of identifying different data types for a Web browser. In this context it is not necessary to go into detail about how MIME works. You can recognize a MIME type by the fact that it consists of a general type name, such as application, image, text, audio, or video, and a subtype name, separated from the general type name by a forward slash (/).

These days, most browsers come preconfigured to recognize a long list of MIME types. However, it is still possible to add new types to the list. In Netscape 4.x, select Edit ➪ Preferences, click to expand the Navigation item in the Category list, and select Applications as illustrated in Figure 16-1. You can use this interface to add new items, edit existing ones, or remove old and unwanted MIME types.

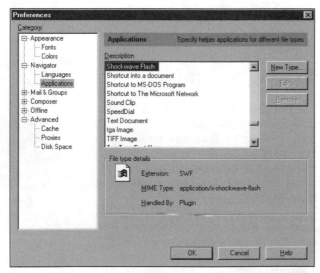

Figure 16-1: Viewing MIME types in Netscape Communicator

In Microsoft IE 4.0, MIME type information is gleaned from the Windows file type information. This can be accessed by opening My Computer, selecting View ➪ Options, and selecting the File Types tab, one portion of whose contents is shown in Figure 16-2.

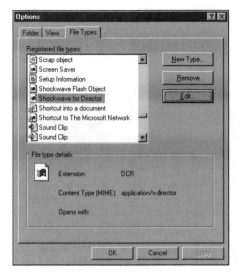

Figure 16-2: File type designations in Windows 95

Beyond the helper application

The helper application method is perhaps better than nothing, but it is not particularly user-friendly or useful. With a helper application every content file must be viewed separately, so any possibility of a complete "multimedia" experience is lost. Not to mention the fact that you have to locate, download, install, and maintain a separate utility for every application.

Note

Although the goal of providing active content seamlessly within your Web experience is a noble one, there are times that it makes more sense to adhere to the helper application model. Consider, for example, the use of streaming audio (discussed later in the chapter). Click the link to an audio stream, and you can listen (for example) to an hour rebroadcast of the evening news. In this case, you might prefer to have the news broadcast running in a separate application, freeing you to continue Web browsing as you listen.

One of the main virtues of the helper application approach is that it makes life for a developer blissfully easy. All you have to do to make your content file available to users via a helper application is create a hyperlink to it, just as you would to any standard Web page. The rest of the work (making sure they have a proper helper application, and configuring their list of MIME types) is up to the users.

Unfortunately, making life easy for developers is not what drives innovation on the Internet. Making life easy for users is what counts.

Discovering Plug-Ins

The next stage in the evolution of active content via the Web was Netscape's development of the plug-in, which was first unveiled in Netscape Navigator 2.*x*. The best way to characterize a plug-in is to say that it is a "smarter" helper application that lives inside a Web page. When the user selects content to be displayed in a plug-in, the content downloads to the user, just as in the helper application scenario. In the case of the plug-in, however, the content is handled by an application that works in conjunction with the Web browser. The browser opens the application, which displays itself "inline" just as graphical images typically do (in a sense the browser's ability to display graphics in this fashion is just the first instance of a plug-in).

Note

Currently plug-ins remain principally a Netscape phenomenon, although Internet Explorer, since version 3.0, has also had the ability to display plug-ins. In practice, IE developers typically use ActiveX controls instead, which have some advantages over plug-ins and provide the developer with more flexibility.

How the user interacts with plug-ins

From the user's perspective using a plug-in is very much like using a helper application. To use a plug-in, the user must download it and install it in the browser before encountering a page that requires it. To illustrate the "ease" of installing a new plug-in, let's imagine that we come upon a site that contains an Adobe PDF–format document. We would really like to view this document. Here are the steps to follow:

1. Locate the source of the plug-in. Frequently developers kindly place a handy "Get Plug-In XYZ Now!" button on the page that contains a link to the content. In this case we see the Adobe Acrobat button and we click it.

Caution

In practice this "handy" button can turn out to be more confusing than convenient, since some plug-in makers require developers to link only to their home page rather than to the plug-in download page. Most new Web users find the whole plug-in concept arcane enough. Sending them to a page with little or no visible connection to their mission is usually disorienting and annoying.

2. Assuming that you can find the location from which to download the plug-in, the next step is typically to fill out a registration form. Most plug-ins are distributed freely. How is this possible, you ask? The plug-ins are essentially viewers for content files that are typically proprietary in form. Software companies make money from people who develop content using their software. The more people want to view content in this form, the more people buy the development software. In other words, free plug-ins generate demand for the products the software company sells.

For obvious marketing reasons, however, the plug-in developers like to know who is downloading their plug-ins. So in effect, you trade your e-mail address and/or phone number for the opportunity to use their plug-in.

Note

On the topic of registration forms, it is worth pointing out that two of the most used plug-in technologies, Macromedia's Shockwave and RealNetwork's RealPlayer (formerly RealAudio), have minimal, unobtrusive registration forms. Coincidence? You be the judge.

3. After filling out the form, you are directed to a download page. Assuming that you can find the plug-in version you want on this page, select it and watch it download. (Plug-Ins typically range from about 300K to 1.5MB in size.)

4. Once the file has downloaded, run the installation program. Installation is usually fairly painless. The setup program copies the pertinent files into the plug-in directory of your Web browser and makes some changes to the Windows registry.

5. Assuming that all the while you have kept open your Web browser (remember that we initiated this process because we saw a file we thought we might like to view), you must now shut down the Web browser and restart. Why? Because when the browser starts, it looks into its plug-in directory to see what is in there. The only way to get the browser to detect a recent addition is to restart it.

6. Now, if you can just remember where you saw that document you wanted to view, return to the site and click the file. Assuming that the plug-in installed correctly, the content opens in your Web page, as illustrated in Figure 16-3.

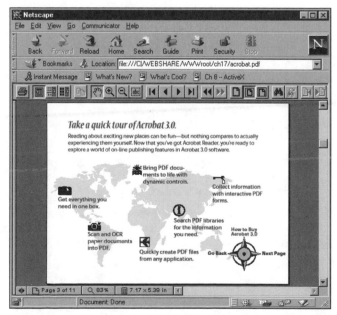

Figure 16-3: Displaying a PDF inline using the Acrobat plug-in

Tip

You can check on the status of your plug-ins in Netscape Navigator by selecting Help ➪ About Plugins. This displays an internal HTML page listing all known plug-ins. An example of the Plug-in page is shown in Figure 16-4. If the plug-in is on the list, it should work (but see the cautionary tale in the sidebar before you bank on this).

Figure 16-4: Everything you ever wanted to know about your Netscape plug-ins in the about:plug-ins page

Plug-in woes: a cautionary tale

Here is another tale from the cross-platform compatibility front lines.

When I first attempted to install the Netscape plug-in for Macromedia Shockwave for Director, I went to the Macromedia site and dutifully downloaded and installed the plug-in.

Every time I attempted to access a Shockwave for Director file, however, I received an error message, indicating that the plug-in was not correctly installed, in spite of the fact that a quick check of the about:Plugins in Netscape indicated that all was fine.

After snooping around and noticing that the registry entry for the Shockwave for Director MIME type did not have a CLSID, on a hunch I decided to check out IE's ability to view these files. It couldn't, and it didn't seem to want to automatically download the control either.

Finally, I reinstalled IE 4.0 and installed its Shockwave controls at the same time. After this, not only did the IE controls work flawlessly, so did Netscape's plug-in (and you thought these guys were in competition).

Inserting plug-ins with FrontPage

Adding a reference to a plug-in is relatively straightforward, and FrontPage makes the task even easier. In this section we describe a simple example of how to do this, using a document in Adobe PDF (Portable Data Format). You can find this sample file in the Chapter 16 Contents section of the CD-ROM that accompanies this book, Content/ch16/hvh2000.pdf.

In order to use the file, first import it into the Web using the File ⇨ Import command. To insert the reference to the plug-in, simply select Insert ⇨ Advanced ⇨ Plug-in, opening the Plug-In Properties dialog box (see Figure 16-5). The most important element of this dialog box is the Data Source. Click the Browse button to locate the file you wish to have displayed via a plug-in. In addition to the Data Source field in this database, there are several other options you can configure:

✦ **Size (Height and Width)** — Indicates the dimensions of the plug-in, in pixels.

✦ **Hide Plug-In** — Check this box to render the plug-in invisible. It is normally used with audio or other plug-ins that need no visible component.

✦ **Layout (Alignment, Border Thickness, Horizontal Spacing, Vertical Spacing)** — These designate various aspects of the location of the plug-in on the page.

✦ **Message for Browser without Plug-In Support** — Insert text and/or HTML to be displayed by browsers that do not recognize the plug-in tag.

When you are happy with your changes, click OK to return to the Editor window.

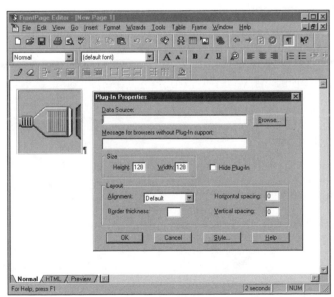

Figure 16-5: Inserting a plug-in using the Plug-in Properties dialog box

As Figure 16-5 also illustrates, FrontPage puts a placeholder plug image in your page to represent the plug-in. You can preview your plug-in by using the Preview tab or by selecting File⇨Preview in Browser. If you click the plug-in image to select it, you can then drag a corner to resize the plug-in window. Double-clicking the plug-in image brings up its Properties dialog box for additional editing.

The plug-in <embed> tag

When you issue the Insert Plug-in command, FrontPage creates an <embed> tag for the plug-in, as shown in the following code:

```
<embed width="489" height="384" src="http://big-dell/ch17/
hvh2000.pdf">
```

FrontPage supports the following <embed> tag attributes via the Plug-In Properties dialog box:

✦ src—This attribute identifies the URL of the file to be displayed by the plug-in. Its type is identified by its filename extension.

✦ height—This is the height of the plug-in window in pixels.

✦ width—This is the width of the plug-in window in pixels.

✦ border—This places a border around the plug-in window with the designated thickness in pixels.

✦ align—This gives the alignment of the plug-in window.

✦ hspace—This is the horizontal space in pixels between the plug-in window and the surrounding elements.

✦ vspace—This is the vertical space in pixels between the plug-in window and the surrounding elements.

✦ hidden—Include this attribute to hide the plug-in element from view. This is most useful for audio plug-ins, when you would like the audio file to play without any visual elements.

The <noembed> tag

In addition to determining the properties (or attributes) of the plug-in, you can use the Plug-In Properties dialog box to create a simple text message to display for users with browsers that do not support the <embed> tag. Any text placed in the "Message for browsers without plug-in support" text box will appear only if the user has an incompatible browser. This message is placed within a <noembed> </noembed> tag set.

Popular plug-ins

When Netscape first introduced the plug-in concept and made available the resources for developers to build their own plug-ins, dozens of companies who had proprietary file formats rushed to create plug-ins for their file types. This has resulted in nearly 200 plug-ins listed on Netscape's site (see the reference that follows). In practice, however, only a handful of plug-ins have achieved any real acceptance. Most of these also exist as ActiveX controls as well. This section profiles some of the major "players," so to speak, organized by common categories.

Animation

The hands-down leader in this category has been Macromedia, which was one of the first companies to capitalize on the plug-in format. They developed a viewer for their Director file format, rechristened Shockwave for the Web community. Since this humble beginning, Macromedia has released versions of Shockwave to run Authorware applications and Frechand presentations. Their most recent entry is Flash, a vector-based animation program that produces compact animations geared toward bandwidth-limited media.

Audio/video/streaming media

The early leaders in this category included Apple's QuickTime and the streaming audio technology originally called RealAudio, the product of RealSystems (formerly Progressive Networks), now expanded to include streaming video and renamed RealVideo. Other popular contenders include VivoActive and VDOLive. In the world of MIDI music, the Crescendo plug-in is frequently used, although there are many options. Of course, Netscape has released its own A/V plug-in modules that work with most standard, nonproprietary formats.

VRML

VRML, short for Virtual Reality Markup Language, and often pronounced "vermel" (isn't that a little North American rodent?), is a programming language for creating 3-D "worlds," or spaces that can be navigated by using the mouse pointer. It is not quite clear whether VRML is a cool technology that has come and gone or whether it is still just a little ahead of its time. It has never quite lived up to its promise, although with the release of version 2.0, VRML has become more flexible and interactive.

The prominent VRML plug-ins are the Cosmo browser, built by Silicon Graphics, VReam's WIRL, and Intervista's WorldView.

Chat

Interactive chat plug-ins—like VRML—represent an attempt to put inside a Web browser not just different file formats but whole new services. Chat plug-ins make possible real-time communication among multiple users, a feat that is just not possible using standard Web pages. The leader in the interactive chat category is iChat. Another interesting contributor in this category is Onlive! Traveler, a 3-D chat environment.

As for formatted documents—no question here, Adobe's Acrobat reader for its own PDF format is the hands-down favorite, although there are certainly other products that perform similar functions.

Where to find plug-ins

Since the plug-in is a Netscape phenomenon, not surprisingly, the main source for plug-ins is the Netscape plug-in site. It is located at:

```
http://home.netscape.com/comprod/products/navigator/version_2.0/
plugins/index.html
```

At last count, there were 176 registered plug-ins available in a variety of categories.

Tip

You can access this site quickly by opening the about:plug-ins page (as described earlier) and clicking the hyperlink at the top of the page.

In addition to the Netscape site, there are several other good sources of plug-ins (although, frankly, Netscape's site is the largest, easiest to use, and best maintained).

✦ Browserwatch plug-in site: `http://browserwatch.internet.com/plug-in.html`

✦ Plug-in Gallery: `http://www2.gol.com/users/oyamada/`

The problem with plug-ins

Although plug-ins have the advantage over helper applications of being able to run inside the Web browser, the preceding example clearly illustrates the main problem with the plug-in model. It is still just too much of a hassle, and there are too many ways for things to go wrong. The plug-in model is also relatively inflexible. Plug-ins tend to be large, static applications that are not typically accessed or manipulated by the Web developer.

There is really much more you can do with plug-ins than we have given them credit for, however. There are several plug-in elements not supported by FrontPage. In addition, plug-ins written to the Netscape LiveConnect specification can communicate with the HTML page and the user via JavaScript. This functionality is not supported by Internet Explorer. For more information on plug-ins, visit Netscape's plug-in guide:

```
http://developer.netscape.com/library/documentation/communicator/
plugin/index.htm
```

Note

An increasing number of companies with plug-ins are developing Java-based versions of their viewer applications. These work much like plug-ins but do not require installation and can be downloaded in advance of the content automatically.

Working with ActiveX

About the time that Netscape was introducing the plug-in innovation, Microsoft (the non-Internet company) was realizing that it needed to remake itself and at the same time remake the Internet if it was not to be left in the dust of the information superhighway. The introduction of the ActiveX technologies is characteristic of Microsoft's efforts to put itself back in the driver's seat.

ActiveX is Microsoft's answer to Netscape plug-ins (as well as to Sun Microsystem's Java programming language, described in the last section of the chapter). To a large degree one could say that the ActiveX name is really just a repackaging of preexisting Microsoft technologies (most notably the Object Linking and Embedding specifications, or OLE), fine-tuned a bit for their new role on the global Internet. These technologies make possible the reuse of application components, and they enable applications to communicate with one another and even to embed parts of themselves in other applications.

Note

Although ActiveX is usually associated with the Internet, it is really just a general-purpose set of technologies that happens to include the Internet. This is both its power — since it can render the computer system, its local applications, and any remote resources on the Internet practically seamless — and its drawback — since all of this is platform- and operating system–dependent.

In somewhat more formal terms, ActiveX refers to any of several technologies that make use of the Microsoft Component Object Model (COM) specification in order to create programming entities that can be combined, reused, scripted, and delivered via a network such as the Internet. The term "ActiveX" encompasses an array of applications that make use of the core concepts of OLE and COM.

ActiveX controls

An ActiveX control is simply a reusable, modular programming component. It can be inserted into another application, such as a Web browser's Web page, and it can be configured or scripted to perform a variety of tasks. It can range in size from something as simple as a radio (option) button to a sophisticated spreadsheet application.

ActiveX controls are really just one segment of the larger ActiveX picture, but they are entities that can be relatively easily used even by nonprogrammers (although a little programming knowledge never hurts). Since ActiveX controls tend to be easier to use than to explain, let's look at some examples.

Inserting an ActiveX control with FrontPage

Let's start with an example of an ActiveX control that is analogous to the Netscape plug-in we inserted in the previous section.

To insert an ActiveX control, select Insert ➪ Advanced ➪ ActiveX Control. In the ActiveX Control Properties dialog box, first select an available ActiveX control from the drop-down list. This list represents all of the controls registered in your system's registry. Items listed may or may not actually be resident on your computer system. For this example, we select the Acrobat control for ActiveX.

Tip

If you do not have the Acrobat control for ActiveX resident on your system, you can obtain it from the Adobe Web site: `http://www.adobe.com/prodindex/acrobat/main.html`.

The ActiveX Properties dialog box, shown in Figure 16-6, enables you to configure several other aspects of how the control is displayed on the Web page. These include:

✦ **Name**—Give your ActiveX control a name if you plan to communicate with it using VBScript or JavaScript.

✦ **Alignment**—This designates how the control is aligned in relation to the elements around it.

✦ **Border Thickness**—This indicates the thickness of the black border element around the control in pixels.

✦ **Horizontal Spacing**—This is the space between the control and elements to its left and right in pixels.

✦ **Vertical Spacing**—This is the space between the control and elements above and below it in pixels.

✦ **Width**—This is the width of the control in pixels.

✦ **Height**—This is the height of the control in pixels.

✦ **Alternative Representation**—Use this text box to designate text that appears in place of the control in browsers that do not support ActiveX controls.

Tip

You can place HTML into the Alternate Representation, including `<embed>` and `<noembed>` tags. This way, if the browser can display an ActiveX control, it will. If not but it can display a plug-in, it will. Otherwise it displays the text contained in the `<noembed>` command.

✦ **Network Location**—This indicates the network location of the ActiveX control if it is not stored locally.

✦ **Code Source**—This indicates the URL to download the ActiveX control when the page is loaded, if the user does not already have the control.

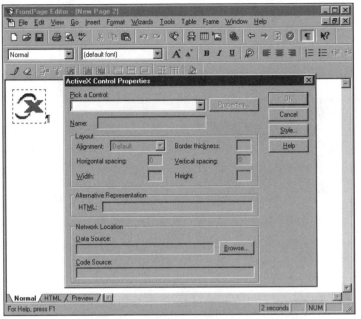

Figure 16-6: The ActiveX Control Properties dialog box

In addition to this set of general options, you can also click Properties to edit the properties of the ActiveX control itself. When you do this, one of two things happens:

✦ If the ActiveX control is resident on your computer and has editable properties, FrontPage opens the ActiveX Control Editor (see Figure 16-7). The editing environment consists of a form editor, shown on the left, and a properties editor, shown on the right. Use this editing environment to configure control properties. To edit a property, click the property to select it, and type changes in the text box at the top of the Properties dialog box. Click Apply to apply changes.

✦ If the ActiveX control is not resident on your computer or is not editable, FrontPage opens the Object Parameters dialog box (see Figure 16-8). You can use this dialog box to add, modify, and remove ActiveX parameter information.

In the case of our Acrobat control, we can access its properties, and we need to edit the source (src) property. This property, like the src attribute of an <image> tag, indicates the URL of the PDF file to display. To edit the property, select the src property and type the filename, **hvh2000.pdf**, into the text box at the top of the Properties dialog box. Click Apply to update the property. Click OK on the main form editor panel to return to the ActiveX Properties dialog box.

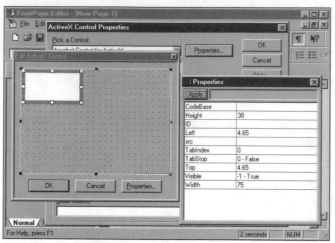

Figure 16-7: Editing the properties for our Acrobat ActiveX control

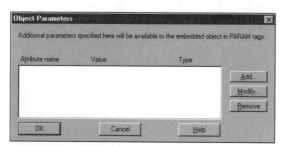

Figure 16-8: The Object Parameters dialog box

Once you have adjusted all settings to your liking, click OK in the ActiveX Properties dialog box to return to Editor. To preview your ActiveX control, select the Preview tab. Alternatively, use the Preview in Browser function to open the page in Internet Explorer.

The ActiveX <object> tag

When FrontPage inserts an ActiveX control into a Web page, it creates an instance of the <object> tag, an example of which is shown here.

```
<object classid="clsid:CA8A9780-280D-11CF-A24D-444553540000"
width="579" height="374">
 <param name="_Version" value="65539">
 <param name="_ExtentX" value="2646">
 <param name="_ExtentY" value="1341">
 <param name="_StockProps" value="0">
 <param name="SRC" value="hvh2000.pdf">
</object>
```

ActiveX controls are somewhat cumbersome to insert into HTML by hand, principally because they must be identified using an excruciatingly long class ID number. Entering this string by hand is both time consuming and error-prone (not to mention the fact that it is hard to memorize too many of these numbers). So in this case, FrontPage does us a favor by automatically inserting the correct ID number.

An ActiveX control is used on three levels. The first is simply to insert the control into an existing page. For those controls whose job is to display a file, this is usually fine, although some small amount of configuration work is necessary.

The second level involves changing properties of the control to suit its current purpose. This activity is roughly similar to your ability to pass parameter names and values to a Java applet. The third level is to use either VBScript or JavaScript to write code that brings these controls to life and makes them useful. In the sections that follow, we demonstrate how to configure the properties of a control and how to script a control.

Editing control properties

Being able to use an ActiveX control like a plug-in is useful, but the real power of ActiveX grows more apparent when you configure a control to your liking. In the last section we saw a brief example of configuring control properties when we entered a source (src) property for our Adobe Acrobat ActiveX control. In the next sections we discuss another example of FrontPage's support for configuring the properties of an ActiveX control. For this example we use the Microsoft Label Object control.

The Label Object control enables us to take a string of text and manipulate it in one of several possible ways:

First, let's change the Label's caption. Select the Caption property (it should have a default value of "Default"). Type some text (for instance, **Now that's some text!** — see Figure 16-9). Click Apply to update the caption.

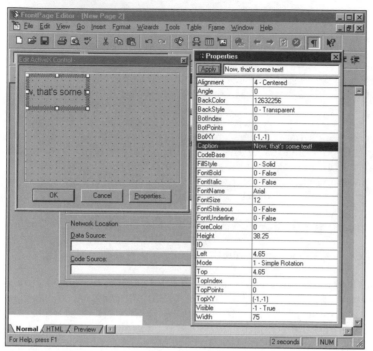

Figure 16-9: The Label Object control, showing this control's long list of properties

Notice that updating the caption creates a small problem with the size of the control (see Figure 16-9). To change the size of the control, select the control object in the form editor and drag a corner of the control to increase its size until you can read the entire caption. If you watch carefully as you do this, you will notice that the width and height properties update to match your adjustments.

Now let's change a couple of other parameters. First select the FontBold property. (If the property window is hidden, click the Properties button in the form editing panel.) When you select this property, the text box at the top of the Properties dialog box changes from a standard text input box to a drop-down menu box. This is because there are only two choices for the FontBold property: 0-false or 1-true. Select true, and note that the form editor text is updated to bold.

Finally, let's change the text angle—something that is a little difficult to do with regular HTML text, by the way. Select the Angle property and change its value from 0 to 45. Click Apply and note the effect on the Label Object control. Adjust the dimensions of the object to accommodate our inclined text. The finished product is shown in Figure 16-10.

Figure 16-10: Take a look at our tilted text!

Scripting a control

Our last example of working with an ActiveX control in FrontPage demonstrates a simple example of combining ActiveX controls with ActiveX scripting (a.k.a. VBScript) in order to create a highly interactive Web page. Our example is simple, but it illustrates the general principles involved in scripting a control.

First we need to create the controls. In this case we are going to combine several ActiveX form controls, as provided by Microsoft. Then we use the Script Wizard to enable these controls to communicate with one another.

First select Insert ⇨ Advanced ⇨ ActiveX Control to open the ActiveX Control Properties dialog box. Select the Microsoft Forms 2.0 Option Button control. Name it **opt1** and select the Properties dialog box. In the Caption property, type **Option 1**, click Apply, and then click OK in the main form editor. Click OK again from the Properties dialog box to return to Editor. Repeat these steps for Options 2–4. Finally, create a Microsoft Forms 2.0 Text Box control, name it **text1**, and return to Editor.

Note

It is important that you give your controls a name so that your VBScript can reference them.

Using the Script Wizard

Now that we have built our form, it is time to activate it using the Script Wizard. We discuss the Script Wizard in detail in Chapter 15. In this example, we assume that you already are familiar with how the Script Wizard operates and are comfortable with the basics of VBScript.

We are going to create a simple procedure called `UpdateText()`. Its purpose is to update the Text property of the text box we created. Then we will call this procedure from each of the radio button's Click events, and we will update the text box with an appropriate and pithy text string.

Here are the steps to follow:

1. Open the Script Wizard by selecting Insert ➪ Advanced ➪ Script and clicking the Script Wizard button in the dialog box.

2. The Script Wizard displays the names, properties, and events for each of the controls we added earlier (see Figure 16-11).

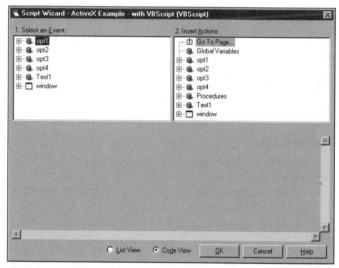

Figure 16-11: Using the Script Wizard to script our ActiveX form

3. Add the `UpdateText()` procedure. Click with the right mouse button on the Procedures item in the right-hand column. Select New Procedure from the drop-down menu. Rename the procedure as follows:

```
Sub updateText(txt)
```

4. Add the following line of code (you can either type this directly or select the Text property of the Text1 object in the right-hand column and double-click it to enter the object name):

```
Text1.Text=txt
```

5. Click to expand the opt1 radio button events in the left-hand column of the Script Wizard. Select Click. Add the following line of code:

```
call updateText("You have selected Option 1")
```

6. Repeat step 5 for each of the radio buttons, supplying appropriate text for each.

7. Click OK to update the page. Switch to Preview mode and test by clicking each of the buttons. An example of the results is shown in Figure 16-12.

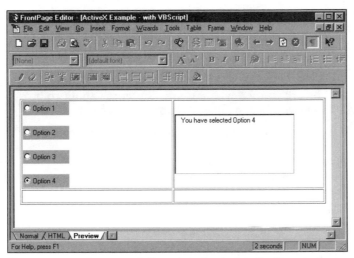

Figure 16-12: A successfully scripted set of ActiveX controls

ActiveX security

When you allow a remote computer to send a program to you to be run on your local computer, as is the case with both ActiveX controls and Java, you open the possibility of security problems. What is to stop someone from sending you a "malicious" program that wreaks havoc with your computer system? The question is always how to safeguard your computer to a reasonable degree of certainty from such attacks without completely forgoing the advantages that the ability to send programming across the Internet affords.

Microsoft has addressed security issues with its ActiveX technologies by creating a method of digitally signing code. This digital signature technology is called Authenticode. When the user arrives at a Web page that contains active content requiring a control not currently resident on the user's system, the page issues a request to download the software. It checks the sender's digital signature, and if that is correct, it displays a certificate-like graphic and asks you for permission to download the control.

Success of this method relies on several assumptions — that the entity who signs the digital certificate is trustworthy and would not cause any harm, that the digital signature has been generated by its actual owner, and that the person receiving the programming can make a reasonable decision about whether or not the owner is deserving of trust. Once you have judged the entity to be legitimate and safe, you are granting the program license to do as it pleases.

In Internet Explorer you can set the level of security of your browser. Internet Explorer 3.*x* has three security options:

✦ **High**—Any potentially unsafe content is not downloaded and a warning is issued to this effect.

✦ **Medium**—You are warned when unsafe content is about to be downloaded and can choose whether to allow the download or not.

✦ **Low**—No safety measures are enacted. All content downloads.

In Internet Explorer 4.0, you can set a similar range of general security levels. In addition, you can customize security options by setting the level of a large number of potential security risks (see Figure 16-13).

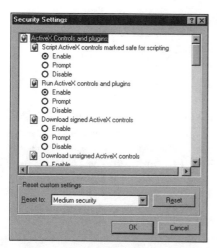

Figure 16-13: So many options, so little time!

All of these options may help to make us feel safe, but it remains the case that if we happen to allow a bad piece of code through, there is no physical layer of security to protect the computer system from this code. This is the main difference between security as it is implemented by Microsoft in its ActiveX technologies and Sun in Java.

Locating controls

For a time, after it first introduced Internet Explorer 3, Microsoft maintained a very useful and informative ActiveX gallery on their Web site. Unfortunately, it has been replaced with a listing of other sites that now maintain repositories of ActiveX controls. (Even more unfortunately, most of those repositories still reference the no-longer-extant Microsoft gallery.) You can find the list of third-party repositories at `http://www.microsoft.com/com/gallery/`. You can also find information on ActiveX at `http://www.microsoft.com/activex/`.

Two other sites worthy of mention are:

✦ C/Net's ActiveX site—`www.activex.com`

✦ Browserwatch ActiveX Arena—`www.browserwatch.com/activex.html`

The problems with ActiveX

As a programming construct, ActiveX is easy to use, versatile, and powerful. It also doesn't hurt that there is a huge developer base of Visual Basic and C/C++ developers who are migrating to Web development seamlessly thanks to ActiveX. One of the main advantages of ActiveX from a user's standpoint is that it configures itself automatically. (The flip side of this coin, of course, is that you can quite rapidly accumulate a large number of controls, either locally resident or cluttering up your registry.) No more hunting around for the software, downloading, installing, and restarting.

The chief drawbacks of ActiveX are (1) that it is a proprietary system that runs on a single operating system and (2) that it has less than stellar security. Microsoft has made some improvement in these areas, but they are likely always to loom over ActiveX to some extent.

Working with Java

OK, you've heard the hype, but what is Java, exactly? Java is a programming language, no more, no less. In that respect it is no different than C or C++, or Visual Basic, or COBOL. You can write regular applications in Java (these are starting to appear on the market as we write), and they operate just like other applications. The thing that makes Java a special kind of programming language is the fact that it was designed with a multiplatform networked environment like the Internet in mind. Several aspects of the Java programming language make it well-suited for Internet use:

✦ **It is object-oriented**—This characteristic helps to make Java code modular, extensible, and highly reusable, especially with the introduction of Java Beans, Java components that are roughly the equivalent of ActiveX controls.

✦ **It is multithreaded**—A multithreaded application is one that can perform several actions simultaneously. This is good in an environment where download times can be a factor.

✦ **It is portable**—Java's claim to fame is the fact that the same programming instructions can be run on a variety of computer platforms without redoing the code.

✦ **It includes automatic garbage collection**—Java is designed to keep track internally of some aspects of programming that normally the developer has to worry about. This helps to make Java a relatively easy language to use. "Garbage collection," the ability of a Java program to take itself out of memory when it is no longer in use, is just one prominent example of this characteristic.

✦ **It offers security restrictions**—Java's security methodology is designed with "untrusted" environments (like the Internet) in mind. This is not to say that Java has not been without its security holes, but in general more people have complained about the over-rigor of security than the lack thereof.

The Java virtual machine

The key element that distinguishes Java from other programming languages is the fact that, from a developer's standpoint, it is entirely platform neutral. In other words, a developer should be able to write his or her program and then give it to someone using a Windows-based PC, someone using a Sun UNIX system, and someone using a Macintosh (I haven't heard of an implementation for the Commodore 64 yet...), and they should all be able to run the application without any "porting" of the code. (You may have noticed the use of "should" here—we are talking about the real world here, where the ideal case is not always realized.)

How can a programming language perform this miracle? Elves? Well not exactly, but the Java programming language does depend on some helpers to do the hard work. What happens is this: Typically, when a computer program is "compiled," it means that a set of instructions written in semi–human readable form (or is that human, semi-readable form?) are converted into specific instructions that the computer understands.

In Java, when the developer compiles a program, the compiler only "semi-compiles" the program into what is known as bytecode. Bytecode cannot be understood directly by any computer operating system. It can only be interpreted by a special entity known as the Java virtual machine. The Java VM, which must reside on your computer system, knows how to read Java bytecode, and it also knows how to speak directly to your computer, translating the non-platform-specific Java bytecode into something your computer can understand.

When you happen upon a Web page with a Java applet embedded in it, the Web server sends the applet's bytecode to your browser. The browser, an expert at delegating, knows to pass the bytecode to the Java virtual machine, where it undergoes some last-minute compiling for your machine and then performs its applet magic.

The Java class library

The other Java "helper" is the set of fundamental Java classes that provide the basic Java functionality. These base classes are used by developers when they build their Java applets and applications, and they come to us as part of the Java-enabled character of your Web browser. (If these classes were not present, they would have to be downloaded to you each time you tried to run an applet.) These base classes perform a number of critical programming functions.

One of the detractions of Java is the fact that these base classes are still evolving. This means that the set of Java base classes you downloaded with your new Web browser last month are not necessarily the current set of base classes in use among Java programmers.

In the first version (1.0.2) of Java, these classes were broken into the following "packages" (Javaspeak for a collection of Java classes put together in a file system subdirectory):

- ✦ **Java.Applet**—These are the classes that generate the foundation of all Java applets.

- ✦ **Java.Awt**—Here, "awt" is short for "Abstract Window Toolkit." These are the classes that produce the Java user interface elements—buttons, lists, scroll bars—as well as graphical elements—rectangles, images, and such.

- ✦ **Java.Io**—These classes enable Java to perform basic input/output operations—that is, to read and write files. Note that applets, because of their security restrictions, cannot read or write local files.

- ✦ **Java.Lang**—These classes include many of the elements essential to the Java language itself—classes related to data types, string functions, multithreading, error trapping, and the like.

- ✦ **Java.Net**—These classes perform basic network operations, including the capability of a Java applet to read and understand URLs.

- ✦ **Java.Util**—This is a handy set of classes used for various purposes, usually associated with some kind of data manipulation.

If you go looking for these Java classes on your computer, you may find them stored in a zip file (if you are using a PC at any rate) called classes.zip.

What is an applet?

First, let's be clear. Java is not just a programming language for building applets. It is quite capable of creating full-scale applications (although there is some disagreement about just how capable "quite capable" is). A Java applet is just one specialized kind of Java application designed especially to operate within a Web browser environment —embedded in a Web page—rather than as a stand-alone application. Usually an applet is smaller and simpler than a Web application, and it is limited in its operations by the security restrictions that Java places on remotely accessed applets. The main difference between an applet and a Java application, however, is the fact that the applet has some special characteristics associated with starting and stopping the applet. This is because an applet is not "run" directly the way a standard application is. It must be able to start when it downloads with a Web page. Likewise, it must respond intelligently when a user stops the Web page from loading, clicks the Back button to return to the page it is on, or the like.

In the next section we illustrate the process of adding Java applets to your Web pages in FrontPage. The simple Java applets we use are from the Java Development Kit demos, available for download from the JavaSoft Web site, `java.sun.com`.

Some of the examples are available only as source code. If you would like to use the examples in this chapter, you will have to do a small amount of compiling. The following sections describe the steps you need to take to be able to run these applets. If you do not plan to try the examples yourself, you can skip this section.

Preparing Java applets

If you would like to follow the Java examples in the next sections, you need to do some preparation. Before you can insert a Java applet into your Web page, you need to locate an applet, compile it (if it comes in its source code format), and then import it into your FrontPage Web. This section details the steps necessary to perform these preparations. If you already have your Java applet class file ready to go and are itching to try it out in FrontPage, you can jump right to the next section, "Inserting a Java applet with FrontPage."

The Java Development Kit (JDK)

If you are going to do any work with Java, you first need to download the JavaSoft JDK. This contains all you need to get started programming with Java. It includes the base Java classes described earlier, as well as a set of tools, including (1) the Java source compiler, `javac.exe`; and (2) an applet viewer, `appletviewer.exe`. It also contains valuable documentation and Java examples. The JDK is available from JavaSoft at `http://java.sun.com/products/jdk/`. Three versions are available at the time of this writing:

✦ **JDK 1.0.2**—This is the baseline standard for Java development, released May 1996. Many applets are still written to the 1.0 release.

✦ **JDK 1.1.5**—This is the current release at time of writing. Most Java applications currently under development are being written to the 1.1 release.

✦ **JDK 1.2**—This is still in beta at the time of this writing.

Once you have obtained the JDK, follow the directions for installing it. Once it is installed, you will find the tools described here in the `bin` subfolder of the main `java` folder.

Using the javac compiler

When a Java program, whether applet or application, is first created, it exists as source code that is just a plain text file with a `*.java` extension. In order to execute the program, you must compile the source code into a bytecode class file (with a `*.class` ending). If you purchase premade Java applets, or even if you are downloading the latest free applet from a site on the Internet, you are likely to receive a class file already compiled for you. However, many of the Java examples that come with the JDK must be compiled before they can be added to your Web page.

To compile a Java source file using the javac compiler, first locate the compiler (usually `/java/bin/javac.exe`) and your Java source file (identified as `*.java`). Open an MS-DOS window by clicking the Start button and selecting Programs ⇨ MS-DOS Prompt. Change to the directory that contains the javac compiler. Use the following syntax, substituting the appropriate source code reference, to run the compiler and compile your source code:

```
javac /full/path/toyour/sourcecode.java
```

If the compiler returns successfully, you should now have a file, `<<sourcecode.class>` in the same directory with the `*.java` file. This class file is a ready-to-run Java applet.

Using the applet viewer

The applet viewer utility that comes with the Java JDK enables you to run Java applets without recourse to a Web browser. The applet viewer is a command line utility, so in order to use it, you must first open an MS-DOS window, which you can do by clicking the Start button in the taskbar and selecting Programs ⇨ MS-DOS Prompt.

Change to the `bin` directory of your Java JDK (which may be `c:\java\bin`). To start the applet viewer, use the following command syntax:

```
appletviewer URL of Web page containing applet
```

Note that the applet viewer does not run class files directly. You must first create a Web page and insert the Java applet into it before using the applet viewer. (You may want to skip ahead to the section on inserting Java applets in FrontPage). Replace the *URL of Web page containing applet* with the full URL to the appropriate Web page, (for example, `http://www.myserver.com/coolapplet.html`). The applet viewer starts, loads, and runs the applet contained in this page. (Note that when you start the applet viewer for the first time, it first displays licensing information, which you must acknowledge before you see your applet.)

Now you are armed with enough tools and information to make inserting a Java applet into your FrontPage Web a breeze.

Inserting a Java applet with FrontPage

The first example of a Java applet we use is a classic version of tic tac toe. This applet displays a 3×3 square playing area. You click a section to record your move, and the applet counters with its move, accompanied by appropriate sounds.

The source code for this applet is available from the JavaSoft Web site in the Applet section. The complete list of available applets is located at `http://www.javasoft.com/applets/js-applets.html`. The tic tac toe example is located at `http://www.javasoft.com/applets/TicTacToe/1.0.2/example1.html`.

The `TicTacToe.java` example is available as source code. Save this file as `TicTacToe.java` and compile it using javac as previously described. Next you need to import the Java file by selecting File ⇨ Import, locating the class file, and adding it to your Web.

Create a new Web page in Editor. Select Insert ⇨ Advanced ⇨ Java Applet, to open the Java Applet Properties dialog box, shown in Figure 16-14. Unfortunately you must type the class filename in the Applet Source text box. You can use the Applet Base URL box to record the URL page to the folder that contains the Java applet. Other options include:

✦ **Message for Browsers without Java Support**—As with the previous types of active content, you can use this box to display a message, including HTML, for any users who do not have a Java-enabled browser.

✦ **Applet Parameters**—Like the ActiveX controls we saw earlier, Java applets can be configured using parameters that are specific to a given applet. The TicTacToe applet does not happen to require any parameters to be set. We examine an applet that does in the next section.

✦ **Size**—Set the width and height of the space allotted to the applet. (Note that this does not change the size of the applet itself.)

✦ **Layout**—Set the horizontal spacing, vertical spacing, and alignment of the applet on the page.

Once you have set the parameters to your liking, click OK to return to the Editor page. FrontPage inserts a large, aquamarine *J* in your page, indicating the presence of a Java applet.

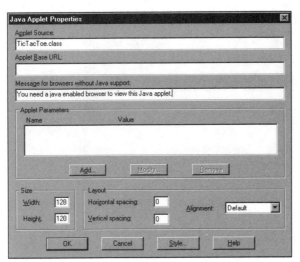

Figure 16-14: The Java Applet Properties dialog box, set for the TicTacToe applet

Before your tic tac toe game works, however, you need to add some support files. Create (or import from the Chapter 16 content, Content/ch16, on the CD-ROM that accompanies this book) two small GIF images, called not.gif (the "O") and cross.gif (the "X"). Place these files in a subfolder called images. If you want your version of tic tac toe to have sound effects, you need to create those as well. The sound files need to be saved in AU format and named yahoo1.au (the sound made when you win), yahoo2.au (the sound made when you lose), return.au (the sound made for a tie), ding.au, and beep.au, which are pretty much self-explanatory and made during the normal course of turn-taking. These sound files need to be placed in an audio subfolder.

Tip

The filenames given in the directions are the ones hard-coded into the TicTacToe.java file. If you want, you can change the names of the files in the source code and then name them anything you like.

Once you have at least the graphic files assembled (otherwise not much will happen when you run your applet), it is time to preview. You can preview your Java applet either in the Preview tab or by selecting File ➪ Preview and opening the page in your favorite Java-enabled Web browser (don't forget to save the page first). If you are savvy enough to outwit the computer, your applet might resemble the one shown in Figure 16-15.

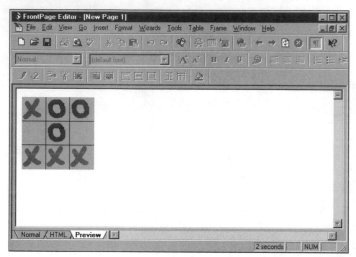

Figure 16-15: A hard-fought victory in the Java version of tic tac toe

The Java <applet> tag

When you insert a Java applet into your Web page, FrontPage generates an
<applet> tag for this element. The applet tag for the TicTacToe.class we
created in the previous section is shown here:

```
<applet width="128" height="128" code="TicTacToe.class">
You need a java enabled browser to view this Java applet.
</applet>
```

Caution

FrontPage 98 uses the old-style Applet tag for Java. This is currently deprecated
in favor of using the more general Object tag for Java as well as other kinds of
active content.

Configuring a Java applet

The Java applet example in this section demonstrates how you can configure some
applets using the parameter settings in the Java Applet Properties dialog box. The
example we use here is called NervousText. It is provided with the 1.1 version of
the JDK. It can be found at http://www.javasoft.com/products/jdk/1.1/
docs/relnotes/demos.html.

This applet takes a text string and, well, makes it look nervous. The text string is
passed to the applet via a parameter. To insert this applet using FrontPage, first
compile the applet NervousText.java as described in previous sections and
import it into the current FrontPage Web.

Select Insert➪Advanced➪Java Applet to open the Java Applet Properties dialog box. Designate the Applet Source as NervousText.class. To add the text parameter, click the Add button under the Parameters list box. In the Set Attribute Value dialog box, type **Text** in the Name box and a text string of your choice in the Value box. Click OK to return to the Java Applet Properties. Check to make sure that the text string appears in the Parameters section, as illustrated in Figure 16-16.

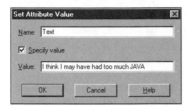

Figure 16-16: Adding a text string to the parameter list for our NervousText applet

That's all there is to it. Now you can preview the results, either in the Preview tab as shown in Figure 16-17 or by using the Preview in Browser function. If you have not adjusted the size parameters, which are by default 128 × 128 pixels, you may find that you need to resize the applet space in order to see all of your text string. To do this, you can select the applet in the Normal tab of the Editor window and drag a corner to resize.

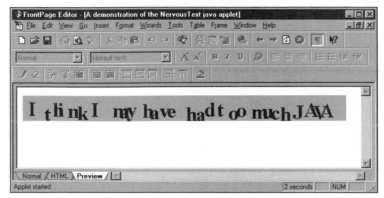

Figure 16-17: Is this your brain on Java?

Java security

Java uses a different security methodology than Microsoft's ActiveX. Java is essentially paranoid. It assumes that any code is potentially vicious, and it therefore limits the capabilities of certain kinds of activities. In Java lingo, the code is said to run in a "sandbox"—it can play with all the toys in the sandbox, but it cannot get out of the sandbox to get at your computer. This is a good idea in that it does not rely on the user to make good choices about which software to allow and which to deny (although of course you can still do this, using the facilities provided by your Web browser). However, it also limits (some would say unduly limits) an applet from doing things that could otherwise be productive. For example, a Java applet under normal circumstances cannot read files or write files.

As a result, Sun has begun to make adjustments to the sandbox methodology in order to allow developers and systems administrators working in a "trusted environment" to enable more functions within their Java code.

Taking the Next Step

This chapter covers the basics of adding various kinds of active content to your Web pages. After reading this chapter, you should be able to make decisions about what kind of active content to include in your pages and how to get that content into the page correctly. We have tried to stay clear of the thornier programming issues of how you actually create active content. However, if you are disappointed that you didn't have a chance to program in this chapter, you are in for a treat in Chapter 17, "Database Connectivity." This upcoming chapter takes you through the process of yet another variety of creating dynamic Web pages—by building the pages on the fly from data drawn from a database.

✦   ✦   ✦

Database Connectivity

$$\text{S}\text{ome of the largest and most widely used Web sites on}$$ the Internet today are built on top of powerful databases. But database systems can be daunting to set up and maintain, not to mention to connect to the Web. As it has developed, FrontPage has added increasing support for creating an online database, and it can take some of the pain out of the process. This chapter focuses on using FrontPage to create relatively simple but useful online resources. This chapter pushes FrontPage a bit. Perhaps it will push you as well, but only gently, and you are sure to find the rewards are worth the effort.

New in 98

FrontPage 98 uses ASP (Active Server Pages) to perform database queries rather than relying on IDC files. The good news is that database queries are now much easier to build, although you may be miffed if you have already become an IDC guru. You can, of course, still use IDC methods to develop your site, but Microsoft has quietly reduced FrontPage's support for the IDC Database Connection Wizard.

Dealing with Databases

Web sites connected to databases are among the most useful and exciting resources on the Internet. They enable users to access information and to add to the share of information in ways simply not possible before the Web took the world by storm. Everything from libraries and galleries to catalog services, job recruiters, travel agencies, real estate and investment brokers, and health care providers are increasingly looking for ways to grant users access to the information they need.

When we think of online databases, we typically conjure images of vast, intricate systems overseen by swarms of database administrators, tending to the system like ants to their queen. There probably are such systems, in fact I am sure there are, but it is also true that the Web has made it possible for anyone to create a database and make it available to anyone who might be interested. If you run a small business with a catalog of products, if you maintain a directory of contacts or customers, or even if you just want to keep track of your family tree, keep your online résumé up to date, or find a place to store all your favorite quotations, a database can help you not only manage your own information but also make it available to others.

The upside

What are some of the advantages of a database-driven Web site over traditional, static Web pages?

- ✦ Real-time updating of information, so users always see up-to-date information
- ✦ Flexible, customizable presentation of information
- ✦ Secure and controllable remote access to existing data, including the ability of remote users, where appropriate, to add to as well as view data

Be forewarned: the secret agenda of this chapter is to convince you that connecting a database to your Web site is within your reach.

The downside

Although databases are powerful tools, they are not necessarily for everyone. They require care and feeding, not to mention a certain level of technical expertise. Some of the reasons not to embark on a database-related project?

- ✦ An online database requires more resources: more software, and thus more money.
- ✦ The increased number of connections means more overhead and maintenance.
- ✦ With more parts involved, there is more to go wrong.

In sum, most of the potential disadvantages can be mitigated, so you do not need to be scared off from a database project because you think it is too hard, too expensive, or too much work. By the same token, like any effort, a database project often entails more work up front in the interest of bigger rewards down the line. The question you have to ask yourself is: Is it worth it? You should be realistic about the fact that to be successful a database system requires a higher level of commitment than a handful of pretty Web pages.

Note

If you have an existing database with information that you would like to make available on the Web, but you aren't sure you want to embark on an all-out database application, there is a compromise. Both Access 97 and MS SQL Server have Web publishing tools, which enable you to export your data as static HTML pages. They are static presentations of the data, but they are easy to generate, so you can republish as frequently as you need to. And you don't need a database connected to your Web server to do it.

Getting Ready

Before you get too charged up planning all the ways you could use a database on your Web site, you need to think through what is required to implement such a system.

1. **What database do I need?** Using FrontPage, you are going to build Web pages that access your database using ODBC (open database connectivity). ODBC is a standard means of connecting to a database. It is supported by virtually all major databases, and even many minor databases. The important thing is that you must have the appropriate ODBC drivers for your database. (Typically this is not a problem, since any database that supports ODBC comes with the necessary drivers. Most come with the Windows operating system, as does the ODBC manager you use to set up your ODBC data source.) If you are operating on Windows NT or Windows 95, the most likely candidates are Access for small to medium-sized projects, and SQL Server for medium to large undertakings. The examples in this chapter all make use of an Access database.

2. **What Web server can I user?** Assuming that you want to make use of FrontPage's database capabilities, you need to have a Web server that is capable of processing Active Server Pages, the technology FrontPage uses to build its database connectivity. If you use the services of a Web host provider, check to see if they support database services. Not all do. If you are running your own Web site, you can use Microsoft's IIS server, or O'Reilly's WebSite Pro. You can even use the Personal Web Server (PWS) that comes with FrontPage 98 (although not out of the box, as I explain momentarily).

To review, then, if you want to build a database application using FrontPage, you need:

✦ An ODBC-compliant database system

✦ The appropriate ODBC drivers and an ODBC management utility

✦ An ASP-enabled Web server

✦ FrontPage 98

If you have all that, you are ready to get started.

Microsoft's Active Server Pages

Throughout this book, we have endeavored to focus on the average FrontPage 98 user. For that reason, we have tried to avoid spending too much time talking about technology you may not have. Our assumption is simply that you have at least Windows 95 and the Personal Web Server that comes with FrontPage, and our examples have focused on that configuration.

The Active Server Page (ASP) technology that FrontPage 98 now supports was originally introduced on Microsoft's IIS Server, version 3.0. In a nutshell, this technology provides a means of adding instructions embedded in your Web page that are executed by the server before it sends the page to the user. In the case of database access (there are many other uses for ASP), you embed your database query, or request, in the Web page itself, in addition to the VBScript that manages the connection to the database. FrontPage 98 handles all of this for you. In theory, all you do is provide FrontPage's Database Wizard with some critical pieces of information. It does the rest. (Remember I said, "in theory.")

The problem is that the Personal Web Server, although it in fact supports ASP technology, does not come with that support built in. Nor does PWS or FrontPage come with any documentation that might be helpful in figuring out how to get PWS to support ASP. So if you use Personal Web Server even as a local testing server, what I am about to tell you may be the single most valuable piece of information in this chapter (which is not to suggest that the rest of the chapter isn't chock-full of useful information).

Adding Active Server Extensions to PWS

In order to use Active Server Pages with Personal Web Server, you must install the Active Server Extensions. How do you know if you have them or not? Well, you can try running a database query in FrontPage—if what you see in your browser looks like gibberish, this means that the server has not translated the ASP code into recognizable HTML, and you probably don't have the extensions installed. You can also check for their presence in the Windows Registry, but only if you know what you are doing. Tampering with the Registry, even if you are only looking, is potentially dangerous (there, you've been warned). Open the registry to HKEY_LOCAL_MACHINE\SYSTEM\CurrentControlSet\Services\W3SVC. If there is no ASP folder in the W3SVC folder, then you don't have the extensions installed.

So all you have to do is get them, right? The catch (this *is* Microsoft we are talking about here) is that the only way to get the Server Extensions is by downloading them with Microsoft's IIS. As of this writing, Microsoft has placed IIS 4.0 online for downloading, but only by way of the mega-megabyte download of the NT 4.0 Option Pack. If you have lots of extra time on your hands, I highly recommend this as a way to kill a great deal of it.

A somewhat more feasible option for most people is to download the IIS 3.0 Server. It is smaller, overall, and since you are only interested in the Server Extensions, not in the server itself, smaller is better. More important, you can actually configure the download of IIS 3.0 to install only the Active Server Extensions and not all the other bells and whistles that you aren't interested in anyway.

However, finding IIS 3 is no easy task, since Microsoft has buried it deep in the virtual bowels of their Web site (and by the time you read this, they may well have removed it altogether). Look for it at http://www.microsoft.com/msdownload/iis3. If it's not there, do a search for IIS 3.0. Or try searching for Active Server Extensions.

If you can get IIS 3.0 downloaded, run the installation program, ignoring the fact that you appear to be about to install an NT application on your Windows 95 system. Do a custom installation, adding only the Active Server Extensions. Unlike the ordeal of trying to find the extensions, installation is relatively straightforward. The extensions even come with a fairly thorough set of documentation called "The Active Server Pages Roadmap."

Creating a database

In all likelihood, if you are contemplating an online database application, you probably already have a database set up. If so, you may want to skip ahead. This section describes in very basic terms how we constructed the small sample Access database that we use for the examples in this chapter. Our sample database consists of a single table of contact information. The application we build with this database we have named the Online Phone Directory, or OPD, since what would a database application be without an obscure acronym?

The test database was created using the Windows NT version of Access 97, which includes a handy Table Wizard for quickly creating a wide variety of databases. If you have this wizard, you can build the database yourself, using the following directions. Otherwise, you can create a database by hand with the fields designated in the example, or just use the database provided on the CD-ROM.

1. In the Table Wizard, select the Business option to see a list of data tables appropriate for business. Select Contacts from the list, as shown in Figure 17-1.

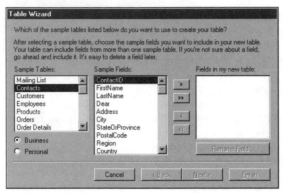

Figure 17-1: The Access Table Wizard, showing the data type, the field size, and where pertinent, the input mask used

2. Add the following fields to your database. If you are using the Table Wizard, you need only add the field names. If you are designing the fields by hand, use the data type, field size, and input mask information provided:

   • ContactID (Autonumber)

   • FirstName (Text, 50)

   • LastName (Text, 50)

   • Address (Text, 255)

   • City (Text, 50)

   • StateOrProvince (Text, 20)

   • PostalCode (Text, 20, Input mask = 00000\-9999)

   • Country (Text, 50)

   • CompanyName (Text, 50)

   • Title (Text, 50)

   • WorkPhone (Text, 30, Input mask = !\(999") "000\-0000)

- WorkExtension (Text, 20)
- HomePhone (Text, 30, Input mask = !\(999") "000\-0000)
- MobilePhone (Text, 30, Input mask = !\(999") "000\-0000)
- FaxNumber (Text, 30, Input mask = !\(999") "000\-0000)
- EmailName (Text, 50)

3. Name the table **Contacts** (the default suggestion), and answer Yes when asked if you want the wizard to generate a primary key for the table.

4. When you finish creating the database, the wizard asks what you want to do next. You will want to enter some data to test your application with. My suggestion is that you let the wizard create a form to simplify data entry for you (see Figure 17-2). Also, this form serves as a handy template for the Web data entry form you are going to build in a moment. If you are designing your table manually, you can enter data directly into the table.

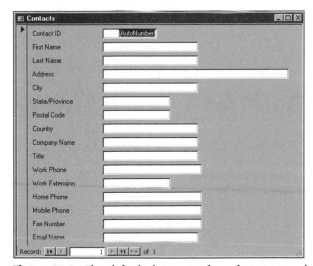

Figure 17-2: The default data entry form for our sample database created by the Access Table Wizard. Use it to enter sample data. Later you build the Web-accessible version of this form.

Importing the database into FrontPage

Once you have created the database and supplied it with some preliminary data, you must import the database into your FrontPage Web. Importing the database file is easy enough, but you may want to take a few extra steps in order to protect your data file from being easily accessible from your Web site. To import the file:

1. Open your Web in Explorer. Create a new folder at the root level of your Web. Name it _db or a name of your own choosing. Naming the folder with an initial underscore character hides it from general view. Be certain that you have configured FrontPage to show you hidden folders, or this folder will disappear from view the moment you name it. To show hidden folders, select Tools ➪ Web Settings in Explorer. Select the Advanced tab, and under the category Options, check the box to Show Documents in Hidden Directories.

2. Click the new folder icon with the right mouse button and select Properties from the pull-down menu. Uncheck the All Files to Be Browsed box. Click OK to return to Explorer.

3. To import the database file to this folder, first select the folder in Explorer. Select File ➪ Import and click the Add File button. Locate the database file, `opd.mdb`, and click OK to import it into the FrontPage Web (be sure that you have quit the application from Access beforehand).

Creating an ODBC data source

Once you have imported the database, the next step is to register your database as an ODBC data source. ODBC (open database connectivity) provides a standard protocol for accessing database information. It is supported by most database systems and is the means that ASP uses to communicate with a database. To create your ODBC data source, use the ODBC Data Source Administrator (see Figure 17-3) found in the Windows Control Panels. To locate this utility, click the Start button on the Windows toolbar and select Settings ➪ Control Panels. Double-click the icon named 32bit ODBC (or perhaps just ODBC).

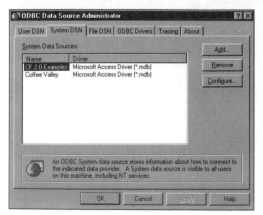

Figure 17-3: The ODBC Data Source Administrator is used to configure your database as an ODBC data source.

The utility contains several tabs:

✦ **User Data Source Name (DSN)**—This is a data source visible only to you, the current user.

✦ **System Data Source Name (DSN)**—This is a data source visible to local users of this computer. The key is that this includes services running on the computer (such as a Web server, for example).

✦ **File Data Source Name (DSN)**—This is used to access remote data sources.

To create a DSN for your application, select the Add button and choose the appropriate ODBC driver for your application. Because we have created our database in Access, we select the Access ODBC Driver (Figure 17-4). Click Finish to continue on to the Access 97 Setup dialog box.

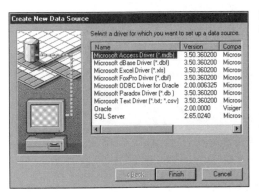

Figure 17-4: Selecting the appropriate ODBC driver in the ODBC Administrator

Next we need to configure our data source using the screen shown in Figure 17-5. Designate a name for your data source (we use the name "OPD"), and provide a short description of the database for posterity. Next configure the data source to use your newly created database. Click Select, locate your database file (such as opd.mdb)—be sure to point to the version you imported into FrontPage—and click OK three times to save your configuration and exit. From now on, whenever you refer to your database, it is by its DSN, that is, "OPD."

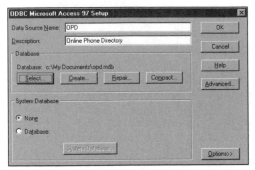

Figure 17-5: Naming and locating your ODBC data source

Note

If you are building a database application that will run on a host computer somewhere else, you should first have the system administrator set up the ODBC configuration on that system. Then set up a DSN with the identical name on the local system where you use FrontPage.

Building a Database Application

At last we are ready to return to FrontPage! Before we dive in and create a Web query to our database, however, we need to think through how you want to present the information to your users. Our Online Phone Directory (OPD) is relatively simple. We would like it to have the following features:

✦ From a listing of records in the database, users can select a record to view in detail.

✦ Users can search for names in the database.

✦ Users can add new records to the database and edit existing records.

Querying the database

For our first effort, we build a simple listing of the database records. After that we illustrate how you can improve somewhat on the user interface.

To create a simple query that returns names and phone numbers in alphabetical order, follow the directions:

Using the Database Region Wizard

First, create a new page in FrontPage Editor. This page will serve to display the results of the database query. Rather than start with a new page, you could also insert your query results into an existing HTML page. In this case, you simply need to rename the page with an .asp extension when you finish (the Database Region Wizard reminds you to do this).

Select Insert ⇨ Database ⇨ Database Region Wizard to start the Database Region Wizard. In the first dialog box, shown in Figure 17-6, indicate the name of the ODBC data source you defined earlier for your database.

Now you see why you were wise to choose a short name for the data source—rather than choose from a list of available data sources, the wizard expects you to type in the name. Spelling counts! Type **OPD** if you have been following the example, leave the username and password boxes empty, since you have not set up your data source to require them, and click Next to continue with the wizard.

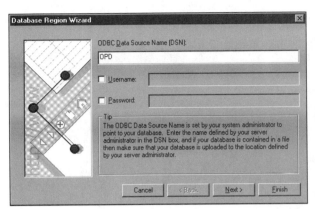

Figure 17-6: Tell the Database Region Wizard the name of your data source.

In FrontPage 97, the database wizard was called Database Connection Wizard. Why is the new one called the Database Region Wizard? I suspect because you are inserting SQL code into a *region* of the HTML page that will be replaced by the actual query results when the page is loaded. This is not unlike the Detail directive used in IDC. Because it returns the data right where it is called, however, it is more efficient than the old method, which performed a query in one file and fed the results back through a second file, the HTX template.

Designating the SQL query

SQL, which stands for structured query language, is the most commonly used language for generating database queries. Don't be alarmed if you don't speak SQL (pronounced "sequel" by people in the know, probably the same ones who call URLs, "earls"). You can create fairly simple queries without much of a learning curve. You can also use a design tool like the one that comes with Access to help you formulate your queries. You just click some boxes and then cut and paste the code that you generated. For this example, just type the following statement into the box designated for the SQL string:

```
SELECT * FROM Contacts
ORDER BY LastName
```

The SELECT SQL statement instructs the database to return all fields (the star [*] is a wildcard, shorthand for all fields in the table) in the Contacts table and to sort them alphabetically by last name. Your screen should look like Figure 17-7. Click Next to continue the wizard.

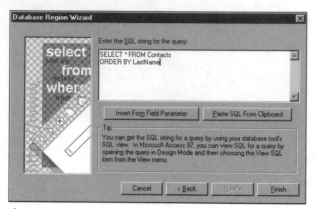

Figure 17-7: Feeding SQL treats to the Database Region Wizard

If this database had many records, using the wildcard character would add unnecessary overhead to our query. As it is, with three records in the database, we can afford a little bit of inefficiency.

The next wizard dialog box asks for the database field names you want to display. Because we used the wildcard character in our SQL query, we could display any or all of the fields in the database. For our first test, though, let's keep it simple and add the LastName, FirstName, HomePhone, WorkPhone, and CompanyName fields (see Figure 17-8). For each field, click the Add Field button and type the name of the field into the dialog box. Be sure that you use the field names as they appear in the design of the database.

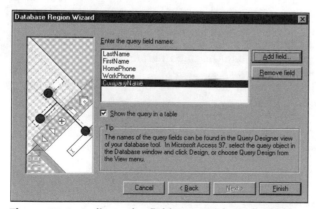

Figure 17-8: Indicate the fields you wish to display in your database results page.

If you need to refresh your memory, open the OPD database in Access and view the Contacts table in Design mode to see the formal field names. Check the box (it is checked by default) to display the results in table format. Click Finish to complete the wizard and build your first query. If you have not yet saved this page, FrontPage reminds you that you will need to save the file with an .asp extension. The Database Region Wizard builds a table to hold your query results and inserts some placeholder text. Compare your results with those in Figure 17-9.

Save your file with the filename extension .asp. Important note: The folder that contains this file must be set to allow program execution. To enable program execution, switch to Explorer, and click with the right mouse button on the folder icon. Select Properties from the pop-up menu, and check the Allow Scripts or Programs to Be Run check box.

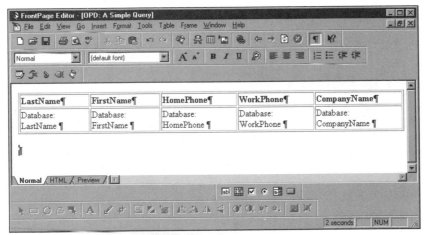

Figure 17-9: A simple data request, as built by the Database Region Wizard

Testing the results

Possibly you are thinking that the page we have just created is not exactly stunning. In a moment, we look at how you can improve the results formatting, but first let's make sure that the ASP database connection really works.

To test your page, you need to use the Preview in Browser command under the File menu. The Editor's Preview tab does not work with ASP. Select File ⇨ Preview in Browser, and select your favorite browser (see Figure 17-10). The results are shown displayed in Netscape in order to emphasize that because all of the work takes place at the server, ASP programming is completely browser independent.

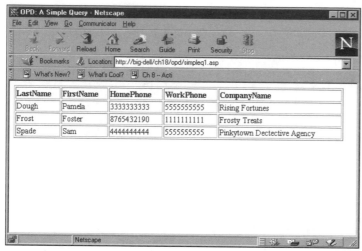

Figure 17-10: The results of your first ASP database request

Editing the SQL query

If you are paying attention, you may have noticed that the phone numbers in our results do not appear quite the way you might want. If you look at these numbers in the Access database, they are nicely formatted, with parentheses around the area code and a dash between the first three and last four main numbers. In our database query, there is no formatting at all. What happened?

This little programming problem illustrates what can happen when dealing with a multitiered application. When we created the Access database, we used a template that included an input mask on the phone numbers (you may have noticed this when you input data into your database). You can see this input mask if you open the database in Design mode and look at the properties of the various phone number fields. The numbers are actually stored in Access as raw ten-digit character strings. Access is smart enough to format them for you whenever it displays them, but when our SQL requests the data, it gets only the raw strings.

There are several approaches to dealing with this. One solution would be to remove the input mask from the field in Access. In this case, whatever you put into the field, you get out, including any formatting. This has the virtue of being simple, but it also makes for less consistent data, since not everyone formats phone numbers the same way. A better approach is to let Access store the raw numbers as it is currently doing, and format them on the fly as they come out of the database. This way, you can ensure that they always look the same, and tomorrow you can change them all if you choose.

You could insert VBScript code into the ASP page to perform this operation, but there is an easier way, and that is to add a Format function to your SQL query. You can edit your data query by clicking with the right mouse button anywhere on the second row of the results table. (The cursor changes to the robot cursor when you are over the ASP content.) Select Database Region Properties from the pop-up menu and edit the SQL as follows:

```
SELECT *, Format(HomePhone, '(000) 000-0000') as fHomePhone,
Format(WorkPhone, '(000) 000-0000') as fWorkPhone
FROM Contacts
ORDER BY LastName
```

Now, in addition to the wildcard (*) field designator, we have added two formatted fields, fHomePhone and fWorkPhone. The Format function for each indicates that it should take the raw data from the designated field and format it according to the template, where each "0" represents a digit. Click Finish to complete the revision and save the changes in Editor.

Editing the database column values

Before we can access our formatted fields, we also have to revise the field names we are displaying. To do this, double-click the "Database: HomePhone" text in the third column of the table. You can also click the HomePhone field with the right mouse button and select Database Column Value Properties. In either case, you are presented with the dialog box shown in Figure 17-11. Add the new field name, fHomePhone, and click OK to update the field name in the ASP table. Do the same for the WorkPhone field, substituting fWorkPhone for WorkPhone.

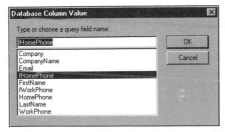

Figure 17-11: Editing the database column values of our database query

By the way, if you find it annoying that you cannot delete the old WorkPhone and HomePhone names from the list of Column Values, there is a way around this. The DatabaseRegionStart component has a parameter, s-columnnames, that lists these names. Switch to the HTML tab and edit this list to your liking.

Just for practice, let's also add a new field to the results display. To add the EmailName field to the end of the table, click the last column of the table. Select Table➪Insert Rows or Columns, and add a new column to the right. Add the field name, EmailName, to the new cell in the first row. Insert the cursor into the new cell in the second row, and select Insert➪Database➪Column Value. Type **EmailName** into the box provided and click OK to record your changes. When you test again, you should see consistently formatted phone numbers, as in Figure 17-12. Congratulations!

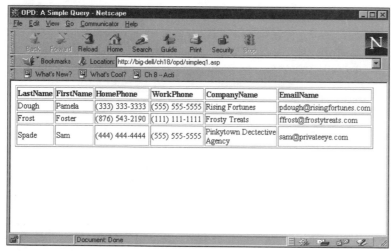

Figure 17-12: A successful and well-formatted database results list

Enhancing the results format

We have seen how you can use the SQL to format the data returned. You can also edit the HTML in the page itself to improve the page layout of the results returned. You can change the table formatting, including the properties of the table and its cells. You can change the font properties of all text, including the text supplied from the database query. You cannot move the column references, however.

You can move column references around, but to do so you must prevent the Wizard from formatting the data in a table (you can create the table yourself and put the data columns in it). In the next section we illustrate this technique as we work on linking our list to a full detail view of a data record.

Adding a detail view

It is common practice in Web database applications to provide two-tiered access to data. The first page provides a summary list of all relevant database entries. Each entry is then linked to detailed information about that particular record. In this section we illustrate two methods of building this kind of structure using the FrontPage Database Region Wizard. Both of these methods require a modicum of customization in order to work. After that, we show how to build a simple search page interface to the database.

First we need to build the ASP page for the detail view of our data. This page displays a single record, based on an ID that is passed to it. Building this page is largely a repeat of techniques we learned earlier in the chapter, so we will keep this short:

1. Create a new file, `query2_detail.asp`, and save it in a directory that has permission to execute programs turned on.

2. Select Insert ⇨ Database ⇨ Database Region Wizard, and proceed as in the earlier example. Use the following SQL statement:

   ```
   SELECT * FROM Contacts
   WHERE ContactID=%%id%%
   ```

   To add the parameter value (`%%id%%`) click the Insert Form Field Parameter button, type **id** into the box, and click OK. Alternatively, you can enter this parameter by hand. If you do so, note that there are no quotation marks around the double percentage signs that encompass the `id` parameter.

3. In the next dialog box add all query fields, since we want to display them all. Do not check the Show the Query in a Table option. Click Finish to return to Editor.

4. Place the cursor inside the Database: Start and Database: End text and create a table large enough to display 16 fields of information. Add the field names to the first column.

5. Next cut and paste each of the Column Value components into their appropriate table cells. Figure 17-13 shows one approach. Save your work.

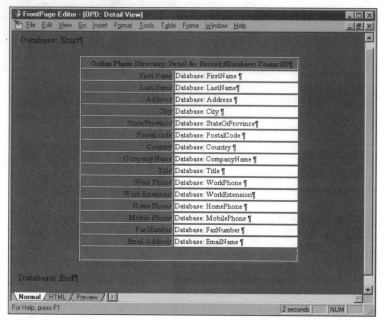

Figure 17-13: The whole enchilada—building a detail view of an OPD record

Linking a results list to a record detail

In the next sections we address two methods of building the initial database list in order to link it to the detail view you have just completed. The first approach involves adding a Form Submit button to each record. The second method uses a standard hyperlink attached to the last name of each person in the results list.

The forms approach

The key to linking a data summary item to its detail is the ability to pass a unique identifier from one data query to the next. The forms approach to this challenge associates a Form Submit button with each record. When the user clicks this button, the application fetches and displays all input for that record.

Start with the formatted version of the ASP query we produced in the last section at the beginning of the chapter. First add a column to the left of the Last Name column (you may need to remove the extra column we added earlier if your table becomes too wide). Leave the top cell blank. In the bottom cell, in the same row with the Column Value components, insert a Form button by selecting Insert ⇨ Form Field ⇨ Push Button. Edit the form field properties by right-clicking the form and selecting Form Field Properties from the pop-up menu. Make the button a Submit button. You can change the label on the button as well. We have selected "Detail."

Next edit the form handler. Right-click the form and select Form Properties from the pop-up list. In the What to Do with Form Results? section, select Send to Other and select Custom ISAPI, NSAPI, CGI, or ASP script. Select Options and in the Action button type the name of the detail ASP page, **query2_detail.asp**. Include any path information necessary to locate the file. Check that the Method box is set to POST. Click OK twice to return to Editor.

Passing a parameter via a hidden field

The last step of the process is to insert the ContactID into this form so that it is passed on to the detail query in `query2_detail.asp`. To do this, we need to create a hidden field and then insert a line of VBScript into the Value attribute of the hidden field.

To create the hidden field, return to the Form Properties dialog box by right-clicking the form element. Click the Advanced button near the bottom of this dialog box. Click Add to add a new hidden field. Give the field the name `id`. In the Value field, insert the following line of code:

```
<% If Not IsEmpty(fp_rs) And Not (fp_rs Is Nothing) Then
Response.Write CStr(fp_rs("ContactID")) %>
```

This is just a long-winded VBScript way of saying if there is a ContactID for this record, put its value into the value attribute of this hidden field.

Tip

You may find it easier to compose the VBScript elsewhere and then cut and paste it into this field.

Click OK twice to return to Editor. Save your work and test the results. The list page should resemble Figure 17-14. When you click a button, you should see full details for that record, as illustrated in Figure 17-15.

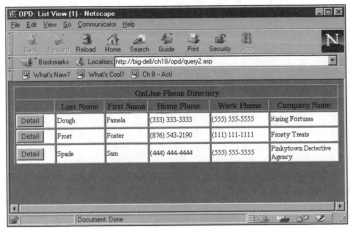

Figure 17-14: The forms approach to listing database records

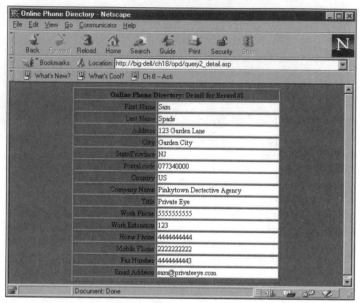

Figure 17-15: All the details at the touch of a button

The hypertext link approach

In this section we walk through a second method of linking a list of records to their detail, using standard HREF hyperlinks. This is actually the more commonly used method. I have saved it for last, however, because it is not very well-supported by the FrontPage Database Region Wizard—in fact you might say that by default it is prevented. In this section we find a way around the wily wizard.

If you are familiar with CGI, you know there are two methods that Web browsers use to pass user input back to the server. The first method is called a POST. The user enters information in a form, and the input is posted to the server behind the scenes, as it were. The second method is to attach the query string to the end of the URL request itself. You have undoubtedly noticed these big, ungainly strings in the URL field of your Web browser. This is not a pretty way to pass data, but it is a relatively easy way to do it using only a standard hyperlink, that is, without requiring the user to fill out a form or click a form button.

Our dilemma in trying to construct a hyperlinked version of our two-page database application is that the ASP code that the Database Region Wizard produces expects its data to arrive via a POST request, that is, from a form. It would be nice if we could tweak this code directly, but alas, we can't. Any attempt to alter the wizard's code produces a warning message that you have tampered with the contents of a FrontPage component and that your changes will be obliterated (OK, so that's not the exact wording—it's just the *spirit* of the message) when you leave the HTML tab. At least FrontPage 98, unlike its earlier incarnations, warns you when it does this.

In case you are interested, the FrontPage components perform a checksum calculation on the contents between the start and end component tags. This is how they detect that you have made a change.

Editing the wizard's ASP code

One way around this shortcoming (in fact the only way I know of) is to edit the template file that the Wizard uses to generate this code in the first place. The code resides in three text files, somewhat unceremoniously dumped in the bin subfolder of your main FrontPage folder. They are named DB_EndBotASP.txt, DB_ResultBotASP.txt, and DB_StartBotASP.txt. The last one is the one we want. (Incidently, DB_ResultBotASP.txt contains the template for the VBScript we added to the hidden field in the previous example.) Since we are about to hack, that is, "patch," this file, now might be a good time to back up all three of these files, in case you later regret having followed me down this path.

To add the patch, open DB_StartBotASP.txt in a text editor such as Notepad. At about line 27 of this file is a line of code that reads:

```
fp_sValue = Request.Form(fp_sField)
```

This code takes the name of a given form field (fp_sField), which it derived from the parameters you placed in your SQL query, and records the value from that form. Right after this, the programming checks this value (fp_sValue), and if it finds it empty, it generates an error message.

What we want to do is add an extra clause that says, in effect, if the value of this form field is 0, first check to see if there is a query string parameter with this name before producing an error message. In other words, if the code does not find a form value for this field, it will look for a corresponding query string value. Just the ticket for our hyperlinking needs.

Immediately after the line quoted previously, add the following lines of code:

```
'try querystring if form doesn't work
If (len(fp_sValue) = 0) Then
    fp_sValue = Request.QueryString(fp_sField)
End If
```

The first line, beginning with the apostrophe, is a comment. The next three lines constitute the conditional clause that performs the work. Save this file with your changes back to its original location, and you are all set. From now on, all of your database queries will work either with form data or with data sent via a hyperlink.

Adding a parameter to a hyperlink

Now we can get back to the business at hand—creating a hyperlink that passes the ContactID on to the detail form we created earlier, query2_detail.asp. We start with the version of the list view we created in the previous section. Delete the extra column that we added for the Form button.

Select the text "Database: LastName," which is used as the preview for the last name column values. Select either Insert ➪ Hyperlink or Edit ➪ Hyperlink or click the Hyperlink icon on the main toolbar to bring up the Create Hyperlink dialog box. In this box, you need to type a rather awkward URL, part regular URL, part query string, and part VBScript (as mentioned earlier, you may find it easier to compose this text first and then cut and paste it into the URL field):

```
query2_detail.asp?id=<%If Not IsEmpty(fp_rs) And Not (fp_rs Is
Nothing) Then Response.Write CStr(fp_rs("ContactID"))%>
```

If you have already created query2_detail.asp as described earlier, then you are all set to test. The initial list page should resemble Figure 17-16. When you click the hyperlinked last name, you should see the detail record for that person, as before.

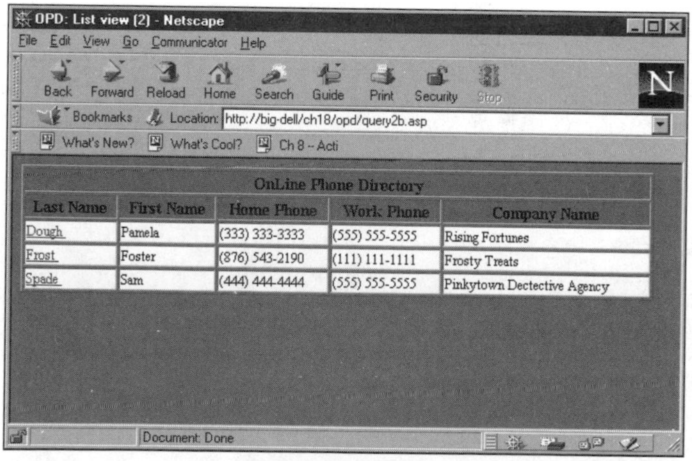

Figure 17-16: The hypertext approach to listing results

Searching the Database

The two examples just described have illustrated techniques for browsing a list of database records. This is a useful technique when dealing with relatively small quantities of data. Clearly, however, if your phone directory had 50,000 entries, you would not want to browse through all of the records each time you wanted to find someone.

In this section we create a basic search interface to the phone directory database. The interface is built using a three-frame set, and it includes two ways to search the database. The top frame consists of graphical representations of the letters of the alphabet. Clicking a letter returns everyone in the database whose last name begins with the selected letter. Results are returned in the middle frame. The bottom frame contains a text input field. Users can enter all or part of a last name, and the database returns anyone whose last name begins with the string entered. The completed interface is shown in Figure 17-17.

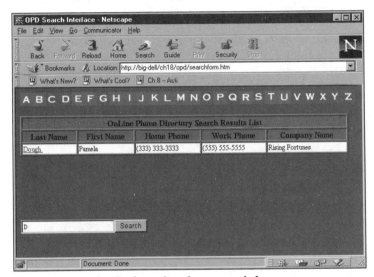

Figure 17-17: The final results of our search form

Many of the techniques used to build this search form are similar to ones introduced in earlier examples. For a more detailed explanation of the procedure described here, look back at those examples.

The frame set interface

The first step is to create the frame set. In Editor, create a new Web page. Select Frame➪New Frames Page and select the Top-Down Hierarchy template. Save the main page as `searchform.htm`. The top frame is `alphabet.htm`. It consists of 26 squares, one for each letter of the alphabet. In a moment we link the graphics to the ASP database query. You can use the samples found on the CD-ROM in `Examples/ch17/images/alphabets`, or you can recreate the interface to your own liking.

The initial middle frame is `searchstart.htm`. It is just a placeholder. Results of our searches are displayed in this frame. The bottom frame is `search1.htm`. It consists of a single text input box and a Submit button. It is also linked to the query page.

The search query

The heart of our search interface is the ASP query page that is called by both the alphabet graphics and the input form. We use the same layout we designed earlier with a hyperlinked list of records that drill down to a detail of a single record. In this example, we rename the query file search1.asp and alter it to its new purpose.

The first thing we need to do is revise the SQL query. Load the existing file, query2b.asp, into Editor and select File ⇨ Save As to save a copy of it with a new name. Next click with the right mouse button in the Database Region table and select Database Region Properties from the pop-up menu. This allows you to edit the SQL statement for this page. Replace the existing query with the following one (or compare with Figure 17-18):

```
SELECT Contacts.*, Format(HomePhone, '(000) 000-0000') as
fHomePhone, Format(WorkPhone, '(000) 000-0000') as fWorkPhone
FROM Contacts
WHERE LastName Like '%%Name%%%'
ORDER BY LastName
```

The principal addition to the SQL is a WHERE clause. This clause defines the conditions that must be met by any rows that the database returns. We used a WHERE clause earlier in creating the detail query.

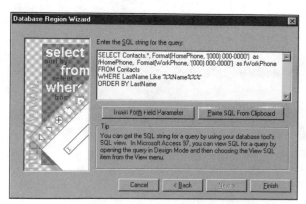

Figure 17-18: The search form SQL statement

This one makes use of a slightly different technique in order to create a database lookup based on the partial contents of a field. We have used the operator LIKE rather than the equals (=) sign and combined it with a wildcard character (%). Perhaps you were thinking that the extra percentage sign after the Name parameter was a typo. In fact it is a SQL wildcard character. In plain English this WHERE clause says, return those rows in the database in which the text in the LastName field begins with the characters in the Name parameter. Thus, if Name is "A," the database returns anyone whose last name begins with A. If "Sh" is input, only those people with last names beginning with "Sh" are returned.

Because we are editing an existing ASP page, you can click Finish at this point and return to the Editor. If this were a new query, the wizard would have asked us to define at least one query field.

Adjusting the URL target frame

While we are editing this file, we may as well make one other necessary adjustment. By default the middle frame of the Nested Hierarchy frame template is configured to load linked pages into the bottom frame. We want it to have a default target of itself, the middle frame. Otherwise, you will get some very odd behavior when you try to view a record's detail page.

To correct this, place the cursor in the middle frame, click with the right mouse button, and select Page Properties from the pop-up menu. Click the General tab and then the button to the right of the Default Target Frame input box. Type **middle** (or use **_self**) into the field and click OK to return to editing. Now unless we specify otherwise, all links from the middle frame should send new pages to this frame as well.

Linking to the query page

With our search1.asp query page in hand, it is time to link it to the two search interfaces described earlier.

Linking from a form

Select the form page we created a moment ago, search1.htm. Select the text input box and click it with the right mouse button. Select Form Field Properties from the pop-up menu. Change the Name of this component to "Name" and click OK to return to Editor. Click the form element with the right mouse button and select Form Properties. Select the Send to Other option for What to Do with Form Results? Click Options and set the Action property to the name of the search query page, search1.asp. Check that the Method designation is POST, and then click OK. Back in the main Form Properties dialog box, click Target Name and type **middle** into the Target Setting dialog box. Click OK to finish.

Linking from a graphic

To link from a graphic to the query form is much like linking from a hyperlink, as described earlier in the chapter. With the alphabetical page in Editor, select one of the letter graphics and click it with the right mouse button. Select Image Properties, and make the following changes:

1. In the Location field in the Default Hyperlink section, type:

   ```
   search1.asp?name=[LETTER]
   ```

   substituting the correct letter of the alphabet for *[LETTER]*. (Thus, for the *D* graphic, use `search1.asp?name=D`).

2. Insert a text Alternative (say, the letter itself) to the graphic into the Text field of the Alternative Representations section of the dialog box.

3. Click the Target Frame selection button and type **middle** into the Target Setting box. Click OK to return to the main dialog box.

4. In the Appearance tab, set the Border Thickness amount to 0 (zero). Click OK to return to Editor.

That's it. Test the interface with different combinations of text, using either the alphabetic search or the free form text search.

Note

By the way, if you are using the sample version of these files on the CD-ROM, only the letters *D, F,* and *S* are actually linked to the query page, since those are the only letters represented in the sample data. You are welcome to add the rest yourself.

Inserting a New Record

So far we have restricted our examples to various ways of searching and displaying the database records using FrontPage's Database Region Wizard. In this section we show how to insert new records into the database.

The New Record Entry form

The first step is simply to create a standard HTML form page with components corresponding to each of the columns in our Online Phone Directory (OPD) database. The one exception is that you do not need to include a field for the ContactID. In this database, the ID field is the primary key, and it is automatically incremented each time a record is inserted. (In fact you will receive an error if you try to insert a new record with a ContactID.) You can use the table we created for our detail view if you like, or create your own. If you are really in a hurry, check out the completed version of the form, `Examples/ch17/opd/insert1.htm`, on the CD-ROM.

Once you have created all of the form fields, you need to provide them with a label that matches their corresponding column in the database. It is not essential that the names match, but it will make your life a lot easier. Also you should establish the form field validation appropriate for each field, using the properties dialog for each input field. For detailed information on creating forms in FrontPage 98, see Chapter 11.

The SQL statement

To add a new record to a table, SQL uses an INSERT statement. We need to create a second page that contains the SQL command to be run, and then link our form to this ASP query page.

First create a new page in Editor. Select Edit ⇨ Database ⇨ Database Region Wizard, and designate the data source name (DSN) for our Online Phone Directory database as in previous examples. The data source name is OPD (if you have been following the example). Click Next, and in the SQL statement input box, insert the following rather ungainly statement:

```
INSERT INTO Contacts
(FirstName, LastName, Address, City, StateOrProvince,
PostalCode, Country, CompanyName, Title, WorkPhone,
WorkExtension, HomePhone, MobilePhone, FaxNumber,EmailName)
VALUES ('%%FirstName%%', '%%LastName%%', '%%Address%%',
'%%City%%', '%%StateOrProvince%%', '%%PostalCode%%',
'%%Country%%', '%%CompanyName%%', '%%Title%%', '%%WorkPhone%%',
'%%WorkExtension%%', '%%HomePhone%%', '%%MobilePhone%%',
'%%FaxNumber%%','%%EmailName%%')
```

Click Finish to complete the wizard. You are instructed that you must enter at least one query form field. This is useless, since your INSERT query does not return any values, but if FrontPage says you must, you must. (You can delete it later.) Save this page as search1.asp, being sure to save it in a directory that permits the execution of programs (see the section on designating the SQL query, earlier in the chapter, for details).

Finally, return to your input form, insert1.htm, and edit the Form Properties to point to this ASP file. In the What to Do with Form Results? section, select Send to Other, and select the Custom ISAPI, NSAPI, CGI, or ASP. Click the Options button, and add the name of the ASP file, search1.asp, in the Action field. Check that the Method is POST. Click OK to return to the dialog box, and OK once more to finish the task. Save your changes, and test. Use the search form created earlier to check that your new entries appear in the database, or you can use Access to peek at the file.

You will notice that we have not attempted in this section to improve the quality of the response page you receive when you insert new records. For suggestions about how to do that, as well as how to edit existing records, read on to the next section.

Editing Existing Records

The FrontPage Database Region Wizard works quite well for generating simple database queries and for inserting records into an existing database. It poses some rather serious limitations when it comes to editing existing records. The main reason for this is that there is no easy way to populate forms fields with the data from a database record. The only way is to cut and paste a small portion of VBScript into each field's value property input box.

In this section, we produce an interface for editing records. The interface consists of a frame set with two frames. The left-hand frame contains a scrollable list of names in the database. Selecting a name and clicking the submit button populates a form in the right-hand frame with data from the selected person's record. From this form, the record can be updated.

Creating the frame set

First we need to create the frame set that will operate this editing application. In FrontPage Editor, select Frame⇨New Frames Page, and select the Contents template. This generates a two-frame page, with a narrow left-hand frame and a wider main frame. Save the left-hand frame as `namelist.asp`. Initially, save the right-hand frame as `editstart.htm`. When the frame set first displays, it will display this start page. When the Select button in the left-hand frame is clicked, it will call `editform.asp` and load it into the main frame. Save the frame set page as `editopd.htm`. Eventually, we will also need a third ASP file, called `updateopd.asp`, whose job it is to update the database from changes made in the edit form.

Creating the scrolling list

Select the name list frame from the frame set you just made. Our plan in this frame is to create a scrollable list of names from the OPD. Clicking a name will cause that record to be loaded into the edit form.

The chief challenge is to populate the list with the names from the database. Thanks to the wonders of the Database Region Wizard, it is apparently impossible to insert data into a list form field element. To solve this shortcoming, we resort to a bit of hand-coding. But don't worry, it will be very painless, and you will be an enlightened person afterward. Plus this gives us a chance to practice some of the scripting skills covered in Chapter 15.

First we create the form into which we insert the database region. Select Insert⇨ Form Field⇨Push Button. This generates a form and places a normal push button at the end of it. Edit the properties of the button to make it a Submit button and change its Value/Label to "Select."

Creating the database query

Next we generate the query. Click inside the form box to set the insertion cursor inside the form. (You may want to enlarge the form somewhat using the Enter key.) Select Insert ⇨ Database ⇨ Database Region Wizard. Type the data source name (DSN) **OPD** where it is requested in the first dialog box. Click Next to continue.

In the next box, insert the following SQL statement:

```
SELECT ContactID, LastName, FirstName
FROM Contacts
ORDER BY LastName
```

Click Next, and in the last dialog box add the field `LastName` to the list of query field names. (We do not bother to add both last name and first name here, since we are just going to undo this in a moment.) Uncheck the Show the Query in a Table box, and click Finish to insert the Database Region component into the page. The results should resemble Figure 17-19.

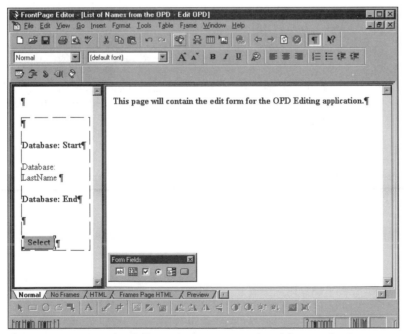

Figure 17-19: Creating a list component populated from a database query

Adding the List component

Now it's time to get our hands dirty. We need to add three small chunks of server-side VBScript to our application. The first is the meat of the matter. It takes the place of the default column value foisted on us by the Database Region Wizard.

Click the "Database: LastName" text (do not double-click!) to select it. Select Insert ⇨ Advanced ⇨ Script or click the Script icon in the Advanced toolbar. This brings up the Script Editor. Select VBScript as the language of choice and check the Run Script on Server check box. Add the following line of code:

```
If Not IsEmpty(fp_rs) And Not (fp_rs Is Nothing) Then Response.
Write CStr("<option value=" & fp_rs("ContactID") & ">" & fp_rs
("LastName") & ", " & fp_rs("FirstName"))
```

This line inserts, for each record returned from the database, an item in a list component. The list will display the person's last name and first name and link them to their ID, which we will use to generate the full record for editing.

Next we need to wrap this procedure with a `<select>` tag, to designate this as a list component. We want to make sure that the `select` tag encompasses and is outside of the database region. Otherwise, we will end up with a separate list component for each item in the database. In theory, we should be able to edit the HTML by hand, adding the requisite beginning and end tags just before the beginning and just after the end of the Database Region component. Alas, FrontPage is once again too smart for us. If you try this, you discover that FrontPage automatically rejoins the beginning and end tags, thus defeating the purpose. For this reason, we once again resort to adding some simple VBScript.

Place the cursor above the bold "**Database: Start**" text but still within the form element dashed lines. Insert a script element as described previously and insert the following code:

```
Response.Write CStr("<SELECT NAME=id>")
```

Repeat the procedure after the "Database: End" text, using this line of code:

```
Response.Write CStr("</SELECT>")
```

You should now have three VBScript icons intermingled within the elements of the Database Region component. Save your work, and let's test what we have so far. Remember that to test an ASP you must save it with an .asp ending in a folder that enables programs to run. You must also use the Preview in Browser feature to test the ASP file, since it does not work correctly in the FrontPage Editor Preview tab. If you have done your work carefully, you should see something resembling Figure 17-20.

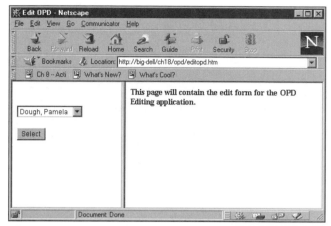

Figure 17-20: Successfully creating a list element for our editing application

Adding a row count

Being able to get the names into a list element is no small feat in itself. However, you may feel that a pop-up list is not the most appropriate for our application. With only a few records in the database it is OK, but with many it would be quite cumbersome. One way to solve this would be to hard-code a size into the list, for example:

```
<SELECT NAME=id SIZE=20>
```

Of course, if we do that, our three records will look mighty small and lonely in a big, long list box. A more elegant solution is to size the list according to the number of records we return, up to some reasonable maximum number. To accomplish this we need to know how many rows we are dealing with.

We can perform a simple database query to tell us this information. Place the cursor near the top of the page (this can be outside the form element). Select Insert ➪ Database ➪ Database Region Wizard and enter the DSN **OPD** as before. Click Next to continue. In the SQL statement screen, insert the following statement:

```
SELECT COUNT(*) as RowCount
FROM Contacts
```

This SQL statement makes use of a Count() function. It returns a single field containing the count of rows in the database. Click Next to continue. Add the field query value RowCount, uncheck the table display option, and click Finish. Now we have retrieved the number of rows in the database. To use that number, however, we first have to store it in a variable. Otherwise its value disappears at the end of the database region.

Select the "Database: RowCount" text inserted by the wizard. Select Insert ➪ Advanced ➪ Script to open the Script Editor. Add the following line of VBScript, which stores the RowCount value in a variable:

```
fpMaxListSize = 20
fpRowCount=fp_rs("RowCount")
fpListSize = fpMaxListSize
If (fpRowCount<fpMaxListSize) Then fpListSize=fpRowCount
```

Finally, edit the VBScript that writes the initial SELECT tag. You can access your script by double-clicking the appropriate VBScript icon. Change the code to the following:

```
Response.Write CStr("<select name=id size=" & fpListSize & ">")
```

Save your work and retest. Now the results should resemble Figure 17-21. When you have more than fpMaxListSize number of rows in the database, the list will get no bigger than the maximum allowable size (which you can change to suit your needs).

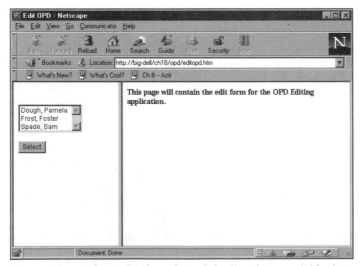

Figure 17-21: The revised version of the list element, with size customized to the number of records

Creating the edit form

So far, you should have completed the list element display and created an introductory HTML page for the main frame of our editing application. Next we need to create editform.asp, the form to use for editing a record. This form is called when the user clicks the Select button in the left-hand frame. It passes along the ID for the selected directory record (from the value of the list item selected) and populates the form with the data.

The easiest way to create the edit form is first to create the database region, insert the form element, then import the edit form, and finally script the form elements to populate them with data.

Create a new page in FrontPage Editor and save it as `editform.asp`. Now add the database region. Select Database⇨Database Region Wizard. Designate the DSN as OPD, and click Next. Enter the following SQL code, the same code used in an earlier example. You can use the Insert Form Field Parameter to add the `id` element to the query, or just type it manually. Be sure to use only the double percentage signs—no quotation marks—since the `id` field is a number, not a text field:

```
SELECT * FROM Contacts
WHERE ContactID=%%id%%
```

In the final screen, designate a field name, for example `LastName`, to make the wizard happy. It doesn't much matter which one you pick, since we are going to delete it anyway.

Once you have added the database region, it is time to insert the table containing a row for each field in the database. First create the form element. Select Insert ⇨ Form Field⇨Push Button to add a form element and a normal button to the page. Edit the button's properties to make it a Submit button. You might also change its Value/Label to Update, since that is what it will do.

Once you have created the form element, if you have followed along the earlier exercises, you may want to import the same table you created previously. The goal is to end up with a two-column table. In the left-hand column are field names. The right-hand column contains input boxes for each field. See Figure 17-22, which shows a portion of this form.

The last step is to insert into the middle of the form input element the VBScript that generates the initial value for the field. The procedure is the same for each field:

Click the form field element, using the right mouse button. Select Form Field Properties. Change the name of the field to match the field name. In the Value box, type the following line of code, replacing the generic *FIELDNAME* with the appropriate fieldname:

```
If Not IsEmpty(fp_rs) And Not (fp_rs Is Nothing) Then
    Response.Write CStr(fp_rs("FIELDNAME"))
```

Click OK to return to the Normal view. FrontPage editor displays this code inside the text input box, a somewhat disconcerting indicator that you have put VBScript into the box. But trust me, it works.

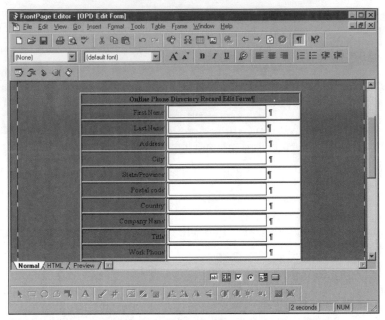

Figure 17-22: The form for editing database records

Repeat this procedure for each form field. When you are finished, you need to create a hidden field to pass along the ContactID, which you do not want the user attempting to edit. To create a hidden field, select the Form Properties, and click the Advanced button. Add a new hidden field, with the name ContactID; assign a value with the same code you used with the other input fields (see Figure 17-23).

Caution FrontPage automatically places hidden fields right after the begin form tag. If you happen to create your database region inside the form (as I learned the hard way the first time I tried this), it will fail because the VBScript command for the hidden field will run before the record set has been instantiated.

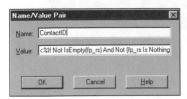

Figure 17-23: Cutting and pasting VBScript code into dialog boxes

You also need to create an Update button to submit the changes to the database. This should be a Submit type button. You may also want to include a standard Reset button. This will restore all fields to their initial value, in case the user changes his or her mind.

When you finish, we need to point the Select button form in the left-hand column to our new editform.asp. Return to the frame set if you are not there already, and click with the right mouse button on the form element in the left-hand frame. Select Form Properties. In the What to Do with Form Results? section, select Send to Other, click the Options button, and designate editform.asp as the program to receive data. Click OK. Click the button next to the Target Frame input box. Insert the name of the editform.asp frame. If you accepted the default frame name when you created the frame set, this frame's name is "main."

Now test the results and compare with Figure 17-24, which shows the form populated with data from Sam Spade's record.

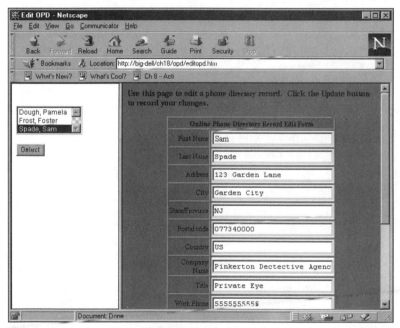

Figure 17-24: Populating the Edit Record form by selecting a name from the list

Creating the Update Query page

The last step in the process is to enable you to update the database with your changes. To do this, you need to create a third ASP page. This page will receive the field input from your edit form, update the database record, and return a confirmation message.

First create a new page and save it as `updateopd.asp`. Select Insert ⇨ Database ⇨ Database Region Wizard, and enter the Data Source Name, **OPD**. Click Next to continue, and enter the following SQL statement:

```
UPDATE Contacts
SET LastName = '%%LastName%%', FirstName='%%FirstName%%',
Address='%%Address%%',
City='%%City%%',
StateOrProvince='%%StateOrProvince%%',
PostalCode='%%PostalCode%%',
Country='%%Country%%',
CompanyName='%%CompanyName%%',
Title='%%Title%%',
WorkPhone='%%WorkPhone%%',
WorkExtension='%%WorkExtension%%',
HomePhone='%%HomePhone%%',
MobilePhone='%%MobilePhone%%',
FaxNumber='%%FaxNumber%%',
EmailName='%%EmailName%%'
WHERE ContactID=%%ContactID%%
```

Caution

Once you add all of the field names to the query, the FrontPage Database Region component expects input for each field. Any fields left blank will generate an error. To resolve this potential problem, you should set the form field validation properties. See Chapter 11 for details on creating forms.

Click Next to proceed to the last wizard dialog box. Designate a query field name. This is required by the wizard but is useless in this case, since the UPDATE statement does not return any values. Consequently, it does not matter which query field name you insert here. Click Finish and save the `updateopd.asp`.

Now return to `editform.asp` and link the form handler to the update query. Click inside the dashed lines of the form element with the right mouse button, and select Form Properties. Select the Send to Other option in the What to Do with Form Results? section of the Form Properties dialog box. Click Options and enter the location of the `updateopd.asp` file in the Action field of the Options dialog box. Check that the Method box contains the word POST. Click OK. Click the Edit button to the right of the Target Frame property, and enter the frame name, **main**, in the Target Setting field of the dialog box. Click OK two times to accept your changes and return to the Editor window. Save your changes.

Now test the update portion of the application. Load the initial HTML frame set. Select a person from the list and click the Select button. In the edit form, try changing the company name. Click Update to record the changes in the database. If all goes well, you should see the message "No Records Returned" in the main window of the frame set.

Editing the default response

Our record editing application is now complete. However, it would be nice to improve the response provided when you update a record, since "No Records Returned," although true enough, sounds like an error message.

This message is supplied by the Database Region component, and to change it requires manually editing the component tag. Switch to the HTML view by clicking the HTML tab. Locate the DatabaseRegionStart Component tag, located near the top of the page. It contains several parameters, one of which reads:

```
s-NoRecordsFound="No Records Returned"
```

Change the text between the quotation marks to a more appropriate response, such as "Record Successfully Updated." You can include HTML tags in this string if you like (FrontPage even converts the tags to their appropriate entity references for you). To test this, try placing a header tag, `<h2>...</h2>`, around the text. Return to the Normal tab view and save the changes.

Inserting field information

Before we test our page again, we are going to make one more improvement on our update confirmation page. It is always reassuring when the database displays some of the information it has updated. Rather than dump all of the data, however, let's select just the name fields.

There are two methods for displaying this information. The best approach is to send another query to the database after the UPDATE statement has executed and return the updated row from the database. If you want to be really sure that the UPDATE statement worked, this is the way to do it. For our purposes, though, we are happy just to give the illusion that the database is working properly. Our plan is to display the information passed to the database from the edit form.

To insert field information from the edit form, do the following:

1. Place the cursor after the end of the "Database: End" text on the updateopd.asp page.

2. Select Insert ⇨ Advanced ⇨ Script to open the Script editor. Select VBScript and check the Run Script on Server check box.

3. Add the following code:

```
Response.Write("Record " & Request.Form("ContactID") & "(" &
Request.Form("LastName") & ", " & Request.Form("FirstName") &
") has been updated.")
```

The command `Request.Form(fieldname)`, where *fieldname* is the name of a form field from the page that calls this script, inserts the value of that form field into the page.

4. Click OK to insert the script into the update page. Save your changes and retest. Now the results should resemble Figure 17-25.

Figure 17-25: The improved edited record confirmation page

Using the Database Connector Wizard

The final section of this chapter discusses the Database Connector Wizard and FrontPage's support for the IDC/HTX method of accessing a database. Prior to the FrontPage 98 release, FrontPage database support was provided by the Database Connector Wizard. This wizard is very similar in operation the Database Region Wizard in FrontPage 98. The difference is that the DCW generates query files using the Internet Database Connection format rather than ASP.

IDC was the initial method Microsoft developed for Internet Information Server (IIS) 1.0 and 2.0 to conduct database transactions. Similar in some ways to ASP, it is not as powerful or flexible. It also requires the use of two separate files for any database transaction. The IDC file contains the actual query information. It in turn references an HTX file that serves as a template for the query response.

You can convert your existing IDC files to ASP format using Microsoft's IDC2ASP utility, available for download from the Microsoft Web site. You can find it at `http://www.microsoft.com/workshop/server/toolbox/toolbox.asp`.

If you have never used IDC, now is not the time to start. It appears to be an outdated technology. ASP is the wave of the future—or at least the present, as of the writing of this book. One sign of this shift is the fact that the FrontPage Database Connector Wizard, although it still installs with the 98 version, does not appear in the list of new file templates. It is, however, still associated by default with `.idc` files in the FrontPage Web settings. In effect, this means that FrontPage enables users who have existing IDC and HTX files to edit them using this wizard, but it is difficult to create a new IDC file.

If you really want to create an IDC file, you can do so simply by creating a blank text file, saving it with an `.idc` extension, and then using it to launch the Database Connector Wizard.

Editing an IDC file

From FrontPage editor, locate and double-click your IDC file. Explorer launches the Database Connector Wizard. In the initial dialog box, you can edit or insert a new data source name, and you can indicate any required username and password information. You also designate the HTX results page to be used from this dialog box. See Figure 17-26.

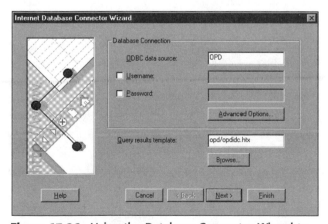

Figure 17-26: Using the Database Connector Wizard to create or edit an IDC page

Click the Browse button to locate the appropriate file or type its name in the field provided. Click the Advanced Options to configure the ODBC connection to your liking—use of these options is, well, optional. Figure 17-27 shows the first tab of this dialog box. Click OK when you are satisfied with your changes to the Advanced Options. Click Next to proceed with the wizard.

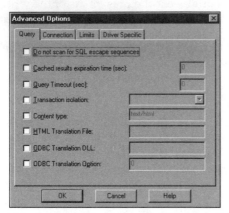

Figure 17-27: The Advanced Options dialog box in the Database Connector Wizard

The next screen allows you to edit your SQL statement or to insert a new SQL statement. You can add multiple SQL calls to the same IDC file. You just need to create an equivalent number of detail sections in your HTX results page. Click Next to continue when you have edited the SQL to your liking.

In the following dialog box, you can add configuration parameters to your IDC file to control various aspects of your query. Examples of parameter directives include:

✦ **MaxRecords**—This specifies the maximum number of records to return.

✦ **RequiredParameters**—This specifies a list of required fields by field name.

✦ **DefaultParameters**—This designates default values for fields with empty values.

✦ **Expires**—This determines the lifetime of cached data in seconds. If it is not set, data is not cached.

To add a parameter, click the Add button and enter the parameter name and associated value. Select an existing parameter and click Modify to edit that parameter's name or value. Select a parameter and click Remove to delete a parameter.

When you are ready, click Finish to save your changes to the IDC file.

Editing the HTX Results page

You can also use FrontPage 98 to edit your HTX results page. An HTX page is basically a standard HTML page plus some special HTML-like code designed for database functions.

To edit your HTX file, open it in FrontPage Editor. You can do this either by selecting File ➪ Open from within Editor or by double-clicking the HTX file icon in FrontPage Explorer. When you open this file, Editor detects the fact that it is dealing with an HTX file, and it adds a new Database menu item to the Edit menu. This item enables you to add custom HTML to the HTX file.

The detail section

The detail section of the HTX file defines the space in which you display record set information from the database query. It consists of a matched set of tags, <%begindetail%> and <%enddetail%>. These are represented as red half-brackets in Editor's Normal tab. Keep in mind that these tags do not display any database information. They simply define the space in which to display information. To define a detail section, place the cursor where you want the section to be and select Edit ➪ Database ➪ Detail Section.

Database column values

This item inserts values from a named database column. To insert a field value into a table cell, for instance, place the cursor in the cell and select Edit ➪ Database ➪ Database Column Values. Type the name of the column and click OK. Editor inserts a tag containing the name of the column surrounded by percentage signs and normal tag brackets. This tag is replaced by the corresponding row set values when the database query is performed.

IDC parameter values

Use this tag to insert form field information from the page that calls this IDC/HTX file. To insert a form field value, select Edit ➪ Database ➪ IDC Parameter Values. Type the name of the form field whose value you want to display. Click OK. The field name is displayed in Editor encompassed by percentage signs and tab brackets. This tag is replaced with the field value when the file is loaded from the Web server.

Conditional operators: if-then and else

You can use these conditional operators to build simple rules into the display of data in your HTX file. Select Edit ➪ Database ➪ If-Then Conditional Section. Select the terms and values you wish to compare, using the simple dialog box seen in Figure 17-28. Select the Else Conditional item to insert the else directive.

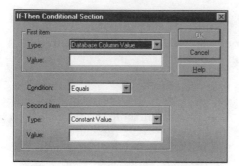

Figure 17-28: The dialog box used to insert conditional code into your HTX file

This mechanism allows you to check the state of several kinds of variables, including:

✦ Database column values

✦ Parameter values

✦ Constants

✦ Current record number

✦ Maximum record number

✦ HTTP variables (a.k.a. CGI environment variables)

Once you have built and edited your IDC and HTX pages, you use them much as we have used the ASP file described in detail throughout this chapter.

Taking the Next Step

This chapter has introduced you to the joys (and pains) of developing database applications using FrontPage 98's support for Active Server Pages. You have created examples of database queries, linking to detail views, searching, adding new records, and editing existing ones. Quite an accomplishment for one chapter, I'd say.

This is the last of the programming chapters. In the final part of this book, we describe how you can use FrontPage as part of a development or maintenance project, and what systems administrators need to know to integrate FrontPage into their Web server environment.

✦   ✦   ✦

Administering and Maintaining Your Site

Managing and Publishing Your Web Project

This chapter looks at the ways FrontPage 98 can assist you in managing a Web project. Whether you are working on your own or as part of a larger development team, you can profit from the many FrontPage features designed to help your project run smoothly. The chapter covers several common scenarios for developing, publishing, and maintaining a project using FrontPage. It demonstrates the use of the Explorer Tasks view, and it explains useful update features such as global spell checking, search and replace, link verification, and link recalculations. It also introduces you to the Project Web template included with FrontPage 98, and it illustrates powerful features that allow you to customize the FrontPage environment to suit the needs of your project.

Managing a Web Project

In the last three or four years, the sum total of Web development talent and expertise has grown exponentially, in step with the feverish pace of increasingly sophisticated Web projects. Whereas a few years ago, a single person could have been counted on to design, develop, and maintain a typical Web site, now it takes a full team of people. Larger, more complex projects also mean an increased need for tools that help keep a project running smoothly. FrontPage has been designed to serve the needs of everything from small-business Web site development to large, coordinated projects in multidepartment corporations.

Whether your Web project involves one or one hundred developers, FrontPage 98 includes several features designed to help manage your project. These include:

✦ A multiuser task list

✦ Web error-checking tools

✦ A Project Web template

✦ Multilevel access control

✦ One-button publishing

✦ A fully customizable environment

This chapter looks at those features that serve the needs of the development team. Chapter 19 describes additional FrontPage features that are typically set up and administered by systems administrators rather than developers (recognizing, of course, that in smaller projects, the same person may perform these roles).

Note See Chapter 19, "Server Administration," for information on configuring the FrontPage settings, establishing access permissions, and using version control software.

Exploring the Development Environment

When you are preparing to begin your Web project, one of the first questions you must consider is where you plan to build your project and how you will get the project from its development location to its "live" site. How you set up your development environment depends on a number of circumstances, including the size of the project, the availability of resources, and the number and location of project team members. FrontPage accommodates any number of development approaches. Some of the more common methods are outlined in the course of this chapter.

Developing a "live" site

Several years ago, it was common wisdom in the software development world that you built your product, tested it thoroughly, and only released it when you were relatively confident that it was as close to error-free as possible. The Internet has changed all that. In part because of the increasing pressure to ship product quickly and also in part because of the ease with which Web projects can be updated, it is now fairly common to release products in "beta" stage (a euphemism for incomplete). Similarly, Web sites often do not hesitate to announce their "under construction" areas.

In such an atmosphere, it is not uncommon to find people developing their "live" Web site directly. In some ways, FrontPage invites this kind of updating, since it is quite easy to open a remote Web in FrontPage and make and save changes directly back to the remote server. Under any circumstances this is easier than having to make a change and then at some later point copying it to a live site.

Of course making changes directly to a live Web site is also risky. You can easily introduce an error that you may not immediately catch. You may also update a page that someone is accessing, causing them some consternation should they happen to reload the page and find it changed. Live updating tends to be most feasible if you are working on a small project, if there is no need for one or more people to authorize changes before they appear in public, and if traffic on the Web site is low. Even under these circumstances, it is more expedient than recommended to operate this way.

Maintaining a "mirror" development site

A much better approach for developing and updating a Web site is to maintain a copy of the site on a development server that is not "live." FrontPage also makes it easy to set up and maintain a mirrored development live site. If you are building primarily HTML pages, without a lot of sophisticated server-side programming, you can use the Microsoft Personal Web Server for your local development Web server and use the Publish feature in Explorer to copy your local Web to a remote server when it is ready to "go live." The first time you publish your Web, all pages are published. Subsequently, you have the option of publishing all pages or just those that have been updated.

Maintaining multiple development servers

If you are managing a multifaceted Web project, such as the development of a corporate intranet, you may find it convenient to divide the development task among several groups, each of which is responsible for a particular portion of the content. In this scenario, it makes sense to have each group maintain its own development version of the content, and then implement a method for updating each portion. Of course, if each group is also maintaining its own live server, then they can use the method described in the previous example. A company, however, will often maintain a single, corporate-level Web server (partly to oversee the content, partly because departments do not always have the technical resources to maintain their own servers). In such a case, there needs to be a method of updating this central, live site. Two general models for doing this are:

✦ Create multiple sub-Webs on the main server, and assign each group the authority to update its sub-Web.

✦ Designate a central administrator (or administrative group) with full access to each development server, and task that person or group with updating all content on the live server.

Managing Tasks

FrontPage 98 Explorer includes a handy Tasks view where you can keep track of development tasks that need doing on your Web. This feature is neither a full-blown project management tool nor an incident tracking system, but for average needs, it provides a convenient way to record and keep track of project tasks that need doing.

The Explorer Tasks view in FrontPage 98 replaces the To Do list feature in FrontPage 97. The functionality is largely the same, although the user interface has been somewhat improved.

To illustrate the use of the Tasks view, we create a new Project Web to help coordinate the Pedigree Pets Web project. Later in the chapter we look at some of the specifics of how to use the Project Web as part of managing your Web project. For the time being, though, the Project Web just serves as an example of a Web that needs some tasks performed.

To create a new Project Web, open FrontPage Explorer and select New ➪ FrontPage Web. In the New FrontPage Web dialog box, first select the From Wizard or Template option and choose the Project Web template. Then create a name for your Project Web (such as "projectweb"). Click OK to create the default Project view, as shown in Figure 18-1.

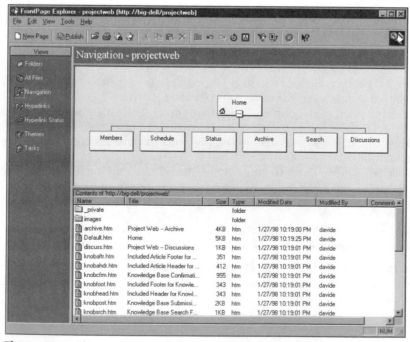

Figure 18-1: The Navigation view of the default Project Web, teeming with tasks to do

Still in Explorer, select Tasks view to see if there are any tasks awaiting you in the Project Web. There aren't. The Tasks view list (see Figure 18-2) is empty, which means that we have to start by adding some tasks.

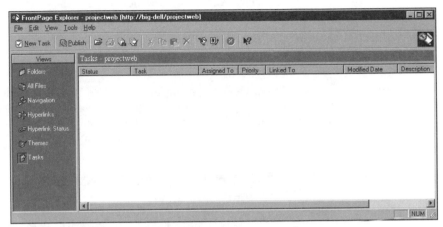

Figure 18-2: The Tasks view awaiting your command

Adding a task

There are two general methods for adding tasks to the Tasks view.

Adding a task from Explorer

From Explorer, you can add a new task directly from the Tasks view list:

1. Select File ➪ New ➪ Task, click the New Task icon in the main toolbar, or use the Ctrl+T key combination to open the New Task dialog box illustrated in Figure 18-3.

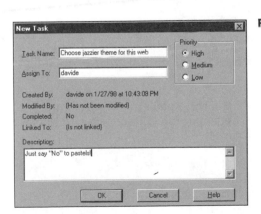

Figure 18-3: The New Task dialog box

2. Give the Task a name (type **Choose jazzier theme for this Web** for this task).

3. Designate its priority, selecting the High, Medium, or Low option (select High for this task).

4. Assign the task to an appropriate Web team member (by default the task is assigned to the current user).

5. Add helpful remarks in the Description text box.

6. Click OK to add the task.

The task is duly added to the Tasks view list, as shown in Figure 18-4. It is assigned a status of "Not Started" and marked with a red dot, signaling that it needs doing. Note that a task added in this fashion is not linked to a particular page. Selecting this task to work on does not initiate any action within FrontPage.

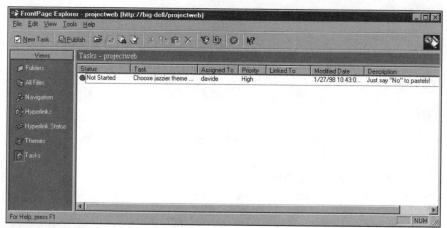

Figure 18-4: Oh look, a new task that needs doing!

Adding a task from Editor

It is appropriate to add general-purpose tasks like the one just illustrated from Explorer. Many tasks you need to perform, however, are associated with a particular page in your Web. For these, it is best to add the task from within Editor with the page open.

To illustrate this procedure, first open the default home page in the Project Web we created earlier. To launch the home page in Editor, switch to Navigator view in Explorer, and double-click the Home Page box.

To add a new task that is linked to the home page:

1. Make the home page the current page in Editor.

2. Select Edit ➪ Add Task.

3. Complete the New Task dialog box as described in the previous section. Be certain that the task you create is pertinent to the current page.

4. Click OK to add the new task. Note that the Linked To column in the Tasks view list for this item includes a reference to the home page.

Adjusting the Tasks view list

Items in the Tasks view list can be sorted on any of the list columns: Status, Task, Assigned To, Priority, Linked To, Modified Date, and Description. Typically, you would sort on the Assigned To column to find the tasks that you are responsible for completing, and perhaps on Priority to find the tasks that really need your attention. To sort on a given column, click the gray column heading once. Clicking a column heading a second time sorts the list in reverse order.

You can also adjust the width of columns. To resize a column, place the cursor on the vertical line between two column headers. The cursor changes to a solid vertical line with arrows pointing left and right. Drag with the mouse to lengthen or shorten the selected columns (OK, so one column lengthens and the other shortens).

Viewing, modifying, or deleting tasks

To view or modify the details or properties of a task, simply double-click that item in the Tasks view list. Alternatively, select a task, and select Edit ⇨ Properties. Yet another method is to click the item with the right mouse button and select Edit Task from the pop-up menu.

Once in the Task Details dialog box, make any desired changes to the task properties, and click OK to save your modifications.

To delete a task, select the task to delete, and then select Edit ⇨ Delete from the Tasks view in Explorer. Or click the task with the right mouse button and select Delete from the pop-up menu.

Completing tasks

Sooner or later, after you have generated enough new tasks to do, the time arrives when you need to do some of the tasks. How you complete a task depends on whether or not the task is linked to a particular page. If you have a general-purpose task, such as the first task we created, simply perform the task. In our case, we select the Themes view in Explorer and locate a jazzier theme. (The Blueprint theme seems appropriate for a Project Web.)

Doing tasks linked to a page

If your task is linked to a particular page, you can use the Tasks view to launch the page and get you started on the task.

Tasks can also be linked to images and other types of files besides Web pages. Selecting the Do Task button for these tasks similarly launches the linked object.

1. Select Tasks view from Explorer.

2. Double-click the task to perform. This opens the Task Details dialog box (which resembles the New Task dialog box).

3. If the task is linked to an object, the Task Details dialog box includes a Do Task button in the lower-left corner. (Tasks that are not linked do not have this button.)

4. Click the Do Task button to launch the page linked to this task.

5. Perform the task.

6. When you have completed your work, select File⇨Save. This initiates a prompt asking if you wish to mark the task as completed. Answer appropriately. If you answer no, FrontPage updates the status of the task to "In Progress." If you answer yes, the task is marked "Completed," and the status button is changed from red to green.

Marking a task completed

Tasks completed using the Do Task button are updated automatically as described in the previous section. You can also manually update the status of a task (although you cannot change the status to "In Progress"). To mark a task completed, select the task from the Tasks view list in Explorer. Select Edit⇨Mark Task Complete. Alternatively, click the task with the right mouse button and select Mark Complete from the pop-up menu.

Once a task is marked completed, it cannot be reopened. All properties of the task, with the exception of the description, become read-only.

Viewing completed tasks and history

When the Tasks view list is refreshed after a task has been marked completed, that task is removed from the view of active tasks. To view completed tasks, use the Task History function.

To view completed tasks, select View⇨Task History from the Tasks view in Explorer. As long as the Task History option is checked in this menu, completed tasks remain visible. To hide completed tasks, select View⇨Task History again to uncheck the menu item. The Task History function can also be accessed by clicking the Tasks view window with the right mouse button and selecting Task History from the pop-up menu.

Checking Your Web for Errors

Now that you know how to create and complete the tasks you must perform before publishing your Web, it's time to examine some of the more common tasks you are likely to perform before initially publishing a Web. One of the truisms of the Web is that it encourages the publishing of unfinished work. This is in part because of an assumption that it is easy to make corrections and partly the result of the breakneck speed of all development on the Internet. At any rate, correcting errors to the content or functionality of a Web site is relatively easy, and a tool like FrontPage makes it even easier.

The problem, typically, is how to identify errors. Checking each page by hand is time consuming and monotonous. You can also rely on users to find problems and report them. However, this is not an especially predictable method for performing quality control, nor does it foster a high degree of confidence in your users. Fortunately, FrontPage includes some simple utilities to help simplify the task of checking for and correcting errors.

The Editor's spell checker

You can check the spelling of your Web pages on a per-page or a per-Web basis. To check the spelling on a given page, open the page in Editor and select Tools ⇨ Spelling from the menu bar. The Editor spell checker is relatively basic. You can check the spell of the entire document or of selected text. To illustrate the spell checker features, we have modified our Web Project Status page slightly, by removing o's from several words.

To find and correct misspellings using Editor, open the page to check in Editor and select Tools ⇨ Check Spelling. The results of the spell check are shown in Figure 18-5.

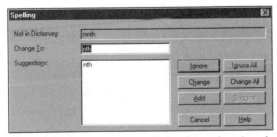

Figure 18-5: The Spelling dialog box, showing that the spell checker may not always offer you the perfect solution to your typos

If the spell checker finds a word not currently in its dictionary, it opens a dialog box with the unknown word in the Not in Dictionary text box. There are several ways to deal with an unrecognized word, as follows:

✦ **Suggest**—Includes a list of close matches on the unknown word. Click a suggested word to put it into the Change To text box. Double-click the suggested word to use it in place of the currently selected unknown word. To extend the list of suggestions, first enter a word into the Change To text box, either by selecting a word from the Suggestion list or by typing in a new word. Then click the Suggest button to generate a new list of suggestions.

✦ **Ignore**—Click Ignore to leave the word as is and continue to check spelling.

✦ **Change**—Click Change to replace the current word with the word currently displayed in the Change To text box.

✦ **Add**—Click Add to add the currently unknown word to the FrontPage word dictionary. FrontPage does not have a provision for creating multiple Custom Dictionaries.

✦ **Ignore All**—Click Ignore All to leave the word as is and ignore all subsequent appearances of the same word.

✦ **Change All**—Click Change All to change every instance of the currently misspelled word on this Web page to the value in the Change To text box.

Spell checking with Explorer

In addition to the spell checker in Editor, you can also use Explorer to check the spelling of several documents at once. In addition, if you choose, this mechanism can add a To Do list item for each misspelled word.

To perform a multipage spell check:

1. Open the Web to be checked in Explorer.

2. To check the spelling of selected Web pages, switch to Folder or All Files view and use the Shift key and the mouse to select a range of pages, or the Control key and the mouse to select specified pages.

3. Select Tools ⇨ Spelling.

4. In the Spelling dialog box, select All Pages or Selected Pages (see Figure 18-6). Note that if you have not selected any pages, the Selected Pages option is not available.

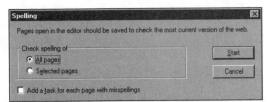

Figure 18-6: The Explorer's spelling options

5. If you would like to record any spelling errors in the To Do list, check the Add a Task for Each Page with Misspellings check box.

6. Click Start. If you have checked the Add a Task for Each Page with Misspellings option, FrontPage checks the page and, if it finds any misspelled words, adds a "Fix misspelled words" task to the list.

7. To view your new task, switch to Tasks view, select the newly added task, and click Do Task. FrontPage opens the Task Details dialog box (see Figure 18-7, which includes a list of all misspelled words in the Description text box).

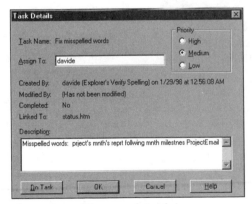

Figure 18-7: More work to do!

8. Select Do Task to open the offending pages in Editor and begin checking errors. At this point FrontPage automatically invokes Editor's spell checker and proceeds as previously described for correcting spelling in Editor.

9. When you have completed the task (or when you tire of correcting spelling errors, whichever comes first), select File ⇨ Save to update the file with your changes. FrontPage prompts you as to whether or not to mark the task as completed.

If you have not elected to have the spelling error recorded in the To Do list, FrontPage uses a different mechanism for alerting you to the fact that misspelled words have been detected. As shown in Figure 18-8, FrontPage lists all pages with misspellings in the Spelling dialog box. From here, you can elect to edit the pages directly by double-clicking an item or by selecting the item and clicking the Edit Page button. Alternatively, you can add items selectively to the task list and worry about them later. To do so, select one item at a time and click the Add Task button. If you click Close without having first either added the errors to a task or corrected them, no record of the errors is kept.

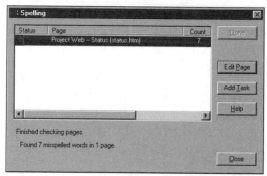

Figure 18-8: The Spelling dialog box, alerting you to the presence of spelling problems on the indicated Web page

Using Editor's thesaurus

In addition to checking spelling in Editor, you can also find synonyms for words using the built-in thesaurus. This function is only available within Editor. To use the thesaurus, select Tools ➪ Thesaurus. The thesaurus looks up the next word in the document and provides a list of alternatives, as illustrated in Figure 18-9. Click the Replace button to substitute the currently looked-up word with a selected word. Click the Look Up button to look up synonyms for the currently selected word. Use the Previous button to back up through a series of look-ups.

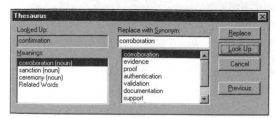

Figure 18-9: Checking the thesaurus for synonyms of confirmation

Using find and replace

It is often the case that you need to make global substitutions of words or phrases in your Web. As with spell checking, text replacements can be performed on a per-file basis or across an entire Web. As with spell checking, too, the replacements can be performed immediately or relegated to a task for later processing.

The Editor's Find feature

To perform an interactive search for a word or string of text, use the Find feature. If you are searching in a single page, open the page in Editor. Select Edit ➪ Find and type the search string into the Find What text box of the Find dialog box, shown in Figure 18-10.

Figure 18-10: Searching for knowledge using the Find dialog box in Editor

You can search from the top of the page down or from the bottom up by selecting either the Up or Down radio button. You can elect to find only whole words. By default, performing a find on the word "know" would match "know," "knows," "knowing," "knowledge," and "unbeknownst" (among other things). In addition, you can limit your find to exact matches on lower- and uppercase. By default, Find is not case-sensitive.

When you have designated the Find criteria, click Find Next. The cursor advances to the next occurrence of the string and selects it. You can click the page and make changes. The Find dialog box remains open so that you can find all occurrences of the string, one at a time. This is the best way to perform a case-by-case substitution.

Explorer's Find feature

Finding text across multiple files in your Web is done using a similar process from Explorer. Open the Web you wish to search in Explorer. If you only want to search a subset of the pages in the Web, select those pages in either Folder or All Files view. Select Tools ➪ Find. Explorer's Find In FrontPage Web dialog box, shown in Figure 18-11, is very similar to that of Editor's. The chief difference is the option to search selected files or all files for the string in question. Note that the option to search selected files is disabled if no files are currently selected.

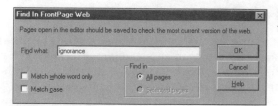

Figure 18-11: The dialog box for Explorer's Find feature

Rather than go straight to matching text when you click OK, Explorer's Find feature creates a list of matching occurrences such as the one shown in Figure 18-12. Matches are listed per page. If you select a page and click Edit Page, Explorer opens the page in Editor and calls Editor's Find function to locate the first instance of the text. If you click Add Task, Explorer saves the find in your Tasks view list for later processing.

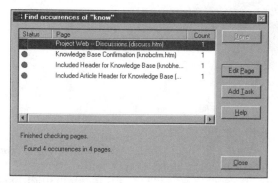

Figure 18-12: Explorer has found four pages in the "know" in the Project Web.

Replacing in Editor

Rather than performing a case-by-case find, you can use the Replace feature to replace occurrences of a text string automatically without cycling through your Web pages. Just be sure when performing a global replacement, especially on more than one file, that you have sufficiently limited your find (for example, globally replacing "the" with "a" is probably not a good idea, since you are likely to change words like "other" to "oar" and so forth). To replace a string in a single Web page, open the page in Editor and select Edit⇨Replace. Type the string to find in the Find What text box and the replacement text in the Replace With text box as shown in Figure 18-13.

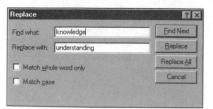

Figure 18-13: Using FrontPage Editor, you can replace "knowledge" with "understanding"—if only it worked on people, too!

You have the following options to help you control the replace action:

✦ **Find Next:** Select this button to perform a find only—with no replacement. This is exactly the same action as using the Find function previously described. Typically, this option would be used in conjunction with the Replace option, allowing you to first locate the string before deciding whether to perform the replacement or not.

✦ **Replace:** This option performs an automatic replacement of the next occurrence of the text.

✦ **Replace All:** Do you feel lucky? Go ahead, replace every occurrence of the string with a single click.

Replacing in Explorer

The Replace feature in Explorer is used to perform text replacements over multiple pages in a Web. It works just like Editor's Find feature. To perform a multipage replace, first open the Web in either view of Explorer, save all open pages, and select Tools ➪ Replace. Type the text to find in the Find What text box and the replacement text in the Replace With text box. Indicate whether you want to search selected pages only or all Web pages. Designate any other options as for the Find feature, and click OK. Explorer produces a list of pages containing matches. Here, as with the multipage find, you can opt to edit a given page immediately by selecting Edit Page or defer the operation by selecting Add Task.

Working with links

Both of the preceding functions, the spell checker and the text replacement feature, are standard word processing features. They provide error checking on the actual content of your Web pages. However, one of the more important and irksome tasks of checking your Web is to make certain that all hyperlinks actually go where they are intended to go. (Anyone who has never encountered a broken link on a Web page is hereby granted permission to skip this section.) FrontPage can perform this task automatically. It also monitors your pages and updates any affected links anytime you move or rename a file.

To illustrate the process of verifying links, we use the Project Web, which conveniently comes with several links already broken.

Hyperlink Status view

To check the status of the hyperlinks in your Web, open the Web in Explorer and select the Hyperlink Status view. By default, internal hyperlinks are automatically verified and any problems are displayed in the Hyperlink Status list marked with a red bullet and the word "Broken." External links are not initially checked and so are marked with a yellow bullet and the word "Unknown." (Note that the Unknown designation does not necessarily mean that FrontPage cannot verify the link. More typically it means FrontPage has not yet checked the link at all. See Figure 18-14.)

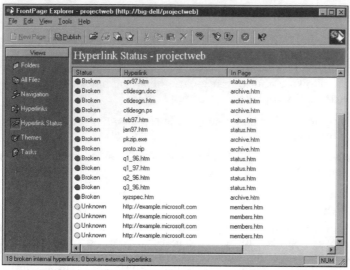

Figure 18-14: Results of an initial check for broken links in the Project Web. Note the as-yet unknown external links.

By default, Hyperlink Status displays only broken and unknown links. You can also display all hyperlinks (this is particularly helpful if your ego is feeling bruised by the number of broken links in your Web). To show all hyperlinks, select View ➪ Show All Hyperlinks. Select this command again to turn off the Show All Hyperlinks option. You can also sort items in the Hyperlink Status list by clicking one of the available column headers: Status, Hyperlink, and In Page.

Verifying external links

In order to check external links, you need to be connected to the Internet, so if you have a dial-up account, you should connect to it before proceeding. Next select Tools ➪ Verify Hyperlinks. FrontPage attempts to check all external links. To interrupt the process, click the Stop icon in the toolbar. (If you interrupt the verification process, it will resume where it left off the next time you try.) The Verify Hyperlinks dialog box is shown in Figure 18-15.

Tip

You can verify individual hyperlinks by clicking the link in question with the right mouse button and selecting Verify from the pop-up menu.

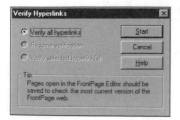

Figure 18-15: The Verify Hyperlinks dialog box

Editing links

Of course locating broken links is only half the battle. The real power of the Hyperlink Status view and the Verify command lies in helping you repair any damage you uncover. For each broken link you have the following options:

✦ **Edit Link:** This allows you to fix the link directly, as described in more detail in the remainder of this section.

✦ **Edit Page:** This takes you to the page, where you can edit the link and/or change the text associated with the link.

✦ **Add Task:** As in earlier error-checking functions, you can defer corrections until a later time by adding the task to the task list.

Editing hyperlinks

To edit a broken link, switch to Hyperlink Status view and double-click a link or click a hyperlink with the right mouse button and select Edit Hyperlink. This opens the dialog box shown in Figure 18-16.

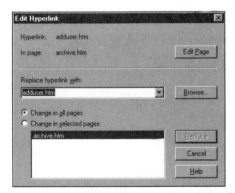

Figure 18-16: The Edit Hyperlink dialog box

You can type the name of the correct link in the Replace Hyperlink With text box or browse within the current Web or anywhere on the World Wide Web to locate the link you want. (In practice, the Browse feature is probably more useful for locating external links than internal ones, since the internal ones may not be linked to anything that would allow you to find them easily. Still this mechanism does allow you to preview the page in question and assure yourself that it exists.) Once you have identified the new link, you can elect to update this link text in all of your Web pages or just selected ones. Click Replace to update the link and return to the Verify Hyperlinks dialog box.

Alternatively, you can click the Edit Page button. This opens the page containing the broken link in Editor and highlights the hyperlink in question.

A final alternative is to postpone any action on the broken link by adding a task to the task list. This is best done by clicking the broken link in Hyperlink Status view and selecting Add Task from the pop-up menu.

If the new hyperlink is a valid internal link, it disappears from the list. External links remain, marked with a yellow light and Unknown status until they are independently verified.

Note

For some reason external hyperlinks remain in the default display list even after they are verified and marked OK.

Recalculating links

While we are speaking of fixing links, it is worth mentioning that FrontPage also automatically updates links whenever you make a change to a filename in your Web. Let's use `archive.htm` as an example.

Imagine that you have decided to rename the archive page "Project Library." You also want to rename the file `library.htm`. Open the Project Web in Explorer and switch to Folder or All Files view. Select `archive.htm` and rename it **library.htm**. When you attempt this change, FrontPage prompts you with the message shown in Figure 18-17, alerting you to the fact that there is one hyperlink in your Web to the old filename and offering to update it with the new filename. This is an offer you cannot refuse.

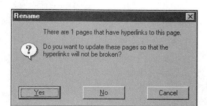

Figure 18-17: FrontPage automatically updates links to files whose names have changed

Under most circumstances, FrontPage automatically recalculates hyperlinks. You can also update links on the current Web manually, using the Recalculate Links command. In Explorer, select Tools ➪ Recalculate Hyperlinks. You are warned that this process could take several minutes, depending on the size of the Web and the bandwidth between you and the server.

Publishing Your Web

The time has come to publish your Web to your viewing audience. First let's be clear about what we mean by "publishing" a Web. This is really only an important-sounding way of saying that you are going to make a copy of your Web on a Web server.

FrontPage can both simplify the publishing task and add administrative controls so that you can manage who has publishing permissions for any given Web on a Web server. FrontPage also simplifies the task of updating a Web on a Web server. For those new to Web development, the standard method of transferring files to a remote Web server is to use a file transfer protocol (FTP) application.

Note

If you are not an Internet whiz, learning FTP may not be high on your list of priorities. Even if you do know how to use FTP, having to use separate applications to develop and publish your Web pages can add time and hassle to the development process.

Publishing options

There are various ways that you can publish information using FrontPage. The typical scenario is one in which you publish the Web from the development Web on a local server to a remote Web server somewhere on the Internet or your company intranet. The following sections cover the possibilities.

Getting ready to publish

In order to publish your Web:

✦ You need your development computer (that is, the computer you have used to develop your Web) connected to the Internet, either on a dedicated line or via a dial-up connection.

✦ You also need access to a Web server. If you are publishing on your own Web server—for example, using the Personal Web Server that comes as part of the Bonus Pack that accompanies FrontPage 98—you may only need to ensure that you have properly installed the PWS.

✦ If you are publishing on an intranet, you need to have an access password to a remote Web server somewhere on your network.

✦ If you are publishing on an intranet, that is, an internal network based on Internet technologies, your development computer is probably on the same network with your Web server.

The most common scenario, however, involves publishing Webs on a server owned and maintained by an external party, such as a Web-hosting service. An external host may or may not directly support the use of FrontPage, a fact that affects the set of FrontPage features you can use.

Note

FrontPage tends to speak interchangeably about copying a Web to a new location and publishing the Web.

You can use the Publish FrontPage Web command in Explorer to access a current list of hosting services that support FrontPage. Select File ⇨ Publish FrontPage Web, and click the More Webs button. This opens the Publish FrontPage Web dialog box. Click the large button with an Internet Explorer icon. This launches your default Web browser and opens the URL on Microsoft's Web site that maintains a list of "authorized" FrontPage hosting services. You can visit this address on your own at `microsoft.saltmine.com/frontpage/wpp/list/`.

To publish your Web to an already-existing site, select File ⇨ Publish FrontPage Web or click the Publish button on the toolbar. Type the URL of the site in the text box provided. Include the name of the Web on the destination site. If you are publishing your Web to a secure server running SSL (secure socket layers), check the box to that effect before proceeding.

If you are publishing the root Web of your current server, you can also publish all of the sub-Webs, or child Webs, of the root at the same time.

Publishing to an established server

Let's start with the simplest scenario. You have created your Web locally and are now ready to publish it to a server where you have already established an account. It might be that you are publishing to an intranet or Internet server that is maintained internally at your place of work. Or perhaps you already have an account with a Web-hosting service that has set you up with a FrontPage account.

To publish your Web under these circumstances requires that you be armed with the following information, all of which should be provided to you by the administrator of the Web server:

✦ **The Internet address of the Web host computer**— This may be a domain name, such as `www.myserver.com`, or an IP number in the form *xxx.xxx.xxx.xxx*, where each set of *x*'s represents a number from 1 to 255.

✦ **A username and password**—These are maintained by FrontPage and allow you to gain access to the remote Web in order to update it.

Once you have this information, follow these steps to publish or update your Web:

1. Connect to the Internet (or intranet) if you have not already done so.

2. Open the Web you are going to publish in Explorer.

3. Make sure that you have saved all files by selecting File ⇨ Save All in Editor.

4. In Explorer, select File ⇨ Publish FrontPage Web or click the Publish icon.

5. In the Publish FrontPage Web dialog box (see Figure 18-18), type the name of the Web server, such as `www.myserver.com`, into the Destination text box. Identify the name of the Web—for example, **mynewweb**. Typically the name of the local version suffices unless you prefer some method of distinguishing your local development version from the remotely accessible, production version. Click OK to continue.

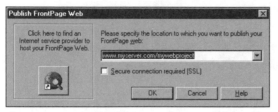

Figure 18-18: Publishing a Web to myserver

6. If you are publishing the root Web of your local server, you have the option of copying all sub-Webs, or child Webs, at the same time. To copy child Webs, check Include Child Webs in the Publish dialog box.

7. If you have already published this Web, you are presented with a Publish dialog box initially, rather than the Publish FrontPage Web dialog box. To select an alternate Web as the destination, click the More Webs button, and designate a new option. You can also indicate whether to update only those pages that have changed since the last time the Web was published, or to update all files.

8. What happens next depends on whether or not the Web to which you are publishing uses passwords to control access and whether or not it is FrontPage-enabled. If the server is FrontPage-enabled and uses passwords, you are prompted for your username and password. Supply these in the respective text boxes. If you are creating this Web, you may need administrator-level access. Otherwise, you need only author-level access. If no passwords are required, FrontPage begins to copy your files.

9. If your server is not FrontPage-enabled but is password-protected, the Web Publishing Wizard walks you through the steps necessary to transfer your pages to the server.

As FrontPage publishes your Web, you can watch the status of the updates in Explorer's status bar (select View ➪ Status Bar to show the status bar if it is not currently visible). When publishing is complete, FrontPage displays a message box announcing its successful updating.

Tip

You should always double-check to see that your Web published as you intended. Using your favorite Web browser, access the newly created Web. Its URL is `www.myserver.com/mynewweb`.

Establishing a Web-hosting account

One of the signs that FrontPage is catching on as a development tool is the growing number of facilities that offer FrontPage as a method of publishing and updating Web sites. The information in this section and the accompanying sidebar tells you how to go about setting up an account and brings up some important issues that bear looking at (and that you can probably resolve) before you proceed.

To set up an account:

1. Establish the account.

2. Obtain access information.

3. Connect to the Internet (if necessary).

4. Access your Web-host account.

5. Publish your Web.

The access information you need consists of the Internet address, that is, the domain name, of the Web host, and a username and password that you use to obtain access to your Web-server directories. When you are ready to publish, first make sure that you are connected to the Internet. If you are connecting via dial-up, connect to your Internet access provider.

Note

How do you know if you are connected? There are lots of ways to tell. One of the easiest is to start your favorite Web browser and see if it connects to Web sites. If it does, you are golden.

The process of publishing your Web is slightly different if your Web server is not set up with direct support for FrontPage. (See Chapter 19 for an explanation of adding the FrontPage server extensions to a Web server and Appendix C for installation instructions.) Keep in mind that although you can publish your Web pages to any server where you have an account, your Web cannot necessarily make use of all of FrontPage's component (WebBot) functionality. Component functionality relies on the presence of the FrontPage server extensions.

New in 98

As mentioned in earlier chapters, what used to be called WebBots in FrontPage 97 are now referred to as components in FrontPage 98. Their HTML codes and names are identical. So if you're familiar with the WebBot feature of previous releases of FrontPage, you're already familiar with components.

A few things to consider

Your hardest decision in setting up a Web site is selecting a provider. Prices and services vary considerably. If you plan to use FrontPage exclusively, one of your main considerations is the level of FrontPage support provided. A number of providers have added FrontPage server extensions because of customer demand but are not providing technical support for FrontPage. The list of providers with qualified, experienced support and technical staff to assist you with FrontPage questions is much smaller. You pay for the privilege, but if your budget permits it, you will not be sorry.

Another consideration is whether of not you need Internet access in addition to Web hosting. What is the difference? In order to publish your Web, you need to be able to connect your development computer to the Internet. If you happen to work for a company or institution whose internal network is directly connected to the Internet, then you have no problem. If you are operating from home or a small office, you probably have a dial-up connection to the Internet, via analog modem or possibly ISDN.

Once you are connected to the Internet, you can publish your Web pages to any server where you have an account. Consequently, if you already have an Internet service provider (ISP) for dial-up access, you do not need to obtain dial-up access from your FrontPage hosting service. All you need is a Web account on their server that allows you to post your pages. If you do not yet have dial-up access, or if you prefer to have multiple dial-up accounts (not a bad idea if you can afford it, particularly if you cannot afford to have your dial-up account busy when you need to publish your pages), then you may find some companies offering the full line of access services at reasonable prices.

Selecting a provider

First, some definitions. In the beginning there were only Internet access providers (IAPs), also known as Internet service providers (ISPs). An ISP offers its customers connectivity to the Internet first and foremost. Second, most ISP accounts come with e-mail, including some amount of online storage space for e-mail messages. Increasingly, ISPs have offered their customers other kinds of space as well, principally Web site space (and sometimes storage for anonymous FTP as well). Typically, however (and there are notable exceptions), ISPs are in the connectivity business first and foremost. They are not as strong in providing support and development services for business-oriented customers.

Enter a new breed of connectivity provider, the Web-hosting company, sometimes also called a Web presence provider. These folks do not deal in access for you to the Internet. They focus on providing a safe and easily accessible home for your Web site on the Internet. In principle, this focus means that they can provide more expertise in the area of Web development, but they assume you can find your own access to the Internet elsewhere.

Note

The divisions discussed in this section are not pure. Many ISPs offer Web-hosting services. Some companies who focus on Web hosting also offer dial-up access, although their facilities are often less robust than those of the better ISPs.

So what do you do?

If you have a Web site with your current Internet access provider, check with them to see if they currently support or have plans to support FrontPage or would be willing to support it if you asked nicely. If they do not, you have three options (besides throwing in the towel on FrontPage, of course):

✦ Select a new service provider.

✦ Keep your current provider and add a Web-hosting provider.

✦ Use FrontPage without the server extensions (as previously described).

Pricing and support

A survey of existing Web-hosting facilities supporting FrontPage also demonstrates a range of pricing and support options. Here are some factors to consider:

✦ Most offer the FrontPage service at no additional charge. Some add an initial setup charge. However, pricing for Web hosting varies dramatically. The average range is roughly between $29 per month and $200 per month. Obviously the features offered vary widely as well.

✦ Options in the support category range from no support ("We do install the FrontPage extension for you, but you are on your own") to extensive, and expensive, on-site training options. A survey of Web sites indicates a range of commitment to and expertise with FrontPage as well.

Note

For more information on Web-hosting services that support FrontPage, see the Microsoft FrontPage Web site, `http://microsoft.saltmine.com/frontpage/wpp/list/`, which as of this writing lists over 260 providers in North America.

Connecting to a FrontPage-enabled Web server

Once your account is established, publishing your Web should be simple. To access your account, you do need the following information:

✦ The location of your Web (if you have ordered your own domain name as part of your account)

✦ A username

✦ A password

These should be provided for you when your account is created. Have them close by, open your newly created Web, and you are ready to publish.

Publishing to a non-FrontPage server

Even if you do not have a Web server that supports FrontPage available to you, there are many reasons to use FrontPage as your primary development tool. As we have seen, you still have to publish your Web to your Web server. However, you cannot make use of all of the extended features, especially some of the components. Some of the things that do not work include:

✦ The Confirmation component

✦ The Discussion component

✦ The Registration component

✦ The Save Results component

✦ The Search component

✦ FrontPage server-side image maps

If you are using FrontPage as a development tool (but do not have access to a Web server that is specifically set up to support FrontPage), you can still use FrontPage to publish your Web—if you are using FrontPage 98 with Bonus Pack. You can also use a standard FTP client to perform the same task.

Using the Web Publishing Wizard

The Web Publishing Wizard is the utility FrontPage supplies to help you publish your Web to a remote Web server that does not have the Microsoft FrontPage server extensions installed. The Web Publishing Wizard is invoked automatically anytime you request to publish a Web to a non-FrontPage-enabled Web server.

New
in 98

The Web Publishing Wizard has been greatly simplified in FrontPage 98.

To use the Web Publishing Wizard, proceed as follows:

1. Make sure that you have saved all changes to your Web. You can do so by opening Editor and selecting File ⇨ Save All.

2. If you have a dial-up Internet connection, make sure that you have established your connection.

3. In Explorer, Select File ⇨ Publish FrontPage Web.

4. In the Publish FrontPage Web dialog box, as shown in Figure 18-19, select the location of the Web server or type it into the input box. Use the complete URL, including any path names, to the location of the Web. Click OK to continue.

Figure 18-19: Identify the URL of the Web you are publishing to.

5. If the Web server you have pointed to does not have the FrontPage server extensions installed, FrontPage starts the Microsoft Web Publishing Wizard so that you can FTP the content to your server. In the first dialog box, type the FTP Server Name and Directory Path (see Figure 18-20). Click Next.

6. In the next dialog box, type the username and password of your Web account on the server.

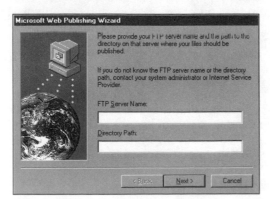

Figure 18-20: Identify the location of your Web server for the Web Publishing Wizard.

Some Web Publishing Wizard tips and tricks

There is a shortcut to all this if you are publishing only one file at a time. Begin by opening and previewing the page in Internet Explorer. When you are satisfied that it is ready to be published, select File ⇨ Send To ⇨ Web Publishing Wizard. This starts the wizard with the page you selected as the default. The only problem with this method is that for some reason, the Web Publishing Wizard translates the name of the HTML Web page into `myfile.url`. This is not a particularly helpful conclusion, and you cannot change it in the wizard because the wizard is operating with a temporary copy of the file. You have to transfer it as is and change the name at the other end.

To work around this, you can perform a similar operation from Windows Explorer. Select the file or folder to send, click the right mouse button, and select Send To from the pop-up menu as described in the previous paragraph. In this case, the wizard retains the correct filename. But of course, you cannot preview a file using this method. You can, however, use this method to upload more than one file at a time by shift-clicking or control-clicking in Explorer.

The Web Publishing Wizard is Microsoft's attempt to simplify the task of publishing Web pages to a non-FrontPage server. In making things simple, however, the wizard also introduces some complications that you should be aware of before entrusting your Web to it. Among the considerations:

✦ *The Web Publishing Wizard cannot delete files from a Web server*—If you delete a file from the local copy of the Web in FrontPage and then try to republish the Web using the wizard, the wizard informs you that nothing has changed. If you have made other changes, the wizard makes these updates, but the deleted file is not removed from the remote server.

✦ *The Web Publishing Wizard does not recognize filename changes of nonlinked Web pages*—If you use Explorer to change the filename of a Web page, Explorer also updates any hyperlinks that refer to this file. If you then republish your Web, the Web Publishing Wizard recognizes that a change has been made and updates your pages correctly. If you happen to change the filename of a page that is not referenced in other pages, the wizard does not register the fact that you have changed the filename. If you try to republish, the wizard informs you that nothing has changed. If you have made other changes, the wizard makes these updates but does not register the changed filename.

You can get around the filename problem by opening the renamed file in Editor and then saving it.

All of which leads to a simple conclusion: The Web Publishing Wizard is fine for basic use, but for industrial use on a non-FrontPage Web, FTP is still preferred. Note that if you do use FTP to publish your Web, be careful not to transfer any of the special `_vti` folders that FrontPage uses to keep track of file information. If you are FTPing to a non-FrontPage Web site, these files are just clutter. If you are using FTP to publish to a FrontPage-enabled Web, you risk overwriting vital information on the Web server.

Using the Project Web

The Project Web template that comes with FrontPage 98 is designed to serve as a communication channel for a Web development team. It is relatively simple-minded, which is a virtue as well as a shortcoming. Use this template if you want a simple way to keep a group apprised of the status and progress of a project, and if you want to centralize implementation discussions, documents, and such.

The Project Web consists of a home page and the following six subsections:

✦ **Members**—This page provides an alphabetical listing of the development team members, including placeholders for a photo, a description, and contact information. This can be a handy reference, particularly if the development team is distributed remotely and you are trying to remember someone's fax number. On the downside, it would be more convenient if this data could be sorted in various ways and searched like a phone directory. (If this sounds appealing, take a peek at Chapter 17, "Database Connectivity.")

✦ **Schedule**—This page lists upcoming events (such as meetings and review sessions) and milestones. It also provides for a priority listing of what is happening in the current and upcoming weeks. This page is organized as a generic text page. It would lend itself to customizing, such that team members could schedule events using a calendar feature.

✦ **Status**—This section lists monthly status reports, on the assumptions (1) that your project is lasting more than one month and (2) that you actually produce such reports. I am sure they are a blessing to all if your project has them.

✦ **Archive**—This archive is really envisioned as something more like a library. It is a place to link documents produced by the project, software code developed by the project, and other tools and utilities that might be of interest to team members.

✦ **Search**—This is the standard FrontPage mechanism for searching HTML pages in a Web.

✦ **Discussions**—The discussion section is divided into two topic areas: (1) Requirements is the place to request, recommend, or dream about features for the project, and (2) Knowledge Base is the place where general question-and-answer discussions are maintained. After the archive, this is probably the potentially most valuable portion of the Project Web, assuming that it is used.

Tip

One element missing from the Web is a mechanism for incident tracking during development of the project. This could easily be implemented as a third discussion track, although ideally one would like something a little more structured than just submitting a discussion item.

Customizing FrontPage

FrontPage 98 comes with a Software Developer's Kit (SDK) that can be used to customize several aspects of the FrontPage environment to suit the needs of a specific development environment. The SDK numerous examples, tools, and utilities will help you develop custom functionality for your Web project. Some of the topics covered in the SDK include:

✦ **Custom menus**—Information on adding custom menu items to Explorer and Editor

✦ **Cgi**—Examples of CGI programs

✦ **Designer HTML**— Examples of "designer" (that is, nonstandard) HTML recognized by FrontPage (covered in Chapter 9)

✦ **Templates**—Examples and instructions on creating your own templates (the utilities directory contains a program for converting an existing Web into a template)

✦ **Themes**— Samples and tools for developing your own themes (covered in Chapter 4)

✦ **Utilities**—Various utilities for adding custom features to your Web

✦ **FrontPage Components (WebBots)**—Examples and tools for developing your own components (covered in Chapter 12)

✦ **Wizards**—Examples and tools for developing your own wizards

✦ **OLE automation**—Information on incorporating FrontPage functionality into your own applications

Tip

For complete contents and instructions on using the SDK, refer to the `FPDEVKIT.DOC` file found in the `SDK` folder.

When might you want to consider customizing FrontPage? Anytime you are using it to perform repetitive tasks or you are working with a variety of team members, some of whom are not necessarily technically inclined:

✦ Updating new pages that are similar

✦ Working in a Web development company producing many Webs

✦ Working on an intranet development project with many departments

In the coming sections, we focus on the SDK issues that are most likely to be of interest to a specific development project. First we create a template page and add it to the list of available templates. Next we create a simple wizard by modifying a sample wizard that comes with the SDK. Finally, we modify the FrontPage Editor menu bar to include a handy item for our newly created wizard.

Developing custom templates

Creating custom templates requires no programming. It is as simple as creating an HTML page and converting it to the template format. FrontPage recognizes three template types:

✦ **Page**—A single-page template, located in the `pages` subfolder of the FrontPage main folder

✦ **Web**—A collection of interconnected pages, stored in the `Webs` subfolder of the FrontPage main folder

✦ **Frame set**—A frame set and all frames, located in the `frames` subfolder of the FrontPage main folder

Creating a page template

To create a page template, first create the HTML page. Select File ➪ Save As, and click the As Template button. This opens the Save As Template dialog box. Select Browse to access the existing template pages in order to make use of an existing description, perhaps. Indicate the title of the template, its name, and a brief description. Click OK to save.

Creating a frame set template

You create a frame set template much as you do a page template. Define the layout of the frame set and select File ➪ Save As, and click the As Template button. Complete the template information as for a page template. Your new frame set template appears in the Frames tab of the New File dialog box.

Creating Web templates

You can create Web templates manually, or if you are using the Microsoft Personal Web Server, you can use the Web Template Maker utility (`webtmpl.exe`) that is part of the SDK.

To create a Web template manually:

1. Create a folder called `[myweb].tem`, where `[myweb]` is the name of the Web template, and place this folder in the `Webs` folder, located in the main FrontPage folder (`\Program Files\Microsoft FrontPage` by default).

2. Create the Web to be used as the basis for the template.

3. Locate the Web files and copy them to the `[myweb].tem` folder. If your Web contains files in `_private` or `images` subfolders, these must be copied as well.

4. Create a `[myweb].inf` file as described in the subsequent section.

To create a Web template using the `webtmpl.exe` utility:

1. Launch the utility.
2. Select the Web to use from the available Webs list.
3. Indicate template information.
4. Click Make Web Template.

The template INF file

When you create a template, FrontPage saves all of the necessary files in the appropriate template directory. In addition it creates an INF file for the template. The INF file is simply a standard Windows INI-format text file that stores configuration information about the template. This file can have several sections:

✦ **Info**—This contains information on the template's title, description, theme, and any shared borders.

✦ **FileList**—This section allows you to map files in a template directory to explicit URLs within the Web that is created. This is the only way to create a Web template with subdirectories.

✦ **MetaInfo**—You can store meta-information variables that can be used in the Web, typically in conjunction with the Substitution component.

✦ **TaskList**—You can store information about initial tasks for your Web template using the TaskList section of the INF file. A task has six attributes: TaskName, Priority (1–3), CreatedBy, URL, Cookie, and Comment.

For more information on the format of the INF file, consult the FrontPage SDK.

Creating custom wizards

Creating your own wizards involves real programming, and it is not for everyone. Using the example wizard source files and utility files provided in the SDK, however, greatly simplifies the task. To illustrate how easy it is to create a customized wizard, we make some minor modifications to the Hello Wizard written in Visual Basic that is part of the SDK in order to create an Email Wizard.

The Hello Wizard that we use as the basis of our Email Wizard is found in the `Wizards/pages` subfolder in the `SDK` folder of the FrontPage CD. The first order of business is to copy the `Hello.wiz` folder into the `[FrontPage Root]/pages` folder. You should also copy the `vb` subfolder to the `[FrontPage Root]` directory.

Open `hello.vbp` in Visual Basic 5.0. Open the form, as shown in Figure 18-21. We have opened up the form in order to view all of the wizard pages at once. We shrink the form back to the size we want before compiling.

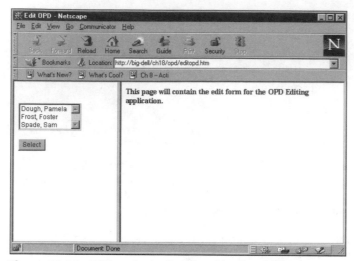

Figure 18-21: Editing the Hello Wizard in Visual Basic 5.0

As it is currently written, the Hello.wiz wizard consists of three screens. The first screen simply introduces the wizard. The second screen takes useful (or potentially useful) information from the user and turns it into Web page content. The third screen merely identifies the name and location of the page to be created.

Editing the wizard form

We make a few simple changes to the wizard form. The introduction screen we leave as is for now, recognizing that the text and graphic should ultimately change to be consistent with the new purpose of the wizard. We also leave the third screen alone.

Next we edit the labels on the second screen, changing the first to "Your name" and the second to "Your email." The default pull-down list is removed and replaced with a text input box for your e-mail address. We rename the name field txtName and the e-mail field txtEmail.

The results of our re-form work can be seen in Figure 18-22.

Editing the wizard code

Corresponding to our minimal changes to the wizard form, we also need to alter the Visual Basic programming. Specifically, we must:

✦ Add to the variables in the LoadSettings subroutine to include our new txtName and txtEmail variables.

✦ Add to the variables in the SaveSettings subroutine, enabling us to save and recall the last values indicated for the name and e-mail fields.

✦ Edit the HTML page that is generated from this wizard in the GeneratePage subroutine to our liking.

Once we have made these changes, we save and recompile the wizard code as `email.exe` and place it in the `email.wiz` subfolder of the `pages` folder. All this wizard does is prompt us for our name and e-mail address and place them into a new page. Not rocket science, perhaps, but you can see how the principles might be applied to create easy-to-follow instructions for anyone generating a Web page. You can see an example of the work produced by the Email Wizard in Figure 18-23.

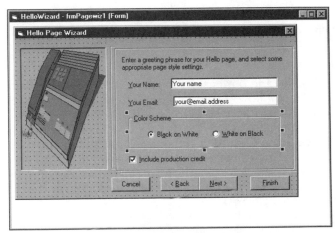

Figure 18-22: Creating a custom wizard

Figure 18-23: A new wizard is born

Adding custom menu items

It is possible to add custom menu items to both FrontPage Explorer and Editor. To do this requires some understanding of the Windows Registry and enough courage to make changes to it manually. The changes are easy to make and, done correctly, perfectly harmless. Anytime you begin editing the Registry, however, it is highly advisable to make a backup copy. Just in case.

By way of illustrating how you can customize FrontPage's menu items, we add a new menu and an item for the custom Email Wizard we created in the previous section.

Adding a new menu

In order to edit the registry and add our custom menu item to FrontPage Editor, you must be familiar with the Windows regedit utility. Start regedit and open the HKEY_CURRENT_USER folder. Menu information for FrontPage Editor is stored in the \Software\Microsoft\FrontPage\Editor\Init Menus folder. Open this folder. If no custom menus have yet been created, it contains only a default entry. To add a new menu item, add a new string value to this folder by selecting Edit ⇨ New ⇨ String Value. Give the string a name, for example, **mymenu1**. Click the new item with the right mouse button and select Modify to designate a value for the item. Menu elements have the following syntax:

```
first_version, last_version, menu_bar_num, menu_name, menu_position
```

✦ **first_version**—This indicates the earliest version of FrontPage that should add this menu (effectively 2, since prior to this the custom menu feature was not supported).

✦ **last_version**—This indicates the latest version which should add the menu item. If left blank, this means all versions up to and including the most recent.

✦ **menu_bar_num**—In theory, this indicates the number of the menu bar to add the new menu to. This should be 1, since there is currently only one menu bar available.

✦ **menu_name**—This indicates the name of the menu as it appears in the menu bar. Place an ampersand (&) before the letter in the word that should be used as the shortcut key.

✦ **menu_position**—This indicates the name of the menu just prior to the new menu and can also be designated as an index number (where the first menu = 1).

To add a new menu called "Wizards" and position it before the Tools menu in Editor, put a value of "2,,1,&Wizards, Tools" in the value field for mymenu1.

Adding a new command

You can add a new command to your custom menu, using a similar technique. String values for menu commands are located in the Init Commands key parallel to the Init Menu key accessed earlier. String values have a syntax as follows:

```
first_version, last_version, menu_bar_num, menu_name,
command_name, command_line, command_position, insert_flag,
status_text, help_reference
```

Some new values in this string include:

✦ **command_name**—This is the command line filename and path to the command to be executed (or in the case of Editor, of a file to be opened).

✦ **command_position**—This value indicates where in the menu list the item is to appear.

✦ **insert_flag**—This value indicates what to do with the command_name file. In Editor 0 = execute, 1 = insert file as HTML, 2= insert literal text as HTML.

✦ **status_text**—This is the text displayed in the status line.

✦ **help_reference**—This links to a help file reference.

As an example, we create an Email menu item linked to the Email Wizard we created earlier:

```
2,,1,Wizards, &Email, C:\Program Files\Microsoft FrontPage\
pages\email.wiz\email.exe, ,0,Email Wizard,,
```

The results of our efforts are highlighted in Figure 18-24.

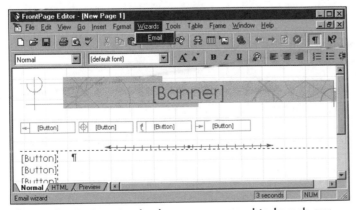

Figure 18-24: A customized menu command to launch our customized Email Wizard

Taking the Next Step

This chapter has covered a multiplicity of ways you can use FrontPage to publish and help manage a Web project. The final chapter addresses server and Web administration issues related to FrontPage.

✦   ✦   ✦

Server Administration

♦   ♦   ♦   ♦

In This Chapter

Configuring
FrontPage settings

Administering users

Changing your
password

Working with Web
servers

Using FrontPage
server extensions

Introducing
FrontPage SERK

Dealing with security
issues

Using Microsoft
Personal Web Server

♦   ♦   ♦   ♦

T his chapter addresses a variety of FrontPage administrative issues, focusing on the installation and use of the FrontPage server extensions. This chapter is of interest to anyone who is responsible for setting up and maintaining a Web server to work with FrontPage. As an introduction to how FrontPage interacts with a Web server, it is also useful to anyone who is creating and maintaining FrontPage Webs. The first section discusses general FrontPage configuration options. The next section describes the FrontPage architecture and introduces the Server Extension Resource Kit. The final section of the chapter explains how to administer the Microsoft Personal Web Server.

Configuring FrontPage Settings

FrontPage allows Web administrators to configure a variety of Web-specific settings from within FrontPage Explorer. For further information on using Explorer, consult Chapter 3 of this book.

Web settings

The Web Settings menu item provides access to some general configuration options for a given Web. Access these settings by selecting Tools ➪ Web Settings. The Web Settings dialog box, shown in Figure 19-1, consists of five tabs, each of which is described here.

New in 98

Several of the Web Settings tabs have been revised in FrontPage 98, and the Navigation tab is entirely new.

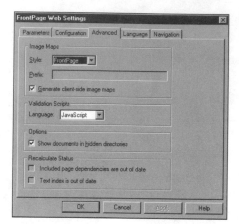

Figure 19-1: Configuring FrontPage using the Web Settings dialog box

Parameters

The Parameters tab enables the administrator or FrontPage user to define variables for the Web. A *variable* consists of a name and a value. Once a variable has been defined, it can be inserted into any page in the Web using the FrontPage Substitution component. This is a convenient way to store and use values that are inserted frequently into your pages. Using a variable helps to ensure that your pages are consistent. It also makes it easier to change a volatile value.

To add a new variable, click the Add button and type the name and value for that variable. Figure 19-2 shows an example involving a multiline parameter value (be sure to read the caution regarding the use of multiline parameters). Click OK to return to the Web Settings dialog box. Your variable is added to the list of available variables.

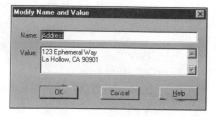

Figure 19-2: Creating a new variable name and value using the Web Settings Parameters tab

It is possible to enter multiple lines in the variable value input field. Use Ctrl+Enter to start a new line without closing the dialog box. FrontPage permits this but does not respond exactly as it should. You can insert this multiline variable using the FrontPage Substitution component. However, the second line of your value appears in the list of variable names. Also, do not use a colon (:) in the name of your variable, or FrontPage interprets the second half of your variable name as a value.

To modify a variable, select the variable and click the Modify button. Make any desired changes. Click OK to save your changes and return to the Web Settings dialog box.

Configuration

The Configuration tab allows you to change the name and title of the current Web (including the name of the root web, the default name for which is `<rootweb>`). In addition, the tab presents useful configuration information that cannot be altered, such as the Web server URL, FrontPage server extensions version number, Web server name and version, IP address, and any proxy server information.

Advanced

This tab contains settings for advanced FrontPage options. These include:

Note

There is nothing particularly "advanced" about these options. Probably a more appropriate name for this set of options would have been "Miscellaneous options that the average user probably doesn't need to worry about," but that might have been hard to fit on the tab.

✦ **Image Maps**—Select the style of image maps to use. Options are FrontPage, NCSA, CERN, Netscape, or None. If you designate a server-side image map style, use the Prefix text box to designate the location of the image map CGI. Check Generate Client-Side Image Maps to have FrontPage do that. See Chapter 5 for more details on creating image maps.

✦ **Validation Scripts**—Select the default scripting language. Options are JavaScript, VBScript, or None. See Chapter 15 for details on scripting languages.

✦ **Options**—Check this option to display files contained in hidden directories. Hidden directories are those directories whose names begin with an underscore.

✦ **Recalculate Status**—This section indicates whether or not included page references or the text index used by the search engine is out of date. See Chapter 18 for information regarding how FrontPage verifies and recalculates hyperlinks.

Language

This tab enables users to customize the FrontPage environment with multiple-language support. It includes options to designate:

✦ **Default Web Language**—The options are English, French, German, Italian, Japanese, and Spanish. This option is used to help FrontPage determine what language to use when it returns error messages from the server.

✦ **Default HTML Encoding**—Select one of the languages from the list of recognized character encodings to generate HTML pages using the character set for that language. This setting defines the default encoding for your Web. You can also change the encoding for a given page in Editor using the Page Properties dialog box for that Web page.

Navigation

This tab allows you to define the text that appears on FrontPage's automatically generated navigation buttons. If you regret your changes, return to the system defaults by clicking the Default button. Buttons and their default titles are shown in Figure 19-3.

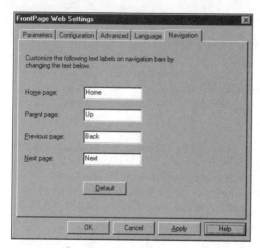

Figure 19-3: Navigation button names and default titles in the Web Settings Navigation tab

Options

The Explorer Options menu item also provides access to basic system configurations. These options relate to the operation of FrontPage itself. Select Tools ➪ Options to open the Options dialog box. This dialog box has three tabs, described here.

✦ **General**—This tab consists of a number of mostly self-explanatory check box options:

- Show Getting Started dialog—checked by default

- Show Toolbar—checked by default

- Show Status Bar—checked by default

- Warn When Included Components Are Out of Date—unchecked by default

- Warn When Text Index Is Out of Date—unchecked by default

- Warn Before Permanently Applying Themes—checked by default

✦ **Proxies**—A proxy server is a security device that causes any Internet traffic to make requests through itself rather than directly. This is one type of a firewall, a mechanism that filters out unwanted activity between the Internet and a company's internal network. Use this tab to designate the name of an HTTP proxy to use if you are inside a firewall. You can also provide FrontPage with a list of hosts to use without the proxy. These would be internal Web servers.

✦ **Configure Editors**—This tab allow you to associate certain types of files (via their file endings) with editing applications capable of dealing with them. There is a long list of defaults, which you can add to, modify, or delete.

FrontPage configuration files

In addition to the options accessed via the FrontPage Explorer Tools menu, you can also set some configuration values directly in the FrontPage INI files. FrontPage maintains two principal INI files: frontpg.ini and fpexplor.ini. These files are located in the Windows folder on the computer running FrontPage.

FrontPage stores Web-specific configuration information in a series of CNF files located in the _vti_pvt subdirectory of the given Web. The main configuration file is services.cnf. Most of the values recorded here can be set using the FrontPage menu items described earlier in the chapter.

Administering Users

In addition to being able to control the Web environment in FrontPage, you can also use Explorer to control access to the Web and its Web pages. Three levels of control are available:

✦ **Browser access**—This allows the user to view pages.

✦ **Author access**—This allows the user to create, edit, and delete pages as well as view them.

✦ **Administrator access**—This allows the user to change settings, add new Webs, and perform other administrative tasks in addition to having full author and browser access.

In order to control permissions, you must have administrator-level authority or be using a site with no active access controls in place.

Select Tools ➪ Permissions to display the Permissions dialog box. The tabs on this dialog box vary, depending on whether you are in the current Web. The root Web, shown in Figure 19-4, has two tabs:

✦ **Users**—This defines a list of users who have access to the Web server and who can make changes on it.

✦ **Computers/Groups**—Depending on the Web server you use, the last tab is either Computers or Groups. Use the Computer tab to define who can and cannot use the service by referring to the IP number, domain name, or the computer used to access the Web. Use the Group tab to collect a designated number of employees into a single, named group.

Figure 19-4: Setting permissions for the root Web

Within each tab, you can add, modify, and delete entries. Users and groups can be granted permission only to browse the Web, to browse and author Web pages, or to browse, author, and administer the Web. Access to a Web can be restricted using either users or groups, or both.

Sub-Webs have a slightly different interface. When you select Tools ➪ Permissions for a sub-Web, it displays an initial Settings tab as shown in Figure 19-5. This tab enables the current Web to use the same password system as the root Web or to keep a list of distinct passwords on a per-Web basis. If you elect to use the same usernames and passwords as the root Web, you can view but not modify users and groups in the additional tabs. To enable these tabs, you should select the Use Unique Permissions for This Web radio button.

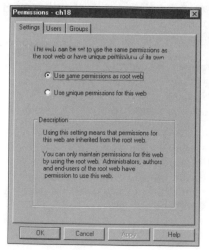

Figure 19-5: For a FrontPage sub-Web, you can elect to use the same permissions in effect for the root Web or to create an independent set of users and groups.

Changing Your Password

In many cases, usernames and passwords are set up by the Web administrators. Even if a user does not have full administrative-level authority, however, once a password has been established, the user can change it.

To change a password for the current user, select Tools ➪ Change Password. In the dialog box, type the current password in the Old Password box. Type the new password once each in the New Password and Confirm Password boxes. Click OK. Assuming you typed the same thing twice, your new password is in effect. Note that if passwords are not in effect on the current Web, the Change Password menu item is unavailable.

Working with Web Servers

The FrontPage client application, composed of Explorer and Editor, interacts with a Web server to provide many of the administrative features as well as the customized programming that FrontPage supports. You can use FrontPage to create and manage Web content on any Web server, even one that cannot communicate directly with FrontPage. There are two drawbacks to using FrontPage with a non-FrontPage-enabled server. Number one, you cannot use the FrontPage components, Active Server Pages, or any other elements requiring server-side processing. In addition you lose the benefit of the integration between client and server that enables automatic updating of hyperlinks, link verification, and so on. (This disadvantage can be mitigated by running FrontPage on a local Web server for development, even if the live server you publish to does not support FrontPage directly.)

File access

When you create a Web page in FrontPage, the client saves both the main file and a small configuration file that stores vital system information about the Web page or content file. When FrontPage connects to the server to open a Web, it draws its information initially from these much smaller files, making for more efficient communications between FrontPage and the server.

File storage

FrontPage organizes content in Webs. A *Web,* in FrontPage terms, is a collection of Web pages, content files, programming, graphics, and such located within a single directory (it may have zero or more subdirectories). A given Web site can have only a single root Web, a Web defined by the root document directory of the Web server. It can have multiple sub-Webs. Sub-Webs are stored as subdirectories within the root document directory of the server. However, they do not appear as part of the root Web. Rather they have their own separate existence within FrontPage. Let's take an example to clarify this.

Suppose you have created a Web site at `www.shapes.com`. Using FrontPage, you have created a root Web and two sub-Webs: `circles` and `squares`. If your server's document root directory is defined as `wwwroot`, and if you look at the physical directory structure on the computer, you see `wwwroot` with two subdirectories, `circles` and `squares`. When you open the root Web in FrontPage, however, you see neither `circles` nor `squares`. You can still add subfolders to your root Web (or to your sub-Webs). So now you add two folders, `polygons` and `ellipses`, to the root Web. In FrontPage, you see these two folders only. In the physical file directory under `wwwroot`, you see all four folders: `circles`, `ellipses`, `polygons`, and `squares`. All four directories are accessed normally from the Web browser.

Dividing the content of your Web into sub-Webs is a good way (1) to minimize download time of the Web from the server and (2) to establish different sets of user permissions on different areas of the Web site. Doing so does somewhat complicate cross-linking among the various sub-Webs, however.

Communicating with the server

The FrontPage client communicates with a server via standard HTTP "POST" requests to a set of CGI programs. Collectively, these CGI programs are referred to as the FrontPage server extensions. Because all communication takes place via standard HTTP protocols, FrontPage is able to work across a firewall, for example, if you are developing content inside the company firewall that is published to a public Web server.

Using FrontPage Server Extensions

The FrontPage server extensions are a set of CGI programs that reside in an executable directory of the Web server and support communication functions between FrontPage and the Web server.

Server extension functions

Functions that the server extensions control include:

✦ **Web page authoring** (`author.dll`/`author.exe`)—Keeps track of the location, hyperlinks, and other aspects of Web pages

✦ **Web administration** (`admin.dll`/`admin.exe`)—Handles user permissions and passwords

✦ **FrontPage components** (`shtml.dll`/`shtml.exe`)—Provides run-time functionality to the Web page, substituting the component tags with valid HTML

Note The FrontPage server extensions are provided on the FrontPage CD-ROM. The Windows versions are in the `ServExt` subfolder. UNIX versions are in the `Unix` subfolder. Current versions of the server extensions can be downloaded from the FrontPage section of the Microsoft Web site `www.microsoft.com/frontpage`.

Supported platforms and servers

Because the server extensions are standard CGI programs, they work with any Web server that supports the CGI standard (which means virtually all Web servers). When you install a Microsoft Web server, such as the Personal Web Server described later in this chapter, or the Internet Information Server, the FrontPage server extensions are automatically installed. On other platforms and/or servers, you must install the extensions by hand. There are really two flavors of the server extensions. Those that run on Windows operating systems are DLLs. The UNIX varieties are standard C executables. Table 19-1 shows the list of supported platforms and servers.

Table 19-1 **Servers supported by UNIX and Windows**	
Operating systems	*Web servers*
UNIX Digital UNIX 3.2c, 4.0 (Alpha) BSD/OS 2.1, 3.0 (Intel x86) Linux 3.03 (Red Hat Software) (Intel x86) HP/UX 9.03, 10.1 (PA-RISC) IRIX 5.3, 6.2 (Silicon Graphics) Solaris 2.4, 2.5 (Sun) SunOS 4.1.3, 4.1.4 (Sun) AIX 3.2.5, 4.1, 4.2 (RS6000, PowerPC) SCO OperServer 5.0 (Intel x86)	Apache 1.1.3, 1.2 CERN 3.0 NCSA 1.5.2 Netscape Commerce Server 1.12 Netscape Enterprise 2.0, 3.0 Netscape FastTrack 2.0
Windows NT (Intel x86)	Microsoft Internet Information Server 2.0, 3.0, 4.0 Netscape Commerce Server 1.12 Netscape Enterprise 2.0, 3.0 Netscape FastTrack 2.0 O'Reilly WebSite FrontPage Personal Web Server
Windows NT Alpha	Microsoft Internet Information Server 2.0, 3.0, 4.0 Microsoft Peer Web Services (on NT Workstation)

(continued)

Table 19-1 *(continued)*	
Operating systems	*Web servers*
Windows 95	Microsoft Personal Web Server FrontPage Personal Web Server Netscape FastTrack 2.0 O'Reilly WebSite

Note   Although not mentioned in this list, Microsoft also has available a Macintosh version of the Personal Web Server for those who want to use FrontPage with a Macintosh Web server. There is no set of server extensions currently for the popular WebStar Web server, however.

Introducing the FrontPage SERK

The FrontPage Server Extensions Resource Kit (SERK) contains detailed documentation in HTML format regarding the components and functionality of the server extensions. If you are going to be maintaining a FrontPage-enabled Web server, the SERK is required reading. It is useful even for end users of FrontPage who want to understand what goes on at the other end of the equation.

A version of the SERK comes with FrontPage on the CD-ROM. The current version of the SERK can be found in the FrontPage area of the Microsoft Web site. In this section of the chapter we review some of the highlights from this resource. For information on installing the server extensions or on upgrading from FrontPage 97 extensions to the FrontPage 98 versions, see Appendix C of this book. For details on other topics, consult the SERK.

Note   As of this writing, the current SERK version was 1.3. The version shipping with the FrontPage 98 CD-ROM is 1.0. Most of the changes pertain to security fixes and patches related to using the extensions on UNIX.

Administering the server extensions

Once installed, the server extensions themselves require very little administration. The primary task of the administrator is to add extensions to new servers or virtual servers, remove the extensions, or upgrade the extensions. In this section we look at the tools available for performing administrative tasks, as well as some platform-specific issues regarding the use of the extensions.

FrontPage Server Administrator

FrontPage comes with a server administrator tool that enables you to configure servers recognized by FrontPage, to install and uninstall the FrontPage server extensions, and to add administrator-level users to the server if you are running a Web server on Windows 95.

There are in fact two server utilities, both located in the `bin` subfolder of the FrontPage main folder (this is the same folder that holds `fpeditor.exe` and `fpexplorer.exe`). The first, `fpserver.exe`, is a command line tool, suitable for batch file use. The more frequently used tool is `fpsrvwin.exe`, a Windows-based utility, shown in Figure 19-6. These utilities are only available for use on the Windows platform. They are essentially an interface to fpsrvadm, the command line tool discussed in the next section.

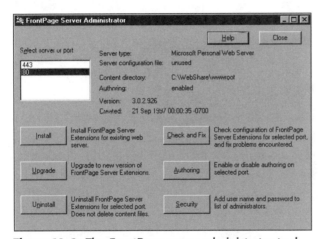

Figure 19-6: The FrontPage server administrator tool

The utility consists of a single interface with buttons for the various functions it performs. On start-up, the tool lists recognized Web servers. Use the administrator tool to perform the following functions:

Install

Use the Install button to install the server extensions on an existing Web server. Note that before you install the server extensions for a Web server, you must have set up and configured the server according to its standard directions. When you click this option, you are asked to select the Web server type on which to install the extensions, as illustrated in Figure 19-7. Click OK to install the extensions and return to the main interface. The newly installed server port displays in the list of active servers.

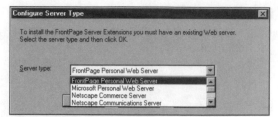

Figure 19-7: Using the FrontPage server administrator tool to install the server extensions on a new Web server

Upgrade

Click the Upgrade button to upgrade the server extensions on servers currently running some version of the extensions. To upgrade a server, select the server from the list of port numbers and click Upgrade.

Uninstall

Uninstall removes the FrontPage server extensions from the selected server port. It does not remove the content associated with that Web server.

Check and Fix

The Check and Fix feature allows you to perform routine repairs on the files stored in FrontPage Webs. Click this option to check and fix the selected Web server. Some of the tasks performed by this utility:

✦ Identify and replace missing files and directories.

✦ Check that all the proper executables are located in each Web.

✦ Check permissions.

✦ Check lock files.

If you are running the Check and Fix feature on a Microsoft Web server (IIS or PWS), you are also given the option of "tightening security." Select this option if you want to limit access to your Web in the most secure way possible.

Authoring

Click the Authoring button to enable or disable authoring capabilities on the currently selected Web.

Security

Use the Security feature to add an administrative username and password. You can also use FrontPage itself to do this, although to use FrontPage, you already need to know a username and password to log on with. Perhaps it is obvious that this server administrator tool should not be generally accessible, since you don't want anyone to use it to create an administrative-level password.

fpsrvadm

The fpsrvadm utility is the main application for administering FrontPage server extensions. It is a command line program on both UNIX and Windows NT. Use this utility to install, update, remove, and repair server extensions on FrontPage Webs. For specifics on the command line operations and options available for this command, consult the SERK.

Remote administration

The FrontPage 98 server extensions package includes a set of HTML forms that can be configured to provide remote administration capabilities. Using these forms, you can perform all of the functions of the command line fpsrvadm utility using a GUI interface.

Permitting remote administration via HTML forms raises some issues about security. As a result, the remote administration capability is not installed by default when you install the server extension package. For instructions on installing and configuring the HTML forms–based administration, consult the SERK.

Dealing with Security Issues

One of the main hesitations of companies considering whether to add FrontPage server extensions to their Web servers is whether or not the mechanism is secure. As in most security-related matters, the key question you need to ask is whether or not FrontPage is secure enough. The fact that it seamlessly updates files between FrontPage and the Web server is a large bonus. The ease with which this can be done is only accomplished by means of some openness in the flow of data.

One advantage of having FrontPage transfer files via HTTP is that FrontPage works with a secure server using Secure Sockets Layer (SSL) to encrypt all content. In this case not only is the content between Web server and users encrypted, but the same is true for content passed between the FrontPage client and the Web server.

UNIX security

On UNIX systems, the FrontPage server extensions make use of the standard Web server access file (.htaccess on NCSA-style servers, including Apache; .nsconfig on Netscape servers). This mechanism allows FrontPage to create sets of users with various levels of authority for each directory of the Web site. In addition, FrontPage uses the SUID (Set User ID) bit on the CGI scripts. Setting this bit ensures that only the owner of that particular CGI, that is, the Web developer, does not have access to any and all files in other user accounts.

Note

Microsoft has identified a security bug in the server extensions designed for use with Apache, a popular NCSA-style UNIX Web server. If you are running an Apache server, you should be sure to download the latest version of the server extensions from the Microsoft Web site.

Security on Windows systems

Windows NT systems running the Internet Information Server (IIS) make use of the NT username and password mechanisms to authenticate users of the Web server. If you are using the NT File System (NTFS), the server extensions validate the current user against their account list. In conjunction with this, NT server extensions offer three possible means of securing Web content:

Basic authentication

Basic authentication consists of using the standard Web server authentication method that causes the browser to display a username/password dialog box. This mechanism is supported by most Web servers. This is a minimal form of security. All usernames and passwords are transmitted encoded, but in a known format easy enough to decode.

Windows challenge/response

Windows NT Challenge/Response (also known as NTLM) is a more secure form of authentication. In this environment, username and password are securely encrypted between the browser and the Web server. There are some limitations to using NT Challenge/Response, however, mostly having to do with the proprietary nature of the security protocol. Specifically, NTLM:

✦ Does not work across a firewall

✦ Is not supported by all browsers

Because of its proprietary nature, NTLM is most viable as an intranet solution, when a company has standardized its operations around the Microsoft product line.

Distributed password authentication

The FrontPage server extensions support the Microsoft Commercial Internet System Membership service, using Microsoft's Distributed Password Authentication (DPA) protocol. DPA uses a challenge-and-response protocol along with a trusted third-party authentication server to establish security. Like NTLM, DPA is proprietary. It requires the installation of either the Microsoft Internet Explorer 3.0 DPA or, if you are running a Netscape server, Microsoft Authentication Proxy for Netscape.

Using the Microsoft Personal Web Server

The Microsoft Personal Web Server (PWS) is a lightweight, easy-to-use Web server designed to run on a local desktop computer or workstation. It is primarily designed for developing and testing Web content before publishing it on a public server. It can also be used for a personal or small departmental intranet Web site.

In addition to its other uses, the Personal Web Server provides a good training tool for using Microsoft's serious Web server, Internet Information Server (IIS 4.0).

Because it is intended for use by end users not necessarily conversant in the technological underpinnings of Web servers and networking, it has scaled-down administration functions with an easy-to-use interface. The latest version also includes wizards to help you build an instant home page, complete with guest book and message box.

At the time of this writing, the FrontPage 98 CD-ROM was still shipping with version 1.0 of the Microsoft Personal Web Server. In order to upgrade to 4.0, you must download the NT 4.0 Option Pak for Windows 95 and Windows NT Workstations. For reasons unknown, there are no versions 2.0 or 3.0 for Personal Web Server.

Installing and using PWS 1.0

The Personal Web Server comes with FrontPage. The installation program does its best to encourage (some might use a slightly stronger word) you to install the server before installing FrontPage. If you did not install the server initially and want to do so later, you can find the setup program on your FrontPage CD-ROM in the pws subfolder.

The PWS installation does not waste any time—or confuse you—by asking you questions. When you click the setup, it installs. So make sure you are really ready to install when you start. (You can change the way PWS behaves later.) By default (since it doesn't ask), PWS installs itself at C:\Program Files\Websrv. The executable to run the server is called Inetsw95.exe and is located in the System subfolder of Websrv. By default, PWS also:

 ✦ Configures itself to start up when you turn on the computer

 ✦ Configures itself to appear in the services tray of your status bar

 ✦ Establishes C:\Webshare\Wwwroot as the root document directory

 ✦ Sets the default home page to default.htm

Tip

For those not familiar with the jargon of Web serving, the "document root" directory of a server is the directory where the Web server begins looking for Web pages. Anything inside that directory, either immediately or in a subdirectory, by default becomes part of the document directory for the server. Anything outside that directory is invisible to the server. For example, if your server, www.myserver.com, is configured to recognize C:\somedir\anotherdir\htmldocs as the root document directory, the file seeme.html placed in htmldocs would have the URL www.myserver.com/seeme.html. If the file were moved to a directory called subone in htmldocs, then its URL would be www.myserver.com/subone/seeme.html. And finally, if you moved the file into the anotherdir directory one level above htmldocs, the file would no longer be accessible from the Web server.

When you install the server, you can elect to have it start automatically when you start your computer. If you decide to start it manually, FrontPage starts the server automatically any time you open a Web on that server, but if someone other than yourself is going to need access to the server, you may want to consider that automatic start. You can also elect to have the server display its icon in the status bar services tray, which is a handy way to keep track of whether the server is up or not. It also provides easy access to the server administration features.

Personal Web Server 1.0 has two different mechanisms for administration: a standard Windows control panel and a browser-based administration interface.

The Properties control panel

To access the Properties control panel, click on the PWS 1.0 icon in the service tray with the right mouse button. Select Properties from the pop-up menu. This opens the tabbed control panel shown in Figure 19-8. Alternatively, you can access Personal Web Server via its icon in the Windows Control Panels. Simply click the Start button, select Settings ⇨ Control Panels, and double-click the PWS icon.

General

The General tab identifies the name of the default home page for the Personal Web Server. Click the Display Home Page button to launch your default browser and view your home page. The More Details button opens user documentation in HTML format. The documentation consists of a Getting Started section, a Personal Web Server administration guide, and an FTP server administration guide.

Startup

The Startup tab controls the Web Server State (Running or Stopped). It also contains check box options to Run the Web Server Automatically at Startup and/or Show the Web Server Icon in the Task Bar.

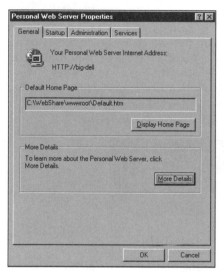

Figure 19-8: The Properties Control Panel for Personal Web Server 3.01

Administration

The Administration tab has a link to the Web-based administration system. This system consists of a set of HTML pages that allow one to configure WWW services, FTP services, and local user administration, if this is enabled. The Web-based administration system is described in more detail later in this chapter.

Services

The Services tab displays the current status of both the HTTP (Web) service and the FTP service. You can start and stop services, or check their properties. To examine and/or edit Web server properties, select HTTP Service and click Properties. In the dialog box that opens you can edit several attributes of the server, including:

- ✦ **Startup Options**—Select Automatic (when the computer boots) or Manual.

- ✦ **Web Server Home Root Settings**—Click the button to change the home directory.

- ✦ **Default Home Page Settings**—Click the button to change the name of the default home page.

HTML-based administration

When you click the Administration button on the tab of the same name in the PWS Control Panel, it opens a local connection to the main page of the Administration Web pages (see Figure 19-9). The main page contains links to the three PWS service areas: WWW, FTP, and local user administration. It also contains links to other PWS resources, surprisingly all links to the Microsoft Web site.

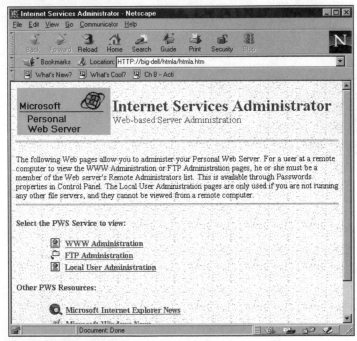

Figure 19-9: The Web-based interface for administering the Personal Web Server

The WWW Administration section contains a page with three tabbed sections: Service, Directories, and Logging.

The Service page provides configuration access to Connection Timeout, Maximum Connections, and Password Authentication Type. See the Security section of this chapter for more information on security options for your Web.

The Directories section, a sample of which is shown in Figure 19-10, provides a complete listing of all Web folders on the server, including all FrontPage _vti folders. Use this section to add, edit, or delete directories from this table.

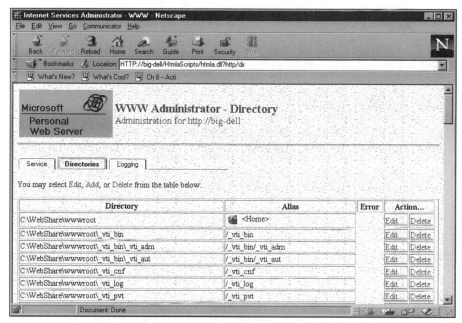

Figure 19-10: A partial listing of files in the PWS document directories

The final section of the WWW Administration system is the Logging tab. It allows an administrator to enable or disable logging as well as to configure the name, location, and frequency with which a log file is refreshed.

Upgrading to Personal Web Server 4.0

At the time of this writing, FrontPage 98 shipped with Personal Web Server 1.0. The latest version of the server, version 4.0, was released at about the same time that IIS 4.0 released. The newer version has several attractive additions, the most prominent of which is the new and greatly improved administrative tool, now called the Personal Web Manager (PWM). A screen from this utility is shown in Figure 19-11.

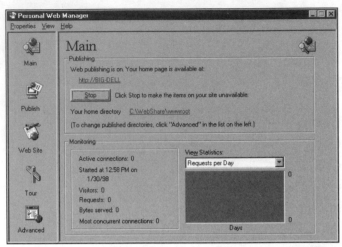

Figure 19-11: The new and improved interface for PWS 4.0

Working with PWS 4.0

PWS 4.0 for Windows has made significant improvements in the interface of the administrative tool, known as the Personal Web Manager (PWM). The PWM also includes several new functions. The interface consists of a left-hand sidebar with icon buttons for each section of the Control Panel, after the manner of FrontPage Explorer. Clicking an icon opens that section in the central window. PWM contains five sections:

✦ **Main**—The Main section is divided into Publishing and Monitoring. The Publishing section identifies the Web server URL and the document root directory. It has a Start/Stop toggle button to control the status of the server. The Monitoring section enables you to quickly review usage statistics for various periods of time.

✦ **Publish**—This section starts the Publishing Wizard, which enables you to publish content to your Web server.

✦ **Web Site**—This section starts the Home Page Wizard (which must be closely related to the Publishing Wizard —see Figure 19-12). This wizard walks you through the creation of a simple but functional Web site, complete with guest book and comment drop box. The first time you click this section, it runs the wizard. Subsequently, you are invited to edit or administer the pages you have created. Figure 19-13 shows a sample of one of the Home Page Wizard's creations.

✦ **Tour**—This offers a slideshow-like overview of the Personal Web Server.

✦ **Advanced**—The Advanced tab enables you to perform many of the functions handled by the Web-based administration pages in previous versions of PWS. It shows, in a simplified tree listing, all of the documents and directories in the site, and it allows you to add, remove, and edit them. You can also designate names for the default documents, enable or disable directory browsing (a feature that lists an index of the directory if there is no default file found in that directory), and enable or disable usage logging.

Figure 19-12: The PWS 4.0 Publishing Wizard and Home Page Wizard — separated at birth?

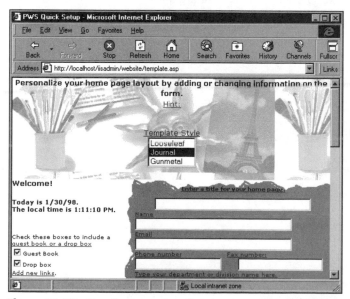

Figure 19-13: Creating a custom home page using the PWS 4.0 Home Page Wizard

Should I upgrade?

As of this writing, there is still at least one good reason to postpone upgrading to PWS 4.0. The main problem is that PWS 4.0 requires the use of Winsock 2.0, Microsoft's updated version of the dynamic link library (DLL) that provides TCP/IP functionality. However, Winsock 2.0 produces a serious problem in FrontPage on Windows 95 systems that are not connected to a network with a DHCP server. Once this issue is resolved, PWS 4.0 will be a valuable upgrade. Until that time, it is not advisable to install the product, unless you are using the product on an NT network.

In addition to this bug, PWS 4.0 has a few new "features" that have presumably been built in to limit the product's flexibility (thereby encouraging you to upgrade to IIS). The main issue in this category is the fact that starting in PWS 4.0, you can no longer configure user permission levels for the server. By default (by decree, actually) all content on an PWS 4.0 server is available for browsing. Authoring and administration can be performed only on the system on which the server is running. The bottom line: Even if you are sure that PWS 4.0 runs on your system, consider whether it continues to serve your server needs before upgrading.

Taking the Next Step

This book has offered detailed instructions on every facet of FrontPage use, from designing graphical elements for your Web pages, to inserting active elements, to administering a simple Web server. You are sure to want to dip into this well of information again, from time to time, but for now, it's time to do what FrontPage makes it easy and fun to do—"go Web, young man" (and woman)!

✦   ✦   ✦

Appendixes

Installing FrontPage

✦ ✦ ✦ ✦

In This Appendix

Dealing with system requirements

Installing Personal Web Server

Installing Image Composer

✦ ✦ ✦ ✦

Before you can begin using all of the power that FrontPage puts at your disposal, you have to actually install the program (that makes sense, right). While the installation program really makes this a breeze, you should read the following walkthrough before you begin so that you can familiarize yourself with your various options.

As with any installation, there is the possibility of a problem arising. It's always a good idea to back up your computer before installing new software.

Dealing with System Requirements

FrontPage's system requirements are fairly modest. Any modern computer should be able to run FrontPage without trouble. To be specific, FrontPage needs:

- ✦ A multimedia computer with a 486 or higher processor

- ✦ Microsoft Windows® 95 or later, Microsoft Windows NT® Workstation 4.0 or later, or Microsoft Windows NT Server 4.0 or later

- ✦ 16MB RAM on Windows 95; 32MB RAM on Windows NT

- ✦ 37MB of available hard disk space required

- ✦ A CD-ROM drive

- ✦ A VGA- or higher-resolution video adapter

- ✦ A mouse or other pointing device such as a pen tablet

Internet features require you to obtain Internet access; Internet and other online access may require payment of a separate fee to a service provider.

To use Microsoft Image Composer, you need all of the items just named, plus an additional 28MB to 44MB of hard disk space (depending on the options you install). In addition, you can use:

✦ A Windows-compatible tablet with mouse emulation for basic mouse support, or a WinTab-compatible tablet for Full Pressure support

✦ TWAIN-compatible scanners or digital cameras

Installing Personal Web Server

To install Personal Web Server:

1. Insert the FrontPage CD in your CD-ROM drive.

   The FrontPage CD-ROM uses the AutoRun feature, so as soon as you put the disk in your drive, the installation program starts. If you have shut off AutoRun, or the installation program doesn't start, select Run from the Start menu, enter **d:/setup.exe**, and click the OK button.

2. If you have never installed FrontPage before, you will first be asked if you want to install Personal Web Server (PWS). This is kind of a silly question— you can't use FrontPage if Personal Web Server (or another Web server) isn't installed on your computer. Answer Yes.

   A license agreement dialog box opens, detailing all of the legal information that you must agree to if you install Personal Web Server.

3. Read the license agreement and, after hours of pondering its implications, click the I Agree button.

   Personal Web Server, along with the FrontPage server extensions, is installed on your computer. A new folder on your C: drive, Webshare, is created. This will be the "home" for the Webs that you create. When this process is done, you will need to reboot your computer before proceeding. Answer Yes when prompted to reboot. (Note that you may be required to insert your Windows 95 CD-ROM or some of its floppy disks during this procedure.)

4. When your computer finishes rebooting, the main installation menu is displayed (see Figure A-1).

5. Select the program you want to install. Since we're installing FrontPage, click the Install FrontPage 98 button. The small Setup dialog box opens and indicates that it is loading the required installation files, and then the full-screen Microsoft FrontPage 98 Setup window opens. This may take a few minutes, depending on the speed of your computer.

Figure A-1: Pick the program you want to install.

FrontPage 98 comes with Internet Explorer 3.02. If you already have Internet Explorer 4 (IE 4) or higher, don't click the Install Internet Explorer text. Since IE 4 has been out for quite a while now, instructions for installing Internet Explorer 3.02 are not included in these instructions.

6. Initially, Personal Web Server has no access restrictions, and a dialog box opens to tell you this. This is fine for now, so click OK to continue. The Welcome dialog box opens, as shown in Figure A-2. (Chapter 19 discusses security and how to set access restrictions.)

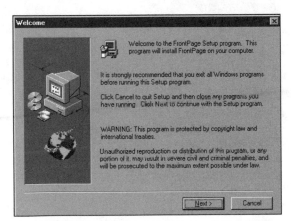

Figure A-2: Welcome to the Microsoft FrontPage setup program.

7. Click Next to continue. The FrontPage Registration dialog box is now displayed.

8. Enter your name and company (if appropriate) in the two text boxes and click the Next button. (Depending on your system and installed software, these text boxes may already be filled in.) A new dialog box opens asking you if the information you entered is correct.

9. Click Yes to continue. The Microsoft FrontPage 98 CD Key dialog box now opens.

10. Enter the CD Key numbers in the two text boxes and click OK to continue. These numbers are located on the orange sticker on the back of the FrontPage 98 CD-ROM jewel case. Yup, another license agreement dialog box opens.

11. Again, contemplate the legal mumbo-jumbo in the license agreement and click the Yes button to continue. The Setup Type dialog box, shown in Figure A-3, opens.

Figure A-3: Select the type of installation you would like.

12. By default, FrontPage is installed in the C:\Program Files\Microsoft FrontPage folder. If you want to install the program in a different folder, or on a different drive, click the Browse button to open the Choose Directory dialog box. Here, type in the path or the new folder in the Path text box, or use the Directories and Drives lists to select the location. Click OK when you have finished to return to the Setup Type dialog box.

13. This walkthrough is based on the Custom selection. Check the Custom radio button and click Next to continue. The Select Components dialog box, shown in Figure A-4, opens.

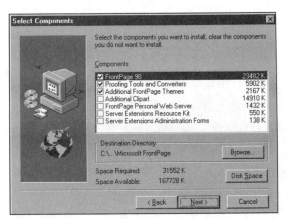

Figure A-4: Select the components you wish to install.

14. Check the check boxes for all of the components that you want to install and then click the Next button. Note that you can come back at a later time and install other components by following these instructions again. You can select from the following components:

- **FrontPage 98**—This installs the main FrontPage programs Explorer and Editor. Editor is explained in Chapter 2 (among others), and Explorer is discussed in Chapter 3.

- **Proofing Tools and Converters**—The Proofing Tools check your spelling, whereas the Converters allow you to import text and graphics from outside FrontPage.

- **Additional FrontPage Themes**—Themes provide a quick method for providing a consistent look for a Web. Themes are discussed in Chapter 4.

- **Additional Clipart**—This adds images to your hard drive that you can quickly access to add to your Web. You can always access this artwork directly from the CD as well.

- **FrontPage Personal Web Server**—This was installed earlier (see previous steps 2, 3, and 4).

- **Server Extensions Resource Kit**—These Web pages provide in-depth technical information about the FrontPage server extensions.

- **Server Extensions Administration Forms**—These Web pages are linked to Personal Web Server and act as the "front end" for changing PWS's settings.

After you have made your selections, FrontPage begins to copy the programs and files onto your computer. The installation progress is indicated by a series of progress bars shown in Figure A-5. (If your machine isn't terribly speedy, feel free to head out to the coffee shop for a while—this process can take a while.)

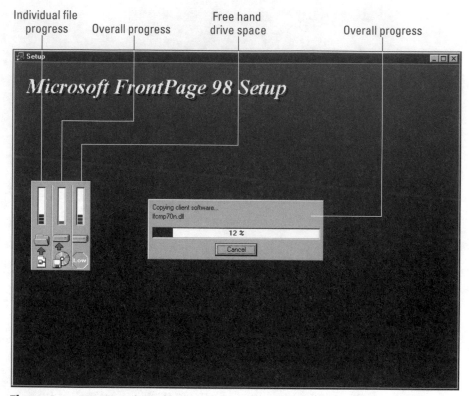

Individual file progress   Overall progress   Free hand drive space   Overall progress

Microsoft FrontPage 98 Setup

Copying client software...
lfcmp70n.dll

12 %

Cancel

Figure A-5: FrontPage is making its way onto your computer system.

15. When the installation is complete, the Restart Windows dialog box opens. Before you can run FrontPage, you need to restart your system, so it's easiest just to leave the Yes, I Want to Restart My Computer Now radio button marked and click OK. (Leave the FrontPage CD-ROM in the drive if you want to install Image Composer or Internet Explorer 3.02 as soon as your computer finishes restarting.)

Windows will now shut down and restart. As Windows is starting up again, a message comes up to indicate that your configuration is being updated. After a few moments Windows starts normally. The Microsoft FrontPage 98 installation dialog box opens again, allowing you to install either Image Composer or Internet Explorer (or to reinstall FrontPage 98, though since you just installed it, what's the point).

Installing Image Composer

Image Composer is a basic image editing tool specifically designed for creating graphics to include in Web pages. Chapter 5 contains an introduction to using Image Composer.

To install Image Composer:

1. Click the Install Image Composer text. The Microsoft Image Composer Setup dialog box opens (see Figure A-6).

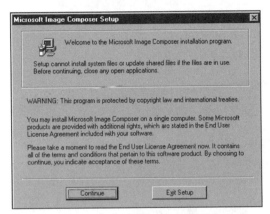

Figure A-6: Begin installing Image Composer.

2. Click the Continue button to proceed with the installation. The Name and Organization Information dialog box opens.

3. Your name and organization should already be filled in with the information you included when installing FrontPage (although the FrontPage installation asked for your company, not organization). If this information isn't included, fill in the two text boxes. Click OK to continue. Click OK again to confirm that the information is correct.

4. The dialog box now displays Image Composer's identification number. Write this number down someplace safe so that it is handy if you ever have to call Microsoft technical support (a good place is the inside cover of your Getting Started with FrontPage 98 book). Click OK to continue. The dialog box now displays the folder where it will install Image Composer.

5. By default, Image Composer is installed in the C:\Program Files\Microsoft Image Composer folder. If you want to install the program in a different folder, or on a different drive, click the Browse button to open the Choose Directory dialog box. Here, type in the path or the new folder in the Path text box, or use the Directories and Drives lists to select the location. Click OK when you have finished to return to the Setup dialog box.

6. Click OK to continue. Setup says that it's looking for installed components, and then yet another License Agreement dialog box opens. As always, study the agreement carefully and click the I Agree button to continue. For some reason, Setup looks for the installed components again before finally displaying a dialog box that lets you choose how you want to install Image Composer.

7. Click the button corresponding to the level of control you want over the installation process:

- **Typical**—This installs the Image Composer components most often used.

- **Complete/Custom**—This provides you with complete control over which components are installed. The Complete/Custom option is used for the remainder of these instructions. When you click this button, the Complete/Custom Install dialog box opens (see Figure A-7).

- **Compact**—This installs only the components necessary to make Image Composer work. This is a good option if you have limited hard drive space or don't intend on using Image Composer very much.

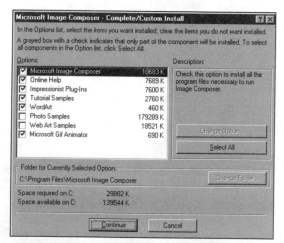

Figure A-7: Choose the Image Composer components you want to install.

8. Check the components that you would like to install, and then click the Continue button to proceed. The Choose Program Group dialog box opens.

While making your selections, keep an eye on the indicator at the bottom of the dialog box that tells you how much space the components need and how much space your selected hard drive has, so that you know they will fit.

9. Choose a Start Menu folder in which to include a shortcut to Image Composer and click Continue. (By default, Image Composer will make its own folder, named `Microsoft Image Composer`.) Setup now checks your hard drive to make sure it has the necessary space and then begins installing the components you chose.

10. When all of the components have been installed, the final dialog box opens letting you know this. Click OK to return to the FrontPage 98 dialog box.

11. If you're all done installing FrontPage programs, click the Exit text to close this dialog box.

Taking the Next Step

You are now ready to begin using FrontPage 98 to create world-class Web sites. The rest of this book explains how to get the best results with this powerful, yet easy-to-use, Web authoring package.

✦   ✦   ✦

Upgrading from FrontPage 97

In order to install the FrontPage 98 upgrade, you must have a previously installed version of FrontPage, either FrontPage 97 or FrontPage 1.1.

Note

You cannot upgrade from the FrontPage 98 beta. If you do not have an earlier version of the program, you must purchase and install the full version of FrontPage 98. Note that if you have replaced an older version with the FrontPage 98 beta, you will have to round up the disks from the old version in order to install the upgrade.

Upgrading FrontPage

To upgrade from FrontPage 1.1 or 97 to FrontPage 98, use the following steps:

1. Place the FrontPage 98 Upgrade CD in your CD-ROM drive.

2. If the automatic setup opens the setup start screen, select Install FrontPage. Otherwise, click the Start button, select Run, and type *<cdrom-drive>*:**setup**, where *<cdrom-drive>* is the drive letter corresponding to your CD-ROM. This starts the setup start screen manually. Select "Install FrontPage" as just described.

3. You are prompted to complete registration information and then to provide the CD KEY number located on the back of the CD-ROM jewel case.

4. The install program searches for a qualifying upgrade product. If it cannot locate one, it offers to let you identify one. Insert the original disks for an earlier version of FrontPage and use the Browse button to locate this disk.

5. Once a qualifying upgrade product is located, the installation displays the license agreement. Agree to the terms, designate a location for the FrontPage files, select Typical or Custom installation, and click OK to begin installation.

6. Once FrontPage has been installed, it installs upgraded FrontPage server extensions to your Personal Web Server.

7. Restart your computer. When you first launch FrontPage 98, it attempts to identify the host name of your computer.

Upgrading Personal Web Server

If you do not have Personal Web Server installed, you will be prompted that this is recommended before installing FrontPage 98. This is a no-frills install—be prepared, it does not ask you any questions after you indicate you want to install it.

Be careful if you answer "no" when asked if you would like to install the server. If you reject this option but then select the Typical installation, PWS is a part of that and will install anyway.

If you already have Personal Web Server installed, the FrontPage 98 installation automatically upgrades the PWS server extensions to the FrontPage 98 version.

If you have a problem with the installation of the server extensions, use the `fpwinsrv.exe` tool (located in the `Version3.0/bin` subdirectory of your FrontPage folder) to investigate and make corrections to the server.

Upgrading Image Composer

FrontPage 98 comes with an updated version of Image Composer, version 1.5. This version includes the Animated Gif tool. To install Image Composer:

1. Place the FrontPage 98 CD in your CD-ROM drive.

2. If the automatic setup opens the setup start screen, select Install Image Composer. Otherwise, click the Start button, select Run, and type *<cdrom-drive>:***setup**, where *<cdrom-drive>* is the drive letter corresponding to your CD-ROM. This starts the setup start screen manually. Select Install Image Composer as above.

3. Enter registration information.

4. Indicate the location for the Image Composer installation.

5. Select Typical, Complete/Custom, or Compact installation.

6. Indicate a name for the Program Group to be placed in the Windows Programs Start menu.

Once the program installs, you can launch it without restarting.

Taking the Next Step

Once you have FrontPage 98 installed, you are ready to benefit from its many new and advanced features. Begin with Chapter 1 and as you work your way through the book, look for the New in 98 icon in the left margin to clue you in to many changes in the current version of FrontPage.

✦   ✦   ✦

Installing FrontPage Server Extensions

This appendix provides a general overview of the installation of the FrontPage server extensions. For more information on using the server extensions, see Chapter 19 of this book. For details on installing the server extensions, consult the Microsoft Server Extensions Resource Kit (SERK), available on the FrontPage CD.

An updated version of the SERK is available on the Microsoft FrontPage Web site, www.microsoft.com/frontpage/wwp/default.htm.

Installing on Windows

The FrontPage server extensions can be installed in one of three ways:

+ The server extensions can be installed when you install FrontPage and the Microsoft Personal Web Server.

+ The server extensions are installed automatically when you install Internet Information Server 4.0.

+ The server extensions can be installed manually on a non-Microsoft Web server.

What gets installed

The following components are installed by the FrontPage server extensions installation process:

✦ FrontPage server extensions DLLs and executables

✦ The three ISAPI or CGI components that constitute the server extensions

✦ FrontPage Server Administrator (fpsvrwin.exe)

✦ The Server Extensions Resource Kit (SERK)

✦ HTML Administration forms

Installing the server extensions

This section describes what's required to install the server extensions manually. Use the following steps:

1. Download the current server extensions from the Microsoft FrontPage Web site, www.microsoft.com/frontpage/wpp/default.htm.

2. Run the server extension setup program.

   If your Web server is running when the installation is started, it is automatically stopped and then restarted when the installation is complete.

3. If your computer is multihosted, the Multi-Hosted Server dialog box is displayed. Select the servers on which to install the extensions. On single-home computers, installation takes place automatically.

4. Provide an administrator username and password. If you are installing IIS, this account must already exist. On other systems, you must designate a username and a password before creating the new account.

Installing on UNIX

The FrontPage server extensions for UNIX are compatible with the following Web sites (see Chapter 19 for a list of supported operating systems):

✦ Apache

✦ Netscape

✦ NCSA

✦ CERN

What gets installed

When you install the FrontPage server extensions for UNIX, the following components are installed:

✦ The FrontPage server extensions

✦ FrontPage Server Administrator (`fpsrvadm.exe`)

✦ HTML Administration forms

✦ Apache server patch (this patch allows the server extensions to install without needing stub versions of the extensions in each FrontPage Web)

Installing the server extensions

Use the following steps to install the server extensions:

1. Log in as root.

2. Run the Installation script, `fp_install.sh`, located in `/usr/local/frontpage` by default.

3. You are reminded to back up all existing content and FrontPage installation files before attempting this installation.

4. Designate a destination for the server extensions.

5. Untar the FrontPage server extensions file, `fp30.<platform>.tar.Z`.

6. At this point the user ID on each FrontPage Web is checked, and the ID of server extensions to ID of owner is set. Content is owned and writable by this user. This step can be performed interactively as part of the installation. Alternatively, the installation program can create a script that can be run at a later time to set the security permissions.

7. You are prompted for an administrator username and password in order to install the server extensions on the root Web.

8. Install the server extensions on each sub-Web.

9. Install the server extensions on any virtual Webs. For each virtual Web, you must supply a username and a password.

10. At the end of the installation, existing Web pages are parsed in order to be used correctly by FrontPage client.

Installing the HTML Administration Forms

The HTML Administration forms allow for remote administration of the server extensions. These forms are copied to your hard drive but are not activated by default. See the SERK for details on how to install these forms without compromising site security.

Taking the Next Step

Now that you've installed the FrontPage server extensions, check out Chapter 19 of this book for more information on how to put them to work. The Microsoft Server Extensions Resource Kit (SERK), which contains detailed information on installing and administering the Microsoft server extensions, is available on the FrontPage CD. A current version of the SERK is available on the Microsoft FrontPage Web site, www.microsoft.com/frontpage/wpp/default.htm.

✦   ✦   ✦

Using the CD-ROM

T he CD-ROM that accompanies this book contains content files and completed Web pages for all of the examples used in the book. In addition it contains numerous applications and helpful utilities for Web developers.

Learning About the Directories

The CD-ROM contains three main directories:

+ Apps—Contains the installation files for several useful applications and utilities.

+ Contents—Contains all content files used in the examples. Content files are organized by chapters of the book.

+ Examples—Contains completed HTML versions of the examples described in the book. Examples are organized by chapters of the book.

Discovering What's on the Disc

The following list briefly describes the main applications and utilities found on the CD-ROM. For detailed information and installation instructions, consult the README files that accompany each application on the CD-ROM. Web addresses are also listed for further information and surfing satisfaction.

+ **Applet Designer**—Converts Visual Basic to Java (demo version).

TV Objects, http://www.tvobjects.com

+ **cgi-lib.pl**—This is a basic Perl CGI library, written by Steven E. Brenner (freeware).

The cgi-lib.pl home page, http://cgi-lib. stanford.edu/cgi-lib/

- ✦ **CSDiff**—Compares two files and reports the differences (freeware).

  Component Software, `http://www.componentsoftware.com/`

- ✦ **CS-RCS**—This is version control software, a port of the UNIX GNU Software Revision Control System (shareware).

  Component Software, `http://www.componentsoftware.com/`

- ✦ **FrameTool**—This is an easy-to-use WYSIWYG frame design tool for Web page authoring (shareware).

  Informatik, Inc., `http://www.informatik.com/framex.html`

- ✦ **HCU95**—This is a search-and-replace tool for HTML files (freeware).

  Michel Verbraak, `http://www.xs4all.nl/~miv/HCU95/HCU95Download.html`

- ✦ **JPadPro**—This is an integrated development environment (IDE) for building Java applications and applets and editing JavaScript and VBScript (shareware).

  Modelworks Software, `http://www.modelworks.com/`

- ✦ **Link*Launch**—This enables you to easily create drop-down menu navigation on your Web site (freeware).

  Web Genie Software, `http://www.webgenie.com/Software/Launch/`

- ✦ **S Ruler**—This is a virtual pixel ruler that can be overlaid on Web pages when laying out designs (shareware).

  Micro Fox Software, Jesse Carneiro, `http://www.kagi.com/microfox/`

- ✦ **StyleMaker**—This aids in the design of cascading style sheets (shareware).

  Danere Group, `http://danere.com/StyleMaker/`

- ✦ **Tape Measure, Jr.**—This is a handy utility that reports the pixel size of images (freeware).

  Robert Elliott, `http://users.aol.com/graphixnut/main.html`

- ✦ **WebBBS**—This is a CGI Web discussion application (freeware).

  Darryl C. Burgdorf, `http://www.awsd.com`

- ✦ **WebBug**—This lets you enter a URL and then displays exactly what it sends to the Web server; when the response is received, it displays exactly what the Web server sends back (freeware).

  Aman Software, `http://www.cyberspyder.com/`

- ✦ **WebTrends**—This is a powerful log file analyzer that can provide reports and graphs of your Web site activity in a variety of formats (demo version).

  e.g. Software, `http://www.egsoftware.com`

Note that several of the applications included are shareware or evaluation versions of commercial software. Please respect the efforts of the authors of these programs. Register and pay for any software you plan to use beyond the evaluation period.

Taking the Next Step

Now that you know what's on the disc, fire it up and get started. If you haven't already worked through the tutorials in this book, now is a good time to begin. Happy Web page building!

✦   ✦   ✦

Index

(continued)

Notes

Notes

Notes

Notes

Notes

Notes

IDG BOOKS WORLDWIDE, INC.
END-USER LICENSE AGREEMENT

4. **Restrictions On Use of Individual Programs.** You must follow the individual requirements and restrictions detailed for each individual program in Appendix D, "Using the CD-ROM," of this Book. These limitations are also contained in the individual license agreements recorded on the Software Media. These limitations may include a requirement that after using the program for a specified period of time, the user must pay a registration fee or discontinue use. By opening the Software packet(s), you will be agreeing to abide by the licenses and restrictions for these individual programs that are detailed in Appendix D and on the Software Media. None of the material on this Software Media or listed in this Book may ever be redistributed, in original or modified form, for commercial purposes.

5. **Limited Warranty.**

   (a) IDGB warrants that the Software and Software Media are free from defects in materials and workmanship under normal use for a period of sixty (60) days from the date of purchase of this Book. If IDGB receives notification within the warranty period of defects in materials or workmanship, IDGB will replace the defective Software Media.

   (b) IDGB AND THE AUTHORS OF THE BOOK DISCLAIM ALL OTHER WARRANTIES, EXPRESS OR IMPLIED, INCLUDING WITHOUT LIMITATION IMPLIED WARRANTIES OF MERCHANTABILITY AND FITNESS FOR A PARTICULAR PURPOSE, WITH RESPECT TO THE SOFTWARE, THE PROGRAMS, THE SOURCE CODE CONTAINED THEREIN, AND/OR THE TECHNIQUES DESCRIBED IN THIS BOOK. IDGB DOES NOT WARRANT THAT THE FUNCTIONS CONTAINED IN THE SOFTWARE WILL MEET YOUR REQUIREMENTS OR THAT THE OPERATION OF THE SOFTWARE WILL BE ERROR FREE.

   (c) This limited warranty gives you specific legal rights, and you may have other rights that vary from jurisdiction to jurisdiction.

6. **Remedies.**

   (a) IDGB's entire liability and your exclusive remedy for defects in materials and workmanship shall be limited to replacement of the Software Media, which may be returned to IDGB with a copy of your receipt at the following address: Software Media Fulfillment Department, Attn.: *FrontPage 98 Bible*, IDG Books Worldwide, Inc., 7260 Shadeland Station, Ste. 100, Indianapolis, IN 46256, or call 1-800-762-2974. Please allow three to four weeks for delivery. This Limited Warranty is void if failure of the Software Media has resulted from accident, abuse, or misapplication. Any replacement Software Media will be warranted for the remainder of the original warranty period or thirty (30) days, whichever is longer.

   (b) In no event shall IDGB or the authors be liable for any damages whatsoever (including without limitation damages for loss of business profits, business interruption, loss of business information, or any other pecuniary loss) arising from the use of or inability to use the Book or the Software, even if IDGB has been advised of the possibility of such damages.

(c) Because some jurisdictions do not allow the exclusion or limitation of liability for consequential or incidental damages, the above limitation or exclusion may not apply to you.

7. **U.S. Government Restricted Rights.** Use, duplication, or disclosure of the Software by the U.S. Government is subject to restrictions stated in paragraph (c)(1)(ii) of the Rights in Technical Data and Computer Software clause of DFARS 252.227-7013, and in subparagraphs (a) through (d) of the Commercial Computer—Restricted Rights clause at FAR 52.227-19, and in similar clauses in the NASA FAR supplement, when applicable.

8. **General.** This Agreement constitutes the entire understanding of the parties and revokes and supersedes all prior agreements, oral or written, between them and may not be modified or amended except in a writing signed by both parties hereto that specifically refers to this Agreement. This Agreement shall take precedence over any other documents that may be in conflict herewith. If any one or more provisions contained in this Agreement are held by any court or tribunal to be invalid, illegal, or otherwise unenforceable, each and every other provision shall remain in full force and effect.

my2cents.idgbooks.com

Register This Book — And Win!

Visit **http://my2cents.idgbooks.com** to register this book and we'll automatically enter you in our fantastic monthly prize giveaway. It's also your opportunity to give us feedback: let us know what you thought of this book and how you would like to see other topics covered.

Discover IDG Books Online!

The IDG Books Online Web site is your online resource for tackling technology — at home and at the office. Frequently updated, the IDG Books Online Web site features exclusive software, insider information, online books, and live events!

10 Productive & Career-Enhancing Things You Can Do at www.idgbooks.com

- Nab source code for your own programming projects.

- Download software.

- Read Web exclusives: special articles and book excerpts by IDG Books Worldwide authors.

- Take advantage of resources to help you advance your career as a Novell or Microsoft professional.

- Buy IDG Books Worldwide titles or find a convenient bookstore that carries them.

- Register your book and win a prize.

- Chat live online with authors.

- Sign up for regular e-mail updates about our latest books.

- Suggest a book you'd like to read or write.

- Give us your 2¢ about our books and about our Web site.

You say you're not on the Web yet? It's easy to get started with IDG Books' *Discover the Internet,* available at local retailers everywhere.

CD-ROM Installation Instructions

Attached to the back cover of this book is a CD-ROM. The disc contains content files and completed Web pages for all of the examples used in the book, as well as numerous applications and helpful utilities for Web developers. The CD-ROM contains three main directories:

+ Apps—Installation files for several useful applications and utilities

+ Contents—Content files, organized by chapter, used in the examples

+ Examples—Completed HTML versions, organized by chapter, of the examples described in the book

Place the CD-ROM disc in your computer and consult the README files for further instructions. For more information on the contents of the disc, other usage, and licencing details, see Appendix D.